The
Supreme
Court
&
the Rights of
the Accused

The Supreme Court & the Rights of the Accused

Edited by John Galloway
Adjunct Assistant Professor of Political Science
Hunter College of the City of New York

FACTS ON FILE, INC.   NEW YORK, N.Y.

The Supreme Court & the Rights of the Accused

© Copyright, 1973, by Facts on File, Inc.

Library of Congress Catalog Card No. 72-80833
ISBN 0-87196-228-4

9 8 7 6 5 4 3 2
PRINTED IN
THE UNITED STATES OF AMERICA

CONTENTS

i

PREFACE

IN DEALING WITH PERSONS ACCUSED of crime, the U.S. judiciary attempts to balance 2 competing concerns. One concern is to safeguard the rights of the relatively weak defendant against injustice from government as represented by the powerful law-enforcement system. The other concern is to protect the persons and property of the members of society against the growing number of criminals who in recent years have been making streets, places of business and even homes increasingly dangerous for innocent citizens.

The U.S. Bill of Rights was framed as a response to centuries of experience with monarchs and their representatives who arbitrarily searched homes and seized persons and property, who imprisoned people without charge or trial, who coerced confessions, who denied the accused counsel and who inflicted excessive punishments on those declared guilty. The Bill of Rights was designed to safeguard the individual against such abuses by

1

government but not to prevent the arrest and fair prosecution of persons accused of crime.

During the 1960s and early 1970s the U.S. experienced an explosive growth of nearly every variety of crime. Almost simultaneously a series of decisions by the Supreme Court has greatly expanded the acknowledged constitutional rights of persons accused of crime. These decisions have extended Bill of Rights protections to suspects in state prosecutions and to children in juvenile courts, have nullified many confessions, have curbed the right of law-enforcement officials to make arrests, to search for and seize evidence and to eavesdrop on alleged criminals, have freed prisoners convicted on convincing evidence and testimony, have barred specific types of police misconduct and have virtually outlawed capital punishment as recently administered.

These Supreme Court decisions have been hailed by many as welcome and even essential additions to the rules of civilized society. But others have denounced the rulings and the court itself as weakening society's ability to protect itself against its criminal enemies. The court has been accused of freeing proven robbers, murderers and rapists to prey on new victims.

This book records the circumstances and facts surrounding the various cases in this ongoing dispute over the Supreme Court and the rights of the accused. A major element of this record consists of comprehensive abridgments of the Supreme Court decisions in the important cases discussed. Much of the material in this book is highly controversial, but as in all FACTS ON FILE books, great pains were taken to present all facts without bias.

THE BILL OF RIGHTS & THE STATES

The 50 states of the Union are required to extend to persons within their borders almost all rights and privileges guaranteed by the U.S. Constitution's first 10 amendments—the Bill of Rights.

But this was not always so. The Bill of Rights does not apply directly and specifically to the states. It was recent Supreme Court decisions that brought most of the Bill of Rights to bear on the states.

Except for the First Amendment, the language of the Bill of Rights does not indicate that its provisions are limited to the federal government. The circumstances surrounding the adoption of the Bill of Rights, however, make it clear that the Bill of Rights was intended to apply only to the federal government. And in 1833, in *Barron v. Baltimore,* the Supreme Court, speaking through Chief Justice John Marshall, in describing the question as "of great importance, but not of much difficulty," held unanimously that the Bill of Rights did not extend to the states.

The change began after the Civil War when the Radical Republicans, in 1868, secured the adoption of the 14th Amendment. This amendment bars the *states* from: (a) abridging "the privileges or immunities of citizens of the United States"; (b) denying "any person life, liberty, or property without due process of law," and (c) denying "to any person within its jurisdiction the equal protection of the laws."

The "privileges and immunities" provision of the 14th Amendment was interpreted by the Supreme Court in the *Slaughter House* cases in 1873 in such a way as to deny it any future significance. But the "due process" and "equal protection" clauses survived to play a vital role in U.S. constitutional history.

Although conceived primarily as protection for the Southern Negro, the due process clause was first used to shield business from state regulation. In *Chicago, Burlington & Quincy Railroad Co. v. Chicago,* the Supreme Court held unanimously in 1897 that the due process clause precluded the states from taking private property for public use without just compensation. In *Lochner v. New York* in 1905, the due process clause was used to invalidate a New York law that, owing to the high rate of tuberculosis among bakers, limited them to a 10-hour day and 60-hour work week. The court viewed the law as a violation of the bakers' right of contract, in particular their right to work more hours than permitted by the New York statute. According to the court, the right of contract was part of the liberty guaranteed by the due process clause. Similar decisions followed until 1937, when the court, shaken by Pres. Franklin D. Roosevelt's court-packing plan, upheld a state minimum wage law on the ground that "the Constitution does not speak of freedom of contract."

Once the Supreme Court interpreted the liberty of the 14th Amendment to include the right of contract, the court was pressed to hold all, or part, of the Bill of Rights binding on the states. The court did not comply with any speed, however, and as late as 1922 it held that "neither the 14th Amendment nor any provision of the Constitution imposes any

restrictions upon the state upon freedom of speech."
2 years earlier, Justice Louis Brandeis, in dissent,
had asserted that it was impossible to believe "that
the liberty guaranteed by the 14th Amendment
includes only liberty to acquire and to enjoy property."

A new era for civil liberties in the U.S. began in
1925 when, for the first time, the court declared a
portion of the Bill of Rights binding on the states. In
Gitlow v. New York the Supreme Court held that,
"for present purposes, we may and do assume that
freedom of speech and of the press—which are protected by the First Amendment"—are "among the
fundamental rights and 'liberties' protected by the
due process clause of the 14th Amendment from
impairment by the states...." By 1940 all First
Amendment rights—freedom of press, speech,
assembly, petition and religion—were made binding
on the states.

In 1948, in *In Re Oliver,* the Supreme Court
required the states to grant criminal defendants a
public trial, as guaranteed by the 5th Amendment.
That was the first instance in which the states were
required to adhere to a provision in the Bill of Rights
concerning the rights of the accused.

Prior to 1948 the Supreme Court did, however,
overrule a number of state convictions, not because
they violated the Bill of Rights but because they
violated certain standards of justice that the court
considered implicit in the concept of due process as
guaranteed by the 14th Amendment. Under that approach, rather than having the states adhere to the
Bill of Rights, the court in effect adopted a
truncated Bill of Rights of its own making wherein
the court, speaking through Justice Benjamin

Cardozo in *Palko v. Connecticut* in 1937, sought to insure that state actions were in keeping with "those canons of decency and fairness which express the notions of English-speaking peoples even toward those charged with the most heinous offenses." Thus, instead of requiring the states to provide counsel as required by the 6th Amendment, the court merely required that state trials be "fair." Similarly, the court ruled that portions of the 5th Amendment pertaining to double jeopardy and the guarantee against self-incrimination were not binding on the states since the failure of the states to honor those principles was not necessarily contrary to what the court considered the "concept of ordered liberty."

An example of the type of state conduct invalidated by the Supreme Court is given in *Brown v. Mississippi,* in which the court in 1936 overruled a conviction based on a confession obtained by torture. In this case a law officer conceded that one of the 2 defendants had been whipped but "not too much for a Negro; not as much as I would have done if it were left to me." *Brown v. Mississippi* was the first instance in which the due process clause was used to disallow a confession obtained by state authorities.

The apparent anomaly wherein the Bill of Rights controlled in federal trials but not in state trials was ended by the Supreme Court in the 1950s and 1960s in a series of decisions in which various provisions of the Bill of Rights were "incorporated" into the due process clause of the 14th Amendment and made binding on the states. These decisions constitute a major portion of the court's work in recent years.

The following decisions, some of which are discussed in other chapters of this book, require the states to adhere to certain provisions of the Bill of Rights in the area of criminal procedure:

In Re Oliver (1948)—right to a public trial.

Wolf v. Colorado (1949)—freedom from unreasonable searches and seizures.

Robinson v. California (1957)—freedom from cruel and unusual punishments.

Gideon v. Wainwright (1963)—right to counsel.

Malloy v. Hogan (1964)—right not to have to testify against one's self.

Pointer v. Texas (1965)—right to confront witnesses.

Klopfer v. North Carolina (1967)—right to a speedy trial.

Washington v. Texas (1967)—right to obtain witnesses in one's favor.

Duncan v. Louisiana (1968)—right to trial by jury.

Benton v. Maryland (1969)—freedom from double jeopardy.

Right to Counsel

The decision that the 6th Amendment right to counsel applied in state criminal trials was made by the Supreme Court Mar. 18, 1963 in *Gideon v. Wainwright.* Previously the states had been required by the court to provide counsel to indigent defendants only in capital cases. 21 years earlier, in *Betts v. Brady,* the court had upheld a felony conviction following a trial in which a state refused to grant an indigent defendant's request for a lawyer.

Justice Hugo L. Black, speaking for the majority in *Gideon,* rejected the court's holding in

Betts that "appointment of counsel is not a fundamental right, essential to a fair trial." According to Black, "that government hires lawyers to prosecute and defendants who have the money hire lawyers to defend are the strongest indications of the widespread belief that lawyers in criminal courts are necessities, not luxuries."

After his conviction was overruled and a new trial ordered, Clarence Gideon, with the aid of counsel, was found not guilty by a jury of having broken and entered a Panama City, Fla. poolroom. While the case was before the Supreme Court, 22 states urged the court to overrule *Betts* as "an anachronism when handed down." When the *Gideon* decision was announced all but 5 states provided trial counsel for indigent defendants in felony cases.

Abridgment of the *Gideon v. Wainwright* decision (372 U.S. 335, Mar. 18, 1963):

Justice Black delivering the opinion of the court:

Petitioner was charged in a Florida state court with having broken and entered a poolroom with intent to commit a misdemeanor. This offense is a felony under Florida law. Appearing in court without funds and without a lawyer, petitioner asked the court to appoint counsel for him, whereupon the following colloquy took place:

"The Court: Mr. Gideon, I am sorry, but I cannot appoint counsel to represent you in this case. Under the laws of the State of Florida, the only time the court can appoint counsel to represent a defendant is when that person is charged with a capital offense. I am sorry, but I will have to deny your request to appoint counsel to defend you in this case.

"The Defendant: The United States Supreme Court says I am entitled to be represented by counsel."

Put to trial before a jury, Gideon conducted his defense about as well as could be expected from a layman. He made an opening statement to the jury, cross-examined the state's witnesses, presented witnesses in his own defense, declined to testify himself, and made a short argument "emphasizing his innocence to the charge contained in the information filed in this case." The jury returned a verdict of guilty, and petitioner was sentenced to serve 5 years in the state prison. Later, petitioner filed in the Florida Supreme Court this *habeas corpus* petition attacking his conviction and sentence on the ground that the trial court's refusal to appoint counsel for him denied him rights "guaranteed by the Constitution and the Bill of Rights by the United States government."... Since 1942, when *Betts v. Brady* was decided by a divided court, the problem of a defendant's federal constitutional right to counsel in a state court has been a continuing source of controversy and litigation in both state and federal courts. To give this problem another review here, we granted *certiorari* [review]. ...

The facts upon which Betts claimed that he had been unconstitutionally denied the right to have counsel appointed to assist him are strikingly like the facts upon which Gideon here bases his federal constitutional claim. Betts was indicted for robbery in a Maryland state court. On arraignment, he told the trial judge of his lack of funds to hire a lawyer and asked the court to appoint one for him. Betts was advised that it was not the practice in that county to appoint counsel for indigent defendants except in murder and rape cases. He then pleaded not guilty, had witnesses summoned, cross-examined the State's witnesses, examined his own and chose not to testify himself. He was found guilty by the judge, sitting without a jury, and sentenced to 8 years in prison. Like Gideon, Betts sought release by *habeas corpus,* alleging that he had been denied the right to assistance of counsel in violation of the 14th Amendment. Betts was denied any relief, and, on review, this court affirmed. It was held that a refusal to appoint counsel for an indigent defendant charged with a felony did not necessarily violate the due process clause of the 14th Amendment... The court said: "Asserted denial [of due process] is to be tested by an appraisal of the totality of facts in a given case. That which may, in one setting, constitute a denial of fundamental fairness, shocking to the universal sense of justice, may, in other circumstances, and in the light of other considerations, fall short of such denial."

Treating due process as "a concept less rigid and more fluid than those envisaged in other specific and particular provisions of the Bill of Rights," the court held that refusal to appoint counsel under the particular facts and circumstances in the *Betts* case was not so "offensive to the common and fundamental ideas of fairness" as to amount to a denial of due process. Since the facts and circumstances of the 2 cases are so nearly indistinguishable, we think the *Betts v. Brady* holding, if left standing, would require us to reject Gideon's claim that the Constitution guarantees him the assistance of counsel. Upon full reconsideration we conclude that *Betts v. Brady* should be overruled.

The 6th Amendment provides, "In all criminal prosecutions, the accused shall enjoy the right ... to have the assistance of counsel for his defence." We have construed this to mean that, in federal courts, counsel must be provided for defendants unable to employ counsel unless the right is competently and intelligently waived. Betts argued that this right is extended to indigent defendants in state courts by the 14th Amendment. In response the court stated that, while the 6th Amendment laid down "no rule for the conduct of the states, the question recurs whether the constraint laid by the Amendment upon the national courts expresses a rule so fundamental and essential to a fair trial and so to due process of law that it is made obligatory upon the states by the 14th Amendment." ... In order to decide whether the 6th Amendment's guarantee of counsel is of this fundamental nature, the court in *Betts* set out and considered "[r]elevant data on the subject ... afforded by constitutional and statutory provisions subsisting in the colonies and the states prior to the inclusion of the Bill of Rights in the national Constitution and in the constitutional, legislative, and judicial history of the states to the present date." ... On the basis of this historical data the court concluded that "appointment of counsel is not a fundamental right, essential to a fair trial." ... It was for this reason the *Betts* court refused to accept the contention that the 6th Amendment's guarantee of counsel for indigent federal defendants was extended to or, in the words of that court, "made obligatory upon the states by the 14th Amendment." Plainly, had the court concluded that appointment of counsel for an indigent criminal defendant was "a fundamental right, essential to a fair trial," it would have held that the 14th Amendment requires appointment of counsel in a state court, just as the 6th Amendment requires in a federal court.

We think the court in *Betts* had ample precedent for acknowledging that those guarantees of the Bill of Rights which are fundamental safeguards of liberty immune from federal abridgment are equally protected against state invasion by the due process clause of the 14th Amendment. This same principle was recognized, explained, and applied in *Powell v. Alabama* ... (1932), a case upholding the right of counsel, where the court held that, despite sweeping language to the contrary in *Hurtado v. California* ... (1884), the 14th Amendment "embraced" those " 'fundamental principles of liberty and justice which lie at the base of all our civil and political institutions,' " even though they had been "specifically dealt with in another part of the federal Constitution."... In many cases other than *Powell* and *Betts,* this court has looked to the fundamental nature of original Bill of Rights guarantees to decide whether the 14th Amendment makes them obligatory on the states. Explicitly recognized to be of this "fundamental nature" and therefore made immune from state invasion by the 14th, or some part of it, are the First Amendment's freedoms of speech, press, religion, assembly, association and petition for redress of grievances. For the same reason ... the court has made obligatory on the states the 5th Amendment's command that private property shall not be taken for public use without just compensation, the 4th Amendment's prohibition of unreasonable searches and seizures, and the 8th's ban on cruel and unusual punishment. On the other hand, this court in *Palko v. Connecticut* ... (1937) refused to hold that the 14th Amendment made the double jeopardy provision of the 5th Amendment obligatory on the states. In so refusing, however, the court, speaking through Mr. Justice Cardozo, was careful to emphasize that "immunities that are valid as against the federal government by force of the specific pledges of particular amendments have been found to be implicit in the concept of ordered liberty, and thus, through the 14th Amendment, become valid as against the states" and that guarantees "in their origin ... effective against the federal government alone" had by prior cases "been taken over from the earlier articles of the federal Bill of Rights and brought within the 14th Amendment by a process of absorption."...

We accept *Betts v. Brady's* assumption, based as it was on
our prior cases, that a provision of the Bill of Rights which is
"fundamental and essential to a fair trial" is made obligatory
upon the states by the 14th Amendment. We think the court in
Betts was wrong, however, in concluding that the 6th Amendment's guarantee of counsel is not one of these fundamental
rights. 10 years before *Betts v. Brady,* this court, after full consideration of all the historical data examined in *Betts,* had un-
equivocally declared that "the right to the aid of counsel is of
this fundamental character." *Powell v. Alabama* ... (1932)....

   ... [I]t is not surprising that the *Betts* court, when faced
with the contention that "one charged with crime, who is
unable to obtain counsel, must be furnished counsel by the
state," conceded that "[e]xpressions in the opinions of this court
lend color to the argument...." ... The fact is that in deciding
as it did—that "appointment of counsel is not a fundamental
right, essential to a fair trial"—the court in *Betts v. Brady*
made an abrupt break with its own well-considered precedents.
In returning to these old precedents, sounder we believe than
the new, we but restore constitutional principles established to
achieve a fair system of justice. Not only these precedents but
also reason and reflection require us to recognize that in our
adversary system of criminal justice, any person haled into
court, who is too poor to hire a lawyer, cannot be assured a fair
trial unless counsel is provided for him.... Governments, both
state and federal, quite properly spend vast sums of money to
establish machinery to try defendants accused of crime.
Lawyers to prosecute are everywhere deemed essential to
protect the public's interest in an orderly society. Similarly,
there are few defendants charged with crime, few indeed, who
fail to hire the best lawyers they can get to prepare and present
their defenses. That government hires lawyers to prosecute and
defendants who have the money hire lawyers to defend are the
strongest indications of the widespread belief that lawyers in
criminal courts are necessities, not luxuries. The right of one
charged with crime to counsel may not be deemed fundamental
and essential to fair trials in some countries, but it is in ours.
From the very beginning, our state and national constitutions
and laws have laid great emphasis on procedural and
substantive safeguards designed to assure fair trials before impartial tribunals in which every defendant stands equal before

the law. This noble ideal cannot be realized if the poor man charged with crime has to face his accusers without a lawyer to assist him. A defendant's need for a lawyer is nowhere better stated than in the moving words of Mr. Justice [George] Sutherland in *Powell v. Alabama:* "The right to be heard would be, in many cases, of little avail if it did not comprehend the right to be heard by counsel. Even the intelligent and educated layman has small and sometimes no skill in the science of law. If charged with crime, he is incapable, generally, of determining for himself whether the indictment is good or bad. He is unfamiliar with the rules of evidence. Left without the aid of counsel he may be put on trial without a proper charge, and convicted upon incompetent evidence, or evidence irrelevant to the issue or otherwise inadmissible. He lacks both the skill and knowledge adequately to prepare his defense, even though he have a perfect one. He requires the guiding hand of counsel at every step in the proceedings against him. Without it, though he be not guilty, he faces the danger of conviction because he does not know how to establish his innocence."...

The court in *Betts v. Brady* departed from the sound wisdom upon which the court's holding in *Powell v. Alabama* rested. Florida, supported by 2 other states, has asked that *Betts v. Brady* be left intact. 22 states, as friends of the court, argue that *Betts* was "an anachronism when handed down" and that it should now be overruled. We agree....

Justice William O. Douglas concurring:

While I join the opinion of the court, a brief historical resume of the relation between the Bill of Rights and the first section of the 14th Amendment seems pertinent. Since the adoption of that Amendment, 10 justices have felt that it protects from infringement by the states the privileges, protections and safeguards granted by the Bill of Rights.... Unfortunately it has never commanded a court. Yet, happily, all constitutional questions are always open.... And what we do today does not foreclose the matter.

Justice John Marshall Harlan concurring:

... When we hold a right or immunity valid against the federal government to be "implicit in the concept of ordered liberty" and thus valid against the states, I do not read our past decisions to suggest that by so holding we automatically carry over an entire body of federal law and apply it in full sweep to the states. Any such concept would disregard the frequently wide disparity between the legitimate interests of the states and of the federal government, the divergent problems that they face and the significantly different consequences of their actions.... In what is done today I do not understand the court to depart from the principles laid down in *Palko v. Connecticut* (1937), or to embrace the concept that the 14th Amendment "incorporates" the 6th Amendment as such.

On these premises I join in the judgment of the court.

Since *Gideon v. Wainwright* involved a felony conviction, the court's ruling in that case did not extend the right of counsel to poor people accused of lesser crimes the penalty for which is generally limited to 6 months in jail. 9 years after *Gideon* the court ruled 7-2 June 13, 1972, in *Argersinger v. Hamlin,* that the states must furnish counsel to poor people on trial for any offense for which the trial judge intends to consider imprisonment. The case involved a Florida man, Jon Richard Argersinger, who had been sentenced to jail for 90 days for carrying a concealed weapon.

At the time of the ruling, most states generally limited the granting of free legal counsel to poor persons facing a minimum sentence of 6 months in jail. Only 7 states—New York, California, Illinois, Massachusetts, Minnesota, New Hampshire and Texas—provided free counsel to all poor persons faced with the prospects of imprisonment. It has been estimated that 4 to 5 million persons are arrested each year for non-traffic misdemeanor offenses, $\frac{1}{3}$ of them for drunkenness. (By comparison, there are about 350,000 felony prosecutions a year.) But only the cases in which the judge intends to consider imprisonment for the defendant are covered by the new rule. Justice Lewis F. Powell Jr., joined by Justice William H. Rehnquist, in a dissenting opinion, questioned the availability of enough lawyers to handle the needs created by the majority's decision. They asserted that it would have been better for the court to have left it to the trial judge to determine whether the circumstances of a particular case required granting free counsel to poor persons accused of petty crimes.

The Supreme Court June 22, 1970, affirmed a U.S. Court of Appeals decision not to review the adequacy of legal counsel provided by a Legal Aid Society lawyer on behalf of an indigent defendant. The case, *Chambers v. Maroney,* involved a defendant who first met his trial lawyer *en route* to the courtroom, a few minutes before his 2d trial began. Although a different Legal Aid lawyer had represented the defendant at his first trial, neither the first lawyer nor any one else from Legal Aid had conferred with the defendant in the interval between the 2 trials. As the court defined the issue, "no charge is made that the attorney was incompetent or inexperienced; rather the claim is that his appearance for petitioner was so belated that he could not have furnished effective legal assistance at the 2d trial."

In refusing to grant a hearing to determine the adequacy of counsel, the Court of Appeals had rejected the petitioner's claim. Its decision was upheld by the Supreme Court. The claim that the petitioner's counsel was unprepared centered on his failure to have certain allegedly illegally seized items excluded from evidence. The Court of Appeals had held that either these items were admissable or that their admission constituted a harmless error. Therefore, said Justice Byron R. White on behalf of the Supreme Court, "the claim of prejudice from the substitution of counsel was without substantial basis. In this posture of the case we are not inclined to disturb the judgment of the Court of Appeals as to what the state record shows with respect to the adequacy of counsel. We are not disposed to fashion a *per se* rule requiring reversal of every conviction following tardy appointment of counsel or to hold that, whenever a *habeas corpus* petition alleges a belated appointment, an evidentiary hearing must be held to determine whether the defendant has been denied his constitutional right to counsel."

Justice John Marshall Harlan, dissenting, asserted that "counsel's last-minute entry into the case precluded his compliance with the state rule requiring that motions to suppress evidence be made before trial, even assuming that he had sufficient acquaintance with the case to know what arguments were worth making. Furthermore, the record suggests that he may have had virtually no such acquaintance.... It is not an answer to petitioner's claim that he has failed after the fact to show that, with adequate assistance, he would have prevailed at trial...."

Following *Gideon,* the Supreme Court ruled that indigents had the right to post-conviction counsel on first appeal *(Douglas v. California,* 1963), the post-indictment right to counsel during police interrogations *(Miranda v. Arizona,* 1966), the right to counsel at police lineups *(United States v. Wade,* 1967) and the right to counsel at preliminary hearings in states in which the preliminary hearing constitutes a "critical stage" of the criminal process *(Coleman v. Alabama,* 1970).

In an earlier effort to reduce the disparity of justice available to the poor, the Supreme Court had ruled in *Griffin v. Illinois* (1956) that a state must furnish a poor convicted felon, who wished to appeal his conviction, with a transcript of his trial. Such transcripts can cost thousands of dollars. In *Mayer v. Chicago* (1971), the court unanimously extended that ruling to poor persons who wished to appeal misdemeanor convictions, including cases involving only fines. The issue was presented by Jack L. Mayer, a medical student, who had been arrested during antiwar demonstrations in Chicago in 1969. Mayer, arrested while serving as a medical volunteer, was convicted of disorderly conduct and interference with a policeman. He was fined $500. Although the Illinois courts agreed that he could not afford the $300 for the transcript, they refused to provide him with one because a State Supreme Court rule guaranteed transcripts only in felony cases. Chicago officials warned the Supreme Court that the cost might be extreme if all persons in petty cases were granted a constitutional right to free transcripts. Chief Justice Warren Burger, in a concurring opinion, said that if lawyers for poor clients violated the new ruling by making "excessive demands" for transcripts, they could be disciplined for unethical conduct.

In *Johnson v. Avery* (1969), the Supreme Court held that a state may not prevent prison inmates from furnishing legal assistance to other inmates unless the state provided an alternative source of legal advice. In *Tate v. Short* (1971), the court ruled that a state may not jail persons unable to pay a fine. The case involved an indigent who had owed $425 in fines for 9 traffic offenses.

Freedom from Self-Incrimination

In a landmark criminal-law decision, *Malloy v. Hogan,* the Supreme Court June 15, 1964 extended the 5th Amendment protections against self-incrimination to state proceedings. The ruling was 5-4, but 2 of the justices dissented on the facts of the case and did not necessarily disagree with the constitutional ruling.

The case involved William Malloy, convicted on a gambling charge in Hartford, Conn. in 1959, sentenced to 90 days in jail and fined $500. In 1961 Malloy was called to testify before an inquiry into alleged gambling and other criminal activity in Hartford County. Malloy refused to answer any questions concerning his earlier arrest and his association with a person whose activities were under investigation on the ground that "it may tend to incriminate me." Malloy, judged in contempt, was sent to prison until he agreed to answer the questions. He appealed on the ground that Connecticut had denied him his 5th Amendment rights.

The majority decision by Justice William J. Brennan Jr. accepted Malloy's contention in holding that "the 5th Amendment's exception from compulsory self-incrimination is also protected by the 14th Amendment against abridgment by the states." That decision overruled 1908 and 1947 decisions that the right against self-incrimination did not involve due process. The court also rejected Connecticut's contention that the 5th Amendment should be applied less stringently in state proceedings. In rejecting that "watered-down, subjective version of the Bill of Rights," the court held that it "would be incongruous to have different standards determine the validity of a claim of privilege based on the same feared prosecution, depending on whether the claim was asserted in a state or federal court." Therefore, the court said, "the same standards must determine whether an accused's silence in either a federal or state proceeding is justified."

Justice Harlan, dissenting, held that the court's decision "carries extremely mischievous, if not dangerous consequences for our federal system in the realm of criminal law enforcement." Harlan opposed the procedure employed by the majority, wherein a provision of the Bill of Rights was incorporated into the due process clause along with its entire body of related case law. According to Harlan, it was preferable, when applying a part of the Bill of Rights to the states, to enforce on the states only those aspects of the privilege that meet "the demands of fundamental fairness which due process embodies." "Why should it be thought, as an *a priori* matter," he asked, "that limitations on the investigative power of the states are in all respects identical with limitations on the investigative power of the federal government?" The "ultimate results" of such actions, he warned, "is compelled uniformity which is inconsistent with the purpose of our federal system and which is achieved either by encroachment on the states' sovereign powers or by dilution in federal law enforcement of the specific protections found in the Bill of Rights."

The same day that it extended the 5th Amendment protection against self-incrimination to the states in *Malloy v. Hogan,* the court in *Murphy v. Waterfront Commission* ruled that if a state granted a man immunity and then forced him to testify, that testimony could not be used in a federal prosecution.

Abridgment of the *Malloy v. Hogan* decision (378 U.S. 1, June 15, 1964):

Justice Brennan delivering the opinion of the court:

In this case we are asked to reconsider prior decisions holding that the privilege against self-incrimination is not safeguarded against state action by the 14th Amendment. *Twining v. New Jersey* [1908], ... *Adamson v. California* [1947]....

The petitioner was arrested during a gambling raid in 1959 by Hartford, Conn. police. He pleaded guilty to the crime of pool-selling, a misdemeanor, and was sentenced to one year in jail and fined $500. The sentence was ordered to be suspended after 90 days at which time he was to be placed on probation for 2 years. About 16 months after his guilty plea, petitioner was ordered to testify before a referee appointed by the Superior Court of Hartford County to conduct an inquiry into alleged gambling and other criminal activities in the county. The petitioner was asked a number of questions related to events surrounding his arrest and conviction. He refused to answer any question "on the grounds it may tend to incriminate me." The Superior Court adjudged him in contempt and committed him to prison until he was willing to answer the questions. Petitioner's application for a writ of *habeas corpus* was denied by the Superior Court, and the Connecticut Supreme Court of Errors affirmed.... The latter court held that the 5th Amendment's privilege against self-incrimination was not available to a witness in a state proceeding, that the 14th Amendment extended no privilege to him and that the petitioner had not properly invoked the privilege available under the Connecticut Constitution. We granted *certiorari.* We reverse. We hold that the 14th Amendment guaranteed the petitioner the protection of the 5th Amendment's privilege against self-incrimination and that, under the applicable federal standard, the Connecticut Supreme Court of Errors erred in holding that the privilege was not properly invoked.

The extent to which the 14th Amendment prevents state invasion of rights enumerated in the first 8 Amendments has been considered in numerous cases in this court since the amendment's adoption in 1868. Although many justices have deemed the amendment to incorporate all 8 of the amendments, the view which has thus far prevailed dates from the decision in 1897 in *Chicago, B. & Q. R. Co. v. Chicago* ... which held that the due process clause requires the states to pay just compensation for private property taken for public use. It was on the authority of that decision that the court said in 1908 in *Twining v. New Jersey* ... that "it is possible that some of the personal rights safeguarded by the first 8 amendments against national action may also be safeguarded against state action, because a denial of them would be a denial of due process of law." ...

The court has not hesitated to re-examine past decisions according the 14th Amendment a less central role in the preservation of basic liberties than that which was contemplated by its framers when they added the amendment to our constitutional scheme. Thus, although the court as late as 1922 said that "neither the 14th Amendment nor any other provision of the Constitution of the United States imposes upon the States any restrictions about 'freedom of speech'...," *Prudential Ins. Co. v. Cheek*, ... 3 years later *Gitlow v. New York* [1925] ... initiated a series of decisions which today holds immune from state invasion every First Amendment protection for the cherished rights of mind and spirit—the freedoms of speech, press, religion, assembly, association and petition for redress of grievances.

Similarly, *Palko v. Connecticut*, ... decided in 1938, suggested that the rights secured by the 4th Amendment, were not protected against state action, citing ... the statement of the court in 1914 in *Weeks v. United States* ... that "the 4th Amendment is not directed to individual misconduct of [state] officials." In 1961, however, the court held that in the light of later decisions, it was taken as settled that "... the 4th Amendment's right of privacy has been declared enforceable against the states through the due process clause of the 14th...." *Mapp v. Ohio*.... Again, although the court held in 1942 that in a state prosecution for a noncapital offense, "appointment of counsel is not a fundamental right," *Betts v. Brady;* ... cf. *Powell v. Alabama* [1932], ... only last term this decision was re-examined, and it was held that provision of counsel in all criminal cases was "a fundamental right essential to a fair trial" and thus was made obligatory on the States by the 14th Amendment. *Gideon v. Wainwright* [1963]. . . .

We hold today that the 5th Amendment's exception from compulsory self-incrimination is also protected by the 14th Amendment against abridgment by the states. Decisions of the court since *Twining* and *Adamson* have departed from the contrary view expressed in those cases. . . .

This conclusion is fortified by our recent decision in *Mapp v. Ohio* [1961], . . . overruling *Wolf v. Colorado, supra,* which had held "that in a prosecution in a state court for a state crime the 14th Amendment does not forbid the admission of evidence obtained by an unreasonable search and seizure." . . . *Mapp* held that the 5th Amendment privilege against self-incrimination implemented the 4th Amendment in such cases and that the 2 guarantees of personal security conjoined in the 14th Amendment to make the exclusionary rule obligatory upon the states. We relied upon the great case of *Boyd v. United States,* . . . decided in 1886, which, considering the 4th and 5th Amendments as running "almost into each other," . . . held that "breaking into a house and opening boxes and drawers are circumstances of aggravation; but any forceable and compulsory extortion of a man's own testimony or of his private papers to be used as evidence to convict him of crime or to forfeit his goods is within the condemnation of [those amendments]. . . ." . . . In thus returning to the *Boyd* view that the privilege is one of the "principles of a free government," . . . *Mapp* necessarily repudiated the *Twining* concept of the privilege as a mere rule of evidence "best defended not as an unchangeable principle of universal justice but as a law proved by experience to be expedient." . . .

The respondent state of Connecticut concedes in its brief that under our decisions, particularly those involving coerced confessions, "the accusatorial system has become a fundamental part of the fabric of our society and, hence, is enforceable against the states." The state urges, however, that the availability of the federal privilege to a witness in a state inquiry is to be determined according to a less stringent standard than is applicable in a federal proceeding. We disagree. We have held that the guarantees of the First Amendment, ... the prohibition of unreasonable searches and seizures of the 4th Amendment ... and the right to counsel guaranteed by the 6th Amendment ... are all to be enforced against the states under the 14th Amendment according to the same standards that protect those personal rights against federal encroachment. In the coerced confession cases, involving the policies of the privilege itself, there has been no suggestion that a confession might be considered coerced if used in a federal but not a state tribunal. The court thus has rejected the notion that the 14th Amendment applies to the states only a "watered-down, subjective version of the Bill of Rights." ... It would be incongruous to have different standards determine the validity of a claim of privilege based on the same feared prosecution, depending on whether the claim was asserted in a state or federal court. Therefore, the same standards must determine whether an accused's silence in either a federal or state proceeding is justified. ...

Justice Harlan, whom Justice Thomas C. Clark joined, dissenting:

... Believing that the reasoning behind the court's decision carries extremely mischievous, if not dangerous consequences for our federal system in the realm of criminal law enforcement, I must dissent. ...

I can only read the court's opinion as accepting in fact what it rejects in theory: the application to the states, via the 14th Amendment, of the forms of federal criminal procedure embodied within the first 8 amendments to the Constitution. While it is true that the court deals today with only one aspect of state criminal procedure and rejects the wholesale "incorporation" of such federal constitutional requirements, the logical gap between the court's premises and its novel constitutional conclusion can, I submit, be bridged only by the additional premise that the due process clause of the 14th Amendment is a shorthand directive to this court to pick and choose among the provisions of the first 8 amendments and apply those chosen, freighted with their entire accompanying body of federal doctrine, to law enforcement in the states.

I accept and agree with the proposition that continuing re-examination of the constitutional conception of 14th Amendment due process of law is required, and that development of the community's sense of justice may in time lead to expansion of the protection which due process affords. In particular, in this case, I agree that principles of justice to which due process gives expression, as reflected in decisions of this court, prohibit a state, as the 5th Amendment prohibits the federal government, from imprisoning a person *solely* because he refuses to give evidence which may incriminate him under the laws of the state. I do not understand, however, how this process of re-examination, which must refer always to the guiding standard of due process of law, including, of course, reference to the particular guarantees of the Bill of Rights, can be short-circuited by the simple device of incorporating into due process, without critical examination, the whole body of law which surrounds a specific prohibition directed against the federal government. The consequence of such an approach to due process as it pertains to the states is inevitably disregard of all relevant differences which may exist between state and federal criminal law and its enforcement. The ultimate result is compelled uniformity, which is inconsistent with the purpose of our federal system and which is achieved either by encroachment on the states' sovereign powers or by dilution in federal law enforcement of the specific protections found in the Bill of Rights. . . .

The court's undiscriminating approach to the due process clause carries serious implications for the sound working of our federal system in the field of criminal law.

The court concludes, almost without discussion, that "the same standards must determine whether an accused's silence in either a federal or state proceeding is justified.". . . About all that the court offers in explanation of this conclusion is the observation that it would be "incongruous" if different standards governed the assertion of a privilege to remain silent in state and federal tribunals. Such "incongruity," however, is at the heart of our federal system. The powers and responsibilities of the state and federal governments are not congruent; under our Constitution, they are not intended to be. Why should it be thought, as an *a priori* matter, that limitations on the investigative power of the states are in all respects identical with limitations on the investigative power of the federal government? This certainly does not follow from the fact that

we deal here with constitutional requirements; for the provisions of the Constitution which are construed are different.

As the court pointed out in *Abbate v. United States* [1959],
... "the states under our federal system have the principal
responsibility for defining and prosecuting crimes." The court
endangers this allocation of responsibility for the prevention of
crime when it applies to the states doctrines developed in the
context of federal law enforcement, without any attention to
the special problems which the states as a group or particular
states may face. If the power of the states to deal with local
crime is unduly restricted, the likely consequence is a shift of
responsibility in this area to the federal government, with its
vastly greater resources. Such a shift, if it occurs, may in the
end serve to weaken the very liberties which the 14th Amendment safeguards by bringing us closer to the monolithic society
which our federalism rejects. Equally dangerous to our liberties
is the alternative of watering down protections against the
federal government embodied in the Bill of Rights so as not
unduly to restrict the powers of the states. The dissenting
opinion in *Aguilar v. Texas* [1964] ... evidences that this danger
is not imaginary.

Rather than insisting, almost by rote, that the Connecticut
court, in considering the petitioner's claim of privilege, was
required to apply the "federal standard," the court should have
fulfilled its responsibility under the due process clause by in-
quiring whether the proceedings below met the demands of
fundamental fairness which due process embodies. Such an
approach may not satisfy those who see in the 14th Amendment
a set of easily applied "absolutes" which can afford a haven
from unsettling doubt. It is, however, truer to the spirit which
requires this court constantly to re-examine fundamental
principles and at the same time enjoins it from reading its own
preferences into the Constitution....

Justice Byron White, whom Justice Potter Stewart joined, dissenting:

The 5th Amendment safeguards an important complex of
values, but it is difficult for me to perceive how these values are
served by the court's holding that the privilege was properly invoked in this case. While purporting to apply the prevailing
federal standard of incrimination—the same standard of

incrimination that the Connecticut courts applied—the court has all but stated that a witness' invocation of the privilege to any question is to be automatically, and without more, accepted.... I prefer the rule permitting the judge rather than the witness to determine when an answer sought is incriminating.

The established rule has been that the witness' claim of the privilege is not final, for the privilege qualifies a citizen's general duty of disclosure only when his answers would subject him to danger from the criminal law. The privilege against self-incrimination or any other evidentiary privilege does not protect silence which is solely an expression of political protest, a desire not to inform, a fear of social obloquy or economic disadvantage or fear of prosecution for future crimes.... If the general duty to testify when subpoenaed is to remain and the privilege is to be retained as a protection against compelled incriminating answers, the trial judge must be permitted to make a meaningful determination of when answers tend to incriminate....

... Under this test, Malloy's refusals to answer some, if not all, of the questions put to him were clearly not privileged.

Right to Cross-Examine Witnesses

The 6th Amendment right of a defendant to confront witnesses against him was held binding on the states in *Pointer v. Texas,* decided by the Supreme Court Apr. 5, 1965. There were no dissenting opinions. The case involved a Texan convicted on the basis of a statement by a witness who had since moved and was not available for cross-examination at the trial.

Abridgment of the *Pointer v. Texas* decision (380 U.S. 400, Apr. 5, 1965):

Justice Hugo L. Black delivering the opinion of the court:

...2 years ago in *Gideon v. Wainwright* ... we held that

the 14th Amendment makes the 6th Amendment's guarantee of right to counsel obligatory upon the states. The question we find necessary to decide in this case is whether the amendment's guarantee of a defendant's right "to be confronted with the witnesses against him," which has been held to include the right to cross-examine those witnesses, is also made applicable to the states by the 14th Amendment.

The petitioner [Robert Granville] Pointer and one Dillard were arrested in Texas and taken before a state judge for a preliminary hearing (in Texas called the "examining trial") on a charge of having robbed Kenneth W. Phillips of $375 "by assault, or violence, or by putting in fear of life or bodily injury." ... At this hearing an assistant district attorney conducted the prosecution and examined witnesses, but neither of the defendants, both of whom were laymen, had a lawyer. Phillips, as chief witness for the state, gave his version of the alleged robbery in detail, identifying petitioner as the man who had robbed him at gunpoint. Apparently Dillard tried to cross-examine Phillips but Pointer did not, although Pointer was said to have tried to cross-examine some other witnesses at the hearing. Petitioner was subsequently indicted on a charge of having committed the robbery. Some time before the trial was held, Phillips moved to California. After putting in evidence to show that Phillips had moved and did not intend to return to Texas, the state at the trial offered the transcript of Phillips' testimony given at the preliminary hearing as evidence against petitioner. Petitioner's counsel immediately objected to introduction of the transcript, stating, "Your Honor, we will object to that, as it is a denial of the confrontment of the witnesses against the defendant." Similar objections were repeatedly made by petitioner's counsel but were overruled by the trial judge, apparently in part because, as the judge viewed it, petitioner had been present at the preliminary hearing and therefore had been "accorded the opportunity of cross-examining the witnesses there against him." The Texas Court of Criminal Appeals, the highest state court to which the case could be taken, affirmed petitioner's conviction, rejecting his contention that use of the transcript to convict him denied him rights guaranteed by the 6th and 14th Amendments.... We granted *certiorari* to consider the important constitutional question the case involves....

...In *Gideon v. Wainwright, supra,* in which this court
held that the 6th Amendment's right to the assistance of counsel
is obligatory upon the states, we did so on the ground that "a
provision of the Bill of Rights which is 'fundamental and
essential to a fair trial' is made obligatory upon the states by
the 14th Amendment."... And last term in *Malloy v. Hogan,*
... in holding that the 5th Amendment's guarantee against self-
incrimination was made applicable to the states by the 14th, we
reiterated the holding of *Gideon* that the 6th Amendment's
right-to-counsel guarantee is " 'a fundamental right, essential to
a fair trial,'" and "thus was made obligatory on the states by
the 14th Amendment."... We hold today that the 6th Amendment's right of an accused to confront the witnesses against
him is likewise a fundamental right and is made obligatory on
the states by the 14th Amendment.

It cannot seriously be doubted at this late date that the
right of cross-examination is included in the right of an accused
in a criminal case to confront the witnesses against him. And
probably no one ... would deny the value of cross-examination
in exposing falsehood and bringing out the truth in the trial of
a criminal case.... The fact that this right appears in the 6th
Amendment of our Bill of Rights reflects the belief of the
framers of those liberties and safeguards that confrontation
was a fundamental right essential to a fair trial in a criminal
prosecution. Moreover, the decisions of this court and other
courts throughout the years have constantly emphasized the
necessity for cross-examination as a protection for defendants
in criminal cases....

There are few subjects, perhaps, upon which this court and
other courts have been more nearly unanimous than in their
expressions of belief that the right of confrontation and cross-
examination is an essential and fundamental requirement for
the kind of fair trial which is this country's constitutional
goal....

...Under this court's prior decisions, the 6th Amendment's
guarantee of confrontation and cross-examination was unquestionably denied petitioner in this case....

...This court has recognized the admissibility against an
accused of dying declarations, ... and of testimony of a
deceased witness who has testified at a former trial.... Nothing
we hold here is to the contrary. The case before us would be

quite a different one had Phillips' statement been taken at a full-fledged hearing at which petitioner had been represented by counsel who had been given a complete and adequate opportunity to cross-examine.... There are other analogous situations which might not fall within the scope of the constitutional rule requiring confrontation of witnesses. The case before us, however, does not present any situation like those mentioned above or others analogous to them. Because the transcript of Phillips' statement offered against petitioner at his trial had not been taken at a time and under circumstances affording petitioner through counsel an adequate opportunity to cross-examine Phillips, its introduction in a federal court in a criminal case against Pointer would have amounted to denial of the privilege of confrontation guaranteed by the 6th Amendment. Since we hold that the right of an accused to be confronted with the witnesses against him must be determined by the same standards whether the right is denied in a federal or state proceeding, it follows that use of the transcript to convict petitioner denied him a constitutional right, and that his conviction must be reversed.

Justice Harlan concurring in the result:

I agree that in the circumstances the admission of the statement in question deprived the petitioner of a right of "confrontation" assured by the 14th Amendment. I cannot subscribe, however, to the constitutional reasoning of the court.

The court holds that the right of confrontation guaranteed by the 6th Amendment in federal criminal trials is carried into state criminal cases by the 14th Amendment. This is another step in the onward march of the long-since discredited "incorporation" doctrine ... which for some reason that I have not yet been able to fathom has come into the sunlight in recent years....

For me this state judgment must be reversed because a right of confrontation is "implicit in the concept of ordered liberty," *Palko v. Connecticut* [1937], ... reflected in the due process clause of the 14th Amendment independently of the 6th.

While either of these constitutional approaches brings one to the same end result in this particular case, there is a basic difference between the 2 in the kind of future constitutional development they portend. The concept of 14th Amendment

due process embodied in *Palko* and a host of other thoughtful
past decisions now rapidly falling into discard recognizes that
our Constitution tolerates, indeed encourages, differences
between the methods used to effectuate legitimate federal and
state concerns, subject to the requirements of fundamental fairness "implicit in the concept of ordered liberty." The philosophy
of "incorporation," on the other hand, subordinates all such
state differences to the particular requirements of the federal
Bill of Rights ... and increasingly subjects state legal processes
to enveloping federal judicial authority. "Selective" incorporation or "absorption" amounts to little more than a diluted form
of the full incorporation theory. Whereas it rejects full
incorporation because of recognition that not all of the guarantees of the Bill of Rights should be deemed "fundamental," it
at the same time ignores the possibility that not all phases of
any given guaranty described in the Bill of Rights are
necessarily fundamental.

It is too often forgotten in these times that the American
federal system is itself constitutionally ordained, that it
embodies values profoundly making for lasting liberties in this
country and that its legitimate requirements demand
continuing solid recognition in all phases of the work of this
court. The "incorporation" doctrines, whether full blown or
selective, are both historically and constitutionally unsound and
incompatible with the maintenance of our federal system on
even course.

Right to a Speedy Trial

The 6th Amendment right to a speedy trial in
state proceedings was established by the Supreme
Court Mar. 13, 1967 in *Klopfer v. North Carolina.*
The decision was unanimous. The case involved an
unusal procedure in North Carolina wherein a
prosecutor, on releasing a suspect from custody, was
permitted to postpone his trial indefinitely. A trial,

however, could be ordered at any time in the future by the prosecution.

Prior to *Klopfer* most state constitutions had guaranteed the right to a speedy trial. The great majority of the states, moreover, had enacted statutes setting forth a period in which a defendant must be brought to trial. A defendant, however, may waive that right.

In *United States v. Ewell* (1966), the Supreme Court, *per* Justice Byron R. White, defined the right to a speedy trial as follows: "This guarantee is an important safeguard to prevent undue and oppressive incarceration prior to trial, to minimize anxiety and concern accompanying public accusation and to limit the possibilities that long delay will impair the ability of the accused to defend himself. However, in large measure because of the many procedural safeguards provided an accused, the ordinary procedures for criminal prosecution are designed to move at a deliberate pace. A requirement of unreasonable speed would have a deleterious effect both upon the rights of the accused and upon the ability of society to protect itself. Therefore, this court has consistently been of the view that 'The right of a speedy trial is necessarily relative. It is consistent with delays and depends upon circumstances. It secures rights to a defendant. It does not preclude the rights of public justice.' ... 'Whether delay in completing a prosecution ... amounts to an unconstitutional deprivation of rights depends upon all the circumstances.... The delay must not be purposeful or oppressive.... [T]he essential ingredient is orderly expedition and not mere speed.' "

In *United States v. Marion,* decided Dec. 20, 1971, the Supreme Court ruled that the 6th Amendment guarantee of a speedy trial applies only after a person has been accused of a crime. In this instance it had taken the federal government 3 years to bring charges formally against 2 men suspected of consumer fraud. Justices William O. Douglas, William J. Brennan Jr. and John Marshall Harlan disagreed, stating that the government's failure to indict a suspect until years after it knew about his alleged offense can violate the right to a speedy trial.

Abridgment of the *Klopfer v. North Carolina* decision (386 U.S. 213, Mar. 13, 1967):

Chief Justice Earl Warren delivering the opinion of the court:

... We hold here that the right to a speedy trial is as fundamental as any of the rights secured by the 6th Amendment. That right has its roots at the very foundation of our English law heritage. Its first articulation in modern jurisprudence appears to have been made in Magna Carta (1215), wherein it was written, "We will sell to no man, we will not deny or defer to any man either justice or right"; but evidence of recognition of the right to speedy justice in even earlier times is found in the Assize of Clarendon (1166). By the late 13th century, justices, armed with commissions of gaol delivery and/or *Oyer* and *Terminer,* were visiting the countryside 3 times a year. These justices, Sir Edward Coke wrote in Part II of his *Institutes,* "have not suffered the prisoner to be long detained, but at their next coming have given the prisoner full and speedy justice, ... without detaining him long in prison." To Coke, prolonged detention without trial would have been contrary to the law and custom of England; but he also believed that the delay in trial, by itself, would be an improper denial of justice. In his explication of Chapter 29 of the Magna Carta, he wrote that the words "We will sell to no man, we will not deny or defer to any man either justice or right" had the following effect: "And therefore, every subject of this realme, for injury done to him *in bonis, terris, vel persona,* by any other subject, be he ecclesiasticall, or temporall, free, or bond, man, or woman, old, or young, or be he outlawed, excommunicated, or any other without exception, may take his remedy by the course of the law, and have justice, and right for the injury done to him, freely without sale, fully without any deniall, and speedily without delay."

Coke's *Institutes* were read in the American Colonies by virtually every student of the law. Indeed, Thomas Jefferson wrote that at the time he studied law (1762-1767), *"Coke Lyttleton* was the universal elementary book of law students." And to John Rutledge of South Carolina, the *Institutes* seemed "to be almost the foundation of our law." To Coke, in turn, Magna Carta was one of the fundamental bases of English liberty. Thus, it is not suprising that when George Mason drafted the first of the colonial bills of rights, he set forth a principle of Magna Carta, using phraseology similar to that of Coke's explication: "[I]n all capital or criminal prosecutions," the Virginia Declaration of Rights of 1776 provided, "a man hath a right ... to a speedy trial...." That this right was considered fundamental at this early period in our history is evidenced by its guarantee in the constitutions of several of the states of the new nation, as well as by its prominent position in the 6th Amendment. Today, each of the 50 states guarantees the right to a speedy trial to its citizens.

The history of the right to a speedy trial and its reception in this country clearly establish that it is one of the most basic rights preserved by our Constitution....

Justice Harlan concurring in the result:

While I entirely agree with the result reached by the court, I am unable to subscribe to the constitutional premises upon which that result is based—quite evidently the viewpoint that the 14th Amendment "incorporates" or "absorbs" *as such* all or some of the specific provisions of the Bill of Rights. I do not believe that this is sound constitutional doctrine....

I would rest decision of this case not on the "speedy trial" provision of the 6th Amendment, but on the ground that this unusual North Carolina procedure, which in effect allows state prosecuting officials to put a person under the cloud of an un-liquidated criminal charge for an indeterminate period, violates the requirement of fundamental fairness assured by the due process clause of the 14th Amendment. To support that conclusion I need only refer to the traditional concepts of due process set forth in the opinion of the Chief Justice.

Right to Obtain Witnesses

The 6th Amendment right to compel witnesses to testify on behalf of the defense was held binding on the states in *Washington v. Texas,* decided by the Supreme Court June 12, 1967.

Justice Harlan, in a separate opinion, reiterated his long-held view that the due process clause does not "incorporate" specific provisions of the Bill of Rights. The clause, he said, in quoting from a 1961 decision, is not reducible to "a series of isolated points" but is rather "a rational continuum which, broadly speaking, includes a freedom from all substantial arbitrary impositions and purposeless restraints." Harlan concurred in the result of the case, however, on the ground that the due process clause, independently of the Bill of Rights, did not permit Texas to prevent coparticipants in a crime from testifying on each other's behalf.

Abridgment of the *Washington v. Texas* decision (388 U.S. 14, June 12, 1967):

Chief Justice Warren delivering the opinion of the court:

We granted *certiorari* in this case to determine whether the right of a defendant in a criminal case under the 6th Amendment to have compulsory process for obtaining witnesses in his favor is applicable to the states through the 14th Amendment and whether that right was violated by a state procedural statute providing that persons charged as principals, accomplices or accessories in the same crime cannot be introduced as witnesses for each other.

Petitioner, Jackie Washington, was convicted in Dallas County, Texas, of murder with malice and was sentenced by a jury to 50 years in prison. The prosecution's evidence showed that petitioner, an 18-year-old youth, had dated a girl named Jean Carter until her mother had forbidden her to see him. The girl thereafter began dating another boy, the deceased. Evidently motivated by jealousy, petitioner with several other boys began driving around the City of Dallas on the night of Aug. 29, 1964, looking for a gun. The search eventually led to one Charles Fuller, who joined the group with his shotgun. After obtaining some shells ..., [the] boys proceeded to Jean Carter's home, where Jean, her family and the deceased were having supper. Some of the boys threw bricks at the house and then ran back to the car, leaving petitioner and Fuller alone in front of the house with the shotgun. At the sound of the bricks the deceased and Jean Carter's mother rushed out on the porch to investigate. The shotgun was fired by either petitioner or Fuller, and the deceased was fatally wounded. Shortly afterward petitioner and Fuller came running back to the car where the other boys waited, with Fuller carrying the shotgun.

Petitioner testified in his own behalf. He claimed that Fuller, who was intoxicated, had taken the gun from him, and that he had unsuccessfully tried to persuade Fuller to leave before the shooting. Fuller had insisted that he was going to shoot someone, and petitioner had run back to the automobile. He saw the girl's mother come out of the door as he began running, and he subsequently heard the shot. At the time, he had thought that Fuller had shot the woman. In support of his version of the facts, petitioner offered the testimony of Fuller. The record indicates that Fuller would have testified that petitioner pulled at him and tried to persuade him to leave and that petitioner ran before Fuller fired the fatal shot.

It is undisputed that Fuller's testimony would have been relevant and material and that it was vital to the defense. Fuller was the only person other than petitioner who knew exactly who had fired the shotgun and whether petitioner had at the last minute attempted to prevent the shooting. Fuller, however, had been previously convicted of the same murder and sentenced to 50 years in prison, and he was confined in the Dallas County jail. 2 Texas statutes provided at the time of the trial in this case that persons charged or convicted as coparticipants in the same crime could not testify for one another, although there was no bar to their testifying for the state. On the basis of these statutes the trial judge sustained the state's objection and refused to allow Fuller to testify. Petitioner's conviction followed, and it was upheld on appeal by the Texas Court of Criminal Appeals.... We reverse.

We have not previously been called upon to decide whether the right of an accused to have compulsory process for obtaining witnesses in his favor, guaranteed in federal trials by the 6th Amendment, is so fundamental and essential to a fair trial that it is incorporated in the due process clause of the 14th Amendment. At one time it was thought that the 6th Amendment had no application to state criminal trials. That view no longer prevails, and in recent years we have increasingly looked to the specific guarantees of the 6th Amendment to determine whether a state criminal trial was conducted with due process of law. We have held that due process requires that the accused have the assistance of counsel for his defense, that he be confronted with the witnesses against him and that he have the right to a speedy and public trial.

The right of an accused to have compulsory process for obtaining witnesses in his favor stands on no lesser footing than the other 6th Amendment rights that we have previously held applicable to the states. This court had occasion in *In re Oliver* ... to describe what it regarded as the most basic ingredients of due process of law. It observed that: "A person's right to reasonable notice of a charge against him and an opportunity to be heard in his defense—a right to his day in court—are basic in our system of jurisprudence; and these rights include, as a minimum, a right to examine the witnesses against him, to offer testimony, and to be represented by counsel."...

The right to offer the testimony of witnesses, and to compel their attendance, if necessary, is in plain terms the right to present a defense, the right to present the defendant's version of the facts as well as the prosecution's to the jury so it may decide where the truth lies. Just as an accused has the right to confront the prosecution's witnesses for the purpose of challenging their testimony, he has the right to present his own witnesses to establish a defense. This right is a fundamental element of due process of law....

The [Texas] rule disqualifying an alleged accomplice from testifying on behalf of the defendant cannot even be defended on the ground that it rationally sets apart a group of persons who are particularly likely to commit perjury. The absurdity of the rule is amply demonstrated by the exceptions that have been made to it. For example, the accused accomplice may be called by the prosecution to testify against the defendant. Common sense would suggest that he often has a greater interest in lying in favor of the prosecution rather than against it, especially if he is still awaiting his own trial or sentencing. To think that criminals will lie to save their fellows but not to obtain favors from the prosecution for themselves is indeed to clothe the criminal class with more nobility than one might expect to find in the public at large. Moreover, under the Texas statutes the accused accomplice is no longer disqualified if he is acquitted at his own trial. Presumably, he would then be free to testify on behalf of his comrade, secure in the knowledge that he could incriminate himself as freely as he liked in his testimony, since he could not again be prosecuted for the same offense. The Texas law leaves him free to testify when he has a great incentive to perjury, and bars his testimony in situations where he has a lesser motive to lie.

We hold that the petitioner in this case was denied his right to have compulsory process for obtaining witnesses in his favor because the state arbitrarily denied him the right to put on the stand a witness who was physically and mentally capable of testifying to events that he had personally observed, and whose testimony would have been relevant and material to the defense. The framers of the Constitution did not intend to commit the futile act of giving to a defendant the right to secure the attendance of witnesses whose testimony he had no right to use. The judgment of conviction must be reversed.

Justice Harlan concurring in the results:

For reasons that I have stated in my concurring opinions in *Gideon v. Wainwright* ... and *Pointer v. Texas* ... and in my dissenting opinion in *Poe v. Ullman* [1961] ..., I cannot accept the view that the due process clause of the 14th Amendment "incorporates," in its terms, the specific provisions of the Bill of Rights. In my view the due process clause is not reducible to "a series of isolated points" but is rather "a rational continuum which, broadly speaking, includes a freedom from all substantial arbitrary impositions and purposeless restraints...." *Poe v. Ullman....*

I concur in the result in this case because I believe that the state may not constitutionally forbid the petitioner, a criminal defendant, from introducing on his own behalf the important testimony of one indicted in connection with the same offense, who would not, however, be barred from testifying if called by the prosecution....

In my opinion this is not, then, really a problem of "compulsory process" at all, although the court's incorporationist approach leads it to strain this constitutional provision to reach these peculiar statutes. Neither is it a situation in which the state has determined, as a matter of valid state evidentiary law, on the basis of general experience with a particular class of persons, as for example, the mentally incompetent or those previously convicted of perjury, that the pursuit of truth is best served by an across-the-board disqualification as witnesses of persons of that class.... This is rather a case in which the state has recognized as relevant and competent the testimony of this type of witness, but arbitrarily barred its use by the defendant. This, I think, the due process clause forbids....

Juries in State Trials

The Supreme Court May 20, 1968, in *Duncan v. Louisiana,* extended the 6th Amendment right to a jury trial to state criminal proceedings. "Because we believe that trial by jury in criminal cases is fundamental to the American scheme of justice," Justice Byron White said in his majority opinion, "we hold that the 14th Amendment guarantees a right of jury trial in all criminal cases which—were they to be tried in a federal court—would come within the 6th Amendment's guarantee." The case concerned Gary Duncan, who had been charged with simple battery, under Louisiana law a misdemeanor punishable by a maximum penalty of 2 years' imprisonment and a fine of $300. Duncan was convicted and sentenced to 60 days in jail and fined $150.

The majority opinion concluded that "the deep commitment of the nation to the right of jury trial in serious criminal cases as a defense against arbitrary law enforcement qualifies for protection under the due process clause ... and must therefore be respected by the states."

Justice Hugo L. Black, in a concurring opinion, set forth his view that the 14th Amendment was meant to apply the entire Bill of Rights to the states. Although willing to go along with the court's policy in recent years of selectively "incorporating" various provisions of the Bill of Rights into the due process clause of the 14th Amendment, Black took particular issue with Justice John Marshall Harlan's dissenting opinion.

According to Harlan, the question before the court was not whether trial by jury is an ancient institution but whether the due process clause barred Louisiana from trying charges of simple battery without a jury. The due process clause, Harlan said, requires that trials be "fair" and does not necessarily demand a jury trial. "Neither history, nor sense, supports using the 14th Amendment to put the states in a constitutional straightjacket with respect to their own development in the administration of criminal or civil law," he said. What was required in the current case, he maintained, was a finding of whether the Louisiana procedure was fundamentally unfair. Harlan asserted that juries were not necessarily indispensable to a fair trial. On the contrary, he said, each state should be encouraged to decide for itself when jury trials are appropriate. Harlan cited Justice Louis Brandeis' assertion that it is "one of the happy incidents of the federal system that a single courageous state may, if its citizens choose, serve as a laboratory." The courts, Harlan continued, would be available to correct "any experiments in criminal procedure that prove fundamentally unfair to defendants. That is not being done today: instead, and quite without reason, the court has chosen to impose upon every state one means of trying criminal cases; it is a good means, but it is not the only fair means, and it is not demonstrably better than the alternatives states might devise."

The notion that the states should be afforded latitude in designing their systems of criminal justice, subject to judicial veto, was held by Justice Black to be an invitation for judges to interject their "predilections and understandings of what is best for the country" into a reading of due process.

Abridgment of the *Duncan v. Louisiana* decision (391 U.S. 145, May 20, 1968):

Justice White delivering the opinion of the court:

...Appellant, Gary Duncan, was convicted of simple battery in the 25th Judicial District Court of Louisiana. Under Louisiana law simple battery is a misdemeanor, punishable by a maximum of 2 years' imprisonment and a $300 fine. Appellant sought trial by jury, but because the Louisiana constitution grants jury trials only in cases in which capital punishment or imprisonment at hard labor may be imposed, the trial judge denied the request. Appellant was convicted and sentenced to serve 60 days in the parish prison and pay a fine of $150. Appellant sought review in the Supreme Court of Louisiana, asserting that the denial of jury trial violated rights guaranteed to him by the United States Constitution. The Supreme Court, finding "[n]o error of law in the ruling complained of," denied appellant a writ of *certiorari.* ... [A]ppellant sought review in this court, alleging that the 6th and 14th Amendments to the United States Constitution secure the right to jury trial in state criminal prosecutions where a sentence as long as 2 years may be imposed. . . .

Appellant was 19 years of age when tried. While driving on Highway 23 in Plaquemines Parish on Oct. 18, 1966, he saw 2 younger cousins engaged in a conversation by the side of the road with 4 white boys. Knowing his cousins, Negroes who had recently transferred to a formerly all-white high school, had reported the occurrence of racial incidents at the school, Duncan stopped the car, got out, and approached the 6 boys. At trial the white boys and a white onlooker testified, as did appellant and his cousins. The testimony was in dispute on many points, but the witnesses agreed that appellant and the white boys spoke to each other, that appellant encouraged his cousins to break off the encounter and enter his car, and that appellant was about to enter the car himself for the purpose of driving away with his cousins. The whites testified that just before getting in the car appellant slapped Herman Landry, one of the white boys, on the elbow. The Negroes testified that appellant had not slapped Landry, but had merely touched him. The trial judge concluded that the state had proved beyond a reasonable doubt that Duncan had committed simple battery and found him guilty.

. . . The 14th Amendment denies the states the power to "deprive any person of life, liberty or property, without due process of law." In resolving conflicting claims concerning the meaning of this spacious language, the court has looked increasingly to the Bill of Rights for guidance; many of the rights guaranteed by the first 8 amendments to the Constitution have been held to be protected against state action by the due process clause of the 14th Amendment. That clause now protects the right to compensation for property taken by the state; the rights of speech, press and religion covered by the First Amendment; the 4th Amendment rights to be free from unreasonable searches and seizures and to have excluded from criminal trials any evidence illegally seized; the right guaranteed by the 5th Amendment to be free of compelled self-incrimination; and the 6th Amendment rights to counsel, to a speedy and public trial, to confrontation of opposing witnesses and to compulsory process for obtaining witnesses.

The test for determining whether a right extended by the 5th and 6th Amendments with respect to federal criminal proceedings is also protected against state action by the 14th Amendment has been phrased in a variety of ways in the opinions of this court. The question has been asked whether a right is among those "'fundamental principles of liberty and justice which lie at the base of all our civil and political institutions,'" *Powell v. Alabama* ... (1932); whether it is "basic in our system of jurisprudence," *In re Oliver* (1948) ...; and whether it is "a fundamental right, essential to a fair trial," *Gideon v. Wainwright* (1963) ...; *Malloy v. Hogan* (1964) ...; *Pointer v. Texas* (1965) .... The claim before us is that the right to trial by jury guaranteed by the 6th Amendment meets these tests. The position of Louisiana, on the other hand, is that the Constitution imposes upon the states no duty to give a jury trial in any criminal case, regardless of the seriousness of crime or the size of the punishment which may be imposed. Because we believe that trial by jury in criminal cases is fundamental to the American scheme of justice, we hold that the 14th Amendment guarantees a right of jury trial in all criminal cases which— were they to be tried in a federal court—would come within the 6th Amendment's guarantee. Since we consider the appeal before us to be such a case, we hold that the Constitution was violated when appellant's demand for jury trial was refused.

The history of trial by jury in criminal cases has been frequently told. It is sufficient for present purposes to say that by the time our Constitution was written, jury trial in criminal cases had been in existence in England for several centuries and carried impressive credentials traced by many to Magna Carta. Its preservation and proper operation as a protection against arbitrary rule were among the major objectives of the revolutionary settlement which was expressed in the Declaration and Bill of Rights of 1689....

Jury trial came to America with English colonists and received strong support from them. Royal interference with the jury trial was deeply resented. Among the resolutions adopted by the First Congress of the American Colonies (the Stamp Act Congress) on Oct. 19, 1765—resolutions deemed by their authors to state "the most essential rights and liberties of the colonists"—was the declaration: "That trial by jury is the inherent and invaluable right of every British subject in these colonies." The First Continental Congress, in the resolve of Oct. 14, 1774, objected to trials before judges dependent upon the crown alone for their salaries and to trials in England for alleged crimes committed in the colonies; the Congress therefore decalred: "That the respective colonies are entitled to the common law of England, and more especially to the great and inestimable privilege of being tried by their peers of the vicinage, according to the course of that law." The Declaration of Independence stated solemn objections to the king's making "judges dependent on his will alone, for the tenure of their offices, and the amount and payment of their salaries," to his "depriving us in many cases, of the benefits of trial by jury," and to his "transporting us beyond seas to be tried for pretended offenses." The Constitution itself, in Art. III, § 2, commanded: "The trial of all crimes, except in cases of impeachment, shall be by jury; and such trial shall be held in the state where the said crimes shall have been committed." Objections to the Constitution because of the absence of a bill of rights were met by the immediate submission and adoption of the Bill of Rights. Included was the 6th Amendment which, among other things, provided: "In all criminal prosecutions, the accused shall enjoy the right to a speedy and public trial, by an impartial jury of the state and district wherein the crime shall have been committed."

The constitutions adopted by the original states guaranteed jury trial. Also, the constitution of every state entering the Union thereafter in one form or another protected the right to jury trial in criminal cases.

Even such skeletal history is impressive support for considering the right to jury trial in criminal cases to be fundamental to our system of justice, an importance frequently recognized in the opinions of this Court. For example, the Court has said [*Thompson v. Utah,* 1898]: "Those who emigrated to this country from England brought with them this great privilege 'as their birthright and inheritance, as a part of that admirable common law which had fenced around and interposed barriers on every side against the approaches of arbitrary power.'"

... The laws of every state guarantee a right to jury trial in serious criminal cases; no state has dispensed with it; nor are there significant movements under way to do so....

... We are aware of prior cases in this court in which the prevailing opinion contains statements contrary to our holding today that the right to jury trial in serious criminal cases is a fundamental right and hence must be recognized by the states as part of their obligation to extend due process of law to all persons within their jurisdiction. Louisiana relies especially on *Maxwell v. Dow* ... (1900); *Palko v. Connecticut* ... (1937); and *Snyder v. Massachusetts* ... (1934). None of these cases, however, dealt with a state which had purported to dispense entirely with a jury trial in serious criminal cases. *Maxwell* held that no provision of the Bill of Rights applied to the states—a position long since repudiated—and that the due process clause of the 14th Amendment did not prevent a state from trying a defendant for a noncapital offense with fewer than 12 men on the jury. It did not deal with a case in which no jury at all had been provided. In neither *Palko* nor *Snyder* was jury trial actually at issue, although both cases contain important *dicta* asserting that the right to jury trial is not essential to ordered liberty and may be dispensed with by the states regardless of the 6th and 14th Amendments. These observations, though weighty and respectable, are nevertheless *dicta,* unsupported by holdings in this court that a state may refuse a defendant's demand for a jury trial when he is charged with a serious crime. Perhaps because the right to jury trial was not directly at stake, the court's remarks about the jury in *Palko* and *Snyder* took no note of past or current developments regarding jury trials, did not consider its purposes and functions, attempted no inquiry into how well it was performing its job, and did not discuss possible distinctions between civil and criminal cases. In *Malloy v. Hogan* [1964] ..., the court rejected *Palko's* discussion of the self-incrimination clause. Respectfully, we reject the prior *dicta* regarding jury trial in criminal cases.

The guarantees of jury trial in the federal and state constitutions reflect a profound judgment about the way in which law should be enforced and justice administered. A right to jury trial is granted to criminal defendants in order to prevent oppression by the government. Those who wrote our constitutions knew from history and experience that it was necessary to protect against unfounded criminal charges brought to eliminate enemies and against judges too responsive to the voice of higher authority. The framers of the constitutions strove to create an independent judiciary but insisted upon further protection against arbitrary action. Providing an accused with the right to be tried by a jury of his peers gave him an inestimable safeguard against the corrupt or over-zealous prosecutor and against the compliant, biased, or eccentric judge. If the defendant preferred the common-sense judgment of a jury to the more tutored but perhaps less sympathetic reaction of the single judge, he was to have it. Beyond this, the jury trial provisions in the federal and state constitutions reflect a fundamental decision about the exercise of official power—a reluctance to entrust plenary powers over the life and liberty of the citizen to one judge or to a group of judges. Fear of unchecked power, so typical of our state and federal governments in other respects, found expression in the criminal law in this insistence upon community participation in the determination of guilt or innocence. The deep commitment of the nation to the right of jury trial in serious criminal cases as a defense against arbitrary law enforcement qualifies for protection under the due process clause of the 14th Amendment and must therefore be respected by the states.

Of course jury trial has "its weaknesses and the potential for misuse," *Singer v. United States* ... (1965). We are aware of the long debate, especially in this century, among those who write about the administration of justice, as to the wisdom of permitting untrained laymen to determine the facts in civil and criminal proceedings. ... Most of the controversy has centered on the jury in civil cases. ... At the heart of the dispute have been express or implicit assertions that juries are incapable of adequately understanding evidence or determining issues of fact, and that they are unpredictable, quixotic and little better than a roll of dice. Yet, the most recent and exhaustive study of the jury in criminal cases concluded that juries do understand the evidence and come to sound conclusions in most of the cases presented to them and that when juries differ with the result at which the judge would have arrived, it is usually because they are serving some of the very purposes for which they were created and for which they are now employed.

The state of Louisiana urges that holding that the 14th Amendment assures a right to jury trial will cast doubt on the integrity of every trial conducted without a jury. Plainly, this is not the import of our holding. Our conclusion is that in the

American states, as in the federal judicial system, a general grant of jury trial for serious offenses is a fundamental right, essential for preventing miscarriages of justice and for assuring that fair trials are provided for all defendants. We would not assert, however, that every criminal trial—or any particular trial—held before a judge alone is unfair or that a defendant may never be as fairly treated by a judge as he would be by a jury. Thus we hold no constitutional doubts about the practices, common in both federal and state courts, of accepting waivers of jury trial and prosecuting petty crimes without extending a right to jury trial. ... Even where defendants are satisfied with bench trials, the right to a jury trial very likely serves its intended purpose of making judicial or prosecutional unfairness less likely.

Louisiana's final contention is that even if it must grant jury trials in serious criminal cases, the conviction before us is valid and constitutional because here the petitioner was tried for simple battery and was sentenced to only 60 days in the parish prison. We are not persuaded. It is doubtless true that there is a category of petty crimes or offenses which is not subject to the 6th Amendment jury trial provision and should not be subject to the 14th Amendment jury trial requirement here applied to the states. Crimes carrying possible penalties up to 6 months do not require a jury trial if they otherwise qualify as petty offenses, *Cheff v. Schnackenberg* ... (1966). But the penalty authorized for a particular crime is of major relevance in determining whether it is serious or not and may in itself, if severe enough, subject the trial to the mandates of the 6th Amendment. *District of Columbia v. Clawans* ... (1937). The penalty authorized by the law of the locality may be taken "as a guage of its social and ethical judgment" ... of the crime in question. In *Clawans* the defendant was jailed for 60 days, but it was the 90-day authorized punishment on which the court focused in determining that the offense was not one for which the Constitution assured trial by jury. In the case before us the Legislature of Louisiana has made simple battery a criminal offense punishable by imprisonment for up to 2 years and a fine. The question, then, is whether a crime carrying such a penalty is an offense which Louisiana may insist on trying without a jury.

We think not. So-called petty offenses were tried without juries both in England and in the colonies and have always been held to be exempt from the otherwise comprehensive language of the 6th Amendment's jury trial provisions. There is no substantial evidence that the framers intended to depart from this established common-law practice, and the possible consequences to defendants from convictions for petty offenses have been thought insufficient to outweigh the benefits to efficient law enforcement and simplified judicial administration resulting from the availability of speedy and inexpensive nonjury adjudications. These same considerations compel the same result under the 14th Amendment. Of course the boundaries of the petty offense category have always been ill-defined, if not ambulatory. In the absence of an explicit constitutional provision, the definitional task ncessarily falls on the courts, which must either pass upon the validity of legislative attempts to identify those petty offenses which are exempt from jury trial or, where the legislature has not addressed itself to the problem, themselves face the question in the first instance. In either case it is necessary to draw a line in the spectrum of crime, separating petty from serious infractions. This process, although essential, cannot be wholly satisfactory, for it requires attaching different consequences to events which, when they lie near the line, actually differ very little.

In determining whether the length of the authorized prison term or the seriousness of other punishment is enough in itself to require a jury trial, we are counseled by *District of Columbia v. Clawans* ... to refer to objective criteria, chiefly the existing laws and practices in the nation. In the federal system, petty offenses are defined as those punishable by no more than 6 months in prison and a $500 fine. In 49 of the 50 states crimes subject to trial without a jury, which occasionally include simple battery, are punishable by no more than one year in jail. Moreover, in the late 18th century in America crimes triable without a jury were for the most part punishable by no more than a 6-month prison term, although there appear to have been exceptions to this rule. We need not, however, settle in this case the exact location of the line between petty offenses and serious crimes. It is sufficient for our purposes to hold that a crime punishable by 2 years in prison is, based on past and contemporary standards in this country, a serious crime and not a petty offense. Consequently, appellant was entitled to a jury trial and it was error to deny it.

The judgment below is reversed and the case is remanded for proceedings not inconsistent with this opinion.

Justice Black, whom Douglas joined, concurring:

The court today holds that the right to trial by jury guaranteed defendants in criminal cases in federal courts by Art. III of the United States Constitution and by the 6th Amendment is also guaranteed by the 14th Amendment to defendants tried in state courts. With this holding I agree for reasons given by the court. I also agree because of reasons given in my dissent in *Adamson v. California* [1947].... In that dissent I took the position, contrary to the holding in *Twining v. New Jersey* [1908], ... that the 14th Amendment made all of the provisions of the Bill of Rights applicable to the states. This court in *Palko v. Connecticut* ..., decided in 1937, although saying "[t]here is no such general rule," went on to add that the 14th Amendment may make it unlawful for a state to abridge by its statutes the "freedom of speech which the First Amendment safeguards against encroachment by the Congress ... or the like freedom of the press ... or the free exercise of religion ... or the right of peaceable assembly ... or the right of one accused of crime to the benefit of counsel.... In these and other situations immunities that are valid as against the federal government by force of the specific pledges of particular amendments have been found to be implicit in the concept of ordered liberty, and thus, through the 14th Amendment, become valid as against the states."... And the *Palko* opinion went on to explain ... that certain Bill of Rights' provisions were made applicable to the states by bringing them "within the 14th Amendment by a process of absorption." Thus *Twining v. New Jersey* ... refused to hold that any one of the Bill of Rights' provisions was made applicable to the states by the 14th Amendment, but *Palko,* which must be read as overruling *Twining* on this point, concluded that the Bill of Rights amendments that are "implicit in the concept of ordered liberty" are "absorbed" by the 14th as protections against state invasion. In this situation I said in *Adamson v. California* ... that while "I would ... extend to all the people of the nation the complete protection of the Bill of Rights," that "[i]f the choice must be between the selective process of the *Palko* decision applying some of the Bill of Rights to the states, or the *Twining* rule applying none of them, I would choose the *Palko* selective process." ...And I am very happy to support this selective process through which our court has since the *Adamson* case held most of the specific Bill of Rights' protections applicable to the states to the same extent they are applicable to the federal government. Among these are the right to trial by jury decided today, the right against compelled self-incrimination, the right to counsel, the right to compulsory process for witnesses, the right to confront witnesses, the right to a speedy and public trial and the right to be free from unreasonable searches and seizures.

All of these holdings making Bill of Rights' provisions applicable as such to the states mark, of course, a departure from the *Twining* doctrine holding that none of those provisions were enforceable as such against the states. The dissent in this case, however, makes a spirited and forceful defense of that now discredited doctrine. I do not believe that it is necessary for me to repeat the historical, and logical reasons for my challenge to the *Twining* holding contained in my *Adamson* dissent and appendix to it. What I wrote there in 1947 was the product of years of study and research. My appraisal of the legislative history followed 10 years of legislative experience as a Senator of the United States, not a bad way, I suspect, to learn the value of what is said in legislative debates, committee discussions, committee reports, and various other steps taken in the course of passage of bills, resolutions and proposed constitutional amendments. My brother Harlan's objections to my *Adamson* dissent history, like that of most of the objectors, relies most heavily on a criticism written by Prof. Charles Fairman and published in the *Stanford Law Review* ... (1949). ...In my view [this article] has completely failed to refute the inferences and arguments that I suggested in my *Adamson* dissent. Prof. Fairman's "history" relies very heavily on what was not said in the state legislatures that passed on the 14th Amendment. Instead of relying on this kind of negative pregnant, my legislative experience has convinced me that it is far wiser to rely on what *was* said, and most importantly, said by the men who actually sponsored the amendment in the

Congress. I know from my years in the United States Senate that it is to men like Congressman Bingham, who steered the Amendment through the House, and Sen. Howard, who introduced it in the Senate, that members of Congress look when they seek the real meaning of what is being offered. And they vote for or against a bill based on what the sponsors of that bill and those who oppose it tell them it means. The historical appendix to my *Adamson* dissent leaves no doubt in my mind that both its sponsors and those who opposed it believed the 14th Amendment made the first 8 amendments of the Constitution (the Bill of Rights) applicable to the states.

... The dissent states that "the great words of the 4 clauses of the first section of the 14th Amendment would have been an exceedingly peculiar way to say that 'The rights heretofore guaranteed against federal intrusion by the first 8 amendments are henceforth guaranteed against state intrusion as well.'"

... I can say only that the words "No state shall make or enforce any law which shall abridge the privileges or immunities of citizens of the United States" seem to me an eminently reasonable way of expressing the idea that henceforth the Bill of Rights shall apply to the states. What more precious "privilege" of American citizenship could there be than that privilege to claim the protections of our great Bill of Rights? I suggest that any reading of "privileges or immunities of citizens of the United States" which excludes the Bill of Rights' safeguards renders the words of this section of the 14th Amendment meaningless....

... [Justice Harlan's] view, as was indeed the view of *Twining*, is that "due process is an evolving concept" and therefore that it entails a "gradual process of judicial inclusion and exclusion" to ascertain those "immutable principles of free government which no member of the Union may disregard." Thus the due process clause is treated as prescribing no specific and clearly ascertainable constitutional command that judges must obey in interpreting the Constitution, but rather as leaving judges free to decide at any particular time whether a particular rule or judicial formulation embodies an "immutable principl[e] of free government" or is "implicit in the concept of ordered liberty," or whether certain conduct "shocks the judge's conscience" or runs counter to some other similar, undefined and undefinable standard. Thus due process, according to my brother Harlan, is to be a word with no permanent meaning but one which is found to shift from time to time in accordance with judges' predilections and understandings of what is best for the country. If due process means this, the 14th Amendment, in my opinion, might as well have been written that "no person shall be deprived of life, liberty or property except by laws that the judges of the United States Supreme Court shall find to be consistent with the immutable principles of free government." It is impossible for me to believe that such unconfined power is given to judges in our Constitution that is a written one in order to limit governmental power.

Another tenet of the *Twining* doctrine as restated by my brother Harlan is that "due process of law requires only fundamental fairness." But the "fundamental fairness" test is one on a par with that of shocking the conscience of the court. Each of such tests depends entirely on the particular judge's idea of ethics and morals instead of requiring him to depend on the boundaries fixed by the written words of the Constitution. Nothing in the history of the phrase "due process of law" suggests that constitutional controls are to depend on any particular judge's sense of values. The origin of the due process clause is Chapter 39 of Magna Carta which declares that "No free man shall be taken, outlawed, banished, or in any way destroyed, nor will we proceed against or prosecute him, except by the lawful judgment of his peers and by the law of the land."... As early as 1354 the words "due process of law" were used in an English statute interpreting Magna Carta, and by the end of the 14th century "due process of law" and "law of the land" were interchangeable. Thus the origin of this clause was an attempt by those who wrote Magna Carta to do away with the so-called trials of that period where people were liable to sudden arrest and summary conviction in courts and by judicial commissions with no sure and definite procedural protections and under laws that might have been improvised to try their particular cases. Chapter 39 of Magna Carta was a guarantee that the government would take neither life, liberty nor property without a trial in accord with the law of the land that already existed at the time the alleged offense was committed. This means that the due process clause gives all Americans, whoever they are and wherever they happen to be, the right to be tried by independent and unprejudiced courts using established procedures and applying valid pre-existing laws. There is not one word of legal history that justifies making the term "due process of law" mean a guarantee of a trial free from laws and conduct which the courts deem at the time to be "arbitrary," "unreasonable," "unfair" or "contrary to civilized standards." The due process of law standard for a trial is one tried in accordance with the Bill of Rights and laws passed pursuant to constitutional power, guaranteeing to all alike a trial under the general law of the land.

... I am not bothered by the argument that applying the Bill of Rights to the states, "according to the same standards that protect those personal rights against federal encroachment," interferes with our concept of federalism in that it may prevent states from trying novel social and economic experiments. I have never believed that under the guise of federalism the states should be able to experiment with the protections afforded our citizens through the Bill of Rights.... It seems to me totally inconsistent to advocate on the one hand, the power of this Court to strike down any state law or practice which it finds "unreasonable" or "unfair," and on the other hand urge that the states be given maximum power to develop their own laws and procedures. Yet the due process approach of my brothers Harlan and Fortas ... does just that since in effect it restricts the states to practices which a majority of this court is willing to approve on a case-by-case basis....

In closing I want to emphasize that I believe as strongly as ever that the 14th Amendment was intended to make the Bill of Rights applicable to the states. I have been willing to support the selective incorporation doctrine, however, as an alternative, although perhaps less historically supportable than complete incorporation. The selective incorporation process, if used properly, does limit the Supreme Court in the 14th Amendment field to specific Bill of Rights' protections only and keeps judges from roaming at will in their own notions of what policies outside the Bill of Rights are desirable and what are not. And, most importantly for me, the selective incorporation process has the virtue of having already worked to make most of the Bill of Rights' protections applicable to the states.

Justice Harlan, whom Stewart joined, dissenting:

Every American jurisdiction provides for trial by jury in criminal cases.... The question in this case is whether the state of Louisiana, which provides trial by jury for all felonies, is prohibited by the Constitution from trying charges of simple battery to the court alone. In my view, the answer to that question, mandated alike by our constitutional history and by the longer history of trial by jury, is clearly "no."

The states have always borne primary responsibility for operating the machinery of criminal justice within their borders and adapting it to their particular circumstances. In exercising this responsibility, each state is compelled to conform its procedures to the requirements of the federal Constitution. The due process clause of the 14th Amendment requires that those procedures be fundamentally fair in all respects. It does not, in my view, impose or encourage nationwide uniformity for its own sake; it does not command adherence to forms that happen to be old; and it does not impose on the states the rules that may be in force in the federal courts except where such rules are also found to be essential to basic fairness.

The court's approach to this case is an uneasy and illogical compromise among the views of various justices on how the due process clause should be interpreted. The court does not say that those who framed the 14th Amendment intended to make the 6th Amendment applicable to the states. And the court concedes that it finds nothing unfair about the procedure by which the present appellant was tried. Nevertheless, the court reverses his conviction: it holds, for some reason not apparent to me, that the due process clause incorporates the particular clause of the 6th Amendment that requires trial by jury in federal criminal cases—including, as I read its opinion, the sometimes trivial accompanying baggage of judicial interpretation in federal contexts....

I believe I am correct in saying that every member of the court for at least the last 135 years has agreed that our founders did not consider the requirements of the Bill of Rights so fundamental that they should operate directly against the states. They were wont to believe rather that the security of liberty in America rested primarily upon the dispersion of governmental power across a federal system. The Bill of Rights was considered unnecessary by some but insisted upon by others in

order to curb the possibility of abuse of power by the strong
central government they were creating.

The Civil War amendments dramatically altered the
relation of the federal government to the states. The first
section of the 14th Amendment imposes highly significant
restrictions on state action. But the restrictions are couched in
very broad and general terms: citizenship, privileges and
immunities; due process of law; equal protection of the laws.
Consequently, for 100 years this court has been engaged in the
difficult process Prof. Jaffe has well called "the search for
intermediate premises." ...

A few members of the court have taken the position that
the intention of those who drafted the first section of the 14th
Amendment was simply, and exclusively, to make the provisions of the first 8 amendments applicable to state action.
This view has never been accepted by this court. In my view, ...
the first section of the 14th Amendment was meant neither to
incorporate, nor to be limited to, the specific guarantees of the
first 8 amendments. The overwhelming historical evidence
marshalled by Prof. Fairman demonstrates, to me conclusively,
that the Congressmen and state legislators who wrote, debated,
and ratified the 14th Amendment did not think they were
"incorporating" the Bill of Rights and the very breadth and
generality of the amendment's provisions suggest that its
authors did not suppose that the nation would always be limited
to mid-19th century conceptions of "liberty" and "due process
of law" but that the increasing experience and evolving conscience of the American people would add new "intermediate
premises." In short, neither history, nor sense, supports using
the 14th Amendment to put the states in a constitutional straitjacket with respect to their own development in the administration of criminal or civil law.

Although I therefore fundamentally disagree with the total
incorporation view of the 14th Amendment, it seems to me that
such a position does at least have the virtue, lacking in the
court's selective incorporation approach, of internal consistency: we look to the Bill of Rights, word for word, clause
for clause, precedent for precedent because, it is said, the men
who wrote the amendment wanted it that way. For those who
do not accept this "history," a different source of "intermediate
premises" must be found. The Bill of Rights is not necessarily

irrelevant to the search for guidance in interpreting the 14th Amendment, but the reason for and the nature of its relevance must be articulated.

Apart from the approach taken by the absolute incorporationists, I can see only one method of analysis that has any internal logic. That is to start with the words "liberty" and "due process of law" and attempt to define them in a way that accords with American traditions and our system of government. This approach, involving a much more discriminating process of adjudication than does "incorporation," is, albeit difficult, the one that was followed throughout the 19th and most of the present century. It entails a "gradual process of judicial inclusion and exclusion" [*Davidson v. New Orleans,* 1878], seeking, with due recognition of constitutional tolerance for state experimentation and disparity, to ascertain those "immutable principles ... of free government which no member of the Union may disregard" [*Holden v. Hardy,* 1898]. Due process was not restricted to rules fixed in the past, for that "would be to deny every quality of the law but its age, and to render it incapable of progress or improvement" [*Hurtado v. California,* 1884]. Nor did it impose nationwide uniformity in details, for "[t]he 14th Amendment does not profess to secure to all persons in the United States the benefit of the same laws and the same remedies. Great diversities in these respects may exist in 2 states separated only by an imaginary line. On one side of this line there may be a right of trial by jury, and on the other side no such right. Each state prescribes its own modes of judicial proceeding" [*Missouri v. Lewis,* 1880].

Through this gradual process, this court sought to define "liberty" by isolating freedoms that Americans of the past and of the present considered more important than any suggested countervailing public objective. The court also, by interpretation of the phrase "due process of law," enforced the Constitution's guarantee that no state may imprison an individual except by fair and impartial procedures.

The relationship of the Bill of Rights to this "gradual process" seems to me to be 2-fold. In the first place it has long been clear that the due process clause imposes some restrictions on state action that parallel Bill of Rights restrictions on federal action. 2d, and more important than this accidental overlap, is the fact that the Bill of Rights is evidence, at various points, of the content Americans find in the term "liberty" and of American standards of fundamental fairness....

...[In previous cases] the right guaranteed against the states by the 14th Amendment was one that had also been guaranteed against the federal government by one of the first 8 amendments. The logically critical thing, however, was not that the rights had been found in the Bill of Rights, but that they were deemed, in the context of American legal history, to be fundamental. This was perhaps best explained by Mr. Justice [Benjamin] Cardozo, speaking for a court that included Chief Justice [Charles Evans] Hughes and Justices [Louis] Brandeis and [Harlan Fiske] Stone, in *Palko v. Connecticut* [1937] ...: "If the 14th Amendment has absorbed them, the process of absorption has had its source in the belief that neither liberty nor justice would exist if they were sacrificed." Referring to *Powell v. Alabama,* ... Mr. Justice Cardozo continued: "The decision did not turn upon the fact that the benefit of counsel would have been guaranteed to the defendants by the provisions of the 6th Amendment if they had been prosecuted in a federal court. The decision turned upon the fact that in the particular situation laid before us in the evidence the benefit of counsel was essential to the substance of a hearing." ... Mr. Justice Cardozo then went on to explain that the 14th Amendment did not impose on each state every rule of procedure that some other state, or the federal courts, thought desirable, but only those rules critical to liberty....

Today's court still remains unwilling to accept the total incorporationists' view of the history of the 14th Amendment. This, if accepted, would afford a cogent reason for applying the 6th Amendment to the states. The court is also, apparently, unwilling to face the task of determining whether denial of trial by jury in the situation before us, or in other situations, is fundamentally unfair. Consequently, the court has compromised on the ease of the incorporationist position, without its internal logic. It has simply assumed that the question before us is whether the jury trial clause of the 6th Amendment should be incorporated into the 14th, jot-for-jot and case-for-case, or ignored. Then the court merely declares that the clause in question is "in" rather than "out."

The court has justified neither its starting place nor its conclusion. If the problem is to discover and articulate the rules of

fundamental fairness in criminal proceedings, there is no reason
to assume that the whole body of rules developed in this court
constituting 6th Amendment jury trial must be regarded as a
unit. The requirement of trial by jury in federal criminal cases
has given rise to numerous subsidiary questions respecting the
exact scope and content of the right. It surely cannot be that
every answer the court has given, or will give, to such a
question is attributable to the founders; or even that every rule
announced carries equal conviction of this court; still less can it
be that every such subprinciple is equally fundamental to
ordered liberty....

Since, as I see it, the court has not even come to grips with
the issues in this case, it is necessary to start from the
beginning. When a criminal defendant contends that his state
conviction lacked "due process of law," the question before this
court, in my view, is whether he was denied any element of
fundamental procedural fairness. Believing, as I do, that due
process is an evolving concept and that old principles are
subject to re-evaluation in light of later experience, I think it
appropriate to deal on its merits with the question whether
Louisiana denied appellant due process of law when it tried him
for simple assault without a jury....

The argument that jury trial is not a requisite of due
process is quite simple. The central proposition of *Palko, ...* a
proposition to which I would adhere, is that "due process of
law" requires only that criminal trials be fundamentally fair.
As stated above, apart from the theory that it was historically
intended as a mere shorthand for the Bill of Rights, I do not see
what else "due process of law" can intelligibly be thought to
mean. If due process of law requires only fundamental fairness,
then the inquiry in each case must be whether a state trial
process was a fair one. The court has held, properly I think,
that in an adversary process it is a requisite of fairness, for
which there is no adequate substitute, that a criminal defendant
be afforded a right to counsel and to cross-examine opposing
witnesses. But it simply has not been demonstrated, nor, I
think, can it be demonstrated, that trial by jury is the only fair
means of resolving issues of fact....

It can hardly be gainsaid ... that the principal original
virtue of the jury trial—the limitations a jury imposes on a
tyrannous judiciary—has largely disappeared....

The jury system can also be said to have some inherent defects, which are multiplied by the emergence of the criminal law from the relative simplicity that existed when the jury system was devised. It is a cumbersome process, not only imposing great cost in time and money on both the state and the jurors themselves, but also contributing to delay in the machinery of justice. Untrained jurors are presumably less adept at reaching accurate conclusions of fact than judges, particularly if the issues are many or complex. And it is argued by some that trial by jury, far from increasing public respect for law, impairs it: the average man, it is said, reacts favorably neither to the notion that matters he knows to be complex are being decided by other average men, nor to the way the jury system distorts the process of adjudication.

That trial by jury is not the only fair way of adjudicating criminal guilt is well attested by the fact that it is not the prevailing way, either in England or in this country....

... [The court has said:] "We would not assert ... that every criminal trial—or any particular trial—held before a judge alone is unfair or that a defendant may never be as fairly treated by a judge as he would be by a jury." I agree. I therefore see no reason why this court should reverse the conviction of appellant, absent any suggestion that his particular trial was in fact unfair, or compel the state of Louisiana to afford jury trial in an as yet unbounded category of cases that can, without unfairness, be tried to a court....

... There is a wide range of views on the desirability of trial by jury and on the ways to make it most effective when it is used; there is also considerable variation from state to state in local conditions such as the size of the criminal caseload, the ease or difficulty of summoning jurors, and other trial conditions bearing on fairness. We have before us, therefore, an almost perfect example of a situation in which the celebrated dictum of Mr. Justice Brandeis should be invoked. It is, he said, "one of the happy incidents of the federal system that a single courageous State may, if its citizens choose, serve as a laboratory...." *New State Ice Co. v. Liebmann* [1932] ... (dissenting opinion). This court, other courts and the political process are available to correct any experiments in criminal procedure that prove fundamentally unfair to defendants. That is not what is being done today: instead, and quite without reason, the court has chosen to impose upon every state one means of trying criminal cases. . . .

I would affirm the judgment of the Supreme Court of Louisiana.

In *DeStefano v. Woods,* announced June 17, 1968, the Supreme Court denied retroactive application to the rule announced in *Duncan.* "The values implemented by the right to jury trial would not measurably be served by requiring retrial of all persons convicted in the past by procedures not consistent with the 6th Amendment right to a jury trial," the court said. Justice Douglas, joined by Justice Black, dissented.

In *Baldwin v. New York,* decided June 22, 1970 the court extended the right of trial by jury to all cases that could result in more than 6 months of imprisonment. New York City by then was the only jurisdiction in the U.S. to deny jury trials for offenses carrying a possible prison term of greater than 6 months. Justices Douglas and Black, in a concurring opinion, asserted that the 6th Amendment required trial by jury in·all criminal cases, regardless of penalty. Chief Justice Burger, dissenting, argued that the states should be permitted latitude in determining whether a crime should be considered serious enough to warrant trial by jury.

The Supreme Court held June 22, 1970, in *Williams v. Florida,* that trial by jury in state criminal cases does not require a jury of 12 members. The decision upheld a Florida law that provided for 6-member juries. The majority opinion by Justice Byron R. White asserted that, although the framers of the Bill of Rights probably anticipated the use of 12-member juries, they did not intend to mandate such a requirement. The purpose of a jury, White

said, is to interpose the judgment of a group of laymen against that of the government. Accordingly,
"the performance of this role is not a function of the
particular number of the body that makes up the
jury." "Neither currently available evidence nor
theory suggests that the 12-man jury is necessarily
more advantageous to the defendant than a jury
composed of fewer members," he declared.

Justices Thurgood Marshall and John Marshall
Harlan dissented in upholding the use of 12-member
juries. According to Harlan, "the necessary consequence of this decision is that 12-member juries are
not constitutionally required in *federal* trials either."
That, he said, underscores his previous warnings that
in applying the Bill of Rights to the states, the court
was inviting the dilution of those rights in an effort
to accommodate the law enforcement needs of the
states.

Abridgment of the *Williams v. Florida* decision
(399 U.S. 78, June 22, 1970):

*Justice White delivering the opinion of the
court:*

In *Duncan v. Louisiana* ... we held that the 14th Amendment guarantees a right to trial by jury in all criminal cases
which—were they to be tried in a federal court—would come
within the 6th Amendment's guarantee. Petitioner's trial for
robbery on July 3, 1968, clearly falls within the scope of that
holding.... The question in this case then is whether the constitutional guarantee of a trial by "jury" necessarily requires trial
by exactly 12 persons, rather than some lesser number—in this
case 6. We hold that the 12-man panel is not a necessary
ingredient of "trial by jury" and that respondent's refusal to
impanel more than the 6 members provided for by Florida law
did not violate petitioner's 6th Amendment rights as applied to
the states through the 14th.

We had occasion in *Duncan v. Louisiana* ... to review briefly the oft-told history of the development of trial by jury in criminal cases. That history revealed a long tradition attaching great importance to the concept of relying on a body of one's peers to determine guilt or innocence as a safeguard against arbitrary law enforcement. That same history, however, affords little insight into the considerations that gradually led the size of that body to be generally fixed at 12....

We do not pretend to be able to divine precisely what the word "jury" imported to the framers, the first Congress, or the states in 1789.... But there is absolutely no indication in "the intent of the framers" of an explicit decision to equate the constitutional and common-law characteristics of the jury. Nothing in this history suggests, then, that we do violence to the letter of the Constitution by turning to other than purely historical considerations to determine which features of the jury system, as it existed at common law, were preserved in the Constitution. The relevant inquiry, as we see it, must be the function that the particular feature performs and its relation to the purposes of the jury trial. Measured by this standard, the 12-man requirement cannot be regarded as an indispensable component of the 6th Amendment.

The purpose of the jury trial, as we noted in *Duncan,* is to prevent oppression by the government.... Given this purpose, the essential feature of a jury obviously lies in the interposition between the accused and his accuser of the commonsense judgment of a group of laymen and in the community participation and shared responsibility that results from that group's determination of guilt or innocence. The performance of this role is not a function of the particular number of the body that makes up the jury. To be sure, the number should probably be large enough to promote group deliberation, free from outside attempts at intimidation, and to provide a fair possibility for obtaining a representative cross-section of the community. But we find little reason to think that these goals are in any meaningful sense less likely to be achieved when the jury numbers 6, than when it numbers 12—particularly if the requirement of unanimity is retained. And, certainly the reliability of the jury as a fact finder hardly seems likely to be a function of its size.

It might be suggested that the 12-man jury gives a defendant a greater advantage since he has more "chances" of finding a juror who will insist on acquittal and thus prevent conviction. But the advantage might just as easily belong to the state, which also needs only one juror out of 12 insisting on guilt to prevent acquittal. What few experiments have occurred— usually in the civil area—indicate that there is no discernible difference between the results reached by the 2 different-sized juries. . . .

Similarly, while in theory the number of viewpoints represented on a randomly selected jury ought to increase as the size of the jury increases, in practice the difference between the 12-man and the 6-man jury in terms of the cross-section of the community represented seems likely to be negligible. Even the 12-man jury cannot insure representation of every distinct voice in the community, particularly given the use of the preemptory challenge. As long as arbitrary exclusions of a particular class from the jury rolls are forbidden, ... the concern that the cross-section will be significantly diminished if the jury is decreased in size from 12 to 6 seems an unrealistic one.

We conclude, in short, as we began: the fact that the jury at common law was composed of precisely 12 is a historical accident, unnecessary to effect the purposes of the jury system and wholly without significance "except to mystics." ... To read the 6th Amendment as forever codifying a feature so incidental to the real purpose of the amendment is to ascribe a blind formalism to the framers which would require considerably more evidence than we have been able to discover in the history and language of the Constitution or in the reasoning of our past decisions. We do not mean to intimate that legislatures can never have good reasons for concluding that the 12-man jury is preferable to the smaller jury, or that such conclusions— reflected in the provisions of most states and in our federal system—are in any sense unwise. Legislatures may well have their own views about the relative value of the larger and smaller juries, and may conclude that, wholly apart from the jury's primary function, it is desirable to spread the collective responsibility for the determination of guilt among the larger group. In capital cases, for example, it appears that no state provides for less than 12 jurors—a fact that suggests implicit recognition of the value of the larger body as a means of legitimating society's decision to impose the death penalty. Our holding does no more than leave these considerations to Congress and the states, unrestrained by an interpretation of the 6th Amendment that would forever dictate the precise number that can constitute a jury. Consistent with this holding, we conclude that petitioner's 6th Amendment rights, as applied to the states through the 14th Amendment, were not violated by Florida's decision to provide a 6-man rather than a 12-man jury. The judgment of the Florida District Court of Appeal is affirmed.

Justice Black, whom Douglas joined, concurring on the issue of a 6-man jury:

... I agree with ... [the] decision for substantially the same reasons given by the court. My brother Harlan, however, charges that the court's decision on this point is evidence that the "incorporation doctrine," through which the specific provisions of the Bill of Rights are made fully applicable to the states under the same standards applied in federal courts, will somehow result in a "dilution" of the protections required by those provisions. He asserts that this court's desire to relieve the states from the rigorous requirements of the Bill of Rights is bound to cause re-examination and modification of prior decisions interpreting those provisions as applied in federal courts in order simultaneously to apply the provisions equally to the state and federal governments and to avoid undue restrictions on the states. This assertion finds no support in today's decision or any other decision of this court. We have emphatically "rejected the notion that the 14th Amendment applies to the states only a 'watered-down, subjective version of the individual guarantees of the Bill of Rights.'" ... Today's decision is in no way attributable to any desire to dilute the 6th Amendment in order more easily to apply it to the states, but follows solely as a necessary consequence of our duty to re-examine prior decisions to reach the correct constitutional meaning in each case. The broad implications in early cases indicating that only a body of 12 members could satisfy the 6th Amendment requirement arose in situations where the issue was not squarely presented and were based, in my opinion, on an improper interpretation of that amendment. Had the question presented here arisen in a federal court before our decision in *Duncan v. Louisiana* ... (1968), this court would still, in my view, have reached the result announced today. In my opinion the danger of diluting the Bill of Rights protections lies not in the "incorporation doctrine," but in the "shock the conscience" test on which my brother Harlan would rely instead—a test which depends, not on the language of the Constitution, but solely on the views of a majority of the court as to what is "fair" and "decent." ...

Justice Marshall dissenting on the issue of the 6-man jury:

...[S]ince I believe that the 14th Amendment guaranteed Williams a jury of 12 to pass upon the question of his guilt or innocence before he could be sent to prison for the rest of his life, I dissent from the affirmance of his conviction.

I adhere to the holding of *Duncan v. Louisiana* ... that "[b]ecause ... trial by jury in criminal cases is fundamental to the American scheme of justice ..., the 14th Amendment guarantees a right of jury trial in all criminal cases which— were they to be tried in a federal court—would come within the 6th Amendment's guarantee." And I agree with the court that the *same* "trial by jury" is guaranteed to state defendants by the 14th Amendment as to federal defendants by the 6th. "Once it is decided that a particular Bill of Rights guarantee is 'fundamental to the American scheme of justice' ..., the same constitutional standards apply against both the state and federal governments." *Benton v. Maryland* ... (1969).

At the same time, I adhere to the decision of the court in *Thompson v. Utah* ... (1898), that the jury guaranteed by the 6th Amendment consists "of 12 persons, neither more nor less." As I see it, the court has not made out a convincing case that the 6th Amendment should be read differently than it was in *Thompson* even if the matter were now before us *de novo*— much less that an unbroken line of precedent going back over 70 years should be overruled. The arguments made by Mr. Justice Harlan in ... his opinion persuade me that *Thompson* was right when decided and still states sound doctrine. I am equally convinced that the requirement of 12 should be applied to the states.

Justice Harlan dissenting in Williams v. Florida

and concurring in Baldwin v. New York:

In *Duncan v. Louisiana*, ... the court held, over my dissent, joined by Mr. Justice Stewart, that a state criminal defendant is entitled to a jury trial in any case which, if brought in a federal court, would require a jury under the 6th Amendment. Today the court concludes, in ... *Baldwin v. New York,* that New York cannot constitutionally provide that misdemeanors carrying sentences up to one year shall be tried in New York City without a jury. At the same time the court holds in ... *Williams v. Florida* that Florida's 6-member-jury statute satisfies the 6th Amendment as carried to the states by the *Duncan* holding. The necessary consequence of this decision is that 12-member juries are not *constitutionally* required in *federal* criminal trials either.

The historical argument by which the court undertakes to justify its view that the 6th Amendment does not require 12-member juries is, in my opinion, much too thin to mask the true thrust of this decision. The decision evinces, I think, a recognition that the "incorporationist" view of the due process clause of the 14th Amendment, which underlay *Duncan* and is now carried forward into *Baldwin,* must be tempered to allow the states more elbow room in ordering their own criminal systems. With that much I agree. But to accomplish this by diluting constitutional protections within the federal system itself is something to which I cannot possibly subscribe. Tempering the rigor of *Duncan* should be done forthrightly, by facing up to the fact that at least in this area the "incorporation" doctrine does not fit well with our federal structure, and by the same token that *Duncan* was wrongly decided. ...

Unanimous Verdicts Not Required in State Trials

In 2 decisions May 22, 1972, the Supreme Court held, 5-4, that jury verdicts need not be unanimous to secure a conviction in a state trial. In *Johnson v. Louisiana* the court upheld a robbery conviction based upon a 9-3 jury verdict, and in *Apodaca v.*

Oregon it upheld 2 felony convictions obtained by 11-1 and 10-2 votes.

Justice Byron R. White, joined by Chief Justice Warren Earl Burger and Justices Lewis F. Powell Jr., William H. Rehnquist and Harry A. Blackmun, Pres. Richard M. Nixon's 4 appointees to the Supreme Court, wrote the majority opinion in both cases. 6th Amendment restrictions involving trial by jury imposed on the states through the due process clause of the 14th Amendment are not as stringent as those imposed directly on the federal government by the 6th Amendment, the court declared. Due process in this instance, White wrote, requires only that a state prove its cases beyond a reasonable doubt. The "disagreement of 3 jurors does not alone establish reasonable doubt, particularly when such a heavy majority of the jury, after having considered the dissenters' views, remains convinced of guilt," the court said. "That rational men disagree is not in itself equivalent to the reasonable doubt standard."

Justice William O. Douglas, in the major dissenting opinion, called the result of the majority's decision "anomalous." "[T]hough unanimous jury decisions are not required in state trials, they are constitutionally required in federal prosecutions," he said. "How can that be when both decisions stem from the 6th Amendment?" He criticized "advocates of the view that the duties imposed on the states by reason of the Bill of Rights operating through the 14th Amendment are a watered-down version of those guarantees."

Abridgment of the *Johnson v. Louisiana* decision (406, U.S. 356, May 22, 1972):

Justice White delivering the opinion of the

court:

Under both the Louisiana Constitution and Code of Criminal Procedure, criminal cases in which the punishment is necessarily at hard labor are tried to a jury of 12, and the vote of 9 jurors is sufficient to return either a guilty or not guilty verdict. The principal question in this case is whether these provisions allowing less than unanimous verdicts in certain cases are valid under the due process and equal protection clauses of the 14th Amendment.

... Appellant Johnson was arrested at his home on Jan. 20, 1968. There was no arrest warrant, but the victim of an armed robbery had identified Johnson from photographs as having committed the crime. He was then identified at a lineup, at which he had counsel, by the victim of still another robbery. The latter crime is involved in this case. Johnson pleaded not guilty, was tried on May 14, 1968, by a 12-man jury and was convicted by a 9-to-3 verdict. His due process and equal protection challenges to the Louisiana constitutional and statutory provisions were rejected by the Louisiana courts, ... and he appealed here....

... This court has never held jury unanimity to be a requisite of due process of law. Indeed, the court has more than once expressly said that "[i]n criminal cases due process of law is not denied by a state law ... which dispenses with the necessity of a jury of 12, or unanimity in the verdict." *Jordan v. Massachusetts* ... (1912) (*dictum*). Accord, *Maxwell v. Dow* ... (1900) (*dictum*). These statements, moreover, coexisted with cases indicating that proof of guilt beyond a reasonable doubt is implicit in constitutions recognizing "the fundamental principles that are deemed essential for the protection of life and liberty."...

Entirely apart from these cases, however, it is our view that the fact of 3 dissenting votes to acquit raises no question of constitutional substance about either the integrity or the accuracy of the majority verdict of guilt. Appellant's contrary argument breaks down into 2 parts, each of which we shall consider separately: first, that 9 individual jurors will be unable to vote conscientiously in favor of guilt beyond a reasonable doubt when 3 of their colleagues are arguing for acquittal, and 2d, that guilt cannot be said to have been proved beyond a reasonable doubt when one or more of a jury's members at the

conclusion of deliberation still possess such a doubt. Neither
argument is persuasive. . . .

In considering the first branch of appellant's argument, we
can find no basis for holding that the 9 jurors who voted for his
conviction failed to follow their instructions concerning the
need for proof beyond such a doubt or that the vote of any one
of the 9 failed to reflect an honest belief that guilt had been so
proved. Appellant, in effect, asks us to assume that, when
minority jurors express sincere doubts about guilt, their fellow
jurors will nevertheless ignore them and vote to convict even if
deliberation has not been exhausted and minority jurors have
grounds for acquittal which, if pursued, might persuade
members of the majority to acquit. But the mere fact that 3
jurors voted to acquit does not in itself demonstrate that, had
the 9 jurors of the majority attended further to reason and the
evidence, all or one of them would have developed a reasonable
doubt about guilt. We have no grounds for believing that
majority jurors, aware of their responsibility and power over
the liberty of the defendant, would simply refuse to listen to
arguments presented to them in favor of acquittal, terminate
discussion and render a verdict. On the contrary it is far more
likely that a juror presenting reasoned argument in favor of
acquittal would either have his arguments answered or would
carry enough other jurors with him to prevent conviction. A
majority will cease discussion and outvote a minority only after
reasoned discussion has ceased to have persuasive effect or to
serve any other purpose—when a minority, that is, continues to
insist upon acquittal without having persuasive reasons in
support of its position. At that juncture there is no basis for
denigrating the vote of so large a majority of the jury or for
refusing to accept their decision as being, at least in their
minds, beyond a reasonable doubt. Indeed, at this point, a
"dissenting juror should consider whether his doubt was a
reasonable one . . . [when it made] no impression upon the minds
of so many men, equally honest, equally intelligent with
himself." *Allen v. United States* . . . (1896). Appellant offers no
evidence that majority jurors simply ignore the reasonable
doubts of their colleagues or otherwise act irresponsibly in
casting their votes in favor of conviction. . . .

We conclude, therefore, that, as to the 9 jurors who voted
to convict, the state satisfied its burden of proving guilt beyond

any reasonable doubt. The remaining question under the due process clause is whether the vote of 3 jurors for acquittal can be said to impeach the verdict of the other 9 and to demonstrate that guilt was not in fact proved beyond such doubt. We hold that it cannot.

Of course, the state's proof could perhaps be regarded as more certain if it had convinced all 12 jurors instead of only 9; it would have been even more compelling if it had been required to convince and had, in fact, convinced 24 or 36 jurors. But the fact remains that 9 jurors—a substantial majority of the jury— were convinced by the evidence. In our view disagreement of 3 jurors does not alone establish reasonable doubt, particularly when such a heavy majority of the jury, after having considered the dissenters' views, remains convinced of guilt. That rational men disagree is not in itself equivalent to a failure of proof by the state, nor does it indicate infidelity to the reasonable doubt standard....

...If the doubt of a minority of jurors indicates the existence of a reasonable doubt it would appear that a defendant should receive a directed verdict of acquittal rather than a retrial. We conclude, therefore, that verdicts rendered by 9 out of 12 jurors are not automatically invalidated by the disagreement of the dissenting 3. Appellant was not deprived of due process of law....

Justice Blackman concurring:

...I add only the comment, which should be obvious and should not need saying, that in so doing I do not imply that I regard a state's split verdict system as a wise one. My vote means only that I cannot conclude that the system is constitutionally offensive. Were I a legislator, I would disfavor it as a matter of policy. Our task here, however, is not to pursue and strike down what happens to impress us as undesirable legislative policy.

I do not hesitate to say, either, that a system employing a 7–5 standard, rather than a 9–3 or 75% minimum, would afford me great difficulty. As Mr. Justice White points out..., "a substantial majority of the jury are to be convinced." That is all that is before us in each of these cases.

Justice Powell concurring:

The reasoning which runs throughout this court's 6th

Amendment precedents is that, in amending the Constitution to guarantee the right to jury trial, the framers desired to preserve the jury safeguard as it was known to them at common law. At the time the Bill of Rights was adopted, unanimity had long been established as one of the attributes of a jury conviction at common law. It therefore seems to me, in accord both with history and precedent, that the 6th Amendment requires a unanimous jury verdict to convict in a federal criminal trial.

But it is the 14th Amendment, rather than the 6th, which imposes upon the states the requirement that they provide jury trials to those accused of serious crimes. This court has said, in cases decided when the intendment of that Amendment was not as clouded by the passage of time, that due process does not require that the states apply the federal jury trial right with all its gloss....

The question, therefore, which should be addressed in this case is whether unanimity is in fact so fundamental to the essentials of jury trial that this particular requirement of the 6th Amendment is necessarily binding on the states under the due process clause of the 14th Amendment....

... There is no reason to believe, on the basis of experience in Oregon or elsewhere, that a unanimous decision of 12 jurors is more likely to serve the high purpose of jury trial, or is entitled to greater respect in the community, than the same decision joined in by 10 members of a jury of 12. The standard of due process assured by the Oregon constitution provides a sufficient guarantee that the government will not be permitted to impose its judgment on an accused without first meeting the full burden of its prosecutorial duty....

Justice Douglas, whom William J. Brennan Jr. and Thurgood Marshall joined, dissenting:

... The result of today's decision is anomalous: though unanimous jury decisions are not required in state trials, they are constitutionally required in federal prosecutions. How can that be possible when both decisions stem from the 6th Amendment?

We held unanimously in 1948 that the Bill of Rights requires a unanimous jury verdict....

There have, of course, been advocates of the view that the duties imposed on the states by reason of the Bill of Rights operating through the 14th Amendment are a watered-down version of those guarantees. . . .

Only once has this court diverged from the doctrine of co-extensive coverage of guarantees brought within the 14th Amendment, and that aberration was later rectified. In *Wolf v. Colorado* [1949] . . . it was held that the 4th Amendment ban against unreasonable and warrantless searches was enforceable against the states, but the court declined to incorporate the 4th Amendment exclusionary rule of *Weeks v. United States* [1914]. . . . Happily, however, that gap was partially closed in *Elkins v. United States* . . . (1960) and then completely bridged in *Mapp v. Ohio* . . . . (1961) *Mapp* we observed that "this court has not hesitated to enforce as strictly against the state as it does against the federal government the rights of free speech and of a free press, the rights to notice and to a fair, public trial. . . ." We concluded that "the same rule" should apply where the 4th Amendment was concerned. . . .

It is said, however, that the 6th Amendment, as applied to the states by reason of the 14th, does not mean what it does in federal proceedings, that it has a "due process" gloss on it, and that that gloss gives the states power to experiment with the explicit or implied guarantees in the Bill of Rights. . . .

These civil rights . . . extend of course to everyone, but in cold reality touch mostly the lower castes in our society. I refer of course to the blacks, the Chicanos, the one-mule farmers, the agricultural workers, the off-beat students, the victims of the ghetto. Are we giving the states the power to experiment in diluting their civil rights? It has long been thought that the Thou Shalt Nots in the Constitution and Bill of Rights protect everyone against governmental intrusion or overreaching. The idea has been obnoxious that there are some who can be relegated to 2d-class citizenship. But if we construe the Bill of Rights and the 14th Amendment to permit states to "experiment" with the basic rights of people, we open a veritable Pandora's box. For hate and prejudice are versatile forces that can degrade the constitutional scheme.

That, however, is only one of my concerns when we make the Bill of Rights, as applied to the states, a "watered-down" version of what that charter guarantees. My chief concern is one often expressed by the late Justice Black, who was alarmed at the prospect of 9 men appointed for life sitting as a super-legislative body to determine whether government has gone too far. The balancing was done when the Constitution and Bill of Rights were written and adopted. For this court to determine, say, whether one person but not another is entitled to free speech is a power never granted it. But that is the ultimate reach of a decision that lets the states, subject to our veto, to experiment with rights guaranteed by the Bill of Rights.

I would construe the 6th Amendment, when applicable to the states, precisely as I would when applied to the federal government.

... The plurality approves a procedure which diminishes the reliability of jury. First, it eliminates the circumstances in which a minority of jurors (a) could have rationally persuaded the entire jury to acquit, or (b) while unable to persuade the majority to acquit, nonetheless could have convinced them to convict only on a lesser-included offense. 2d, it permits prosecutors in Oregon and Louisiana to enjoy a conviction-acquittal ratio substantially greater than that ordinarily returned by unanimous juries.

The diminution of verdict reliability flows from the fact that nonunanimous juries need not debate and deliberate as fully as must unanimous juries. As soon as the requisite majority is attained, further consideration is not required either by Oregon or by Louisiana even though the dissident jurors might, if given the chance, be able to convince the majority. Such persuasion does in fact occasionally occur in states where the unanimous requirement applies: "In roughly one case in 10, the minority eventually succeeds in reversing an initial majority, and these may be cases of special importance."* One explanation for this phenomenon is that because jurors are often not permitted to take notes and because they have imperfect memories, the forensic process of forcing jurors to defend their conflicting recollections and conclusions flushes out many nuances which otherwise would go overlooked. This collective effort to piece together the puzzle of historical truth, however, is cut short as soon as the requisite majority is reached in Oregon and Louisiana. Indeed, if a necessary majority is immediately obtained, then no deliberation at all is required in these states. (There is a suggestion that this may have happened

---

* Kalven & Zeisel, *The American Jury* (1960).

in the 10–2 verdict rendered in only 41 minutes in Apodaca's case.) To be sure, in jurisdictions other than these 2 states, initial majorities normally prevail in the end, but about a 10th of the time the rough and tumble of the juryroom operates to reverse completely their preliminary perception of guilt or innocence. The court now extracts from the juryroom this automatic check against hasty fact-finding by relieving jurors of the duty to hear out fully the dissenters. . . .

Justice Brennan, whom Marshall joined, dissenting:

. . . Emotions may run high at criminal trials. Although we can fairly demand that jurors be neutral until they have begun to hear evidence, it would surpass our power to command that they remain unmoved by the evidence that unfolds before them. What this means is that jurors will often enter the jury deliberations with strong opinions on the merits of the case. If at that time a sufficient majority is available to reach a verdict, those jurors in the majority will have nothing but their own common sense to restrain them from returning a verdict before they have fairly considered the positions of jurors who would reach a different conclusion. Even giving all reasonable leeway to legislative judgment in such matters, I think it simply ignores reality to imagine that most jurors in these circumstances would or even could fairly weigh the arguments opposing their position.

It is in this context that we must view the constitutional requirement that all juries be drawn from an accurate cross-section of the community. When verdicts must be unanimous, no member of the jury may be ignored by the others. When less than unanimity is sufficient, consideration of minority views may become nothing more than a matter of majority grace. In my opinion, the right of all groups in this nation to participate in the criminal process means the right to have their voices heard. A unanimous verdict vindicates that right. Majority verdicts could destroy it.

Justice Marshall dissenting:

I respectfully reject the suggestion of my brother Powell that the doubts of minority jurors may be attributable to "irrationality" against which some protection is needed. For if the jury has been selected properly, and every juror is a competent and rational person, then the "irrationality" that enters into the deliberation process is precisely the essence of the right to a jury trial. Each time this court has approved a change in the familiar characteristics of the jury, we have reaffirmed the principle that its fundamental characteristic is its capacity to render a common-sense, laymen's judgment, as a representative body drawn from the community. To fence out a dissenting juror fences out a voice from the community and undermines the principle on which our whole notion of the jury now rests. My dissenting brothers have pointed to the danger, under a less-than-unanimous rule, of excluding from the process members of minority groups, whose participation we have elsewhere recognized as a constitutional requirement. It should be emphasized, however, that the fencing-out problem goes beyond the problem of identifiable minority groups. The juror whose dissenting voice is unheard may be a spokesman, not for any minority viewpoint, but simply for himself—and that, in my view, is enough. The doubts of a single juror are in my view evidence that the government has failed to carry its burden of proving guilt beyond a reasonable doubt. I dissent.

Double Jeopardy

The 5th Amendment protection against double jeopardy—being retried for an offense for which a defendant already has been acquitted—was made a duty of the states in *Benton v. Maryland,* decided by the Supreme Court June 23, 1969. The case involved John Dalmer Benton, a Maryland man found not guilty of larceny but guilty of burglary. Since the jury had been drawn incorrectly, Benton was offered a new trial, and he was then found guilty of both offenses. Justice Marshall wrote the majority opinion. Harlan and Stewart dissented.

Abridgment of the *Benton v. Maryland* decision
(395 U.S. 784, June 23, 1969):

Justice Marshall delivering the opinion of the court:

In Aug. 1965, petitioner was tried in a Maryland state
court on charges of burglary and larceny. The jury found
petitioner not guilty of larceny but convicted him on the
burglary count. He was sentenced to 10 years in prison. Shortly
after his notice of appeal was filed in the Maryland Court of
Appeals, that court handed down its decision in the case of
Schowgurow v. State ... (1965). In *Schowgurow* the Maryland
Court of Appeals struck down a section of the state constitution
which required jurors to swear their belief in the existence of
God. As a result of this decision, petitioner's case was remanded
to the trial court. Because both the grand and petit juries in
petitioner's case had been selected under the invalid constitutional provision, petitioner was given the option of demanding re-indictment and retrial. He chose to have his conviction set aside, and a new indictment and new trial followed. At
this 2d trial, petitioner was again charged with both larceny
and burglary. Petitioner objected to retrial on the larceny
count, arguing that because the first jury had found him not
guilty of larceny, retrial would violate the constitutional
prohibition against subjecting persons to double jeopardy for
the same offense. The trial judge denied petitioner's motion to
dismiss the larceny charge, and petitioner was tried for both
larceny and burglary. This time the jury found petitioner guilty
of both offenses, and the judge sentenced him to 15 years on the
burglary count and 5 years for larceny, the sentences to run
concurrently....

After consideration of all the questions before us, we find
no bar to our decision of the double jeopardy issue. On the
merits, we hold that the double jeopardy clause of the 5th
Amendment is applicable to the states through the 14th Amendment, and we reverse petitioner's conviction for larceny....

In 1937, this court decided the landmark case of *Palko v.
Connecticut.* ... Palko, although indicted for first-degree
murder, had been convicted of murder in the 2d degree after a
jury trial in a Connecticut state court. The state appealed and

won a new trial. Palko argued that the 14th Amendment
incorporated, as against the states, the 5th Amendment requirement that no person "be subject for the same offence to be
twice put in jeopardy of life or limb." The court disagreed.
Federal double jeopardy standards were not applicable against
the states. Only when a kind of jeopardy subjected a defendant
to "a hardship so acute and shocking that our polity will not
endure it" ... did the 14th Amendment apply. The order for a
new trial was affirmed. In subsequent appeals from state
courts, the court continued to apply this lesser *Palko*
standard....

Recently, however, this court has "increasingly looked to
the specific guarantees of the [Bill of Rights] to determine
whether a state criminal trial was conducted with due process
of law." *Washington v. Texas*...(1967). In an increasing
number of cases, the court "has rejected the notion that the 14th
Amendment applies to the states only a 'watered-down,
subjective version of the individual guarantees of the Bill of
Rights....'" *Malloy v. Hogan* ... (1964). Only last term we
found that the right to trial by jury in criminal cases was
"fundamental to the American scheme of justice," *Duncan v.
Louisiana* ... (1968), and held that the 6th Amendment right to
a jury trial was applicable to the states through the 14th
Amendment. For the same reasons, we today find that the
double jeopardy prohibition of the 5th Amendment represents a
fundamental ideal in our constitutional heritage and that it
should apply to the states through the 14th Amendment.
Insofar as it is inconsistent with this holding, *Palko v.
Connecticut* is overruled.

Palko represented an approach to basic constitutional
rights which this court's recent decisions have rejected. It was
cut of the same cloth as *Betts v. Brady* ... (1942), the case
which held that a criminal defendant's right to counsel was to
be determined by deciding in each case whether the denial of
that right was "shocking to the universal sense of justice." ... It
relied upon *Twining v. New Jersey* ... (1908), which held that
the right against compulsory self-incrimination was not an
element of 14th Amendment due process. *Betts* was overruled
by *Gideon v. Wainwright* ... (1963); *Twining,* by *Malloy v.
Hogan* ... (1964). Our recent cases have thoroughly rejected the
Palko notion that basic constitutional rights can be denied by

the states as long as the totality of the circumstances does not disclose a denial of "fundamental fairness." Once it is decided that a particular Bill of Rights guarantee is "fundamental to the American scheme of justice," *Duncan v. Louisiana, ...* (1968) the same constitutional standards apply against both the state and federal governments. *Palko's* roots had thus been cut away years ago. We today only recognize the inevitable.

The fundamental nature of the guarantee against double jeopardy can hardly be doubted. Its origins can be traced to Greek and Roman times, and it became established in the common law of England long before this nation's independence.... Today, every state incorporates some form of the prohibition in its constitution or common law....

... The validity of petitioner's larceny conviction must be judged, not by the watered-down standard enunciated in *Palko,* but under this court's interpretations of the 5th Amendment double jeopardy provision....

Justice Harlan, whom Stewart joined, dissenting:

... I would hold, in accordance with *Palko v. Connecticut* ..., that the due process clause of the 14th Amendment does not take over the double jeopardy clause of the 5th, as such. Today *Palko* becomes another casualty in the so far unchecked march toward "incorporating" much, if not all, of the federal Bill of Rights into the due process clause. This march began, with a court majority, in 1961 when *Mapp v. Ohio* ... was decided and, before the present decision, found its last stopping point in *Duncan v. Louisiana* ... decided at the end of last term. I have at each step in the march expressed my opposition.... Under the pressures of the closing days of the term, I am content to rest on what I have written in prior opinions, save to raise my voice again in protest against a doctrine which so subtly, yet profoundly, is eroding many of the basics of our federal system.

More broadly, that this court should have apparently become so impervious to the pervasive wisdom of the constitutional philosophy embodied in *Palko,* and that it should have felt itself able to attribute to the perceptive and timeless words of Mr. Justice Cardozo nothing more than a "watering down" of constitutional rights, are indeed revealing symbols of the

extent to which we are weighing anchors from the funda-
mentals of our constitutional system....

The same day that it held the double-jeopardy
provision of the Bill of Rights binding on the states,
the Supreme Court, in *North Carolina v. Pearce,*
held that it was contrary to that principle for a judge
to refuse to credit a prisoner for the time served in
jail when the prisoner succeeded in securing a new
trial. The court also held that a judge could impose a
heavier penalty at the 2d trial only on the basis of
"objective information" concerning the prisoner's
behavior following his original conviction. The court
pointed out that increased sentences on reconviction
were not uncommon and that prisoners were sometimes afraid to appeal their original conviction for
fear of angering the sentencing judge.

In *Ashe v. Swenson,* the Supreme Court held
Apr. 6, 1970 that the double-jeopardy ban meant that
a person acquitted on charges of robbing one person
in a multi-victim robbery could not be tried on
charges of robbing another of the victims. Chief
Justice Burger, in dissent, characterized the ruling as
"decision by slogan." In *Price v. Georgia,* the court
held unanimously June 15, 1970 that a person once
tried for murder but found guilty of the lesser crime
of involuntary manslaughter could not be tried again
for murder after successfully appealing the
manslaughter conviction.

CONFESSIONS

Use of Confessions Limited by Court

One of the most controversial series of rulings in Supreme Court history concerns pre-trial confessions.

In *Escobedo v. Illinois,* decided June 22, 1964, the court ruled, 5-4, that a confession obtained from a suspect in police custody may not be used in court if the police failed to inform him of his constitutional right to remain silent and refused his request to consult an attorney.

That ruling was expanded in another 5-4 decision, *Miranda v. Arizona,* decided June 13, 1966. In *Miranda,* the court ruled that a confession could not be used in court if the suspect, once in police custody, was not informed of his right to counsel and of his right to remain silent. In *Orozco v. Texas,* the court said Mar. 25, 1969 that *Miranda* applied to questioning undertaken before the suspect was brought to the police station.

The impact of these 3 Warren court decisions was blunted by the Burger court in *Harris v. New York,* handed down Feb. 24, 1971. In *Harris,* the court ruled, 6-2, that a defendant who takes the witness stand can be contradicted by what he said earlier at the police station even though the suspect had not been informed, as required by *Miranda,* of his right to counsel and of his right to remain silent. Thus, although a confession obtained contrary to *Miranda* may not be used directly in court, these same confessional statements may be cited by the prosecution when cross-examining the defendant. The effect of *Harris,* therefore, is to discourage defendants from taking the witness stand lest they be confronted with pretrial statements that cannot be excluded under *Miranda.*

The most controversial aspect of *Miranda* concerns the so-called exclusionary rule prohibiting the use in court of evidence obtained by unconstitutional methods. Some authorities deem that prohibition essential where confessions are concerned because of the possibility that a coerced confession may not be true. In other areas, however, as in the case of physical evidence, that issue is not presented. A gun used to shoot a man is trustworthy evidence regardless of how the police obtained it.

2 theories have been advanced on behalf of a comprehensive exclusionary rule. One view holds that the prestige and moral authority of the government is undermined when the government uses evidence that, although valid, had been obtained by unconstitutional methods. Expressing this position, Justice Louis Brandeis said: "Our government is potent, the omnipresent teacher. For good or for ill, it teaches the whole people by its example. Crime is contagious. If the government becomes a law breaker, it breeds contempt for law."

Others see the exclusionary rule primarily as a means of regulating the police. This view was set forth by Justice Frank Murphy in 1949 in his dissenting opinion in *Wolf v. Colorado.* Murphy said: "Only by exclusion can we impress upon the zealous prosecutor that violation of the Constitution will do him no good. And only when that point is driven home can the prosecutor be expected to emphasize the importance of observing constitutional demands in his instructions to the police." The difficulty of this position was described by Justice Benjamin Cardozo.: "The criminal is to go free because the constable has blundered.... A room is searched against the law, and the body of a murdered man is found.... The privacy of the home has been infringed, and the murderer goes free."

The ability of the exclusionary rule to deter unconstitutional police behavior has been questioned by a number of authorities. In some 80% of all felony cases there is no trial from which evidence can be excluded because the defendant chooses to plead guilty in the hope of receiving a lesser sentence. As Chief Justice Warren Earl Burger pointed out in 1971 in his dissent in *Bivens v. 6 Unknown Named Agents:* "The prosecutor who loses his case because of police misconduct is not an official of the police department.... He does not have control or direction over police procedures or police action that lead to the exclusion of evidence."

A "bad" policeman, according to some authorities, moreover, is unlikely to be deterred by a Supreme Court decision. According to this view, a policeman who relied on coercion to obtain confessions prior to *Miranda* is likely to continue the practice and perjure himself by insisting that the defendant waived his right to remain silent and to consult an attorney.

To some critics, the most unsatisfactory aspect of the exclusionary rule is its heavy-handedness. An honest, relatively insignificant error on the part of a policeman can lead to the exclusion of valuable evidence just as does deliberate, wholesale violation of a defendant's rights. An example concerned a Detroit policeman who admitted shooting one of 3 blacks killed during the 1967 Detroit riots. The policeman's statement was not admitted in evidence because his fellow police officers did not think it necessary to inform him of his rights under *Miranda.* According to Justice Burger in *Bivens,* "freeing either a tiger or a mouse in a schoolroom is an illegal act, but no rational person would suggest that these 2 acts should be punished in the same way."

Defenders of the exclusionary rule, while acknowledging its defects, argue that police practices have improved throughout the country in recent years as a result of the exclusionary rule and that the Supreme Court was forced to regulate police behavior because of the failure of state and local governments to discharge their responsibilities.

Miranda has led to increased scrutiny as to the value of confessions in obtaining convictions and reducing crime. Many studies indicate that the importance of confessions has been exaggerated by the public and the police.

Most crimes, for example, do not lead to arrest. Only about 19% of all burglaries reported to the police lead to arrest. It is doubtful, moreover, whether even one burglary in 5 is reported to the police. Only about 27% of all robberies lead to arrest. For the 3 most common crimes included in the FBI crime index—burglary, larceny and car theft—fewer than one in 5 lead to arrest. In some instances the police may fail to make an arrest because they suspect that their evidence will not be admitted in court. In most cases, however, the criminal remains at large because the police have been unable to solve the crime.

In cases in which the police have a suspect, confessions often are not needed since the evidence that led to the suspect is sufficient to convict. Such confessions are considered superfluous, therefore, since they are obtained from persons whose guilt is apparent. *Miranda* is typical in that regard. Ernesto A. Miranda's conviction of kidnap and rape was overturned by the Supreme Court on the ground that his confession should not have been admitted into evidence. But Miranda was retried, found guilty and sentenced to 30 years in jail on the basis of other evidence.

Most defendants who do not confess when questioned by the police end up "confessing" in court by pleading guilty in hope of a lesser penalty. Abraham S. Blumberg points out in *Criminal Justice* "that the process of criminal law enforcement has always depended ... on confessions obtained judicially in open court *(i.e.,* pleas of guilty) rather than on confessions wrung from the accused in the back room of a police station." The impact of *Miranda* is blunted, moreover, by the realization that many criminals prior to *Miranda* already knew of their right to remain silent when interrogated by the police.

In *Escobedo v. Illinois,* the Supreme Court ruled that a pretrial confession should not have been introduced in evidence since it was obtained after the police refused Danny Escobedo's request that he be allowed to consult his attorney, who was waiting outside the interrogation room, and after the police failed to inform Escobedo of his right to remain silent. Justice Arthur J. Goldberg, speaking for the majority, said that such actions were in violation of the 6th Amendment right of counsel. According to Goldberg, the right of counsel would be "hollow" if it did not extend to events that preceded the trial. Escobedo, 22, a Mexican-American, was convicted of shooting and killing his brother-in-law.

Discussing the possibility that the number of confessions would decline if suspects were permitted to consult with their lawyers, Goldberg asserted that "if the exercise of constitutional rights will thwart the effectiveness of a system of law enforcement, then there is something very wrong with that system."

Justice Potter Stewart, in a dissenting opinion, called Escobedo's confession "voluntary" and asserted that the Supreme Court "has never held that the Constitution requires the police to give any 'advice' regarding constitutional rights." Justice Byron R. White, in a dissenting opinion, predicted that law enforcement would be "crippled and its task made a great deal more difficult" by *Escobedo*.

Abridgment of the *Escobedo v. Illinois* decision (378 U.S. 478, June 22, 1964):

Justice Goldberg delivering the majority opinion:

The critical question in this case is whether, under the circumstances, the refusal by the police to honor petitioner's request to consult with his lawyer during the course of an interrogation constitutes a denial of "the assistance of counsel" in violation of the 6th Amendment to the Constitution as "made obligatory upon the states by the 14th Amendment," *Gideon v. Wainwright* [1963], ... and thereby renders inadmissible in a state criminal trial any incriminating statement elicited by the police during the interrogation.

On the night of Jan. 19, 1960, petitioner's brother-in-law was fatally shot. In the early hours of the next morning, at 2:30

a.m., petitioner was arrested without a warrant and interrogated. Petitioner made no statement to the police and was released at 5 that afternoon pursuant to a state court writ of *habeas corpus* obtained by Mr. Warren Wolfson, a lawyer who had been retained by petitioner.

On Jan. 30, Benedict DiGerlando, who was then in police custody and who was later indicted for the murder along with petitioner, told the police that petitioner had fired the fatal shots. Between 8 and 9 that evening, petitioner and his sister, the widow of the deceased, were arrested and taken to police headquarters. En route to the police station, the police "had handcuffed the defendant behind his back," and "one of the arresting officers told defendant that DiGerlando had named him as the one who shot" the deceased. Petitioner testified, without contradiction, that the "detectives said they had us pretty well, up pretty tight, and we might as well admit to this crime," and that he replied, "I am sorry but I would like to have advice from my lawyer." A police officer testified that although petitioner was not formally charged, "he was in custody" and "couldn't walk out the door."

Shortly after petitioner reached police headquarters, his retained lawyer arrived. . . .

Petitioner testified that during the course of the interrogation he repeatedly asked to speak to his lawyer and that the police said that his lawyer "didn't want to see" him. The testimony of the police officers confirmed these accounts in substantial detail.

Notwithstanding repeated requests by each, petitioner and his retained lawyer were afforded no opportunity to consult during the course of the entire interrogation. At one point . . . petitioner and his attorney came into each other's view for a few moments but the attorney was quickly ushered away. Petitioner testified "that he heard a detective telling the attorney the latter would not be allowed to talk to [him] 'until they were done'" and that he heard the attorney being refused permission to remain in the adjoining room. A police officer testified that he had told the lawyer that he could not see petitioner until "we were through interrogating" him.

There is testimony by the police that during the interrogation, petitioner, . . . with no record of previous experience with the police, "was handcuffed" in a standing position and that he "was nervous, he had circles under his eyes and he was upset" and was "agitated" because "he had not slept well in over a week."

It is undisputed that during the course of the interrogation Officer Montejano, who "grew up" in petitioner's neighborhood, who knew his family, and who uses "Spanish language in [his] police work," conferred alone with petitioner "for about a quarter of an hour...." Petitioner testified that the officer said to him "in Spanish that my sister and I could go home if I pinned it on Benedict DiGerlando," that "he would see to it that we would go home and be held only as witnesses, if anything, if we had made a statement against DiGerlando..., that we would be able to go home that night." Petitioner testified that he made the statement in issue because of this assurance. Officer Montejano denied offering any such assurance.

A police officer testified that during the interrogation the following occurred: "I informed him of what DiGerlando told me, and when I did, he told me that DiGerlando was [lying] and I said, 'Would you care to tell DiGerlando that?' and he said, 'Yes, I will.' So, I brought ... Escobedo in and he confronted DiGerlando and he told him that he was lying and said, 'I didn't shoot Manuel, you did it.' "

In this way, petitioner, for the first time, admitted to some knowledge of the crime. After that he made additional statements further implicating himself in the murder plot. At this point an assistant state's attorney, Theodore J. Cooper, was summoned "to take" a statement. Mr. Cooper, an experienced lawyer who was assigned to the Homicide Division to take "statements from some defendants and some prisoners that they had in custody," "took" petitioner's statement by asking carefully framed questions apparently designed to assure the admissibility into evidence of the resulting answers. Mr. Cooper testified that he did not advise petitioner of his constitutional rights, and it is undisputed that no one during the course of the interrogation so advised him.

Petitioner moved both before and during trial to suppress the incriminating statement, but the motions were denied. Petitioner was convicted of murder and he appealed the conviction....

Petitioner, a layman, was undoubtedly unaware that under Illinois law an admission of "mere" complicity in the murder plot was legally as damaging as an admission of firing of the fatal shots.... The "guiding hand of counsel" was essential to advise petitioner of his rights in this delicate situation. *Powell v. Alabama* [1932].... This was the "stage when legal aid and advice" were most critical to petitioner. *Massiah v. United States* [1914]....

In *Gideon v. Wainwright* [1963] ... we held that every person accused of a crime, whether state or federal, is entitled to a lawyer at trial. The rule sought by the state here, however, would make the trial no more than an appeal from the interrogation; and the "right to use counsel at the formal trial [would be] a very hollow thing [if], for all practical purposes, the conviction is already assured by pretrial examination." *In re Groban* [1957].... "One can imagine a cynical prosecutor saying: 'Let them have the most illustrious counsel, now. They can't escape the noose. There is nothing that counsel can do for them at the trial.'" *Ex parte Sullivan*....

It is argued that if the right to counsel is afforded prior to indictment, the number of confessions obtained by the police will diminish significantly because most confessions are obtained during the period between arrest and indictment and "any lawyer worth his salt will tell the suspect in no uncertain terms to make no statement to police under any circumstances." *Watts v. Indiana* [1949].... This argument, of course, cuts 2 ways. The fact that many confessions are obtained during this period points up its critical nature as a "stage when legal aid and advice" are surely needed. *Massiah v. United States*.... The right to counsel would indeed be hollow if it began at a period when few confessions were obtained. There is necessarily a direct relationship between the importance of a stage to the police in their quest for a confession and the criticalness of that stage to the accused in his need for legal advice. Our Constitution, unlike some others, strikes the balance in favor of the right of the accused to be advised by his lawyer of his privilege against self-incrimination....

We have learned the lesson of history, ancient and modern, that a system of criminal law enforcement which comes to depend on the "confession" will, in the long run, be less reliable and more subject to abuses than a system which depends on extrinsic evidence independently secured through skillful investigation....

We have also learned the companion lesson of history that no system of criminal justice can, or should, survive if it comes to depend for its continued effectiveness on the citizens' abdication through unawareness of their constitutional rights. No system worth preserving should have to *fear* that if an accused is permitted to consult with a lawyer, he will become aware of, and exercise, these rights. If the exercise of constitutional rights will thwart the effectiveness of a system of law enforcement, then there is something very wrong with that system.

We hold, therefore, that where, as here, the investigation is no longer a general inquiry into an unsolved crime but has begun to focus on a particular suspect, the suspect has been taken into police custody, the police carry out a process of interrogations that lends itself to eliciting incriminating statements, the suspect has requested and been denied an opportunity to consult with his lawyer, and the police have not effectively warned him of his absolute constitutional right to remain silent, the accused has been denied "the assistance of counsel" in violation of the 6th Amendment to the Constitution as "made obligatory upon the states by the 14th Amendment," *Gideon v. Wainwright, . . . and that no statement elicited by the police during the interrogation may be used against him at a criminal trial. . . .*

Justice John Marshall Harlan dissenting:

I think the rule announced today is most ill-conceived and that it seriously and unjustifiably fetters perfectly legitimate methods of criminal law enforcement.

Justice Potter Stewart dissenting:

. . . The confession which the court today holds inadmissible was a voluntary one. It was given during the course of a perfectly legitimate police investigation of an unsolved murder. The court says that what happened during this investigation "affected" the trial. I had always supposed that the whole purpose of a police investigation of a murder was to "affect" the trial of the murderer, and that it would be only an incompetent, unsuccessful, or corrupt investigation which would not do so. The court further says that the Illinois police officers did not advise the petitioner of his "constitutional rights" before he confessed to the murder. This court has never held that the Constitution requires the police to give any "advice" under circumstances such as these.

Supported by no stronger authority than its own rhetoric, the court today converts a routine police investigation of an unsolved murder into a distorted analogue of a judicial trial. It imports into this investigation constitutional concepts historically applicable only after the onset of formal prosecutorial proceedings. By doing so, I think the court perverts those precious constitutional guarantees, and frustrates the vital interests of society in preserving the legitimate and proper function of honest and purposeful police investigation.

Like my brother [Thomas C.] Clark, I cannot escape the logic of my brother [Byron] White's conclusions as to the extraordinary implications which emanate from the court's opinion in this case, and I share their views as to the untold and highly unfortunate impact today's decision may have upon the fair administration of criminal justice. I can only hope we have completely misunderstood what the court has said.

Justice White, whom Clark and Stewart joined, dissenting:

... By abandoning the voluntary-involuntary test for admissibility of confessions, the court seems driven by the notion that it is uncivilized law enforcement to use an accused's own admissions against him at his trial. It attempts to find a home for this new and nebulous rule of due process by attaching it to the right to counsel guaranteed in the federal system by the 6th Amendment and binding upon the states by virtue of the due process guarantee of the 14th Amendment. *Gideon v. Wainwright, supra.* The right to counsel now not only entitles the accused to counsel's advice and aid in preparing for trial but stands as an impenetrable barrier to any interrogation once the accused has become a suspect. From that very moment apparently his right to counsel attaches, a rule wholly unworkable and impossible to administer unless police cars are equipped with public defenders and undercover agents and police informants have defense counsel at their side. I would not abandon the court's prior cases defining with some care and analysis the circumstances requiring the presence or aid of counsel and substitute the amorphous and wholly unworkable principle that counsel is constitutionally required whenever he would or could be helpful.... These cases dealt with the requirement of counsel at proceedings in which definable rights could be won or lost, not with stages where probative evidence might be obtained. Under this new approach one might just as well argue that a potential defendant is constitutionally entitled to a lawyer before, not after, he commits a crime, since it is then that crucial incriminating evidence is put within the reach of the government by the would-be accused. Until now there simply has been no right guaranteed by the federal Constitution to be free from the use at trial of a voluntary admission made prior to indictment....

The court may be concerned with a narrower matter: the unknowing defendant who responds to police questioning because he mistakenly believes that he must and that his admissions will not be used against him. But this worry hardly calls for the broadside the court has now fired. The failure to inform an accused that he need not answer and that his answers may be used against him is very relevant indeed to whether the disclosures are compelled. Cases in this court, to say the least, have never placed a premium on ignorance of constitutional rights. If an accused is told he must answer and does not know better, it would be very doubtful that the resulting admissions could be used against him. When the accused has not been informed of his rights at all, the court characteristically and properly looks very closely at the surrounding circumstances.... I would continue to do so. But in this case Danny Escobedo knew full well that he did not have to answer and knew full well that his lawyer had advised him not to answer.

I do not suggest for a moment that law enforcement will be destroyed by the rule announced today. The need for peace and order is too insistent for that. But it will be crippled and its task made a great deal more difficult, all in my opinion, for unsound, unstated reasons, which can find no home in any of the provisions of the Constitution.

The Supreme Court expanded the *Escobedo* ruling in *Miranda v. Arizona* June 13, 1966. The decision requires police to inform a suspect of his 5th Amendment right against self-incrimination and his 6th Amendment right of counsel. Under *Miranda,* if the police do not inform a suspect of these rights, any confession that may be obtained may not be introduced in court.

In the *Miranda* ruling the court held: "Prior to any questioning, the person must be warned that he has a right to remain silent, that any statement he does make may be used as evidence against him and that he has a right to the presence of an attorney, either retained or appointed. The defendant may waive effectuation of these rights, provided the waiver is made voluntarily, knowingly and intelligently. If, however, he indicates in any manner and at any stage of the process that he wishes to consult with an attorney before speaking, there can be no questioning. Likewise, if the individual is alone and indicates in any manner that he does not wish to be interrogated, the police may not question him. The mere fact that he may have answered some questions or volunteered some statements on his own does not deprive him of the right to refrain from answering any further inquiries until he has consulted with an attorney and thereafter consents to be questioned."

Chief Justice Earl Warren wrote the majority opinion in *Miranda*. In it he said that while some policemen may resort to physical violence to obtain confessions, the more common practice was to resort to trickery. While conceding that it was difficult to determine what actually transpires in the majority of police interrogations, Warren pointed to material contained in police manuals and texts recommending various psychological "ploys" for use in interrogating suspects. One example cited by Warren involved the so-called "reverse line-up," described thus in a police manual: "The accused is placed in a line-up, but this time he is identified by several fictitious witnesses or victims who associated him with different offenses. It is expected that the suspect will become desperate and confess to the offense under investigation in order to escape the false accusation." Such tactics, Warren said, enable the police to "persuade, trick or cajole" a suspect "out of exercising his constitutional rights." Warren rejected the contention that requiring the police to inform suspects of their rights would unduly hamper the police.

Justice Thomas C. Clark, dissenting, said the majority had failed to demonstrate that police interrogations followed the advice of the cited police manuals and texts. Justice Harlan, in his dissenting opinion, accused the majority of largely ignoring the interests of society by establishing a new code that "would markedly decrease the number of confessions." He said that the court was "taking a real risk with society's welfare." Harlan asserted that, contrary to the majority contention, interrogation procedures employed by the FBI, the military and other nations were not as restrictive as *Miranda.* Harlan said he preferred to let the courts continue to determine the voluntariness of confessions.

In *Miranda,* the court sanctioned the use of confessions obtained from persons who, after being told of their rights, agreed, nevertheless, to answer questions. The court insisted, however, that such waivers be "made voluntarily, knowingly and intelligently." This raised 2 questions: How can a person "intelligently" waive his right to an attorney? "Hell, if he waives his right to a lawyer, what's intelligent about that?" one policeman asked. Other observers argued that it was inconsistent for the court to permit waivers. *Miranda,* they pointed out, was based to a considerable degree on the court's distrust of police interrogation practices. Ploys that had been used to secure confessions could now be used to obtain waivers, critics contended. One criminal law text asks, therefore, whether *Miranda* simply shifted "the 'swearing contest' from the 'voluntariness' of the confession to the adequacy of the warnings and the validity of the waiver."

Abridgment of the *Miranda v. Arizona* decision (384 U.S. 436, June 13, 1966):

Chief Justice Warren delivering the opinion:

... Our holding ... briefly stated ... is this: the prosecution may not use statements, whether exculpatory or inculpatory, stemming from custodial interrogation of the defendant unless it demonstrates the use of procedural safeguards effective to secure the privilege against self-incrimination. By custodial interrogation, we mean questioning initiated by law enforcement officers after a person has been taken into custody or otherwise deprived of his freedom of action in any significant way. As for the procedural safeguards to be employed, unless other fully effective means are devised to inform accused persons of their right of silence and to assure a continuous opportunity to exercise it, the following measures are required. Prior to any questioning, the person must be warned that he has a right to remain silent, that any statement he does make may be used as evidence against him and that he has a right to the presence of an attorney, either retained or appointed. The defendant may waive effectuation of these rights, provided the waiver is made voluntarily, knowingly and intelligently. If, however, he indicates in any manner and at any stage of the process that he wishes to consult with an attorney before speaking, there can be no questioning. Likewise, if the individual is alone and indicates in any manner that he does not wish to be interrogated, the police may not question him. The mere fact that he may have answered some questions or volunteered some statements on his own does not deprive him of the right to refrain from answering any further inquiries until he has consulted with an attorney and thereafter consents to be questioned.

... The constitutional issue we decide in each of these cases is the admissibility of statements obtained from a defendant questioned while in custody and deprived of his freedom of action. In each, the defendant was questioned by police officers, detectives, or a prosecuting attorney in a room in which he was cut off from the outside world. In none of these cases was the defendant given a full and effective warning of his rights at the outset of the interrogation process. In all the cases, the questioning elicited oral admissions, and in 3 of them signed statements as well which were admitted at their trials. They all thus share salient features—incommunicado interrogation of individuals in a police-dominated atmosphere, resulting in self-incriminating statements without full warnings of constitutional rights.

An understanding of the nature and setting of this in-custody interrogation is essential to our decisions today. The difficulty in depicting what transpires at such interrogations stems from the fact that in this country they have largely taken place incommunicado. From extensive factual studies undertaken in the early 1930s, ... it is clear that police violence and the "3rd degree" flourished at that time. In a series of cases decided by this court long after these studies, the police resorted to physical brutality—beating, hanging, whipping—and to sustained and protracted questioning incommunicado in order to extort confessions. The 1961 Commission on Civil Rights found much evidence to indicate that "some policemen still resort to physical force to obtain confessions." ...

... Unless a proper limitation upon custodial interrogation is achieved—such as these decisions will advance—there can be no assurance that practices of this nature will be eradicated in the foreseeable future....

Again we stress that the modern practice of in-custody interrogation is psychologically rather than physically oriented. As we have stated before, "Since *Chambers v. Florida* [1940]..., this court has recognized that coercion can be mental as well as physical and that the blood of the accused is not the only hallmark of an unconstitutional inquisition." *Blackburn v. Alabama* ... (1960). Interrogation still takes place in privacy. Privacy results in secrecy and this in turn results in a gap in our knowledge as to what in fact goes on in the interrogation rooms. A valuable source of information about present police practices, however, may be found in various police manuals and texts which document procedures employed with success in the past, and which recommend various other effective tactics. These texts are used by law enforcement agencies themselves as guides. It should be noted that these texts professedly present the most enlightened and effective means presently used to obtain statements through custodial interrogation. By considering these texts and other data, it is possible to describe procedures observed and noted around the country.

The officers are told by the manuals that the "principal psychological factor contributing to a successful interrogation is *privacy*—being alone with the person under interrogation." The efficacy of this tactic has been explained as follows: "If at all practicable, the interrogation should take place in the investigator's office or at least in a room of his own choice. The subject should be deprived of every psychological advantage. In his own home he may be confident, indignant or recalcitrant. He is more keenly aware of his rights and more reluctant to tell of his indiscretions or criminal behavior within the walls of his home. Moreover, his family and other friends are nearby, their presence lending moral support. In his own office, the investigator possesses all the advantages. The atmosphere suggests the invincibility of the forces of the law."

To highlight the isolation and unfamiliar surroundings, the manuals instruct the police to display an air of confidence in the suspect's guilt and from outward appearance to maintain only an interest in confirming certain details. The guilt of the subject is to be posited as a fact. The interrogator should direct his comments toward the reasons why the subject committed the act, rather than to court failure by asking the subject whether he did it. Like other men, perhaps the subject has had a bad family life, had an unhappy childhood, had too much to drink, had an unrequited attraction to women. The officers are instructed to minimize the moral seriousness of the offense, to cast blame on the victim or on society. These tactics are designed to put the subject in a psychological state where his story is but an elaboration of what the police purport to know already—that he is guilty. Explanations to the contrary are dismissed and discouraged.

The texts thus stress that the major qualities an interrogator should possess are patience and perseverance. One
writer describes the efficacy of these characteristics in this
manner: "In the preceding paragraphs emphasis has been
placed on kindness and stratagems. The investigator will, however, encounter many situations where the sheer weight of his
personality will be the deciding factor. Where emotional
appeals and tricks are employed to no avail, he must rely on an
oppressive atmosphere of dogged persistence. He must
interrogate steadily and without relent, leaving the subject no
prospect of surcease. He must dominate his subject and over-
whelm him with his inexorable will to obtain the truth. He
should interrogate for a spell of several hours, pausing only for
the subject's necessities in acknowledgment of the need to avoid
a charge of duress that can be technically substantiated. In a
serious case, the interrogation may continue for days, with the
required intervals for food and sleep, but with no respite from
the atmosphere of domination. It is possible in this way to
induce the subject to talk without resorting to duress or
coercion. The method should be used only when the guilt of the
subject appears highly probable."

The manuals suggest that the suspect be offered legal
excuses for his actions in order to obtain an initial admission of
guilt. Where there is a suspected revenge-killing, for example,
the interrogator may say: "Joe, you probably didn't go out
looking for this fellow with the purpose of shooting him. My
guess is, however, that you expected something from him and
that's why you carried a gun—for your own protection. You
knew him for what he was, no good. Then when you met him he
probably started using foul, abusive language and he gave some
indication that he was about to pull a gun on you, and that's
when you had to act to save your own life. That's about it, isn't
it, Joe?" . . .

. . . One ploy often used has been termed the "friendly-
unfriendly" or the "Mutt and Jeff" act: ". . . In this technique, 2
agents are employed. Mutt, the relentless investigator, who
knows the subject is guilty and is not going to waste any
time. . . . Jeff, on the other hand, is obviously a kindhearted
man. He has a brother who was involved in a little scrape like
this. He disapproves of Mutt and his tactics and will arrange to
get him off the case if the subject will cooperate. . . . The

technique is applied by having both investigators present while Mutt acts out his role. Jeff may stand by quietly and demur at some of Mutt's tactics. When Jeff makes his plea for cooperation, Mutt is not present in the room."

The interrogators sometimes are instructed to induce a confession out of trickery.... In the identification situation, the interrogator may take a break in his questioning to place the subject among a group of men in a line-up. "The witness or complainant (previously coached, if necessary) studies the line-up and confidently points out the subject as the guilty party." Then the questioning resumes "as though there were now no doubt about the guilt of the subject."...

The manuals also contain instructions for police on how to handle the individual who refuses to discuss the matter entirely, or who asks for an attorney or relatives. The examiner is to concede him the right to remain silent. "This usually has a very undermining effect. First of all, he is disappointed in his expectation of an unfavorable reaction on the part of the interrogator. Secondly, a concession of this right to remain silent impresses the subject with the apparent fairness of his interrogator." After this psychological conditioning, however, the officer is told to point out the incriminating significance of the suspect's refusal to talk: "Joe, you have a right to remain silent. That's your privilege and I'm the last person in the world who'll try to take it away from you.... But let me ask you this. Suppose you were in my shoes and I were in yours and you called me in to ask me about this and I told you, 'I don't want to answer any of your questions.' You'd think I had something to hide.... That's exactly what I'll have to think about you, and so will everybody else. So let's sit here and talk this whole thing over." Few will persist in their initial refusal to talk, it is said, if this monologue is employed correctly.

In the event that the subject wishes to speak to a relative or an attorney, the following advice is tendered: "[T]he interrogator should respond by suggesting that the subject first tell the truth to the interrogator himself rather than get anyone else involved in the matter. If the request is for an attorney, the interrogator may suggest that the subject save himself or his family the expense of any such professional service, particularly if he is innocent...."

From these representative samples of interrogation techniques, the setting prescribed by the manuals and observed in practice becomes clear. In essence, it is this: To be alone with the subject is essential to prevent distraction and to deprive him of any outside support. The aura of confidence in his guilt undermines his will to resist. He merely confirms the preconceived story the police seek to have him describe. Patience and persistence, at times relentless questioning, are employed. To obtain a confession, the interrogator must "patiently maneuver himself or his quarry into a position from which the desired objective may be attained." When normal procedures fail to produce the needed result, the police may resort to deceptive stratagems such as giving false legal advice. It is important to keep the subject off balance, for example, by trading on his insecurity about himself or his surroundings. The police then persuade, trick, or cajole him out of exercising his constitutional rights.

Even without employing brutality, the "3d degree" or the specific stratagems described above, the very fact of custodial interrogation exacts a heavy toll on individual liberty and trades on the weakness of individuals.*...

... The potentiality for compulsion is forcefully apparent, for example, in *Miranda,* where the indigent Mexican defendant was a seriously disturbed individual with pronounced sexual fantasies....

From the foregoing, we can readily perceive an intimate connection between the privilege against self-incrimination and police custodial questioning....

It is impossible for us to foresee the potential alternatives for protecting the privilege which might be devised by

---

* Interrogation procedures may even give rise to a false confession. The most recent conspicuous example occurred in New York, in 1964, when a Negro of limited intelligence [George Whitmore] confessed to 2 brutal murders and a rape which he had not committed. When this was discovered, the prosecutor was reported as saying: "Call it what you want—brain-washing, hypnosis, fright. They made him give an untrue confession. The only thing I don't believe is that Whitmore was beaten."

Congress or the states in the exercise of their creative rule-making capacities. Therefore, we cannot say that the Constitution necessarily requires adherence to any particular solution for the inherent compulsions of the interrogation process as it is presently conducted. Our decision in no way creates a constitutional straitjacket which will handicap sound efforts at reform, nor is it intended to have this effect. We encourage Congress and the states to continue their laudable search for increasingly effective ways of protecting the rights of the individual while promoting efficient enforcement of our criminal laws. . . .

If the interrogation continues without the presence of an attorney and a statement is taken, a heavy burden rests on the government to demonstrate that the defendant knowingly and intelligently waived his privilege against self-incrimination and his right to retained or appointed counsel. . . . This court has always set high standards of proof for the waiver of constitutional rights . . ., and we re-assert these standards as applied to in-custody interrogation. Since the state is responsible for establishing the isolated circumstances under which the interrogation takes place and has the only means of making available corroborated evidence of warnings given during incommunicado interrogation, the burden is rightly on its shoulders.

An express statement that the individual is willing to make a statement and does not want an attorney followed closely by a statement could constitute a waiver. But a valid waiver will not be presumed simply from the silence of the accused after warnings are given or simply from the fact that a confession was in fact eventually obtained. . . .

Whatever the testimony of the authorities as to waiver of rights by an accused, the fact of lengthy interrogation or incommunicado incarceration before a statement is made is strong evidence that the accused did not validly waive his rights. In these circumstances the fact that the individual eventually made a statement is consistent with the conclusion that the compelling influence of the interrogation finally forced him to do so. It is inconsistent with any notion of a voluntary relinquishment of the privilege. Moreover, any evidence that the accused was threatened, tricked or cajoled into a waiver will, of course, show that the defendant did not voluntarily waive his privilege. The requirement of warnings and waiver of rights is a fundamental with respect to the 5th Amendment privilege and not simply a preliminary ritual to existing methods of interrogation....

Our decision is not intended to hamper the traditional function of police officers in investigating crime.... When an individual is in custody on probable cause, the police may, of course, seek out evidence in the field to be used at trial against him. Such investigation may include inquiry of persons not under restraint. General on-the-scene questioning as to facts surrounding a crime or other general questioning of citizens in the fact-finding process is not affected by our holding. It is an act of responsible citizenship for individuals to give whatever information they may have to aid in law enforcement. In such situations the compelling atmosphere inherent in the process of in-custody interrogation is not necessarily present.

In dealing with statements obtained through interrogation, we do not purport to find all confessions inadmissible. Confessions remain a proper element in law enforcement. Any statement given freely and voluntarily without any compelling influences is, of course, admissible in evidence. The fundamental import of the privilege while an individual is in custody is not whether he is allowed to talk to the police without the benefit of warnings and counsel but whether he can be interrogated. There is no requirement that police stop a person who enters a police station and states that he wishes to confess to a crime, or a person who calls the police to offer a confession or any other statement he desires to make. Volunteered statements of any kind are not barred by the 5th Amendment, and their admissibility is not affected by our holding today.

To summarize, we hold that when an individual is taken into custody or otherwise deprived of his freedom by the authorities and is subjected to questioning, the privilege against self-incrimination is jeopardized. Procedural safeguards must be employed to protect the privilege, and unless other fully effective means are adopted to notify the person of his right of silence and to assure that the exercise of the right will be scrupulously honored, the following measures are required. He must be warned prior to any questioning that he has the right to remain silent, that anything he says can be used against him in a court of law, that he has the right to the presence of an attorney, and that if he cannot afford an attorney one will be appointed for him prior to any questioning if he so desires. Opportunity to exercise these rights must be afforded to him throughout the interrogation. After such warnings have been given and such opportunity afforded him, the individual may knowingly and intelligently waive these rights and agree to answer questions or make a statement. But unless and until such warnings and waiver are demonstrated by the prosecution at trial, no evidence obtained as a result of interrogation can be used against him. . . .

. . . Over the years the Federal Bureau of Investigation has compiled an exemplary record of effective law enforcement while advising any suspect or arrested person, at the outset of an interview, that he is not required to make a statement, that any statement may be used against him in court, that the individual may obtain the services of an attorney of his own choice and, more recently, that he has a right to free counsel if he is unable to pay. . . .

The experience in some other countries also suggests that the danger to law enforcement in curbs on interrogation is overplayed. The English procedure since 1912 under the Judges' Rules is significant. As recently strengthened, the Rules require that a cautionary warning be given an accused by a police officer as soon as he has evidence that affords reasonable grounds for suspicion; they also require that any statement made be given by the accused without questioning by police. . . . The right of the individual to consult with an attorney during this period is expressly recognized. . . . Similarly, in our country the Uniform Code of Military Justice has long provided that no suspect may be interrogated without first being warned of his right not to make a statement and that any statement he makes may be used against him. Denial of the right to consult counsel during interrogation has also been proscribed by military tribunals. There appears to have been no marked detrimental effect on criminal law enforcement in these jurisdictions as a result of these rules.

Justice Clark dissenting:

. . . I am unable to join the majority because its opinion goes too far on too little, while my dissenting brethren do not go quite far enough. Nor can I join in the court's criticism of the present practices of police and investigatory agencies as to custodial interrogation. The materials it refers to as "police manuals" are, as I read them, merely writings in this field by professors and some police officers. Not one is shown by the record here to be the official manual of any police department, much less in universal use in crime detection. Moreover, the examples of police brutality mentioned by the court are rare exceptions to the thousands of cases that appear every year in the law reports. The police agencies—all the way from municipal and state forces to the federal bureaus—are responsible for law enforcement and public safety in this country. I am proud of their efforts, which in my view are not fairly characterized by the court's opinion. . . .

. . . [Here] the court fashions a constitutional rule that the police may engage in no custodial interrogation without additionally advising the accused that he has a right under the 5th Amendment to the presence of counsel during interrogation and that, if he is without funds, counsel will be furnished him. When at any point during an interrogation the accused seeks affirmatively or impliedly to invoke his rights to silence or counsel, interrogation must be forgone or postponed. The court further holds that failure to follow the new procedures requires inexorably the exclusion of any statement by the accused, as well as the fruits thereof. Such a strict constitutional specific inserted at the nerve center of crime detection may well kill the patient. Since there is at this time a paucity of information and an almost total lack of empirical knowledge on the practical operation of requirements, truly comparable to those announced by the majority, I would be more restrained lest we go too far too fast. . . .

Justice Harlan, whom Stewart and White joined, dissenting:

I believe the decision of the court represents poor constitutional law and entails harmful consequences for the country at large. How serious these consequences may prove to be only time can tell. . . .

. . . The new rules are not designed to guard against police brutality or other unmistakably banned forms of coercion. Those who use 3d-degree tactics and deny them in court are equally able and destined to lie as skillfully about warnings and waivers. Rather, the thrust of the new rules is to negate all pressures, to reinforce the nervous or ignorant suspect, and ultimately to discourage any confession at all. The aim in short is toward "voluntariness" in a utopian sense, or, to view it from a different angle, voluntariness with a vengeance.

To incorporate this notion into the Constitution requires a strained reading of history and precedent and a disregard of the very pragmatic concerns that alone may on occasion justify such strains. I believe that reasoned examination will show that the due process clauses provide an adequate tool for coping with confessions and that, even if the 5th Amendment privilege against self-incrimination be invoked, its precedents taken as a whole do not sustain the present rules....

The court's opening contention, that the 5th Amendment governs police station confessions, is perhaps not an impermissible extension of the law, but it has little to commend itself in the present circumstances. Historically, the privilege against self-incrimination did not bear at all on the use of extra-legal confessions, for which distinct standards evolved....

... The court's opinion in my view reveals no adequate basis for extending the 5th Amendment's privilege against self-incrimination to the police station. Far more important, it fails to show that the court's new rules are well supported, let alone compelled, by 5th Amendment precedents. Instead, the new rules actually derive from quotation and analogy drawn from precedents under the 6th Amendment, which should properly have no bearing on police interrogation....

Without at all subscribing to the generally black picture of police conduct painted by the court, I think it must be frankly recognized at the outset that police questioning allowable under due process precedents may inherently entail some pressure on the suspect and may seek advantage in his ignorance or weaknesses. The atmosphere and questioning techniques, proper and fair though they be, can in themselves exert a tug on the suspect to confess, and in this light "[t]o speak of any confessions of crime made after arrest as being 'voluntary' or 'uncoerced' is somewhat inaccurate, although traditional. A confession is wholly and incontestably voluntary only if a guilty person gives himself up to the law and becomes his own accuser." *Ashcraft v. Tennessee* [1944].... Until today, the role of the

Constitution has been only to sift out *undue* pressure, not to assure spontaneous confessions.

The court's new rules aim to offset these minor pressures and disadvantages intrinsic to any kind of police interrogation. The rules do not serve due process interests in preventing blatant coercion since ... they do nothing to contain the policeman who is prepared to lie from the start....

What the court largely ignores is that its rules impair, if they will not eventually serve wholly to frustrate, an instrument of law enforcement that has long and quite reasonably been thought worth the price paid for it. There can be little doubt that the court's new code would markedly decrease the number of confessions. To warn the suspect that he may remain silent and remind him that his confession may be used in court are minor obstructions. To require also an express waiver by the suspect and an end to questioning whenever he demurs must heavily handicap questioning. And to suggest or provide counsel for the suspect simply invites the end of the interrogation....

How much harm this decision will inflict on law enforcement cannot fairly be predicted with accuracy. Evidence on the role of confessions is notoriously incomplete.... We do know that some crimes cannot be solved without confessions, that ample expert testimony attests to their importance in crime control, and that the court is taking a real risk with society's welfare in imposing its new regime on the country. The social costs of crime are too great to call the new rules anything but a hazardous experimentation.

While passing over the costs and risks of its experiment, the court portrays the evils of normal police questioning in terms which I think are exaggerated. Albeit stringently confined by the due process standards, interrogation is no doubt often inconvenient and unpleasant for the suspect. However, it is no less so for a man to be arrested and jailed, to have his house searched or to stand trial in court, yet all this may properly happen to the most innocent given probable cause, a warrant or an indictment. Society has always paid a stiff price for law and order, and peaceful interrogation is not one of the dark moments of the law.

This brief statement of the competing considerations seems to me ample proof that the court's preference is highly debatable at best and therefore not to be read into the Constitution. However, it may make the analysis more graphic to consider the actual facts of one of the 4 cases reversed by the court. *Miranda v. Arizona* serves best....

On Mar. 3, 1963, an 18-year-old girl was kidnapped and forcibly raped near Phoenix, Arizona. 10 days later, on the morning of Mar. 13, petitioner [Ernesto A.] Miranda was arrested and taken to the police station. At this time Miranda was 23 years old, indigent, and educated to the extent of completing half the 9th grade. He had "an emotional illness" of the schizophrenic type, according to the doctor who eventually examined him; the doctor's report also stated that Miranda was "alert and oriented as to time, place and person," intelligent within normal limits, competent to stand trial and sane within the legal definition. At the police station, the victim picked Miranda out of a line-up, and 2 officers then took him into a separate room to interrogate him, starting about 11:30 a.m. Though at first denying his guilt, within a short time Miranda gave a detailed oral confession and then wrote out in his own hand and signed a brief statement admitting and describing the crime. All this was accomplished in 2 hours or less without any force, threats or promises and—I will assume this though the record is uncertain...—without any effective warnings at all.

Miranda's oral and written confessions are now held inadmissible under the court's new rules. One is entitled to feel astonished that the Constitution can be read to produce this result. These confessions were obtained during brief, daytime questioning conducted by 2 officers and unmarked by any of the traditional indicia of coercion. They assured a conviction for a brutal and unsettling crime, for which the police had and quite possibly could obtain little evidence other than the victim's identifications, evidence which is frequently unreliable. There was, in sum, a legitimate purpose, no perceptible unfairness and certainly little risk of injustice in the interrogation. Yet the resulting confessions, and the responsible course of police practice they represent, are to be sacrificed to the court's own finespun conception of fairness which I seriously doubt is shared by many thinking citizens in this country....

The court in closing its general discussion invokes the practice in federal and foreign jurisdictions as lending weight to its new curbs on confessions for all the states. A brief resume will suffice to show that none of these jurisdictions has struck so one-sided a balance as the court does today. Heaviest reliance is placed on the FBI practice. Differing circumstances may make this comparison quite untrustworthy, but in all events the FBI falls sensibly short of the court's formalistic rules. For example, there is no indication that FBI agents must obtain an affirmative "waiver" before they pursue their questioning. Nor is it clear that one invoking his right to silence may not be prevailed upon to change his mind. And the warning as to appointed counsel apparently indicates only that one will be assigned by the judge when the suspect appears before him; the thrust of the court's rules is to induce the suspect to obtain appointed counsel before continuing the interview.... Apparently American military practice, briefly mentioned by the court, has these same limits and is still less favorable to the suspect than the FBI warning, making no mention of appointed counsel....

The law of the foreign countries described by the court also reflects a more moderate conception of the rights of the accused as against those of society when other data are considered....

In closing this necessarily truncated discussion of policy considerations attending the new confession rules, some reference must be made to their ironic untimeliness. There is now in progress in this country a massive reexamination of criminal law enforcement procedures on a scale never before witnessed. Participants in this undertaking include a special committee of the American Bar Association, under the chairmanship of Chief Judge Lumbard of the Court of Appeals for the 2d Circuit; a distinguished study group of the American Law Institute, headed by Profs. Vorenberg and Bator of the Harvard Law School; and the President's Commission on Law Enforcement & Administration of Justice, under the leadership of the Attorney General of the United States. Studies are also being conducted by the District of Columbia Crime Commission, the Georgetown Law Center, and by others equipped to do practical research. There are also signs that legislatures in some of the states may be preparing to reexamine the problem before us....

... For the reasons stated in this opinion, I would adhere to the due process test and reject the new requirements inaugurated by the court....

In conclusion: Nothing in the letter or the spirit of the Constitution or in the precedents squares with the heavy-handed and one-sided action that is so precipitously taken by the court in the name of fulfilling its constitutional responsibilities. The foray which the court takes today brings to mind the wise and farsighted words of Mr. Justice [Robert H.] Jackson in *Douglas v. Jeannette...:* "This court is forever adding new stories to the temples of constitutional law, and the temples have a way of collapsing when one story too many is added."

Justice White, whom Harlan and Stewart joined, dissenting:

That the court's holding today is neither compelled nor even strongly suggested by the language of the 5th Amendment, is at odds with American and English legal history, and involves a departure from a long line of precedent does not prove either that the court has exceeded its powers or that the court is wrong or unwise in its present reinterpretation of the 5th Amendment. It does, however, underscore the obvious—that the court has not discovered or found the law in making today's decision, nor has it derived it from some irrefutable sources; what it has done is to make new law and new public policy in much the same way that it has in the course of interpreting other great clauses of the Constitution. This is what the court historically has done. Indeed, it is what it must do and will continue to do until and unless there is some fundamental change in the constitutional distribution of governmental powers.

But if the court is here and now to announce new and fundamental policy to govern certain aspects of our affairs, it is wholly legitimate to examine the mode of this or any other constitutional decision in this court and to inquire into the advisability of its end product in terms of the long-range interest of the country. At the very least the court's text and reasoning should withstand analysis and be a fair exposition of the constitutional provision which its opinion interprets. Decisions like these cannot rest alone on syllogism, metaphysics or some ill-defined notions of natural justice, although each will perhaps play its part. In proceeding to such constructions as it now announces, the court should also duly consider all the factors and interests bearing upon the cases, at least insofar as the relevant materials are available; and if the necessary considerations are not treated in the record or obtainable from some other reliable source, the court should not proceed to formulate fundamental policies based on speculation alone....

... Rather than asserting new knowledge, the court concedes that it cannot truly know what occurs during custodial questioning, because of the innate secrecy of such proceedings. It extrapolates a picture of what it conceives to be the norm from police investigatorial manuals, published in 1959 and 1962 or earlier, without any attempt to allow for adjustments in police practices that may have occurred in the wake of more recent decisions of state appellate tribunals or this court. But even if the relentless application of the described procedures could lead to involuntary confessions, it most assuredly does not follow that each and every case will disclose this kind of interrogation or this kind of consequence.* Insofar as it appears from the court's opinion, it has not examined a single transcript of any police interrogation, let alone the interrogation that took place in any one of these cases which it decides today. Judged by any of the standards for empirical investigation utilized in the social sciences, the factual basis for the court's premise is patently inadequate....

... Even if one were to postulate that the court's concern is not that all confessions induced by police interrogation are coerced but rather that some such confessions are coerced and present judicial procedures are believed to be inadequate to identify the confessions that are coerced and those that are not, it would still not be essential to impose the rule that the court has now fashioned. Transcripts or observers could be required, specific time limits, tailored to fit the cause, could be imposed, or other devices could be utilized to reduce the chances that

---

* In fact, the type of sustained interrogation described by the court appears to be the exception rather than the rule. A survey of 399 cases in one city found that in almost half of the cases the interrogation lasted less than 30 minutes.... Questioning tends to be confused and sporadic and is usually concentrated on confrontations with witnesses or new items of evidence, as these are obtained by officers conducting the investigation.

otherwise indiscernible coercion will produce an inadmissible confession.

On the other hand, even if one assumed that there was an adequate factual basis for the conclusion that all confessions obtained during in-custody interrogation are the product of compulsion, the rule propounded by the court would still be irrational, for, apparently, it is only if the accused is also warned of his right to counsel and waives both that right and the right against self-incrimination that the inherent compulsiveness of interrogation disappears. But if the defendant may not answer without a warning a question such as "Where were you last night?" without having his answer be a compelled one, how can the court ever accept his negative answer to the question of whether he wants to consult his retained counsel or counsel whom the court will appoint? And why if counsel is present and the accused nevertheless confesses, or counsel tells the accused to tell the truth, and that is what the accused does, is the situation any less coercive insofar as the accused is concerned? The court apparently realizes its dilemma of foreclosing questioning without the necessary warnings but at the same time permitting the accused, sitting in the same chair in front of the same policemen, to waive his right to consult an attorney. It expects, however, that not too many will waive the right; and if it is claimed that he has, the state faces a severe, if not impossible, burden of proof....

...I believe that a good many criminal defendants, who otherwise would have been convicted on what this court has previously thought to be the most satisfactory kind of evidence, will now, under this new version of the 5th Amendment, either not be tried at all or acquitted if the state's evidence, minus the confession, is put to the test of litigation....

In some unknown number of cases the court's rule will return a killer, a rapist or other criminal to the streets and to the environment which produced him, to repeat his crime whenever it pleases him. As a consequence, there will not be a gain, but a loss, in human dignity. The real concern is not the unfortunate consequences of this new decision on the criminal law as an abstract, disembodied series of authoritative proscriptions, but the impact on those who rely on the public authority for protection and who without it can only engage in violent self-help with guns, knives and the help of their neighbors similarly inclined....

Nor can this decision do other than have a corrosive effect on the criminal law as an effective device to prevent crime. A major component in its effectiveness in this regard is its swift and sure enforcement. The easier it is to get away with rape and murder, the less the deterrent effect on those who are inclined to attempt it....

And what about the accused who has confessed or would confess in response to simple, noncoercive questioning and whose guilt could not otherwise be proved? Is it so clear that release is the best thing for him in every case? Has it so unquestionably been resolved that in each and every case it would be better for him not to confess and to return to his environment with no attempt whatsoever to help him? I think not....

... The rule announced today will measurably weaken the ability of the criminal law to perform in these tasks. It is a deliberate calculus to prevent interrogations, to reduce the incidence of confessions and pleas of guilty and to increase the number of trials. Criminal trials, no matter how efficient the police are, are not sure bets for the prosecution, nor should they be if the evidence is not forthcoming. Under the present law, the prosecution fails to prove its case in about 30% of the criminal cases actually tried in the federal courts.... But it is something else again to remove from the ordinary criminal case all those confessions which heretofore have been held to be free and voluntary acts of the accused and to thus establish a new constitutional barrier to the ascertainment of truth by the judicial process....

... Today's decision leaves open such questions as whether the accused was in custody, whether his statements were spontaneous or the product of interrogation, whether the accused has effectively waived his rights, and whether nontestimonial evidence introduced at trial is the fruit of statements made during a prohibited interrogation, all of which are certain to prove productive of uncertainty during investigation and litigation during prosecution. For all these reasons, if further restrictions on police interrogation are desirable at this time, a more flexible approach makes much more sense than the court's constitutional straitjacket which forecloses more discriminating treatment by legislative or rule-making pronouncements....

One week after the *Miranda* decision, the Supreme Court announced June 20, 1966, in *Johnson v. New Jersey,* that the new rules derived from *Miranda* would not be applied retroactively. These rules were held to apply only in trials that began on or after June 13, 1966, the date of the *Miranda* decision. The same principle was extended also to the more limited rules set forth June 22, 1964 in *Escobedo.*

By contrast, in *Gideon v. Wainwright* (1963) the right to counsel was applied retroactively. Under that principle, persons who had been convicted months or even years before *Gideon* were permitted to appeal their convictions and, if successful, to secure new trials. In limiting *Miranda* to trials that started on or after the date of the *Miranda* decision, the court still prohibited the use of a number of confessions obtained prior to *Miranda* from suspects whose trials did not commence until after *Miranda.* A number of these cases were publicized and contributed to widespread unpopularity of *Miranda* among the public. A different approach had been used in *Stovall v. Denno* (1967), under which the right to counsel at a line-up, established in *United States v. Wade* (1967), was limited to line-ups convened after the date of the Wade decision.

Justices Clark, Harlan, Stewart and White concurred in the *Johnson* opinion and judgment and reiterated their opposition to the court's decision in *Miranda.* Justices Black and Douglas dissented, without writing an opinion, "for substantially the same reasons" as stated in their dissenting opinion in *Linkletter v. Walker* (1965).

Abridgment of the *Johnson v. New Jersey*

decision (384 U.S. 719, June 20, 1966):

Chief Justice Warren delivering the opinion of the court:

In this case we are called upon to determine whether *Escobedo v. Illinois* ... and *Miranda v. Arizona* ... should be applied retroactively. We hold that *Escobedo* affects only those cases in which the trial began after June 22, 1964, the date of that decision. We hold further that *Miranda* applies only to cases in which the trial began after the date of our decision one week ago. The convictions assailed here were obtained at trials completed long before *Escobedo* and *Miranda* were rendered, and the rulings in those cases are therefore inapplicable to the present proceeding....

In the past year we have twice dealt with the problem of retroactivity in connection with other constitutional rules of criminal procedure. *Linkletter v. Walker* ... (1965); *Tehan v. Shott* ... (1966). These cases establish the principle that in criminal litigation concerning constitutional claims, "the court may in the interest of justice make the rule prospective ... where the exigencies of the situation require such an application."... These cases also delineate criteria by which such an issue may be resolved. We must look to the purpose of our new standards governing police interrogation, the reliance which may have been placed upon prior decisions on the subject, and the effect on the administration of justice of a retroactive application of *Escobedo* and *Miranda*....

In *Linkletter* we declined to apply retroactively the rule laid down in *Mapp v. Ohio,* ... (1961), by which evidence obtained through an unreasonable search and seizure was excluded from state criminal proceedings. In so holding, we relied in part on the fact that the rule affected evidence "the reliability and relevancy of which is not questioned." Likewise in *Tehan* we declined to give retroactive effect to *Griffin v. California* ... (1965), which forbade prosecutors and judges to comment adversely on the failure of a defendant to testify in a state criminal trial. In reaching this result, we noted that the basic purpose of the rule was to discourage courts from penalizing use of the privilege against self-incrimination....

As *Linkletter* and *Tehan* acknowledged, however, we have given retroactive effect to other constitutional rules of criminal procedure laid down in recent years, where different guarantees were involved. For example, in *Gideon v. Wainwright* ..., which concerned the right of an indigent to the advice of counsel at trial, we reviewed a denial of *habeas corpus.* Similarly, *Jackson v. Denno* ... (1964), which involved the right of an accused to effective exclusion of an involuntary confession from trial, was itself a collateral attack. In each instance we concluded that retroactive application was justified because the rule affected "the very integrity of the fact-finding process" and averted "the clear danger of convicting the innocent."...

We here stress that the choice between retroactivity and nonretroactivity in no way turns on the value of the constitutional guarantee involved. The right to be represented by counsel at trial, applied retroactively in *Gideon v. Wainwright,* ... has been described by Justice Schaefer of the Illinois Supreme Court as "by far the most pervasive ... [o]f all of the rights that an accused person has." Yet Justice [Louis] Brandeis even more boldly characterized the immunity from unjustifiable intrusions upon privacy, which was denied retroactive enforcement in *Linkletter,* as "the most comprehensive of rights and the right most valued by civilized men." To reiterate what was said in *Linkletter,* we do not disparage a constitutional guarantee in any manner by declining to apply it retroactively....

We also stress that the retroactivity or nonretroactivity of a rule is not automatically determined by the provision of the Constitution on which the dictate is based. Each constitutional rule of criminal procedure has its own distinct functions, its own background of precedent and its own impact on the administration of justice, and the way in which these factors combine must inevitably vary with the dictate involved. Accordingly, as *Linkletter* and *Tehan* suggest, we must determine retroactivity "in each case" by looking to the peculiar traits of the specific "rule in question."...

Finally, we emphasize that the question whether a constitutional rule of criminal procedure does or does not enhance the reliability of the fact-finding process at trial is necessarily a matter of degree. We gave retroactive effect to *Jackson v. Denno,* ... because confessions are likely to be highly persuasive with a jury, and if coerced they may well be untrustworthy by their very nature. On the other hand, we denied retroactive application to *Griffin v. California* ... despite the fact that comment on the failure to testify may sometimes mislead the jury concerning the reasons why the defendant has refused to take the witness stand. We are thus concerned with a question of probabilities and must take account, among other factors, of the extent to which other safeguards are available to protect the integrity of the truth-determining process at trial.

Having in mind the course of the prior cases, we turn now to the problem presented here: whether *Escobedo* and *Miranda* should be applied retroactively. Our opinion in *Miranda* makes it clear that the prime purpose of these rulings is to guarantee full effectuation of the privilege against self-incrimination, the mainstay of our adversary system of criminal justice.... They are designed in part to assure that the person who responds to interrogation while in custody does so with intelligent understanding of his right to remain silent and of the consequences which may flow from relinquishing it. In this respect the rulings secure scrupulous observance of the traditional principle, often quoted but rarely heeded to the full degree, that "the law will not suffer a prisoner to be made the deluded instrument of his own conviction." Thus, while *Escobedo* and *Miranda* guard against the possibility of unreliable statements in every instance of in-custody interrogation, they encompass situations in which the danger is not necessarily as great as when the accused is subjected to overt and obvious coercion.

At the same time, our case law on coerced confessions is available for persons whose trials have already been completed, providing, of course, that the procedural prerequisites for direct or collateral attack are met.... Prisoners may invoke a substantive test of voluntariness which, because of the persistence of abusive practices, has become increasingly meticulous through the years.... That test now takes specific account of the failure to advise the accused of his privilege against self-incrimination or to allow him access to outside assistance.... Prisoners are also entitled to present evidence anew on this aspect of the voluntariness of their confessions if a full and fair hearing has not already been afforded them.... Thus, while *Escobedo* and *Miranda* provide important new safeguards against the use of unreliable statements at trial, the nonretroactivity of these decisions will not preclude persons whose trials have already been completed from invoking the same safeguards as part of an involuntariness claim.

Nor would retroactive application have the justifiable effect of curing errors committed in disregard of constitutional rulings already clearly foreshadowed. We have pointed out above that past decisions treated the failure to warn accused persons of their rights, or the failure to grant them access to outside assistance, as factors tending to prove the involuntariness of the resulting confessions.... Prior to *Escobedo* and *Miranda,* however, we had expressly declined to condemn an entire process of in-custody interrogation solely because of such conduct by the police.... Law enforcement agencies fairly relied on these prior cases, now no longer binding, in obtaining incriminating statements during the intervening years preceding *Escobedo* and *Miranda.* This is in favorable comparison to the situation before *Mapp v. Ohio* ... (1961), where the states at least knew that they were constitutionally forbidden from engaging in unreasonable searches and seizures under *Wolf v. Colorado* ... (1949).

At the same time, retroactive application of *Escobedo* and *Miranda* would seriously disrupt the administration of our criminal laws. It would require the retrial or release of numerous prisoners found guilty by trustworthy evidence in conformity with previously announced constitutional standards....

In the light of these various considerations, we conclude that *Escobedo* and *Miranda* ... should not be applied retroactively. The question remains whether *Escobedo* and *Miranda* shall affect cases still on direct appeal when they were decided or whether their application shall commence with trials begun after the decisions were announced. Our holdings in *Linkletter* and *Tehan* were necessarily limited to convictions which had become final by the time *Mapp* and *Griffin* were rendered. Decisions prior to *Linkletter* and *Tehan* had already established without discussion that *Mapp* and *Griffin* applied to cases still on direct appeal at the time they were announced.... On the other hand, apart from the application of the holdings in *Escobedo* and *Miranda* to the parties before the court in those cases, the possibility of applying the decisions only prospectively is yet an open issue.

All of the reasons set forth above for making *Escobedo* and *Miranda* nonretroactive suggest that these decisions should apply only to trials begun after the decisions were announced. Future defendants will benefit fully from our new standards governing in-custody interrogation, while past defendants may still avail themselves of the voluntariness test. Law enforcement officers and trial courts will have fair notice that statements taken in violation of these standards may not be used against an accused....

...We do not find any persuasive reason to extend *Escobedo* and *Miranda* to cases tried before those decisions were announced, even though the cases may still be on direct appeal....

...We conclude that *Escobedo* and *Miranda* should apply only to cases commenced after those decisions were announced....

The Supreme Court ruled Mar. 25, 1969, in *Orozco v. Texas,* that the *Miranda* rule on admissions by suspects applied as soon as the suspect was arrested—even before he was taken to the police station. The case involved Reyes Arias Orozco, who had been sentenced to prison for from 2 to 10 years after being found guilty of murder.

Orozco had left the scene of the murder, had returned to his boarding house and had gone to sleep. He was awakened at 4:00 a.m. by police officers, whom he led to a hidden gun. Orozco told the officers that he owned the gun. Ballistics tests later indicated that the gun was the murder weapon. During the trial one of the policemen testified that Orozco had admitted owning the gun.

Orozco appealed his conviction on the ground that the testimony about his ownership of the gun should not have been admitted because he had not been informed of his rights under *Miranda* before admitting to owning the gun.

Orozco's conviction was reversed by the Supreme Court. The dissenting opinion argued that *Miranda* was directed only at police-station interrogations and that it had not been shown that coercive elements associated with police-station interrogations were necessarily present when a suspect was questioned at home or at the scene of the crime.

Abridgment of the *Orozco v. Texas* decision (394 U.S. 325, Mar. 25, 1969):

Justice Black delivering the opinion of the court:

The petitioner, Reyes Arias Orozco, was convicted in the Criminal District Court of Dallas County, Texas, of murder without malice and was sentenced to serve in the state prison not less than 2 nor more than 10 years. The Court of Criminal Appeals of Texas affirmed the conviction, rejecting petitioner's contention that a material part of the evidence against him was obtained in violation of the provision of the 5th Amendment ..., made applicable to the states by the 14th Amendment, that: "No person ... shall be compelled in any criminal case to be a witness against himself."

The evidence introduced at trial showed that petitioner and the deceased had quarreled outside the El Farleto Cafe in Dallas shortly before midnight on the date of the shooting.... In the heat of the quarrel ..., the deceased is said to have beaten petitioner about the face and called him "Mexican grease." A shot was fired, killing the deceased. Petitioner left the scene.... At about 4 a.m. 4 police officers arrived at petitioner's boarding house, were admitted by an unidentified woman and were told that petitioner was asleep in the bedroom. All 4 officers entered the bedroom and began to question petitioner. From the moment he gave his name, according to the testimony of one of the officers, petitioner was not free to go where he pleased but was "under arrest." The officers asked him if he had been to the El Farleto restaurant that night and when he answered "yes," he was asked if he owned a pistol. Petitioner admitted owning one. After being asked a 2d time where the pistol was located, he admitted that it was in the washing machine in a back room of the boarding house. Ballistics tests indicated that the gun found in the washing machine was the gun that fired the fatal shot. At petitioner's trial, held after the effective date of this court's decision in *Miranda v. Arizona* ..., the trial court allowed one of the officers, over the objection of petitioner's lawyer, to relate the statements made by petitioner concerning the gun and petitioner's presence at the scene of the shooting. The trial testimony clearly shows that the officers questioned petitioner about incriminating facts without first informing him of his right to remain silent, his right to have the advice of a lawyer before making any statement, and his right to have a lawyer appointed to assist him if he could not afford to hire one. The Texas Court of Criminal Appeals held, with one judge dissenting, that the admission of testimony concerning the statements petitioner had made without the above warnings was not precluded by *Miranda.* We disagree and hold that the use of these admissions obtained in the absence of the required warnings was a flat violation of the self-incrimination clause of the 5th Amendment as construed in *Miranda.*

The state has argued here that since petitioner was interrogated on his own bed, in familiar surroundings, our *Miranda* holding should not apply.... The court did say in *Miranda* that "compulsion to speak in the isolated setting of the police station may well be greater than in courts or other official investigations, where there are often impartial observers to guard against intimidation or trickery."... But the opinion iterated and reiterated the absolute necessity for officers interrogating people "in custody" to give the described warnings.... According to the officer's testimony, petitioner was under arrest and not free to leave when he was questioned in his bedroom in the early hours of the morning. The *Miranda* opinion declared that the warnings were required when the person being interrogated was "in custody at the station or otherwise deprived of his freedom of action in any significant way."... We do not, as the dissent implies, expand or extend to the slightest extent our *Miranda* decision. We do adhere to our well-considered holding in that case and therefore reverse the conviction below.

Justice Harlan issued a short concurring opinion in which he stated his opposition to *Miranda* but said that in view of that decision he was reluctantly compelled "to acquiesce in today's decision of the court, at the same time observing that the constitutional condemnation of this perfectly understandable, sensible, proper, and indeed commendable piece of police work highlights the unsoundness of *Miranda*."

Justice White, whom Stewart joined, dissenting:

This decision carries the rule of *Miranda v. Arizona* ... (1966) to a new and unwarranted extreme. I continue to believe that the original rule amounted to a "constitutional straitjacket" on law enforcement which was justified neither by the words or history of the Constitution, nor by any reasonable view of the likely benefits of the rule as against its disadvantages.... Even accepting *Miranda,* the court extends the rule here and draws the straitjacket even tighter.

The opinion of the court in *Miranda* was devoted in large part to an elaborate discussion of the subtle forms of psychological pressure which could be brought to bear when an accused person is interrogated at length in unfamiliar surroundings....

The court now extends the same rules to all instances of in-custody questioning outside the station house. Once arrest occurs, the application of *Miranda* is automatic. The rule is simple but it ignores the purpose of *Miranda* to guard against what was thought to be the corrosive influence of practices which station-house interrogation makes feasible. The court wholly ignores the question whether similar hazards exist or even are possible when police arrest and interrogate on the spot.... No predicate is laid for believing that practices outside the station house are normally prolonged, carried out in isolation or often productive of the physical or psychological coercion made so much of in *Miranda.* It is difficult to imagine the police duplicating in a person's home or on the street those conditions and practices which the court found prevalent in the station house and which were thought so threatening to the right to silence. Without such a demonstration, *Miranda* hardly reaches this case or any cases similar to it.

Here there was no prolonged interrogation, no unfamiliar surroundings, no opportunity for the police to invoke those procedures which moved the majority in *Miranda*. In fact, the conversation was by all accounts a very brief one. According to uncontradicted testimony, petitioner was awake when the officers entered his room, and they asked him 4 questions: his name, whether he had been at the El Farleto, whether he owned a pistol and where it was. He gave his name, said he had been at the El Farleto and admitted he owned a pistol without hesitation. He was slow in telling where the pistol was, and the question was repeated. He then took the police to the nearby washing machine where the gun was hidden.

It is unquestioned that this sequence of events in their totality would not constitute coercion in the traditional sense or lead any court to view the admissions as involuntary within the meaning of the rules by which we even now adjudicate claims of coercion relating to pre-*Miranda* trials.... The police had petitioner's name and description, had ample evidence that he had been at the night club and suspected that he had a gun. Surely, had he refused to give his name or answer any other questions, they would have arrested him anyway, searched the house and found the gun, which would have been clearly admissible under all relevant authorities. But the court insists that this case be reversed for failure to give *Miranda* warnings.

I cannot accept the dilution of the custody requirements of *Miranda* to this level, where the hazards to the right to silence are so equivocal and unsupported by experience in a recurring number of cases. Orozco was apprehended in the most familiar quarters, the questioning was brief, and no admissions were made which were not backed up by other evidence. This case does not involve the confession of an innocent man, or even of a guilty man from whom a confession has been wrung by physical abuse or the modern psychological methods discussed in *Miranda*. These are simply the terse remarks of a man who has been caught, almost in the act. Even if there were reason to encourage suspects to consult lawyers to tell them to be silent before quizzing at the station house, there is no reason why police in the field should have to preface every casual question of a suspect with the full panoply of *Miranda* warnings. The same danger of coercion is simply not present in such circumstances, and the answers to the questions may as often clear a suspect as help convict him. If the *Miranda* warnings have their intended effect, and the police are able to get no answers from suspects, innocent or guilty, without arresting them, then a great many more innocent men will be making unnecessary trips to the station house. Ultimately it may be necessary to arrest a man, bring him to the police station and provide a lawyer just to discover his name. Even if the man is innocent the process will be an unpleasant one.

Since the court's extension of *Miranda*'s rule takes it into territory where even what rationale there originally was disappears, I dissent.

Congress & Court Limit Miranda

In Title III of the 1968 Omnibus Crime Control & Safe Streets Act, Congress sought to repeal *Miranda* in federal prosecutions by holding that confessions would be admissible in evidence if rendered voluntarily.

Under the 1968 statute: "Before such confession is received in evidence, the trial judge shall, out of presence of the jury, determine any issue as to voluntariness. If the trial judge determines that the confession was voluntarily made, it shall be admitted in evidence and the trial judge shall permit the jury to hear relevant evidence on the issue of voluntariness and shall instruct the jury to give such weight to the confession as the jury feels it deserves under all the circumstances."

The Supreme Court itself limited the application of *Miranda* when, in a 5-4 decision in the case of *Harris v. New York,* it ruled Feb. 23, 1971 that statements made to police officers by a suspect not informed of his *Miranda* rights can be used in court to impugn his courtroom testimony. Chief Justice Burger wrote the majority opinion, which acknowledged that Harris' confession could not be used in court as evidence of his guilt. But it stated that Harris' confessional statements, nevertheless, could be used to judge the truthfulness of his testimony at his trial.

During his trial Harris had testified that he had not sold narcotics to an undercover police officer as charged. Yet, when arrested, Harris had admitted to having made 2 such sales. The decision of the trial judge to admit evidence concerning Harris' pretrial admission of guilt for the purpose of enabling the jury to judge the truthfulness of his courtroom testimony was upheld by the court on the ground that "the shield provided by *Miranda* cannot be perverted into a license to use perjury by way of a defense, free from the risk of confrontation with prior inconsistent utterances."

Justice Brennan, dissenting, called it "monstrous that courts should aid or abet the law-breaking police officer." According to Brennan, "the court today tells the police that they may freely interrogate an accused incommunicado and without counsel and know that although any statement they obtain in violation of *Miranda* can't be used on the state's direct case, it may be introduced if the defendant has the temerity to testify in his own defense. This goes far toward undoing much of the progress made in conforming police methods to the Constitution."

Abridgment of the *Harris v. New York* decision (401 U.S. 222, Feb. 23, 1971):

Chief Justice Burger delivering the opinion of the court:

We granted the writ in this case to consider petitioner's claim that a statement made by him to police under circumstances rendering it inadmissible to establish the prosecution's case in chief under *Miranda v. Arizona* ... may not be used to impeach his credibility.

The State of New York charged petitioner in a 2-count indictment with twice selling heroin to an undercover police officer. At a subsequent jury trial the officer was the state's chief witness, and he testified as to details of the 2 sales. A 2d officer verified collateral details of the sales, and a 3d offered testimony about the chemical analysis of the heroin.

Petitioner took the stand in his own defense. He admitted knowing the undercover police officer but denied a sale on Jan. 4. He admitted making a sale of contents of a glassine bag to the officer on Jan. 6 but claimed it was baking powder and part of a scheme to defraud the purchaser.

On cross-examination petitioner was asked *seriatim* whether he had made specified statements to the police immediately following his arrest on Jan. 7—statements that partially contradicted petitioner's direct testimony at trial. In response to the cross-examination, petitioner testified that he could not remember virtually any of the questions or answers recited by the prosecutor. At request of petitioner's counsel the written statement from which the prosecutor had read questions and answers in his impeaching process was placed in the record for possible use on appeal; the statement was not shown to the jury.

The trial judge instructed the jury that the statements attributed to petitioner by the prosecution could be considered only in passing on petitioner's credibility and not as evidence of guilt. In closing summations, both counsel argued the substance of the impeaching statements. The jury then found petitioner guilty of the 2d count of the indictment. [No agreement was reached on the first count. That count was later dropped by the state.]...

At trial, the prosecution made no effort in its case in chief to use the statements allegedly made by petitioner, conceding that they were inadmissible under *Miranda*.... The transcript of the interrogation used in the impeachment, but not given to the jury, shows that no warning of a right to appointed counsel was given before questions were put to petitioner when he was taken into custody. Petitioner makes no claim that the statements made to the police were coerced or involuntary.

Some comments in the *Miranda* opinion can indeed be read as indicating a bar to use of an uncounseled statement for any purpose, but discussion of that issue was not at all necessary to the court's holding and cannot be regarded as controlling. *Miranda* barred the prosecution from making its case with statements of an accused made while in custody prior to having or effectively waiving counsel. It does not follow from *Miranda* that evidence inadmissible against an accused in the prosecution's case in chief is barred for all purposes, provided of course that the trustworthiness of the evidence satisfies legal standards....

... The conflict between petitioner's testimony in his own behalf concerning the events of Jan. 7 contrasted sharply with what he told the police shortly after his arrest. The impeachment process here undoubtedly provided valuable aid to the jury in assessing petitioner's credibility, and the benefits of this process should not be lost, in our view, because of the speculative possibility that impermissible police conduct will be encouraged thereby. Assuming that the exclusionary rule has a deterrent effect on proscribed police conduct, sufficient deterrence flows when the evidence in question is made unavailable to the prosecution in its case in chief.

Every criminal defendant is privileged to testify in his own defense, or to refuse to do so. But that privilege cannot be construed to include the right to commit perjury.... Having voluntarily taken the stand, petitioner was under an obligation to speak truthfully and accurately, and the prosecution here did no more than utilize the traditional truth-testing devices of the adversary process. Had inconsistent statements been made by the accused to some 3d person, it could hardly be contended that the conflict could not be laid before the jury by way of cross-examination and impeachment.

The shield provided by *Miranda* cannot be perverted into a license to use perjury by way of a defense, free from the risk of confrontation with prior inconsistent utterances. We hold, therefore, that petitioner's credibility was appropriately impeached by use of his earlier conflicting statements.

Justice Brennan, whom Douglas and Marshall joined, dissenting:

It is conceded that the question-and-answer statement used

to impeach petitioner's direct testimony was, under *Miranda v. Arizona*, ... constitutionally inadmissible as part of the state's direct case against petitioner. I think that the Constitution also denied the state the use of the statement on cross-examination to impeach the credibility of petitioner's testimony given in his own defense. ...

The state's case against Harris depended upon the jury's belief of the testimony of the undercover agent that petitioner "sold" the officer heroin on Jan. 4 and again on Jan. 6. Petitioner took the stand and flatly denied having sold anything to the officer on Jan. 4. He countered the officer's testimony as to the Jan. 6 sale with testimony that he had sold the officer 2 glassine bags containing what appeared to be heroin, but that actually the bags contained only baking powder intended to deceive the officer in order to obtain $12. The statement contradicted petitioner's direct testimony as to the events of both days. The statement's version of the events on Jan. 4 was that the officer had used petitioner as a middleman to buy some heroin from a 3d person with money furnished by the officer. The version of the events on Jan. 6 was that petitioner had again acted for the officer in buying 2 bags of heroin from a 3d person for which petitioner received $12 and a part of the heroin. Thus, it is clear that the statement was used to impeach petitioner's direct testimony not on collateral matters but on matters directly related to the crimes for which he was on trial. ...

The objective of deterring improper police conduct is only part of the larger objective of safeguarding the integrity of our adversary system. The "essential mainstay" of that system, *Miranda v. Arizona*, ... is the privilege against self-incrimination, which for that reason has occupied a central place in our jurisprudence since before the nation's birth. Moreover, "we may view the historical development of the privilege as one which groped for the proper scope of governmental power over the citizen. ... All these policies point to one overriding thought: the constitutional foundation underlying the privilege is the respect a government ... must accord to the dignity and integrity of its citizens." *Ibid.* These values are plainly jeopardized if an exception against admission of tainted statements is made for those used for impeachment purposes. Moreover, it is monstrous that courts should aid or abet the law-breaking police officer. It is abiding truth that "[n]othing can destroy a government more quickly than its failure to observe its own laws, or worse, its disregard of the charter of its own existence." *Mapp v. Ohio*.... Thus, even to the extent that *Miranda* was aimed at deterring police practices in disregard of the Constitution, I fear that today's holding will seriously undermine the achievement of that objective....

4TH AMENDMENT: SEARCH & SEIZURE

A number of recent, far-reaching Supreme Court decisions have involved the Constitution's 4th Amendment, which reads: "The right of people to be secure in their persons, houses, papers, and effects, against unreasonable searches and seizures, shall not be violated, and no Warrants shall issue, but upon probable cause, supported by Oath or affirmation, and particularly describing the place to be searched, and the persons or things to be seized."

Some authorities consider the 4th Amendment the most important provision of the Bill of Rights. According to Prof. Monrad Paulsen, "the other freedoms, freedom of speech, of assembly, of religion, of political action, presuppose that arbitrary and capricious police action has been restrained. Security in one's home and person is the fundamental right without which there can be no liberty."

The 4th Amendment seeks to guard against "unreasonable searches and seizures" by requiring government agents to obtain search warrants. In general, in order to obtain a warrant the police must present to a magistrate sufficient evidence to demonstrate "probable cause" that a crime was or is about to be committed.* A warrant under the 4th Amendment, moreover, must be specific "in

---

* The Supreme Court permits the search of an auto if there is probable cause to believe that it contains contraband or that it is being used to violate the law. Another exception to the general rule requiring search warrants permits the police to search a person placed under arrest.

127

particularly describing the place to be searched and the persons or things to be seized." A warrant that does not meet this requirement is referred to as a general warrant. It is considered a license for the authorities to engage in a "fishing expedition" or to spy on people. The 4th Amendment's ban on general warrants relates directly to the use of such warrants by the British prior to the American Revolution.

The text of the 4th Amendment leaves these questions unanswered: Can evidence obtained without a valid search warrant be used in court? Does the 4th Amendment bar the police from searching persons on the street or frisking them for weapons? Does the 4th Amendment extend to wiretapping and the use of electronic eavesdropping devices? Can a valid search warrant be obtained on the basis of information supplied by an anonymous informer? Can the authorities, without a search warrant, search the immediate area in which they have arrested a person?

Use of Illegally Seized Evidence

The Supreme Court in *Weeks v. United States* held in 1914 that evidence produced by illegal searches could not be used in federal trials. Since the Bill of Rights was not applied to the states at that time, the question of whether such evidence could be introduced in state trials did not arise.

In *Wolf v. Colorado,* the Supreme Court held June 27, 1949 that the 4th Amendment was binding on the states. The case involved Dr. Julius A. Wolf of Denver, who had been convicted of conspiring to commit abortions. State officials had arrested Wolf and had taken possession of his appointment books. The latter gave the name and address of a woman whose transactions with Wolf had previously been unknown to the authorities. Wolf objected to the introduction of the appointment books as evidence at his trial. In requiring the states to adhere to the 4th Amendment, the court, however, refused to prohibit the use of unconstitutionally seized evidence in state trails. Justice Felix Frankfurter noted in the majority opinion that such evidence could be used in most English-speaking countries and that in the U.S. only 17 states followed the *Weeks* principle of barring the use in court of illegally obtained evidence. According to Frankfurter:

> We cannot, therefore, regard it as a departure from basic standards to remand such persons, together with those who emerge scatheless from a search, to the remedies of private action and such protection as the internal discipline of the police, under the eyes of an alert public opinion, may afford. Granting that in practice the exclusion of evidence may be an effective way of deterring unreasonable searches, it is not for this court to condemn as falling below the minimum standards assured by the due process clause a state's reliance upon other methods which, if consistently enforced, would be equally effective.... There are, moreover, reasons for excluding evidence unreasonably obtained by the federal police which are less compelling in the case of police under state or local authority. The public opinion of a community can far more effectively be exerted against oppressive conduct on the part of the police directly responsible to the community itself than can local opinion, sporadically aroused, be brought to bear upon remote authority pervasively exerted throughout the country.

3 years after *Wolf* the Supreme Court Jan. 17, 1952, in *Rochin v. California,* overruled a state conviction secured on the basis of evidence that, it held, was obtained in a particularly outrageous manner. Under the so-called "shock the conscience"

test, the use of such evidence in state trials was deemed a violation of the due process clause of the 14th Amendment.

Rochin was a case in which 3 Los Angeles deputy sheriffs, "having some evidence" that Antonio R. Rochin was selling narcotics, entered his home and found him sitting partly dressed on a bed on which his wife was lying. The officers saw 2 capsules on a night stand, and Rochin quickly seized and swallowed the capsules. A struggle ensued and the 3 officers "jumped" on Rochin in an unsuccessful effort to extract the capsules. Rochin was then handcuffed and taken to a hospital. A doctor forced a solution through a tube into Rochin's stomach, and he vomited up the 2 capsules, which were found to contain morphine. The capsules were introduced in evidence against Rochin at his trial, and he was found guilty of possessing morphine in violation of California law.

In ruling that the capsules should not have been used as evidence against Rochin, Justice Frankfurter declared: "This is conduct that shocks the conscience ..., methods too close to the rack and screw...."

In *Breithaupt v. Abram,* the Supreme Court refused in 1957 to exclude evidence obtained when the police ordered a blood sample taken from an unconscious person who had been involved in a fatal auto accident. The blood sample indicated that the suspect was intoxicated. The court upheld the procedure in noting what it said was the lack of Rochin-type "coercion" or "brutality." (The use of blood tests to secure evidence was again upheld by the court in 1965 in *Schmerber v. California.)*

In *Irvine v. California,* the court refused Feb. 8, 1954 to extend the "shock the conscience" test to situations, however "shocking," that did not involve coercion or brutality. In *Irvine,* the police made several illegal entries to place a hidden microphone in gambler Patrick E. Irvine's bedroom. The microphone was used to monitor bedroom conversations for more than a month, and Irvine was convicted under a local ban on gambling. The Supreme Court, 5-4, upheld the conviction. Justice Frankfurter, dissenting, said the evidence should have been excluded under the terms of *Rochin.* Justice William O. Douglas, in a separate dissent, asserted that the responsibility for such police misconduct lay with the court's refusal to apply the *Wolf* exclusionary rule to the states.

In *Elkins v. United States,* the Supreme Court in 1960 overruled the so-called "silver platter" doctrine under which evidence illegally obtained by federal authorities, and consequently inadmissible in federal trials, could be turned over to state authorities for use in state trials. Justice Potter Stewart, in the majority opinion, said in justifying the exclusionary rule that "its purpose is to deter—to compel respect for the constitutional guaranty in the only effectively available way—by removing the incentive to disregard it." "[T]here is another consideration— the imperative of judicial integrity," he continued, in asserting that the use of illegally seized evidence in court undermines the integrity of the judicial process.

The exclusionary rule, barring the use of evidence obtained in violation of the 4th Amendment, was extended to the states June 19, 1961 in *Mapp v. Ohio.* The 5-4 decision reversed the court's *Wolf v. Colorado* position. Justice Thomas C. Clark, in the majority opinion, said: "There is no war between the Constitution and common sense. Presently, a federal prosecutor may make no use of evidence illegally seized, but a state's attorney across the street may, although he supposedly is operating under the enforcement prohibitions of the same amendment. Thus the state, by admitting evidence unlawfully seized, serves to encourage disobedience to the federal Constitution which it is bound to uphold."

In conceding the truth of Justice Benjamin Cardozo's remark that under the exclusionary rule the "criminal is to go free because the constable has blundered," Clark asserted that the integrity of the judicial process demanded such a course. "Nothing can destroy a government more quickly than its failure to observe its own laws, or worse, its disregard of the charter of its own existence," he said. Clark predicted, moreover, that the exclusionary rule would not unduly hamper state and local officials. Only the previous year, in *Elkins,* he wrote, "this court expressly considered that contention and found that 'pragmatic evidence of a sort' to the contrary was not wanting" since the federal courts had been operating under the exclusionary rule for nearly 50 years and half the states already had some type of an exclusionary rule of their own.

Justice John Marshall Harlan, dissenting, stressed what he considered the proper role of the court. Harlan, considered a firm believer in judicial restraint, said he preferred to leave it to the states to determine whether to exclude illegally seized evidence from use in court. "In my view this court should continue to forbear from fettering the states with an adamant rule which may embarrass them in coping with their own peculiar problems in criminal law enforcement," he said.

In the *Mapp* case, Dollree Mapp was convicted of keeping obscene material in a trunk in the attic of her boarding house despite her contention that she was merely storing the trunk for a former boarder. In appealing her conviction, Miss Mapp's attorneys argued that the Ohio obscenity law, under which she was convicted, violated the First Amendment.

Although the Supreme Court nearly always decides a case on the basis of the question put before it, in this instance the majority chose to decide on the basis of the 4th Amendment. By then, many observers held, it was apparent that wholesale violations of the 4th Amendment were occurring throughout the country. (A few months before *Mapp,* for example, the court reviewed a case in which 13 Chicago policemen broke into an apartment occupied by Mr. and Mrs. James Monroe and their 6 children. The couple, routed out of bed, was made to stand naked in the living room while the officers ransacked every room in the apartment, emptied drawers and ripped open mattress covers. Monroe was then taken to the police station, detained for 10 hours, questioned about a murder and released.) Before *Mapp,* the police in many cities had seldom bothered to obtain search warrants. In New York, for example, search warrants had rarely been obtained, but in 1963, the year after *Mapp,* 5,132 warrants were issued in that city.

Abridgment of the *Mapp v. Ohio* decision (367 U.S. 643, June 19, 1961):

Justice Clark delivering the opinion of the court:
On May 23, 1957, 3 Cleveland police officers arrived at

appellant's residence ... pursuant to information that "a person
[was] hiding out in the home, who was wanted for questioning
in connection with a recent bombing, and that there was a large
amount of policy paraphernalia being hidden in the home."
Miss Mapp and her daughter ... lived on the top floor of the 2-
family dwelling. Upon their arrival at that house, the officers
knocked on the door and demanded entrance but appellant,
after telephoning her attorney, refused to admit them without a
search warrant. ...

The officers again sought entrance some 3 hours later
when 4 or more additional officers arrived. ... When Miss
Mapp did not come to the door immediately, at least one of the
several doors to the house was forcibly opened and the
policemen gained admittance. Meanwhile Miss Mapp's attorney
arrived, but the officers, having secured their own entry, and
continuing in their defiance of the law, would permit him
neither to see Miss Mapp nor to enter the house. It appears that
Miss Mapp was halfway down the stairs from the upper floor to
the front door when the officers, in this high-handed manner,
broke into the hall. She demanded to see the search warrant. A
paper, claimed to be a warrant, was held up by one of the
officers. She grabbed the "warrant" and placed it in her bosom.
A struggle ensued in which the officers recovered the piece of
paper and as a result of which they handcuffed appellant
because she had been "belligerent" in resisting their official
rescue of the "warrant" from her person. Running roughshod
over appellant, a policeman "grabbed" her, "twisted [her]
hand," and she "yelled [and] pleaded with him" because "it was
hurting." Appellant, in handcuffs, was then forcibly taken upstairs to her bedroom where the officers searched a dresser, a
chest of drawers, a closet and some suitcases. They also looked
into a photo album and through personal papers belonging to
the appellant. The search spread to the rest of the 2d floor,
including the child's bedroom. ... The basement of the building
and a trunk found therein were also searched. The obscene
materials for possession of which she was ultimately convicted
were discovered in the course of that widespread search.

At the trial no search warrant was produced by the
prosecution, nor was the failure to produce one explained or
accounted for. ...

The state says that even if the search were made without authority, or otherwise unreasonably, it is not prevented from using the unconstitutionally seized evidence at trial, citing *Wolf v. Colorado* ... (1949), in which this court did indeed hold "that in a prosecution in a state court for a state crime the 14th Amendment does not forbid the admission of evidence obtained by an unreasonable search and seizure." ...

... [T]his court, in *Weeks v. U.S.* ... [1914], stated that "the 4th Amendment ... put the courts of the United States and federal officials, in the exercise of their power and authority, under limitations and restraints [and] ... forever secure[d] the people, their persons, houses, papers and effects against all unreasonable searches and seizures under the guise of law ... and the duty of giving to it force and effect is obligatory upon all entrusted under our federal system with the enforcement of the laws." ... Specifically dealing with the use of the evidence unconstitutionally seized, the court concluded: "If letters and private documents can thus be seized and held and used in evidence against a citizen accused of an offense, the protection of the 4th Amendment declaring his right to be secure against such searches and seizures is of no value, and, so far as those thus placed are concerned, might as well be stricken from the Constitution. The efforts of the courts and their officials to bring the guilty to punishment, praiseworthy as they are, are not to be aided by the sacrifice of those great principles established by years of endeavor and suffering which have resulted in their embodiment in the fundamental law of the land." ...

Finally, the court in that case clearly stated that use of the seized evidence involved "a denial of the constitutional rights of the accused." Thus, in the year 1914, in the *Weeks* case, this court "for the first time" held that "in a federal prosecution the 4th Amendment barred the use of evidence secured through an illegal search and seizure." ... This court has ever since required of federal law officers a strict adherence to that command which this court has held to be a clear, specific, and constitutionally required—even if judicially implied—deterrent safeguard without insistence upon which the 4th Amendment would have been reduced to "a form of words." Holmes, J., *Silverthorne Lumber Co. v. United States* [1920]. ... It meant, quite simply, that "conviction by means of unlawful seizures and enforced confessions ... should find no sanction in the judgments of the courts...," *Weeks,* ... and that such evidence "shall not be used at all." *Silverthorne Lumber Co....*

In 1949, 35 years after *Weeks* was announced, this court, in *Wolf v. Colorado* (1949)..., for the first time, discussed the effect of the 4th Amendment upon the states through the operation of the due process clause of the 14th Amendment. It said: "[W]e have no hesitation in saying that were a state affirmatively to sanction such police incursion into privacy it would run counter to the guaranty of the 14th Amendment."... Nevertheless, after declaring that the "security of one's privacy against arbitrary intrusion by the police" is "implicit in 'the concept of ordered liberty' and as such enforceable against the states through the due process clause," *cf. Palko v. Connecticut* [1937],... and announcing that it "stoutly adhere[d]" to the *Weeks* decision, the court decided that the *Weeks* exclusionary rule would not then be imposed upon the states as "an essential ingredient of the right."... The court's reasons for not considering essential to the right to privacy, as a curb imposed upon the states by the due process clause, that which decades before had been posited as part and parcel of the 4th Amendment's limitation upon federal encroachment of individual privacy, were bottomed on factual considerations....

The court in *Wolf* first stated that "[t]he contrariety of views of the states" on the adoption of the exclusionary rule of *Weeks* was "particularly impressive"...; and, in this connection, that it could not "brush aside the experience of states which deem the incidence of such conduct by the police too slight to call for a deterrent remedy...by overriding the [states'] relevant rules of evidence."... While in 1949, prior to the *Wolf* case, almost ⅔ of the states were opposed to the use of the exclusionary rule, now, despite the *Wolf* case, more than half of those since passing upon it, by their own legislative or judicial decision, have wholly or partly adopted or adhered to the *Weeks* rule.... Significantly, among those now following the rule is California, which, according to its highest court, was "compelled to reach that conclusion because other remedies have completely failed to secure compliance with the constitutional provisions...."...

...Today we once again examine *Wolf's* constitutional documentation of the right to privacy free from unreasonable state intrusion, and, after its dozen years on our books, are led by it to close the only courtroom door remaining open to evidence secured by official lawlessness in flagrant abuse of that basic right, reserved to all persons as a specific guarantee against that very same unlawful conduct. We hold that all evidence obtained by searches and seizures in violation of the Constitution is, by that same authority, inadmissible in a state court....

... (O)ur holding that the exclusionary rule is an essential part of both the 4th and 14th Amendments is not only the logical dictate of prior cases, but it also makes very good sense. There is no war between the Constitution and common sense. Presently, a federal prosecutor may make no use of evidence illegally seized, but a state's attorney across the street may, although he supposedly is operating under the enforceable prohibitions of the same Amendment. Thus the state, by admitting evidence unlawfully seized, serves to encourage disobedience to the federal Constitution which it is bound to uphold....

... In nonexclusionary states, federal officers, being human, were by it invited to and did, as our cases indicate, step across the street to the state's attorney with their unconstitutionally seized evidence. Prosecution on the basis of that evidence was then had in a state court in utter disregard of the enforceable 4th Amendment....

There are those who say, as did Justice (then Judge) Cardozo, that under our constitutional exclusionary doctrine "[t]he criminal is to go free because the constable has blundered."... In some cases this will undoubtedly be the result. But, as was said in *Elkins* [*v. U.S.,* 1960], "there is another consideration—the imperative of judicial integrity."... The criminal goes free, if he must, but it is the law that sets him free. Nothing can destroy a government more quickly than its failure to observe its own laws, or worse, its disregard of the charter of its own existence. As Mr. Justice [Louis] Brandeis, dissenting, said in *Olmstead v. United States* ... (1928): "Our government is the potent, the omnipresent teacher. For good or for ill, it teaches the whole people by its example.... If the government becomes a lawbreaker, it breeds contempt for law; it invites every man to become a law unto himself; it invites anarchy." Nor can it lightly be assumed that, as a practical matter, adoption of the exclusionary rule fetters law enforcement. Only last year this court expressly considered that contention and found that "pragmatic evidence of a sort" to the contrary was not wanting. *Elkins v. United States....* The court noted that "the federal courts themselves have operated under the exclusionary rule of *Weeks* for almost half a century; yet it has not been suggested either that the Federal Bureau of Investigation has thereby been rendered ineffective, or that the administration of criminal justice in the federal courts has thereby been disrupted. Moreover, the experience of the states is impressive.... The movement towards the rule of exclusion has been halting but seemingly inexorable."

The ignoble shortcut to conviction left open to the state tends to destroy the entire system of constitutional restraints on which the liberties of the people rest. Having once recognized that the right to privacy embodied in the 4th Amendment is enforceable against the states, and that the right to be secure against rude invasions of privacy by state officers is, therefore, constitutional in origin, we can no longer permit that right to remain an empty promise. Because it is enforceable in the same manner and to like effect as other basic rights secured by the due process clause, we can no longer permit it to be revocable at the whim of any police officer who, in the name of law enforcement itself, chooses to suspend its enjoyment. Our decision, founded on reason and truth, gives to the individual no more than that which the Constitution guarantees him, to the police officer no less than that to which honest law enforcement is entitled, and, to the courts, that judicial integrity so necessary in the true administration of justice....

Justices Hugo L. Black and William O. Douglas issued separate concurring opinions. Justice Potter Stewart expressed no view on the constitutional issues but said he would overturn the conviction as in violation of free expression guaranteed by the First Amendment.

Justice John Marshall Harlan, whom Felix Frankfurter and Charles E. Whittaker joined, dissenting:

... From the court's statement of the case one would gather that the central, if not controlling, issue on this appeal is whether illegally state-seized evidence is constitutionally admissible in a state prosecution, an issue which would of course face us with the need for re-examining *Wolf*. However, such is not the situation. For, although that question was indeed raised here and below among appellant's subordinate points, the new and pivotal issue brought to the court by this appeal is whether ... the Ohio Revised Code making criminal the *mere* knowing possession or control of obscene material, and under which appellant has been convicted, is consistent with the rights of free thought and expression assured against state action by the 14th Amendment. That was the principal issue which was decided by the Ohio Supreme Court, which was tendered by appellant's jurisdictional statement and which was briefed and argued in this court.

In this posture of things, I think it fair to say that 5 members of this court have simply "reached out" to overrule *Wolf*. With all respect for the views of the majority, and recognizing that *stare decisis* carries different weight in constitutional adjudication than it does in nonconstitutional decision, I can perceive no justification for regarding this case as an appropriate occasion for re-examining *Wolf*....

I would not impose upon the states this federal exclusionary remedy. The reasons given by the majority for now suddenly turning its back on *Wolf* seem to me notably unconvincing.

First, it is said that "the factual grounds upon which *Wolf* was based" have since changed, in that more states now follow the *Weeks* exclusionary rule than was so at the time *Wolf* was decided. While that is true, a recent survey indicates that at present ½ of the states still adhere to the common-law non-exclusionary rule, and one, Maryland, retains the rule as to felonies.... But in any case surely all this is beside the point, as the majority itself indeed seems to recognize. Our concern here, as it was in *Wolf*, is not with the desirability of that rule but only with the question whether the states are constitutionally free to follow it or not as they may themselves determine, and the relevance of the disparity of views among the states on this point lies simply in the fact that the judgment involved is a debatable one. Moreover, the very fact on which the majority relies, instead of lending support to what is now being done, points away from the need of replacing voluntary state action with federal compulsion.

The preservation of a proper balance between state and federal responsibility in the administration of criminal justice demands patience on the part of those who might like to see things move faster among the states in this respect. Problems of criminal law enforcement vary widely from state to state. One state, in considering the totality of its legal picture, may conclude that the need for embracing the *Weeks* rule is pressing because other remedies are unavailable or inadequate to secure compliance with the substantive constitutional principle involved. Another, though equally solicitous of constitutional rights, may choose to pursue one purpose at a time, allowing all evidence relevant to guilt to be brought into a criminal trial, and dealing with constitutional infractions by other means. Still another may consider the exclusionary rule too rough-and-ready a remedy, in that it reaches only unconstitutional intrusions which eventuate in criminal prosecution of the victims. Further, a state, after experimenting with the *Weeks* rule for a time, may, because of unsatisfactory experience with it, decide to revert to a non-exclusionary rule. And so on.... In my view this court should continue to forbear from fettering the states with an adamant rule which may embarrass them in coping with their own peculiar problems in criminal law enforcement....

...In the last analysis I think this court can increase respect for the Constitution only if it rigidly respects the limitations which the Constitution places upon it and respects as well the principles inherent in its own processes. In the present case I think we exceed both, and that our voice becomes only a voice of power, not of reason.

In a 7-2 ruling June 7, 1965, the Supreme Court held in *Linkletter v. Walker* that the *Mapp* rule did not apply to convictions obtained prior to June 19, 1961, the date of the *Mapp* decision. The decision's effect was to deny new trials to many state prisoners who had been convicted on the basis of unconstitutionally seized evidence. Justice Clark held in the majority opinion that the Constitution neither prohibited nor required that judicial decisions be applied retroactively. Therefore, Clark said, "we must then weigh the merits and demerits in each case by looking to the prior history of the rule in question, its purpose and effect, and whether retrospective application will further retard its operation." In reviewing the background of the exclusionary rule set forth in *Mapp,* Clark concluded that its purpose "was to deter the lawless action of the police and to effectively enforce the 4th Amendment." That purpose, he concluded, "will not at this late date be served by the wholesale release of the guilty victims."

Justice Black, dissenting, pointed out that this was the first time the Supreme Court "ever refused to give a previously convicted defendant the benefit of a new and more expansive Bill of Rights interpretation." According to Black, the court, in extending the exclusionary rule to the states in *Mapp,* was not, as the majority claimed, seeking to police the police but was "construing the Constitution." The fact that the retroactive application of *Mapp* would mean new trials and the release of many guilty persons was not relevant, he said. "It has not been the usual thing to cut down trial protections guaranteed by the Constitution on the basis that some guilty person might escape," he wrote. "There is probably no one of the Bill of Rights that does not make it more difficult to convict defendants." Black also noted the anomaly wherein the benefits of the exclusionary rule that had been extended to Miss Mapp were denied to Linkletter, even though his arrest preceded that of Miss Mapp's by more than a year. Linkletter's appeal in state court, however, was denied prior to *Mapp* and he was thus denied the benefits of the exclusionary rule.

Abridgment of the *Linkletter v. Walker* decision (381 U.S. 618, June 7, 1965):

Justice Clark delivering the opinion of the court:

In *Mapp v. Ohio* ... we held that the exclusion of evidence seized in violation of the search and seizure provisions of the 4th Amendment was required of the states by the due process clause of the 14th Amendment. In so doing we overruled *Wolf v. Colorado* ... to the extent that it failed to apply the exclusionary rule to the states. This case presents the question of whether this requirement operates retrospectively upon cases finally decided in the period prior to *Mapp*. ...

The petitioner was convicted in a Louisiana district court on May 28, 1959 of "simple burglary." ... He was taken to the police station, searched, and keys were taken from his person. After he was booked and placed in jail, other officers took his keys, entered and searched his home and siezed certain property and papers. Later his place of business was entered and searched, and seizures were effected. These intrusions were made without a warrant. ...

On June 19, 1961, *Mapp* was announced. Immediately thereafter petitioner filed an application for *habeas corpus* in the state court on the basis of *Mapp.* The writ being denied in the Louisiana courts, he then filed a like application in the United States District Court. After denial there he appealed and the Court of Appeals affirmed. It found the searches too remote from the arrest and therefore illegal but held that the constitutional requirement of exclusion of the evidence under *Mapp* was not retrospective. Petitioner has 2 points: (1) that the Court of Appeals erred in holding that *Mapp* was not retrospective; and (2) that even though *Mapp* be held not to operate retrospectively, the search in his case was subsequent to that in *Mapp,* and while his final conviction was long prior to our disposition in it, his case should nevertheless be governed by *Mapp.*

... [I]n this case, we are concerned only with whether the exclusionary principle enunciated in *Mapp* applies to state court convictions which had become final before rendition of our opinion. ...

At common law there was no authority for the proposition that judicial decisions made law only for the future. Blackstone stated the rule that the duty of the court was not to "pronounce a new law, but to maintain and expound the old one." ... This court followed that rule in *Norton v. Shelby County*... (1886), holding that unconstitutional action "confers no rights; it imposes no duties; it affords no protection; it creates no office; it is, in legal contemplation, as inoperative as though it had never been passed." ... The judge rather than being the creator of the law was but its discoverer.... In the case of the overruled decision, *Wolf v. Colorado...,* it was thought to be only a failure at true discovery and was consequently never the law; while the overruling one, *Mapp,* was not "new law but the application of what is, and, therefore had been, the true law."...

On the other hand, Austin maintained that judges do in fact do something more than discover law; they make it interstitially by filling in with judicial interpretation the vague, indefinite, or generic statutory or common-law terms that alone are but the empty crevices of the law. Implicit in such an approach is the admission when a case is overruled that the earlier decision was wrongly decided. However, rather than being erased by the later overruling decision it is considered as an existing juridical fact until overruled, and intermediate cases finally decided under it are not to be disturbed....

... [W]e believe that the Constitution neither prohibits nor requires retrospective effect....

Once the premise is accepted that we are neither required to, nor prohibited from applying a decision retrospectively, we must then weigh the merits and demerits in each case by looking to the prior history of the rule in question, its purpose and effect, and whether retrospective operation will further or retard its operation. We believe that this approach is particularly correct with reference to the 4th Amendment's prohibitions as to unreasonable searches and seizures. Rather than "disparaging" the amendment we but apply the wisdom of Justice [Oliver Wendell] Holmes that "[t]he life of the law has not been logic: it has been experience."...

Mapp was announced in 1961. The court in considering "the current validity of the factual grounds upon which *Wolf* was based" pointed out that prior to *Wolf* "almost ⅔ of the states were opposed to the use of the exclusionary rule, now, despite the *Wolf* case, more than half of those since passing upon it... have wholly or partly adopted or adhered to the *Weeks* rule."...

It is clear that the *Wolf* court, once it had found the 4th Amendment's unreasonable search and seizure clause applicable to the states through the due process clause of the 14th Amendment, turned its attention to whether the exclusionary rule was included within the command of the 4th Amendment. This was decided in the negative. It is clear that based upon the factual considerations heretofore discussed the *Wolf* court then concluded that it was not necessary to the enforcement of the 4th Amendment for the exclusionary rule to be extended to the states as a requirement of due process. *Mapp* had as its prime purpose the enforcement of the 4th Amendment through the inclusion of the exclusionary rule within its rights. This, it was found, was the only effective deterrence against lawless police action. Indeed, all of the cases since *Wolf* requiring the exclusion of illegal evidence have been based on the necessity for an effective deterrent to illegal police action.... We cannot say that this purpose would be advanced by making the rule retrospective. The misconduct of the police prior to *Mapp* has already occurred and will not be corrected by releasing the prisoners involved. Nor would it add harmony to the delicate state-federal relationship of which we have spoken as part and parcel of the purpose of *Mapp*. Finally, the ruptured privacy of the victim's homes and effects cannot be restored. Reparation comes too late....

Finally, there are interests in the administration of justice and the integrity of the judicial process to consider. To make the rule of *Mapp* retrospective would tax the administration of justice to the utmost. Hearings would have to be held on the excludability of evidence long since destroyed, misplaced or deteriorated. If it is excluded, the witnesses available at the time of the original trial will not be available or if located their memory will be dimmed. To thus legitimate such an extraordinary procedural weapon that has no bearing on guilt would seriously disrupt the administration of justice....

Nor can we accept the contention of petitioner that the *Mapp* rule should date from the day of the seizure there, rather than that of the judgment of this court. The date of the seizure in *Mapp* has no legal significance. It was the judgment of this court that changed the rule and the date of that opinion is the crucial date....

All that we decide today is that though the error complained of might be fundamental it is not of the nature requiring us to overturn all final convictions based upon it. After full consideration of all the factors we are not able to say that the *Mapp* rule requires retrospective application. *Affirmed.*

Justice Black, whom Douglas joined, dissenting:

... Despite the court's resounding promises throughout the *Mapp* opinion that convictions based on such "unconstitutional evidence" would " 'find no sanction in the judgments of the courts,' " Linkletter, convicted in the state court by use of "unconstitutional evidence," is today denied relief by the judgment of this court because his conviction became "final" before *Mapp* was decided. Linkletter must stay in jail; Miss Mapp, whose offense was committed before Linkletter's, is free. This different treatment of Miss Mapp and Linkletter points up at once the arbitrary and discriminatory nature of the judicial contrivance utilized here to break the promise of *Mapp* by keeping all people in jail who are unfortunate enough to have had their unconstitutional convictions affirmed before June 19, 1961.

Miss Mapp's Ohio offense was committed May 23, 1957; Linkletter's Louisiana offense occurred more than a year later—Aug. 16, 1958. Linkletter was tried in Louisiana, convicted, the State Supreme Court affirmed, and a rehearing was denied Mar. 21, 1960, all within about one year and 7 months after his offense was committed. The Ohio Supreme Court affirmed Miss Mapp's conviction Mar. 23, 1960, approximately 2 years and 10 months after her offense. Thus, had the Ohio courts proceeded with the same expedition as those in Louisiana, or had the Louisiana courts proceeded as slowly as the Ohio courts, Linkletter's conviction would not have been "finally" decided within the court's definition of "finally" until within about 10 days of the time Miss Mapp's case was decided in this court—which would have given Linkletter ample time to petition this court for virtually automatic relief on direct review after the *Mapp* case was decided. The court offers no defense based on any known principle of justice for discriminating among defendants who were similarly convicted by use of evidence unconstitutionally seized. It certainly cannot do so as between Linkletter and Miss Mapp. The crime with which she was charged took place more than a year before his, yet the decision today seems to rest on the fanciful concept that the 4th Amendment protected her 1957 offense against conviction by use of unconstitutional evidence but denied its protection to Linkletter for his 1958 offense. In making this ruling the court assumes for itself the virtue of acting in harmony with a comment of Justice Holmes that "[t]he life of the law has not been logic: it has been experience." Justice Holmes was not there talking about the Constitution; he was talking about the evolving judge-made law of England and of some of our states whose judges are allowed to follow in the common law tradition. It should be remembered in this connection that no member of this court has ever more seriously criticized it than did Justice Holmes for reading its own predilections into the "vague contours" of the due process clause. But quite apart from that, there is no experience of the past that justifies a new court-made rule to perpetrate a grossly invidious and unfair discrimination against Linkletter simply because he happened to be prosecuted in a state that was evidently well up with its criminal court docket. If this discrimination can be excused at all it is not because of experience but because of logic—sterile and formal at that—not, according to Justice Holmes, the most dependable guide in lawmaking. . . .

As the court concedes . . ., this is the first instance on record where this court, having jurisdiction, has ever refused to give a previously convicted defendant the benefit of a new and more expansive Bill of Rights interpretation. I am at a loss to understand why those who suffer from the use of evidence secured by a search and seizure in violation of the 4th Amendment should be treated differently from those who have been denied other guarantees of the Bill of Rights. . . .

One reason—perhaps a basic one—put forward by the court for its refusal to give Linkletter the benefit of the search and seizure exclusionary rule is the repeated statement that the purpose of that rule is to deter sheriffs, policemen and other law officers from making unlawful searches and seizures. The inference I gather from these repeated statements is that the rule is not a right or privilege accorded to defendants charged with crime but is a sort of punishment against officers in order

to keep them from depriving people of their constitutional
rights. In passing I would say that if that is the sole purpose,
reason, object and effect of the law, or of the rule, the court's
action in adopting it sounds more like law-making than
construing the Constitution. ... Both the majority and the
concurring members of the *Boyd* court seemed to believe they
were construing the Constitution. Quite aside from that aspect,
however, the undoubted implication of today's opinion that the
rule is not a safeguard for defendants but is a mere punishing
rod to be applied to law enforcement officers is a rather
startling departure from many past opinions, and even from
Mapp itself. *Mapp* quoted from the court's earlier opinion in
Weeks v. United States..., certainly not with disapproval,
saying that the court "in that case clearly stated that use of the
seized evidence involved 'a denial of the constitutional rights of
the accused.'" ... I have read and reread the *Mapp* opinion but
have been unable to find one word in it to indicate that the
exclusionary search and seizure rule should be limited on the
basis that it was intended to do nothing in th world except to
deter officers of the law. Certainly no such limitation is implied
by the court's statement in *Mapp* that without the rule: "[T]he
assurance against unreasonable ... searches and seizures would
be 'a form of words,' valueless and undeserving of mention in a
perpetual charter of inestimable human liberties...." ... The
court went on to indicate its belief that the rule was "'implicit
in the concept of ordered liberty'" ... and that it is an "essential
ingredient" of the constitutional guarantee. ... If the exclusionary rule has the high place in our constitutional plan of
"ordered liberty," which this court in *Mapp* and other cases has
so frequently said that it does have, what possible valid reason
can justify keeping people in jail under convictions obtained by
wanton disregard of a constitutional protection which the court
itself in *Mapp* treated as being one of the "constitutional rights
of the accused"?

... The court says that the exclusionary rule's purpose of
preventing law enforcement officers from making lawless
searches and seizures "will not at this late date be served by the
wholesale release of the guilty victims." ... It has not been the
usual thing to cut down trial protections guaranteed by the
Constitution on the basis that some guilty persons might escape.
There is probably no one of the Bill of Rights that does not

make it more difficult to convict defendants. But all of them are based on the premise, I suppose, that the Bill of Rights' safeguards should be faithfully enforced by the courts without regard to a particular judge's judgment as to whether more people could be convicted by a refusal of courts to enforce the safeguards. Such has heretofore been accepted as a general maxim. In answer to an argument made in the *Mapp* case, that application of the exclusionary rule to the states might allow guilty criminals to go free, this court conceded that: "In some cases this will undoubtedly be the result. . . . The criminal goes free, if he must, but it is the law that sets him free. Nothing can destroy a government more quickly than its failure to observe its own laws, or worse, its disregard of the charter of its own existence." . . .

The plain facts here are that the court's opinion cuts off many defendants who are now in jail from any hope of relief from unconstitutional convictions. . . . No state should be considered to have a vested interest in keeping prisoners in jail who were convicted because of lawless conduct by the state's officials. Careful analysis of the court's opinion shows that it rests on the premise that the state's assumed interest in the old, repudiated rule outweighs the interests of the states and of the people convicted in having wrongful convictions set aside. . . .

To obtain a search warrant, the 4th Amendment requires a police officer to submit to a magistrate a sworn statement demonstrating that he has "probable cause" to believe that a crime was, or is, about to be committed. The application must be specific "in particularly describing the place to be searched, and the persons or things to be seized." Over the years, however, an exception developed that permitted the police to search the clothing of a person arrested and the immediate vicinity. The Supreme Court expanded the exception in *Rabinowitz v. United States* in 1950 by holding, in effect, that policemen making a valid arrest could, over the suspect's objections, search the premises without a search warrant.

In general, it is easier to obtain an arrest warrant than a search warrant. Often the police will have probable cause that a suspect is guilty of a crime without having probable cause that any specific evidence will be on his person or on his premises. In some instances, therefore, the police apparently were encouraged to arrange to arrest a suspect in his home. Under *Rabinowitz,* a person thus had greater protection against searches of his home when he was *not* at home.

This result was abolished June 23, 1969 by the decision in *Chimel v. California.* In this case, 3 policemen had obtained a warrant to arrest Ted Steven Chimel, a coin collector suspected of stealing coins from other numismatists. The police waited for Chimel at his home. When he arrived, they arrested him, searched his house, garage and workshop and found stolen coins. Chimel was tried, convicted and sentenced to prison for from 5 years to life. He appealed on the ground that the coins should not have been introduced in evidence since they were obtained as a result of an unconstitutional search.

In a 6-2 decision, the court ruled in favor of Chimel. It held that an arresting officer can search only the arrestee's person and the area within his "immediate control." This area was defined by Justice Potter Stewart in the majority opinion to include the area in which the person arrested might obtain a weapon or destructible evidence. Accordingly, it would be reasonable for the police to search a drawer in front of the person arrested to prevent him from seizing a gun, Stewart wrote, although there is no comparable justification "for routinely searching rooms other than that in which an arrest occurs—or, for that matter, for searching through all the desk drawers or other closed or concealed areas in that room itself."

Dissenting, Justice White said it was unreasonable to require the police to leave the scene of an arrest to obtain a search warrant "when there must almost always be a strong possibility that confederates of the arrested man will in the meanwhile remove items for which the police have probable cause to search." In Chimel's case, there apparently was opportunity for the police to obtain a search warrant prior to the arrest, but in many cases an arrest is not planned. The majority decision, however, does not extend to unplanned arrests.

Abridgment of the *Chimel v. California* decision (395 U.S. 752, June 23, 1969):

Justice Stewart delivering the opinion of the court:

This case raises basic questions concerning the permissible scope under the 4th Amendment of a search incident to a lawful arrest.

...3 police officers arrived at the Santa Ana, California, home of the petitioner with a warrant authorizing his arrest for the burglary of a coin shop. The officers knocked on the door, identified themselves to the petitioner's wife, and asked if they might come inside. She ushered them into the house, where they waited 10 or 15 minutes until the petitioner returned home from work. When the petitioner entered the house, one of the officers handed him the arrest warrant and asked for permission to "look around." The petitioner objected but was advised that "on the basis of the lawful arrest," the officers would nonetheless conduct a search. No search warrant had been issued.

Accompanied by the petitioner's wife, the officers then looked through the entire...house, including the attic, the garage and a small workshop. ... In the master bedroom and sewing room...the officers directed the petitioner's wife to open drawers and "to physically move contents of the drawers from side to side so that [they] might view any items that would have come from [the] burglary." After completing the search, they seized numerous items—primarily coins, but also several medals, tokens and a few other objects. The entire search took between 45 minutes and an hour.

At the petitioner's subsequent state trial on 2 charges of burglary, the items taken from his house were admitted into evidence against him, over his objection that they had been unconstitutionally seized. He was convicted, and the judgments of conviction were affirmed by both the California District Court of Appeal... and the California Supreme Court. ... Both courts accepted the petitioner's contention that the arrest warrant was invalid because the supporting affidavit was set out in conclusory terms but held that since the arresting officers had procured the warrant "in good faith," and since in any event they had had sufficient information to constitute probable cause for the petitioner's arrest, that arrest had been lawful. From this conclusion the appellate courts went on to hold that the search of the petitioner's home had been justified, despite the absence of a search warrant, on the ground that it had been incident to a valid arrest....

Without deciding the question, we proceed on the hypothesis that the California courts were correct in holding that the arrest of the petitioner was valid under the Constitution. This brings us directly to the question whether the warrantless search of the petitioner's entire house can be constitutionally justified as incident to that arrest. The decisions of this court bearing upon that question have been far from consistent, as even the most cursory review makes evident....

In 1950, ... came *United States v. Rabinowitz...,* the decision upon which California primarily relies in the case now before us. In *Rabinowitz,* federal authorities had been informed that the defendant was dealing in stamps bearing forged overprints. On the basis of that information they secured a warrant for his arrest, which they executed at his one-room business office. At the time of the arrest, the officers "searched the desk, safe and file cabinets in the office for about an hour and a half" ...and seized 573 stamps with forged overprints. The stamps were admitted into evidence at the defendant's trial, and this court affirmed his conviction, rejecting the contention that the warrantless search had been unlawful. The court held that the search in its entirety fell within the principle giving law enforcement authorities "[t]he right 'to search the place where the arrest is made in order to find and seize things connected with the crime....'" ...The opinion rejected the rule of *Trupiano [v. United States,* 1948] that "in seizing goods and articles, law enforcement agents must secure and use search warrants wherever reasonably practicable." The test, said the court, "is not whether it is reasonable to procure a search warrant but whether the search was reasonable."...

Rabinowitz has come to stand for the proposition, *inter alia,* that a warrantless search "incident to a lawful arrest" may generally extend to the area that is considered to be in the "possession" or under the "control" of the person arrested. And it was on the basis of that proposition that the California courts upheld the search of the petitioner's entire house in this case. That doctrine, however, at least in the broad sense in which it was applied by the California courts in this case, can withstand neither historical nor rational analysis....

Nor is the rationale by which the state seeks here to sustain the search of the petitioner's house supported by a reasoned view of the background and purpose of the 4th Amendment. Mr. Justice Frankfurter wisely pointed out in his *Rabinowitz* dissent that the amendment's proscription of "unreasonable searches and seizures" must be read in light of "the history that gave rise to the words"—a history of "abuses so deeply felt by the Colonies as to be one of the potent causes of the Revolution...." ... The amendment was in large part a reaction to the general warrants and warrantless searches that had so alienated the colonists and had helped speed the movement for independence....

Only last term in *Terry v. Ohio* [1968]... we emphasized that "the police must, whenever practicable, obtain advance judicial approval of searches and seizures through the warrant procedure" ... and that "[t]he scope of [a] search must be 'strictly tied to and justified by' the circumstances which rendered its initiation permissible." ... The search undertaken by the officer in that "stop and frisk" case was sustained under that test, because it was no more than a "protective... search for weapons." ... But in a companion case, *Sibron v. New York...,* we applied the same standard to another set of facts and reached a contrary result, holding that a policeman's action in thrusting his hand into a suspect's pocket had been neither motivated by nor limited to the objective of protection. Rather, the search had been made in order to find narcotics, which were in fact found.

A similar analysis underlies the "search incident to arrest" principle and marks its proper extent. When an arrest is made, it is reasonable for the arresting officer to search the person arrested in order to remove any weapons that the latter might seek to use in order to resist arrest or effect his escape. Otherwise, the officer's safety might well be endangered and the arrest itself frustrated. In addition, it is entirely reasonable for the arresting officer to search for and seize any evidence on the arrestee's person in order to prevent its concealment or destruction. And the area into which an arrestee might reach in order to grab a weapon or evidentiary items must, of course, be governed by a like rule. A gun on a table or in a drawer in front of one who is arrested can be as dangerous to the arresting officer as one concealed in the clothing of the person arrested. There is ample justification, therefore, for a search of the arrestee's person and the area "within his immediate control"— construing that phrase to mean the area from within which he might gain possession of a weapon or destructible evidence.

There is no comparable justification, however, for routinely searching rooms other than that in which an arrest occurs—or, for that matter, for searching through all the desk drawers or other closed or concealed areas in that room itself. Such searches, in the absence of well-recognized exceptions, may be made only under the authority of a search warrant. The "adherence to judicial processes" mandated by the 4th Amendment requires no less. ...

The petitioner correctly points out that one result of decisions such as *Rabinowitz* and *Harris [v. United States, 1947]* is to give law enforcement officials the opportunity to engage in searches not justified by probable cause, by the simple expedient of arranging to arrest suspects at home rather than elsewhere.... [Had the petitioner] been arrested earlier in the day, at his place of employment rather than at home, no search of his house could have been made without a search warrant. In any event, even apart from the possibility of such police tactics, the general point so forcefully made by Judge Learned Hand in *United States v. Kirschenblatt* ... remains: "After arresting a man in his house, to rummage at will among his papers in search of whatever will convict him appears to us to be indistinguishable from what might be done under a general warrant; indeed, the warrant would give more protection, for presumably it must be issued by a magistrate. True, by hypothesis the power would not exist if the supposed offender were not found on the premises; but it is small consolation to know that one's papers are safe only so long as one is not at home."...

Rabinowitz and *Harris* have been the subject of critical commentary for many years and have been relied upon less and less in our own decisions. It is time, for the reasons we have stated, to hold that on their own facts, and insofar as the principles they stand for are inconsistent with those that we have endorsed today, they are no longer to be followed.

Application of sound 4th Amendment principles to the facts of this case produces a clear result. The search here went far beyond the petitioner's person and the area from within which he might have obtained either a weapon or something that could have been used as evidence against him. There was no constitutional justification, in the absence of a search warrant, for extending the search beyond that area. The scope of the search was, therefore, "unreasonable" under the 4th and 14th Amendments, and the petitioner's conviction cannot stand.

Justice White, whom Black joined, dissenting:

... The court must decide whether a given search is reasonable [under the 4th Amendment]. The amendment does not proscribe "warrantless searches" but instead it proscribes "unreasonable searches" and this court has never held nor does the majority today assert that warrantless searches are necessarily unreasonable.

Applying this reasonableness test to the area of searches incident to arrests, one thing is clear at the outset. Search of an arrested man and of the items within his immediate reach must in almost every case be reasonable. There is always a danger that the suspect will try to escape, seizing concealed weapons with which to overpower and injure the arresting officers, and there is a danger that he may destroy evidence vital to the prosecution....

The justifications which make such a search reasonable obviously do not apply to the search of areas to which the accused does not have ready physical access. This is not enough, however, to prove such searches unconstitutional. The court has always held, and does not today deny, that when there is probable cause to search and it is "impracticable" for one reason or another to get a search warrant, then a warrantless search may be reasonable....

This is not to say that a search can be reasonable without regard to the probable cause to believe that seizable items are on the premises. But when there are exigent circumstances, and probable cause, then the search may be made without a warrant, reasonably. An arrest itself may often create an emergency situation making it impracticable to obtain a warrant before embarking on a related search. Again assuming that there is probable cause to search premises at the spot where a suspect is arrested, it seems to me unreasonable to require the police to leave the scene in order to obtain a search warrant when they are already legally there to make a valid arrest and when there must almost always be a strong possibility that confederates of the arrested man will in the meanwhile remove the items for which the police have probable cause to search....

...Petitioner was arrested in his home. ... There was doubtless probable cause not only to arrest petitioner, but to search his house. He had obliquely admitted both to a neighbor and to the owner of the burglarized store that he had committed the burglary. In light of this, and the fact that the neighbor had seen other admittedly stolen property in petitioner's house, there was surely probable cause on which a warrant could have issued to search the house for the stolen coins. Moreover, had the police simply arrested petitioner, taken him off to the station house, and later returned with a warrant, it seems very likely that petitioner's wife, who in view of petitioner's generally garrulous nature must have known of the robbery, would have removed the coins. For the police to search the house while the evidence they had probable cause to search out and seize was still there cannot be considered unreasonable....

If circumstances so often require the warrantless arrest that the law generally permits it, the typical situation will find the arresting officers lawfully on the premises without arrest or search warrant. Like the majority, I would permit the police to search the person of a suspect and the area under his immediate control either to assure the safety of the officers or to prevent the destruction of evidence. And like the majority, I see nothing in the arrest alone furnishing probable cause for a search of any broader scope. However, where as here the existence of probable cause is independently established and would justify a warrant for a broader search for evidence, I would follow past cases and permit such a search to be carried out without a warrant, since the fact of arrest supplies an exigent circumstance justifying police action before the evidence can be removed, and also alerts the suspect to the fact of the search so that he can immediately seek judicial determination of probable cause in an adversary proceeding, and appropriate redress.

This view, consistent with past cases, would not authorize the general search against which the 4th Amendment was meant to guard, nor would it broaden or render uncertain in any way whatsoever the scope of searches permitted under the 4th Amendment. The issue in this case is not the breadth of the search, since there was clearly probable cause for the search which was carried out. No broader search than if the officers had a warrant would be permitted. The only issue is whether a search warrant was required as a precondition to that search. It is agreed that such a warrant would be required absent exigent circumstances. . . .

The majority today proscribes searches for which there is probable cause and which may prove fruitless unless carried out immediately. This rule will have no added effect whatsoever in protecting the rights of the criminal accused at trial against introduction of evidence seized without probable cause. Such evidence could not be introduced under the old rule. Nor does the majority today give any added protection to the right of privacy of those whose houses there is probable cause to search. A warrant would still be sworn out for those houses and the privacy of their owners invaded. The only possible justification for the majority's rule is that in some instances arresting officers may search when they have no probable cause to do so and that such unlawful searches might be prevented if the officers first sought a warrant from a magistrate. Against the possible protection of privacy in that class of cases, in which the privacy of the house has already been invaded by entry to make the arrest—an entry for which the majority does not assert that any warrant is necessary—must be weighed the risk of destruction of evidence for which there is probable cause to search, as a result of delays in obtaining a search warrant. Without more basis for radical change than the court's opinion reveals, I would not upset the balance of these interests which has been struck by the former decisions of this court.

In considering searches incident to arrest, it must be remembered that there will be immediate opportunity to challenge the probable cause for the search in an adversary proceeding. The suspect has been apprised of the search by his very presence at the scene, and having been arrested, he will soon be brought into contact with people who can explain his rights. As Mr. Justice Brennan noted in a dissenting opinion, joined by Justices Black and Douglas, and the Chief Justice [Earl Warren], in *Abel v. United States* ... (1960), a search contemporaneous with a warrantless arrest is specially safeguarded since "[s]uch an arrest may constitutionally be made only upon probable cause, the existence of which is subject to judicial examination, ... and such an arrest demands the prompt bringing of the person arrested before a judicial officer, where the existence of probable cause is to be inquired into...." And since that time the court has imposed on state and federal officers alike the duty to warn suspects taken into custody, before questioning them, of their right to a lawyer. *Miranda v. Arizona* ... (1966); *Orozco v. Texas.* ...

An arrested man, ... provided almost immediately with a lawyer and a judge, is in an excellent position to dispute the reasonableness of his arrest and contemporaneous search in a full adversary proceeding. I would uphold the constitutionality of this search contemporaneous with an arrest since there was probable cause both for the search and for the arrest, exigent circumstances involving the removal or destruction of evidence, and a satisfactory opportunity to dispute the issues of probable cause shortly thereafter. In this case, the search was reasonable.

'Stop & Frisk'

A policeman cannot constitutionally search a "suspicious"-looking person whom he encounters on the street unless he has "probable cause" to arrest him for a crime. But can he constitutionally frisk* a person whom he suspects of carrying a concealed weapon? In *Terry v. Ohio,* decided June 10, 1968, the Supreme Court answered this question in the affirmative, *provided* that the officer "has reason to believe that he is dealing with an armed and dangerous individual, regardless of whether he has probable cause to arrest the individual for a crime." According to the majority opinion, "the officer need not be absolutely certain that the individual is armed; the issue is whether a reasonably prudent man in the circumstances would be warranted in the belief that his safety or that of others was in danger."

The case presented a number of problems. To deny the police the right to frisk persons whom they stopped to interrogate could jeopardize the safety of officers and passersby. A survey of police practices in several large cities, carried out by the President's Commission on Law Enforcement & Administration of Justice (1967), found that one of every 5 persons frisked was carrying a dangerous weapon—about evenly divided between guns and knives. On the other hand, being frisked can cause humiliation, fear and anger. According to the report: "In many communities field interrogations are a major source of friction between the police and minority groups. Many minority group leaders strongly contend that field interrogations are predominantly conducted in slum communities, that they are used indis-

---

* A frisk has been described thus: "The officer must feel with sensitive fingers every portion of the prisoner's body. A thorough search must be made of ... arms and armpits, waistline and back, the groin and the area about the testicles, and entire surface of the legs down to the feet."

criminately and that they are conducted in an abusive and unfriendly manner."

The court acted in the knowledge that any restrictions it sought to impose on frisking practices would be difficult to enforce. Recourse could be had to the exclusionary rule wherein evidence obtained as a result of an unconstitutional frisk could be excluded from evidence, but as Chief Justice Earl Warren pointed out in the majority opinion, "the exclusionary rule has its limitations...as a tool of judicial control." He said: "Regardless of how effective the rule may be where obtaining convictions is an important objective of the police, it is powerless to deter invasions of constitutionally guaranteed rights where the police either have no interest in prosecuting or are willing to forego successful prosecution in the interests of serving some other goal." Because of the limitations of the exclusionary rule, "the wholesale harassment by certain elements of the police community, of which minority groups...frequently complain, will not be stopped by the exclusion of any evidence from any criminal trial. Yet a rigid and unthinking application of the exclusionary rule, in futile protest against practices which it can never be used effectively to control, may exact a high toll in human injury and frustration of efforts to prevent crime."

After announcing its rule permitting a policeman to frisk when he "has reason to believe that he is dealing with an armed and dangerous individual," the court reviewed the circumstances of the case: Cleveland plainclothes policeman Martin McFadden testified that he had been patrolling and that 2 men, Richard Chilton and John W. Terry, "didn't look right to me." McFadden said he saw the men pass and peer inside a store window some 24 times, and he suspected that they were planning a holdup. He approached the men, identified himself as a policeman and frisked Chilton, Terry and a 3d man who had joined them. In patting the outer clothing of the 3 men, the officer found that Chilton and Terry each had a revolver. Both men were arrested and convicted of carrying concealed weapons.

In applying its newly formulated rule, the court upheld this frisk as "the tempered act of a policeman who in the course of an investigation had to make a quick decision as to how to protect himself and others from possible danger and took limited steps to do so."

Justice Douglas, the sole dissenter, asserted that a frisk for weapons was unconstitutional unless the officer had "probable cause"—as opposed to a "reasonable suspicion" as required by the majority—to conclude that a suspect was armed. Since a judge cannot issue a warrant without probable cause, Douglas wrote, "we hold today that the police have greater authority to make a 'seizure' and conduct a 'search' than a judge has to authorize such action." "To give the police greater power than a magistrate is to take a long step down the totalitarian path," he said. If "such a step is desirable to cope with modern forms of lawlessness," it should be taken only by "the deliberate choice of the people through a constitutional amendment."

Abridgement of the *Terry v. Ohio* decision (392 U.S. 1, June 10, 1968):

Chief Justice Warren delivering the opinion of the court:

... Petitioner Terry was convicted of carrying a concealed weapon and sentenced to the statutorily prescribed term of one to 3 years in the penitentiary. Following the denial of a pretrial motion to suppress, the prosecution introduced in evidence 2 revolvers and a number of bullets seized from Terry and a co-defendant, Richard Chilton, by Cleveland Police Detective Martin McFadden. At the hearing on the motion to suppress this evidence, Officer McFadden testified that while he was patrolling... his attention was attracted by... Chilton and Terry, standing on the corner of Huron Road and Euclid Avenue. He had never seen the 2 men before, and he was unable to say precisely what first drew his eye to them. However, he testified that he had been a policeman for 39 years and a detective for 35 and that he had been assigned to patrol this vicinity of downtown Cleveland for shoplifters and pickpockets for 30 years. He explained that he had developed routine habits of observation over the years and that he would "stand and watch people or walk and watch people at many intervals of the day." He added: "Now, in this case when I looked over they didn't look right to me at the time."

...Officer McFadden took up a post of observation in the entrance to a store 300 to 400 feet away from the 2 men.... saw one of the men leave the other one and walk southwest on Huron Road, past some stores. The man paused for a moment and looked in a store window, then walked on a short distance, turned around and walked back toward the corner, pausing once again to look in the same store window. He rejoined his companion at the corner, and the 2 conferred briefly. Then the 2d man went through the same series of motions,... returning to confer with the first man at the corner. The 2 men repeated this ritual alternately between 5 and 6 times apiece.... At one point, while the 2 were standing together on the corner, a 3d man approached them and engaged them briefly in conversation. This man then left the 2 others and walked west on Euclid Avenue. Chilton and Terry resumed their measured pacing, peering, and conferring. After this had gone on for 10 to 12 minutes, the 2 men walked off together,... following the path taken earlier by the 3d man.

...[McFadden] testified that after observing their elaborately casual and oft-repeated reconnaissance of the store window on Huron Road, he suspected the 2 men of "casing a job, a stick-up," and that he considered it his duty as a police officer to investigate further. He added that he feared "they may have a gun." Thus, Officer McFadden followed Chilton and Terry and saw them stop in front of Zucker's store to talk to the same man who had conferred with them earlier on the street corner. ... McFadden approach[ed] the 3 men, identified himself as a police officer and asked for their names. At this point his knowledge was confined to what he had observed. He was not acquainted with any of the 3 men by name or by sight, and he had received no information concerning them from any other source. When the men "mumbled something" in response to his inquiries, Officer McFadden grabbed petitioner Terry, spun him around so that they were facing the other 2, with Terry between McFadden and the others, and patted down the outside of his clothing. In the left breast pocket of Terry's overcoat Officer McFadden felt a pistol. He reached inside the overcoat pocket, but was unable to remove the gun. At this point, keeping Terry between himself and the others, the officer ordered all 3 men to enter Zucker's store. As they went in, he removed Terry's overcoat completely, retrieved a .38 caliber revolver from the pocket and ordered all 3 men to face the wall with their hands raised. Officer McFadden proceeded to pat down the outer clothing of Chilton and the 3d man, Katz. He discovered another revolver in the outer pocket of Chilton's overcoat, but no weapons were found on Katz. The officer testified that he only patted the men down to see whether they had weapons and that he did not put his hands beneath the outer garments of either Terry or Chilton until he felt their guns. So far as appears from the record, he never placed his hands beneath Katz's outer garments. Officer McFadden seized Chilton's gun, asked the proprietor of the store to call a police wagon and took all 3 men to the station, where Chilton and Terry were formally charged with carrying concealed weapons.

On the motion to suppress the guns, the prosecution took the position that they had been seized following a search incident to a lawful arrest. The trial court rejected this theory, stating that it "would be stretching the facts beyond reasonable comprehension" to find that Officer McFadden had had probable cause to arrest the men before he patted them down for weapons. However, the court denied the defendant's motion on the ground that Officer McFadden, on the basis of his experience, "had reasonable cause to believe ... that the defendants were conducting themselves suspiciously, and some interrogation should be made of their action." Purely for his own protection, the court held, the officer had the right to pat down the outer clothing of these men, whom he had reasonable cause to believe might be armed. The court distinguished between an investigatory "stop" and an arrest, and between a "frisk" of the outer clothing for weapons and a full-blown search for evidence of crime. The frisk, it held, was essential to the proper performance of the officer's investigatory duties, for without it, "the answer to the police officer may be a bullet, and a loaded pistol discovered during the frisk is admissible."

After the court denied their motion to suppress, Chilton and Terry waived jury trial and pleaded not guilty. The court adjudged them guilty....

...We granted *certiorari*... to determine whether the admission of the revolvers in evidence violated petitioner's rights under the 4th Amendment.... We affirm the conviction.

...The 4th Amendment provides that "the right of the people to be secure in their persons, houses, papers, and effects, against unreasonable searches and seizures, shall not be violated...." This inestimable right of personal security belongs as much to the citizen on the streets of our great cities as to the homeowner closeted in his study to dispose of his secret affairs....

...This question thrusts to the fore difficult and troublesome issues regarding a sensitive area of police activity—issues which have never before been squarely presented to this court. Reflective of the tensions involved are the practical and constitutional arguments pressed with great vigor on both sides of the public debate over the power of the police to "stop and frisk"... suspicious persons....

...We approach the issues in this case mindful of the limitations of the judicial function in controlling the myriad daily situations in which policemen and citizens confront each other on the street. The state has characterized the issue here as "the right of a police officer... to make an on-the-street stop, interrogate and pat down for weapons (known in the street vernacular as 'stop and frisk')." But this is only partly accurate. For the issue is not the abstract propriety of the police conduct, but the admissibility against petitioner of the evidence uncovered by the search and seizure. Ever since its inception, the rule excluding evidence seized in violation of the 4th Amendment has been recognized as a principal mode of discouraging lawless police conduct. See *Weeks v. United States...* (1914). Thus its major thrust is a deterrent one, see *Linkletter v. Walker...,* and experience has taught that it is the only effective deterrent to police misconduct in the criminal context, and that without it the constitutional guarantee against unreasonable searches and seizures would be a mere "form of words." *Mapp v. Ohio....* The rule also serves another vital function—"the imperative of judicial integrity." *Elkins v. United States....* Courts which sit under our Constitution cannot and will not be made party to lawless invasions of the constitutional rights of citizens by permitting unhindered governmental use of the fruits of such invasions. Thus in our system evidentiary rulings provide the context in which the judicial process of inclusion and exclusion approves some conduct as comporting with constitutional guarantees and disapproves other actions by state agents. A ruling admitting evidence in a criminal trial, we recognize, has the necessary effect of legitimizing the conduct which produced the evidence, while an application of the exclusionary rule withholds the constitutional imprimatur.

The exclusionary rule has its limitations, however, as a tool of judicial control. It cannot properly be invoked to exclude the products of legitimate police investigative techniques on the ground that much conduct which is closely similar involves unwarranted intrusions upon constitutional protections. Moreover, in some contexts the rule is ineffective as a deterrent. Street encounters between citizens and police officers are incredibly rich in diversity. They range from wholly friendly exchanges of pleasantries or mutually useful information to hostile confrontations of armed men involving arrests, or injuries, or loss of life. Moreover, hostile confrontations are not all of a piece. Some of them begin in a friendly enough manner, only to take a different turn upon the injection of some unexpected element into the conversation. Encounters are initiated by the police for a wide variety of purposes, some of which are wholly unrelated to a desire to prosecute for crime. Doubtless some police "field interrogation" conduct violates the 4th Amendment. But a stern refusal by this court to condone such activity does not necessarily render it responsive to the exclusionary rule. Regardless of how effective the rule may be where obtaining convictions is an important objective of the police, it is powerless to deter invasions of constitutionally guaranteed rights where the police either have no interest in prosecuting or are willing to forego successful prosecution in the interest of serving some other goal.

Proper adjudication of cases in which the exclusionary rule is invoked demands a constant awareness of these limitations. The wholesale harassment by certain elements of the police community, of which minority groups, particularly Negroes, frequently complain, will not be stopped by the exclusion of any evidence from any criminal trial. Yet a rigid and unthinking application of the exclusionary rule, in futile protest against practices which it can never be used effectively to control, may exact a high toll in human injury and frustration of efforts to prevent crime. No judicial opinion can comprehend the protean variety of the street encounter, and we can only judge the facts of the case before us. Nothing we say today is to be taken as indicating approval of police conduct outside the legitimate investigative sphere. Under our decision, courts still retain their traditional responsibility to guard against police conduct which is overbearing or harassing, or which trenches upon personal security without the objective evidentiary justification which the Constitution requires. When such conduct is identified, it must be condemned by the judiciary and its fruits must be excluded from evidence in criminal trials. And, of course, our approval of legitimate and restrained investigative conduct undertaken on the basis of ample factual justification should in no way discourage the employment of other remedies than the exclusionary rule to curtail abuses for which that sanction may prove inappropriate.

...We turn our attention to the quite narrow question posed by the facts before us: whether it is always unreasonable for a policeman to seize a person and subject him to a limited search for weapons unless there is probable cause for an arrest....

Our first task is to establish at what point in this encounter the 4th Amendment becomes relevant. That is, we must decide whether and when Officer McFadden "seized" Terry and whether and when he conducted a "search." There is some suggestion in the use of such terms as "stop" and "frisk" that such police conduct is outside the purview of the 4th Amendment because neither action rises to the level of a "search" or "seizure" within the meaning of the Constitution. We emphatically reject this notion. ... The 4th Amendment governs "seizures" of the person which do not eventuate in a trip to the station house and prosecution for crime—"arrests" in traditional terminology. It must be recognized that whenever a police officer accosts an individual and restrains his freedom to walk away, he has "seized" that person. And it is nothing less than sheer torture of the English language to suggest that a careful exploration of the outer surfaces of a person's clothing all over his or her body in an attempt to find weapons is not a "search." Moreover, it is simply fantastic to urge that such a procedure performed in public by a policeman while the citizen stands helpless ... is a "petty indignity." It is a serious intrusion upon the sanctity of the person, which may inflict great indignity and arouse strong resentment, and it is not to be undertaken lightly....

...We therefore reject the notions that the 4th Amendment does not come into play at all as a limitation upon police conduct if the officers stop short of something called a "technical arrest" or a "full-blown search."

In this case there can be no question, then, that Officer McFadden "seized" petitioner and subjected him to a "search" when he took hold of him and patted down the outer surfaces of his clothing. We must decide whether at that point it was reasonable for Officer McFadden to have interfered with petitioner's personal security as he did. And in determining whether the seizure and search were "unreasonable" our inquiry is a dual one—whether the officer's action was justified at its inception, and whether it was reasonably related in scope to the circumstances which justified the interference in the first place....

...In order to assess the reasonableness of Officer McFadden's conduct as a general proposition, it is necessary "first to focus upon the governmental interest which allegedly justifies official intrusion upon the constitutionally protected interests of the private citizen," for there is "no ready test for determining reasonableness other than by balancing the need to search [or seize] against the invasion which the search [or seizure] entails." *Camara v. Municipal Court* ... (1967). And in justifying the particular intrusion the police officer must be able to point to specific and articulable facts which, taken together with rational inferences from those facts, reasonably warrant that intrusion. The scheme of the 4th Amendment becomes meaningful only when it is assured that at some point the conduct of those charged with enforcing the laws can be subjected to the more detached, neutral scrutiny of a judge who must evaluate the reasonableness of a particular search or seizure in light of the particular circumstances. And in making that assessment it is imperative that the facts be judged against an objective standard: would the facts available to the officer at the moment of the seizure or the search "warrant a man of reasonable caution in the belief" that the action taken was appropriate?... Anything less would invite intrusions upon constitutionally guaranteed rights based on nothing more substantial than inarticulate hunches, a result this court has consistently refused to sanction.... And simple " 'good faith on the part of the arresting officer is not enough.'... If subjective good faith alone were the test, the protections of the 4th Amendment would evaporate, and the people would be 'secure in their persons, houses, papers, and effects,' only in the discretion of the police." *Beck v. Ohio* [1964]....

Applying these principles to this case, we consider first the nature and extent of the governmental interests involved. One general interest is, of course, that of effective crime prevention and detection; it is this interest which underlies the recognition that a police officer may in appropriate circumstances and in an appropriate manner approach a person for purposes of investigating possibly criminal behavior even though there is no probable cause to make an arrest. It was this legitimate investigative function Officer McFadden was discharging when he decided to approach petitioner and his companions. He had observed Terry, Chilton, and Katz go through a series of acts, each of them perhaps innocent in itself, but which taken together warranted further investigation.... It would have been poor police work indeed for an officer of 30 years' experience in the detection of thievery from stores in this same neighborhood to have failed to investigate this behavior further.

The crux of this case, however, is not the propriety of Officer McFadden's taking steps to investigate petitioner's suspicious behavior, but rather, whether there was justification for McFadden's invasion of Terry's personal security by searching him for weapons in the course of that investigation. We are now concerned with more than the governmental interest in investigating crime; in addition, there is the more immediate interest of the police officer in taking steps to assure himself that the person with whom he is dealing is not armed with a weapon that could unexpectedly and fatally be used against him. Certainly it would be unreasonable to require that police officers take unnecessary risks in the performance of their duties. American criminals have a long tradition of armed violence, and every year in this country many law enforcement officers are killed in the line of duty, and thousands more are wounded. Virtually all of these deaths and a substantial portion of the injuries are inflicted with guns and knives.

In view of these facts, we cannot blind ourselves to the need for law enforcement officers to protect themselves and other prospective victims of violence in situations where they may lack probable cause for an arrest. When an officer is justified in believing that the individual whose suspicious behavior he is investigating at close range is armed and presently dangerous to the officer or to others, it would appear to be clearly unreasonable to deny the officer the power to take necessary measures to determine whether the person is in fact carrying a weapon and to neutralize the threat of physical harm.

We must still consider, however, the nature and quality of the intrusion on individual rights which must be accepted if police officers are to be conceded the right to search for weapons in situations where probable cause to arrest for crime is lacking. Even a limited search of the outer clothing for weapons constitutes a severe, though brief, intrusion upon cherished personal security, and it must surely be an annoying, frightening and perhaps humiliating experience. Petitioner contends that such an intrusion is permissible only incident to a lawful arrest, either for a crime involving the possession of weapons or for a crime the commission of which led the officer to investigate in the first place....

Petitioner does not argue that a police officer should refrain from making any investigation of suspicious circumstances until such time as he has probable cause to make an arrest; nor does he deny that police officers in properly discharging their investigative function may find themselves confronting persons who might well be armed and dangerous. Moreover, he does not say that an officer is always unjustified in searching a suspect to discover weapons. Rather, he says it is unreasonable for the policeman to take that step until such time as the situation evolves to a point where there is probable cause to make an arrest. When that point has been reached, petitioner would concede the officer's right to conduct a search of the suspect for weapons, fruits or instrumentalities of the crime, or "mere" evidence, incident to the arrest....

Our evaluation of the proper balance that has to be struck in this type of case leads us to conclude that there must be a narrowly drawn authority to permit a reasonable search for weapons for the protection of the police officer, where he has reason to believe that he is dealing with an armed and dangerous individual, regardless of whether he has probable cause to arrest the individual for a crime. The officer need not be absolutely certain that the individual is armed; the issue is whether a reasonably prudent man in the circumstances would be warranted in the belief that his safety or that of others was in danger.... And in determining whether the officer acted reasonably in such circumstances, due weight must be given, not to his inchoate and unparticularized suspicion or "hunch," but to the specific reasonable inferences which he is entitled to draw from the facts in light of his experience....

We conclude that the revolver seized from Terry was properly admitted in evidence against him. At the time he seized petitioner and searched him for weapons, Officer McFadden had reasonable grounds to believe that petitioner was armed and dangerous, and it was necessary for the protection of himself and others to take swift measures to discover the true facts and neutralize the threat of harm if it materialized. The policeman carefully restricted his search to what was appropriate to the discovery of the particular items which he sought. Each case of this sort will, of course, have to be decided on its own facts. We merely hold today that where a police officer observes unusual conduct which leads him reasonably to conclude in light of his experience that criminal activity may be afoot and that the persons with whom he is dealing may be armed and presently dangerous; where in the course of investigating this behavior he identifies himself as a policeman and makes reasonable inquiries; and where nothing in the initial stages of the encounter serves to dispel his reasonable fear for his own or others' safety, he is entitled for the protection of himself and others in the area to conduct a carefully limited search of the outer clothing of such persons in an attempt to discover weapons which might be used to assault him. Such a search is a reasonable search under the 4th Amendment, and any weapons seized may properly be introduced in evidence against the person from whom they were taken.

Justice Black concurred in the judgment and opinion but took exception to the court's reliance on *Katz v. U.S.*

Justice Douglas dissenting:

I agree that petitioner was "seized" within the meaning of the 4th Amendment. I also agree that frisking petitioner and his companions for guns was a "search." But it is a mystery how that "search" and that "seizure" can be constitutional by 4th Amendment standards unless there was "probable cause" to believe that (1) a crime had been committed or (2) a crime was in the process of being committed or (3) a crime was about to be committed.

The opinion of the court disclaims the existence of "probable cause." If loitering were an issue and that was the offense charged, there would be "probable cause" shown. But the crime here is carrying concealed weapons; and there is no basis for concluding that the officer had "probable cause" for believing that crime was being committed. Had a warrant been sought, a magistrate would, therefore, have been unauthorized to issue one, for he can act only if there is a showing of "probable cause." We hold today that the police have greater authority to make a "seizure" and conduct a "search" than a judge has to authorize such action. We have said precisely the opposite over and over again.

In other words, police officers, up to today have been permitted to effect arrests or searches without warrants only when the facts within their personal knowledge would satisfy the constitutional standard of *probable cause.* At the time of their "seizure" without a warrant they must possess facts concerning the person arrested that would have satisfied a magistrate that "probable cause" was indeed present. The term "probable cause" rings a bell of certainty that is not sounded by phrases such as "reasonable suspicion.". . .

The infringement on personal liberty of any "seizure" of a person can only be "reasonable" under the 4th Amendment if we require the police to possess "probable cause" before they seize him. Only that line draws a meaningful distinction between an officer's mere inkling and the presence of facts within the officer's personal knowledge which would convince a reasonable man that the person seized has committed, is committing or is about to commit a particular crime. . . .

To give the police greater power than a magistrate is to take a long step down the totalitarian path. Perhaps such a step is desirable to cope with modern forms of lawlessness. But if it is taken, it should be the deliberate choice of the people through a constitutional amendment. Until the 4th Amendment, which is closely allied with the 5th, is rewritten, the person and the effects of the individual are beyond the reach of all government agencies until there are reasonable grounds to believe (probable cause) that a criminal venture has been launched or is about to be launched. . . .

. . . [If] the individual is no longer to be sovereign, if the police can pick him up whenever they do not like the cut of his gib, if they can "seize" and "search" him in their discretion, we enter a new regime. The decision to enter it should be made only after a full debate by the people of this country.

In 2 companion cases handed down the same day as *Terry v. Ohio,* the court applied the *Terry* rule in 2 diverse situations. In *Sibron v. New York,* the court overturned a drug conviction based on evidence obtained from a street-corner search. A New York policeman had searched a suspect after seeing him talk with 6 or 8 known narcotics addicts over an 8-hour period. The search yielded several envelopes of heroin. The Supreme Court, applying *Terry,* held that the heroin should not have been admitted into evidence.

In *Sibron* the prosecution conceded that the officer lacked "probable cause" to arrest Sibron for a narcotics violation but argued that the search was justified as a self-protective search for weapons. The court ruled, however, that the officer did not have any basis for suspecting that Sibron was armed. Even if he had cause to suspect that Sibron was armed, the court said, the officer was restricted under *Terry* to "a limited patting of the outer clothing of the suspect for concealed objects which might be used as instruments of assault." The court pointed out that "only when he discovered such objects did the officer in *Terry* place his hands in the pockets of the man he searched."

Justice Black, dissenting, noted that the officer had thrust his hand into Sibron's pocket after Sibron had put his own hand into that pocket. Therefore, said Black, the officer had probable cause to believe Sibron was reaching for a gun. Black criticized the majority for 2d-guessing the officer. "A policeman under such circumstances has to act in a split second; delay may mean death for him," Black said. "No one can know when an addict may be moved to shoot or stab, and particularly when he moves his hand hurriedly to a pocket where weapons are known to be carried, it behooves an officer who wants to live to act at once as this officer did."

In the 2d companion case, *Peters v. New York,* a defendant had been convicted of possessing burglary tools under circumstances suggesting an intent to use them to commit a crime. The burglary tools were obtained after an off-duty policeman frisked Peters, who could not account for his presence in the hallway of the officer's apartment building. In patting down Peters' outer clothing, the officer felt a hard object in Peters' pocket. The officer testified later that he thought the object might be a gun or knife. Reaching into Peters' pocket, the officer found an envelope containing burglary tools. Peters' conviction was upheld by a unanimous court.

Abridgment of the *Sibron v. New York* and *Peters v. New York* decision (392 U.S. 40, June 10, 1968):

...Sibron, the appellant..., was convicted of the unlawful possession of heroin. He moved before trial to suppress the heroin seized from his person by the arresting officer, Brooklyn Patrolman Anthony Martin. After the trial court denied his motion, Sibron pleaded guilty to the charge, preserving his right to appeal the evidentiary ruling. At the hearing on the motion to suppress, Officer Martin testified that while he was patrolling his beat in uniform on Mar. 9, 1965, he observed Sibron "continually from the hours of 4:00 p.m. to 12:00 midnight...in the vicinity of 742 Broadway." He stated that during this period of time he saw Sibron in conversation with 6 or 8 persons whom he (Patrolman Martin) knew from past experience to be narcotics addicts. The officer testified that he did not overhear any of these conversations, and that he did not see anything pass between Sibron and any of the others. Late in the evening Sibron entered a restaurant. Patrolman Martin saw Sibron speak with 3 more known addicts inside the restaurant. Once again, nothing was overheard and nothing was seen to pass between Sibron and the addicts. Sibron sat down and ordered pie and coffee, and as he was eating, Patrolman Martin approach[ed] him and told him to come outside. Once outside, the officer said to Sibron, "You know what I am after." According to the officer, Sibron "mumbled something and reached into his pocket." Simultaneously, Patrolman Martin thrust his hand into the same pocket, discovering several glassine envelopes, which, it turned out, contained heroin.

...In his sworn complaint Patrolman Martin stated: "As the officer approached the defendant, the latter being in the direction of the officer and seeing him, he did put his hand in his left jacket pocket and pulled out a tinfoil envelope and did attempt to throw same to the ground. The officer never losing sight of the said envelope seized it from the def[endan]t's left hand, examined it and found it to contain ten glascine *[sic]* envelopes with a white substance alleged to be heroin."

This version of the encounter, however, bears very little resemblance to Patrolman Martin's testimony at the hearing on the motion to suppress. In fact, he discarded the abandonment theory at the hearing. Nor did the officer ever seriously suggest that he was in fear of bodily harm and that he searched Sibron in self-protection to find weapons.

The prosecutor's theory at the hearing was that Patrolman Martin had probable cause to believe that Sibron was in possession of narcotics because he had seen him conversing with a number of known addicts over an 8-hour period. In the absence of any knowledge on Patrolman Martin's part concerning the nature of the intercourse between Sibron and the addicts, how-ever, the trial court was inclined to grant the motion to suppress. As the judge stated, "All he knows about the unknown men: They are narcotics addicts. They might have been talking about the World Series. They might have been talking about prize fights." The prosecutor, however, reminded the judge that Sibron had admitted on the stand, in Patrolman Martin's absence, that he had been talking to the addicts about narcotics. Thereupon, the trial judge changed his mind and ruled that the officer had probable cause for an arrest....

Peters..., was convicted of possessing burglary tools under circumstances evincing an intent to employ them in the commission of a crime. The tools were seized from his person at the time of his arrest, and like Sibron he made a pretrial motion to suppress them. When the trial court denied the motion, he too pleaded guilty, preserving his right to appeal. Officer Samuel Lasky of the New York City Police Department testified at the hearing on the motion that he was at home in his apartment in Mount Vernon, New York, at about 1 p.m. on July 10, 1964. He had just finished taking a shower and was drying himself when he heard a noise at his door. His attempt to investigate was interrupted by a telephone call, but when he returned and looked through the peephole into the hall, Officer Lasky saw "2 men tiptoeing out of the alcove toward the stairway." He immediately called the police, put on some civilian clothes and armed himself with his service revolver.

Returning to the peephole, he saw "a tall man tiptoeing away from the alcove and followed by this shorter man, Mr. Peters, toward the stairway." Officer Lasky testified that he had lived in the 120-unit building for 12 years and that he did not recognize either of the men as tenants. Believing that he had happened upon the 2 men in the course of an attempted burglary, Officer Lasky opened his door, entered the hallway and slammed the door loudly behind him. This precipitated a flight down the stairs on the part of the 2 men, and Officer Lasky gave chase. His apartment was located on the 6th floor, and he apprehended Peters between the 4th and 5th floors. Grabbing Peters by the collar, he continued down another flight in unsuccessful pursuit of the other man. Peters explained his presence in the building to Officer Lasky by saying that he was visiting a girl friend. However, he declined to reveal the girl friend's name, on the ground that she was a married woman. Officer Lasky patted Peters down for weapons, and discovered a hard object in his pocket. He stated at the hearing that the object did not feel like a gun, but that it might have been a knife. He removed the object from Peters' pocket. It was an opaque plastic envelope, containing burglar's tools. . . .

Turning to the facts of Sibron's case, it is clear that the heroin was inadmissible in evidence against him. The prosecution has quite properly abandoned the notion that there was probable cause to arrest Sibron for any crime at the time Patrolman Martin accosted him in the restaurant, took him outside and searched him. The officer was not acquainted with Sibron and had no information concerning him. He merely saw Sibron talking to a number of known narcotics addicts over a period of 8 hours. It must be emphasized that Patrolman Martin was completely ignorant regarding the content of these conversations, and that he saw nothing pass between Sibron and the addicts. . . . The inference that persons who talk to narcotics addicts are engaged in the criminal traffic in narcotics is simply not the sort of reasonable inference required to support an intrusion by the police upon an individual's personal security. Nothing resembling probable cause existed until after the search had turned up the envelopes of heroin. It is axiomatic that an incident search may not precede an arrest and serve as part of its justification. . . . Thus the search cannot be justified as incident to a lawful arrest.

If Patrolman Martin lacked probable cause for an arrest, however, his seizure and search of Sibron might still have been justified at the outset if he had reasonable grounds to believe that Sibron was armed and dangerous. *Terry v. Ohio....* We are not called upon to decide in this case whether there was a "seizure" of Sibron inside the restaurant antecedent to the physical seizure which accompanied the search. The record is unclear with respect to what transpired between Sibron and the officer inside the restaurant. It is totally barren of any indication whether Sibron accompanied Patrolman Martin outside in submission to a show of force or authority which left him no choice, or whether he went voluntarily in a spirit of apparent cooperation with the officer's investigation. In any event, this deficiency in the record is immaterial, since Patrolman Martin obtained no new information in the interval between his initiation of the encounter in the restaurant and his physical seizure and search of Sibron outside.

Although the Court of Appeals of New York wrote no opinion in this case, it seems to have viewed the search here as a self-protective search for weapons. ... But the application of this reasoning to the facts of this case proves too much. The police officer is not entitled to seize and search every person whom he sees on the street or of whom he makes inquiries. Before he places a hand on the person of a citizen in search of anything, he must have constitutionally adequate reasonable grounds for doing so. In the case of the self-protective search for weapons, he must be able to point to particular facts from which he reasonably inferred that the individual was armed and dangerous. *Terry v. Ohio....* Patrolman Martin's testimony reveals no such facts. The suspect's mere act of talking with a number of known narcotics addicts over an 8-hour period no more gives rise to reasonable fear of life or limb on the part of the police officer than it justifies an arrest for committing a crime. Nor did Patrolman Martin urge that when Sibron put his hand in his pocket, he feared that he was going for a weapon and acted in self-defense. His opening statement to Sibron—"You know what I am after"—made it abundantly clear that he sought narcotics, and his testimony at the hearing left no doubt that he thought there were narcotics in Sibron's pocket.

Even assuming *arguendo* that there were adequate grounds to search Sibron for weapons, the nature and scope of the search conducted by Patrolman Martin were so clearly unrelated to that justification as to render the heroin inadmissible. The search for weapons approved in *Terry* consisted solely of a limited patting of the outer clothing of the suspect for concealed objects which might be used as instruments of assault. Only when he discovered such objects did the officer in *Terry* place his hands in the pockets of the men he searched. In this case, with no attempt at an initial limited exploration for arms, Patrolman Martin thrust his hand into Sibron's pocket and took from him envelopes of heroin. His testimony shows that he was looking for narcotics, and he found them. The search was not reasonably limited in scope to the accomplishment of the only goal which might conceivably have justified its inception—the protection of the officer by disarming a potentially dangerous man. Such a search violates the guarantee of the 4th Amendment, which protects the sanctity of the person against unreasonable intrusions on the part of all government agents.

... We think it is equally clear that the search in Peters' case was wholly reasonable under the Constitution.... [We think] that for purposes of the 4th Amendment the search was properly incident to a lawful arrest. By the time Officer Lasky caught up with Peters on the stairway between the 4th and 5th floors of the apartment building, he had probable cause to arrest him for attempted burglary. The officer heard strange noises at his door which apparently led him to believe that someone sought to force entry. When he investigated these noises he saw 2 men, whom he had never seen before in his 12 years in the building, tiptoeing furtively about the hallway. They were still engaged in these maneuvers after he called the police and dressed hurriedly. And when Officer Lasky entered the hallway, the men fled down the stairs. It is difficult to conceive of stronger grounds for an arrest, short of actual eyewitness observation of criminal activity. As the trial court explicitly recognized, deliberately furtive actions and flight at the approach of strangers or law officers are strong indicia of *mens rea,* and when coupled with specific knowledge on the part of the officer relating the suspect to the evidence of crime, they are proper factors to be considered in the decision to make an arrest....

As we noted in Sibron's case, a search incident to a lawful arrest, may not precede the arrest and serve as part of its justification. It is a question of fact precisely when, in each case, the arrest took place.... And while there was some inconclusive discussion in the trial court concerning when Officer Lasky "arrested" Peters, it is clear that the arrest had for purposes of constitutional justification already taken place before the search commenced. When the policeman grabbed Peters by the collar, he abruptly "seized" him and curtailed his freedom of movement on the basis of probable cause to believe that he was engaged in criminal activity.... At that point he had the authority to search Peters, and the incident search was obviously justified "by the need to seize weapons and other things which might be used to assault an officer or effect an escape, as well as by the need to prevent the destruction of evidence of the crime." *Preston v. United States* ... (1964). Moreover, it was reasonably limited in scope by these purposes. Officer Lasky did not engage in an unrestrained and thorough-going examination of Peters and his personal effects. He seized him to cut short his flight, and he searched him primarily for weapons. While patting down his outer clothing, Officer Lasky discovered an object in his pocket which might have been used as a weapon. He seized it and discovered it to be a potential instrument of the crime of burglary.

We have concluded that Peters' conviction fully comports with the commands of the 4th and 14th Amendments and must be affirmed.... [Sibron's conviction], however, must be reversed, on the ground that the heroin was unconstitutionally admitted in evidence against the appellant.

Justice Black, who concurred in Peters, *dissenting in* Sibron:

... First. I think there was probable cause for the policeman to believe that when Sibron reached his hand to his coat pocket, Sibron had a dangerous weapon which he might use if it were not taken away from him. This, according to the court's own opinion, seems to have been the ground on which the Court of Appeals of New York justified the search, since it "affirmed on the basis of § 180-a, which authorizes such a search when the officer 'reasonably suspects that he is in danger of life or limb.' ".... And it seems to me to be a reasonable inference that when Sibron, who had been approaching and talking to addicts for 8 hours, reached his hand quickly to his left coat pocket, he might well be reaching for a gun. And as the court has emphasized today in its opinions in the other stop and frisk cases, a policeman under such circumstances has to act in a split second; delay may mean death for him. No one can know when an addict may be moved to shoot or stab, and particularly when he moves his hand hurriedly to a pocket where weapons are known to be habitually carried, it behooves an officer who wants to live to act at once as this officer did. It is true that the officer might also have thought Sibron was about to get heroin instead of a weapon. But the law enforcement officers all over the nation have gained little protection from the courts through opinions here if they are now left helpless to act in self-defense when a man associating intimately and continuously with addicts, upon meeting an officer, shifts his hand immediately to a pocket where weapons are constantly carried.

... I realize that the court has chosen to draw inferences different from mine and those drawn by the courts below. The court for illustration draws inferences that the officer's testimony at the hearing continued upon the "plain premise that he had been looking for narcotics all the time." ... But this court is hardly, at this distance from the place and atmosphere of the trial, in a position to overturn the trial and appellate courts on its own independent finding of an unspoken "premise" of the officer's inner thoughts.

In acting upon its own findings and rejecting those of the lower state courts, this court ... should be most cautious. Due to our holding in *Mapp v. Ohio* ..., we are due to get for review lierally thousands of cases raising questions like those before us here. If we are setting ourselves meticulously to review all such findings our task will be endless and many will rue the day when *Mapp* was decided. It is not only wise but imperative that where findings of the facts of reasonableness and probable cause are involved in such state cases, we should not overturn state court findings unless in the most extravagant and egregious errors. It seems fantastic to me even to suggest that this is such a case. I would leave these state court holdings alone.

2d, I think also that there was sufficient evidence here on which to base findings that after recovery of the heroin, in particular, an officer could reasonably believe there was probable cause to charge Sibron with violating New York's narcotics laws. As I have previously argued, there was, I think, ample evidence to give the officer probable cause to believe Sibron had a dangerous weapon and that he might use it. Under such circumstances the officer had a right to search him in the very limited fashion he did here. Since, therefore, this was a reasonable and justified search, the use of the heroin discovered by it was admissible in evidence.

In *McCray v. Illinois,* handed down Mar. 20, 1967, the court 6-3 upheld a street-corner search based on information supplied by an anonymous informer. In holding that the police had sufficient cause to conduct such a search without a warrant, the court also upheld the right of the state not to reveal the identity of its informer. The case involved a Chicago man whom police searched on the street after an informer was said to have identified the man as a drug pusher with narcotics on his person. The search yielded a packet of heroin. In upholding the state's refusal to reveal the identity of the informer the court said that nothing in the Constitution "requires a state court judge to assume that the arresting officer is committing perjury."

Justices Douglas, Brennan and Fortas dissented in asserting that the police should have obtained a search warrant. "Instead of going to a magistrate and making a showing of 'probable cause' based on their informant's tip-off, they acted on their own," Douglas wrote. "They, rather than the magistrate, became the arbiters of 'probable cause,'" he said. "What we do today is to encourage arrests and searches without warrants," Douglas warned.

The Supreme Court has not set limits on the right of the police to stop and briefly interrogate a person on the street although they have no legal basis on which to arrest him. It refused to do so in *Wainwright v. New Orleans* (1968), a case involving 2 policemen who had been on the lookout in New Orlean's French Quarter for a suspected killer with "Born to Raise Hell" tattooed on his arm. The policemen, on the street, stopped a young man who answered the suspect's description as sketched by a police artist. The 2 officers asked him to remove his jacket. The young man, who had no identification on his person and who claimed to be a law student, refused to do so. He said that he had an unsightly skin condition and that the law did not require him to remove his jacket on the street. He gave the police his name and address and tried to walk away. Instead, he was taken to the police station, where 6 officers forcibly removed his jacket. The law student, Stephen R. Wainwright, was arrested and convicted of disturbing the peace. In arguing that Wainwright's conviction should be sustained, the lawyer for New Orleans said that "if he can just walk away, the police power in this nation is gone." In supporting Wainwright in his appeal to the Supreme Court, the American Civil Liberties Union and the NAACP Legal Defense & Educational Fund argued that the police should not be permitted to detain anyone, for any period of time, without "probable cause." But the Supreme Court refused to hear Wainwright's appeal.

'Stop & Frisk' Right Extended

In *Adams v. Williams,* the Supreme Court June 12, 1972, in a 5-4 decision, authorized the police to stop and frisk persons on the basis of an informer's tip. In this particular instance, a Bridgeport, Conn. policeman had been informed by an identified informant that a man sitting alone in a nearby car late at night in a high crime area was carrying narcotics and had a pistol in his waistband; the policeman approached the car; reaching in through an open window he removed a handgun from the suspect's waistband. A search then carried out incidental to an arrest for the illegal possession of a weapon yielded a substantial quantity of heroin.

In appealing Robert Williams's subsequent conviction for illegal possession òf a gun and narcotics, his attorneys contended that the initial weapons frisk, which lead to the subsequent weapons arrest and search, violated the standards of *Terry v. Ohio* in that the officer was not justified in frisking a citizen on the sole basis of an informant's tip.

In the majority decision Justice Rehnquist declared that *Terry* did not limit a policeman's authority to frisk suspects to those instances in which the officer, based on his own personal observations, had reason to suspect that a person was armed and dangerous. In upholding the frisk and subsequent search, the majority described the frisk as proper since the officer "had ample reason to fear for his own safety."

The 4 dissenting justices called the frisk unjustifiable on the ground that Connecticut law permitted citizens with permits to carry concealed weapons. On that basis, therefore, they concluded that the police officer had no cause to frisk Williams for possession of what conceivably could have been a legal weapon. Rather than "water down" the 4th Amendment, Justice Douglas suggested that the 2d Amendment be "watered down" to outlaw the possession of handguns. Since Connecticut law authorized persons with permits to carry concealed guns, there "was no reason for the officer to infer from anything that the informant said that the respondent was dangerous," Douglas asserted. "His frisk was, therefore, illegal under *Terry.*"

Abridgment of the *Adams v. Williams* decision (407 U.S. 297, June 12, 1972):

Justice Rehnquist delivering the opinion of the court:

... [W]e reject respondent's argument that reasonable cause for a stop and frisk can only be based on the officer's personal observation, rather than on information supplied by another person. Informants' tips, like all other clues and evidence coming to a policeman on the scene, may vary greatly in their value and reliability. One simple rule will not cover every situation. Some tips, completely lacking in indicia of reliability, would either warrant no police response or require further investigation before a forcible stop of a suspect would be authorized. But in some situations—for example, when the victim of a street crime seeks immediate police aid and gives a description of his assailant, or when a credible informant warns of a specific impending crime—the subtleties of the hearsay rule should not thwart an appropriate police response.

... While properly investigating the activity of a person who was reported to be carrying narcotics and a concealed weapon and who was sitting alone in a car in a high crime area at 2:15 in the morning, Sgt. Connolly had ample reason to fear for his safety. When Williams rolled down his window, rather than complying with the policeman's request to step out of the car so that his movements could more easily be seen, the revolver allegedly at Williams' waist became an even greater threat. Under these circumstances the policeman's action in reaching to the spot where the gun was thought to be hidden constituted a limited intrusion designed to insure his safety, and we conclude that it was reasonable. The loaded gun seized as a result of this intrusion was therefore admissible at Williams' trial....

...Once Sgt. Connolly had found the gun precisely where the informant had predicted, probable cause existed to arrest Williams for unlawful possession of the weapon....

Justice Douglas, whom Marshall joined, dissenting:

...Connecticut allows its citizens to carry weapons, concealed or otherwise, at will, provided they have a permit.... Connecticut law gives its police no authority to frisk a person for a permit. Yet the arrest was for illegal possession of a gun. The only basis for that arrest was the informer's tip on the narcotics. Can it be said that a man in possession of narcotics will not have a permit for his gun? Is that why the arrest for possession of a gun in the free-and-easy state of Connecticut becomes constitutional?

The police problem is an acute one not because of the 4th Amendment but because of the ease with which anyone can acquire a pistol. A powerful lobby dins into the ears of our citizenry that these gun purchases are constitutional rights protected by the 2d Amendment which reads, "A well regulated Militia, being necessary to the security of a free State, the right of the people to keep and bear Arms, shall not be infringed."

There is under our decisions no reason why stiff state laws governing the purchase and possession of pistols may not be enacted....

Critics say that proposals like this water down the 2d Amendment. Our decisions belie that argument, for the 2d Amendment, as noted, was designed to keep alive the militia. But if watering-down is the mood of the day, I would prefer to water down the 2d rather than the 4th Amendment.

Justices Brennan and Marshall issued separate dissenting opinions.

The Supreme Court held Apr. 22, 1969, in *Davis v. Mississippi,* that a state may not introduce, in court, fingerprint evidence obtained during an illegal detention. In its 6-2 decision, the court suggested, however, that it would approve statutes authorizing the taking of fingerprints of suspects for whom there was no probable cause to arrest, provided that such detentions were authorized by a magistrate. The case involved John Davis, then 14, a black youth found guilty of rape on the basis of fingerprints taken during mass, "dragnet" arrests.

Mandatory Blood Tests Valid

In a 5-4 decision the Supreme Court held June 20, 1966, in *Schmerber v. California,* that no 5th Amendment right was violated when the police ordered a blood sample taken over the objections of a person suspected of drunk driving. The court hinted, however, that it would have withheld its approval had the blood sample been drawn by non-medical personnel or had it been taken in a non-medical environment, such as a police station. Since the defendant, Armando Schmerber, according to the court, was not "one of the few who on grounds of fear, concern for health or religious scruple" preferred some other means of testing, such as the "breathalyzer," which Schmerber refused to take, the court said that it need not decide whether such wishes would have to be respected.

Schmerber had argued that the compulsory blood analysis violated his 5th Amendment right not to testify against himself and his 4th Amendment right not to be subject to unreasonable searches and seizures. The court held, however, that the 5th

Amendment banned compulsory "communications" and "testimony" but that it did not apply to efforts to obtain "physical evidence," as for example, when a suspect is compelled to submit "to fingerprinting, photography or measurements, to write or speak for identification, to appear in court, to stand, to assume a stance, to walk or to make a particular gesture."

Prior to conducting a search, the police are generally required, under the 4th Amendment, to obtain a search warrant from a magistrate based on a showing of probable cause. Since the percentage of alcohol in the blood begins to diminish shortly after drinking stops, the court said that a search warrant was not required as in other emergency situations. Justice William J. Brennan Jr. emphasized in his majority opinion that the decision was based wholly on the facts of the specific case. "The integrity of an individual's person is a cherished value of our society," he wrote. "That we today hold that the Constitution does not forbid the states minor intrusions into an individual's body under stingently limited conditions in no way indicates that it permits more substantial intrusions, or intrusions under other conditions."

In the major dissenting opinion, based on the 5th Amendment, Justice Hugo L. Black asserted that "to reach the conclusion that compelling a person to give his blood to help the state convict him is not equivalent to compelling him to be a witness against himself strikes me as quite an extraordinary feat." Justice Abe Fortas, in a short, separate dissent, said that the state "has no right to commit any kind of violence upon the person," and he asserted that "the extraction of blood, over protest, is an act of violence."

Abridgment of the *Schmerber v. California* decision (384 U.S. 757, June 20, 1966):

Justice Brennan delivering the opinion of the court:

Petitioner was convicted in Los Angeles Municipal Court of the criminal offense of driving an automobile while under the influence of intoxicating liquor. He had been arrested at a hospital while receiving treatment for injuries suffered in an accident involving the automobile that he had apparently been driving. At the direction of a police officer, a blood sample was then withdrawn from petitioner's body by a physician at the hospital. The chemical analysis of this sample revealed a percent by weight of alcohol in his blood at the time of the offense which indicated intoxication, and the report of this analysis was admitted in evidence at the trial. Petitioner objected to receipt of this evidence of the analysis on the ground that the blood had been withdrawn despite his refusal, on the advice of his counsel, to consent to the test. He contended that in that circumstance the withdrawal of the blood and the admission of the analysis in evidence denied him due process of law under the 14th Amendment, as well as specific guarantees of the Bill of Rights secured against the states by that amendment: his privilege against self-incrimination under the 5th Amendment; his right to counsel under the 6th Amendment; and his right not to be subjected to unreasonable searches and seizures in violation of the 4th Amendment. The Appellate Department of the California Superior Court rejected these contentions and affirmed the conviction....

Breithaupt [v. Abram (1957)] was also a case in which police officers caused blood to be withdrawn from the driver of an automobile involved in an accident and in which there was ample justification for the officer's conclusion that the driver was under the influence of alcohol. There, as here, the extraction was made by a physician in a simple, medically acceptable manner in a hospital environment. There, however, the driver was unconscious at the time the blood was withdrawn and hence had no opportunity to object to the procedure. We affirmed the conviction there resulting from the use of the test in evidence, holding that under such

circumstances the withdrawal did not offend "that 'sense of justice' of which we spoke in *Rochin v. California* [1952]...."
...*Breithaupt* thus requires the rejection of petitioner's due process argument, and nothing in the circumstances of this case or in supervening events persuades us that this aspect of *Breithaupt* should be overruled....

Breithaupt summarily rejected an argument that the withdrawal of blood and the admission of the analysis report involved in that state case violated the 5th Amendment privilege of any person not to "be compelled in any criminal case to be a witness against himself," citing *Twining v. New Jersey* [1908].... But that case, holding that the protections of the 14th Amendment do not embrace this 5th Amendment privilege, has been succeeded by *Malloy v. Hogan* [1964].... We there held that "[t]he 14th Amendment secures against state invasion the same privilege that the 5th Amendment guarantees against federal infringement—the right of a person to remain silent unless he chooses to speak in the unfettered exercise of his own will, and to suffer no penalty...for such silence." We therefore must now decide whether the withdrawal of the blood and admission in evidence of the analysis involved in this case violated petitioner's privilege. We hold that the privilege protects an accused only from being compelled to testify against himself, or otherwise provide the state with evidence of a testimonial or communicative nature, and that the withdrawal of blood and use of the analysis in question in this case did not involve compulsion to these ends....

It is clear that the protection of the privilege reaches an accused's communications, whatever form they might take, and the compulsion of responses which are also communications, for example, compliance with a subpoena to produce one's papers. *Boyd v. United States* [1892].... On the other hand, both federal and state courts have usually held that it offers no protection against compulsion to submit to fingerprinting, photographing or measurements, to write or speak for identification, to appear in court, to stand, to assume a stance, to walk, or to make a particular gesture. The distinction which has emerged ... is that the privilege is a bar against compelling "communications" or "testimony," but that compulsion which makes a suspect or accused the source of "real or physical evidence" does not violate it.

Although we agree that this distinction is a helpful framework for analysis, we are not to be understood to agree with past applications in all instances. There will be many cases in which such a distinction is not readily drawn. Some tests seemingly directed to obtain "physical evidence," for example, lie detector tests measuring changes in body function during interrogation, may actually be directed to eliciting responses which are essentially testimonial. To compel a person to submit to testing in which an effort will be made to determine his guilt or innocence on the basis of physiological responses, whether willed or not, is to evoke the spirit and history of the 5th Amendment. Such situations call to mind the principle that the protection of the privilege "is as broad as the mischief against which it seeks to guard." *Counselman v. Hitchcock* [1892]. . . .

In the present case, however, no such problem of application is presented. Not even a shadow of testimonial compulsion upon or enforced communication by the accused was involved. . . . Petitioner's testimonial capacities were in no way implicated; indeed, his participation, except as a donor, was irrelevant to the results of the test, which depend on chemical analysis and on that alone. Since the blood test evidence, although an incriminating product of compulsion, was neither petitioner's testimony nor evidence relating to some communicative act or writing by the petitioner, it was not inadmissible on privilege grounds. . . .

This conclusion also answers petitioner's claim that in compelling him to submit to the test in face of the fact that his objection was made on the advice of counsel, he was denied his 6th Amendment right to the assistance of counsel. Since petitioner was not entitled to assert the privilege, he has no greater right because counsel erroneously advised him that he could assert it. . . .

. . . In *Breithaupt,* as here, it was also contended that the chemical analysis should be excluded from evidence as the product of an unlawful search and seizure in violation of the 4th and 14th Amendments. The court did not decide whether the extraction of blood in that case was unlawful but rejected the claim on the basis of *Wolf v. Colorado* [1949]. . . . That case had held that the Constitution did not require, in state prosecutions for state crimes, the exclusion of evidence obtained in violation of the 4th Amendment's provisions. We have since

overruled *Wolf* in that respect, holding in *Mapp v. Ohio* ... that
the exclusionary rule adopted for federal prosecutions in *Weeks
v. United States* [1914]... must also be applied in criminal
prosecutions in state courts. The question is squarely presented
therefore, whether the chemical analysis introduced in evidence
in this case should have been excluded as the product of an
unconstitutional search and seizure....

Although the facts which established probable cause to
arrest in this case also suggested the required relevance and
likely success of a test of petitioner's blood for alcohol, the
question remains whether the arresting officer was permitted to
draw these inferences himself, or was required instead to
procure a warrant before proceeding with the test. Search warrants are ordinarily required for searches of dwellings, and,
absent an emergency, no less could be required where intrusions
into the human body are concerned. The requirement that a
warrant be obtained is a requirement that the inferences to
support the search "be drawn by a neutral and detached magistrate instead of being judged by the officer engaged in the
often competitive enterprise of ferreting out crime." *Johnson v.
United States* [1943].... The importance of informed, detached
and deliberate determinations of the issue whether or not to
invade another's body in search of evidence of guilt is
indisputable and great.

The officer in the present case, however, might reasonably
have believed that he was confronted with an emergency, in
which the delay necessary to obtain a warrant, under the
circumstances, threatened "the destruction of evidence,"
Preston v. United States [1964].... We are told that the
percentage of alcohol in the blood begins to diminish shortly
after drinking stops, as the body functions to eliminate it from
the system. Particularly in a case such as this, where time had
to be taken to bring the accused to a hospital and to investigate
the scene of the accident, there was no time to seek out a
magistrate and secure a warrant. Given these special facts, we
conclude that the attempt to secure evidence of blood-alcohol
content in this case was an appropriate incident to petitioner's
arrest.

Similarly, we are satisfied that the test chosen to measure
petitioner's blood-alcohol level was a reasonable one.
Extraction of blood samples for testing is a highly effective

means of determining the degree to which a person is under the influence of alcohol....

Finally, the record shows that the test was performed in a reasonable manner. Petitioner's blood was taken by a physician in a hospital environment according to accepted medical practices. We are thus not presented with the serious questions which would arise if a search involving use of medical technique, even of the most rudimentary sort, were made by other than medical personnel or in other than a medical environment—for example, if it were administered by police in the privacy of the stationhouse. To tolerate searches under these conditions might be to invite an unjustified element of personal risk of infection and pain.

We thus conclude that the present record shows no violation of petitioner's right under the 4th and 14th Amendments to be free of unreasonable searches and seizures. It bears repeating, however, that we reach this judgment only on the facts of the present record. The integrity of an individual's person is a cherished value of our society. That we today hold that the Constitution does not forbid the states minor intrusions into an individual's body under stringently limited conditions in no way indicates that it permits more substantial intrusions, or intrusions under other conditions.

Chief Justice Warren, dissenting, reiterated his dissenting opinion in *Breithaupt v. Abram.*

Justice Black, whom Douglas joined, dissenting:

I would reverse petitioner's conviction. I agree with the court that the 14th Amendment made applicable to the states the 5th Amendment's provision that "No person ... shall be compelled in any criminal case to be a witness against himself...." But I disagree with the court's holding that California did not violate petitioner's constitutional right against self-incrimination when it compelled him, against his will, to allow a doctor to puncture his blood vessels in order to extract a sample of blood and analyze it for alcoholic content, and then used that analysis as evidence to convict petitioner of a crime.

The court admits that "the state compelled [petitioner] to submit to an attempt to discover evidence [in his blood] that might be [and was] used to prosecute him for a criminal offense." To reach the conclusion that compelling a person to give his blood to help the state convict him is not equivalent to compelling him to be a witness against himself strikes me as quite an extraordinary feat. The court, however, overcomes what had seemed to me to be an insuperable obstacle to its conclusion by holding that "... the privilege protects an accused only from being compelled to testify against himself, or otherwise provide the state with evidence of a testimonial or communicative nature, and that the withdrawal of blood and use of the analysis in question in this case did not involve compulsion to these ends."... I cannot agree that this distinction and reasoning of the court justify denying petitioner his Bill of Rights' guarantee that he must not be compelled to be a witness against himself....

Justice Fortas dissenting:

I would reverse. In my view, petitioner's privilege against self-incrimination applies. I would add that, under the due process clause, the state, in its role as prosecutor, has no right to extract blood from an accused or anyone else, over his protest. As prosecutor, the state has no right to commit any kind of violence upon the person, or to utilize the results of such a tort, and the extraction of blood, over protest, is an act of violence....

'Mere Evidence' Rule Discarded

In *Warden v. Hayden,* the Supreme Court May 29, 1967 overturned the so-called "mere evidence" rule established by the court in 1892. The mere evidence rule had limited searches and seizures under the 4th Amendment to contraband plus the instruments and fruits of a crime. Thus, the police were not permitted to search for strictly evidentiary material such as the bloody shirt worn by the perpetrator of a crime. Nor could they search and seize a diary.

Telford Taylor gave this illustration of the mere evidence rule as it existed prior to *Warden v.*

Hayden: Bluebeard's wives have disappeared one after another. Despite their suspicions, the authorities have no evidence to link Bluebeard to their deaths. Then Bluebeard's latest wife finds a diary in which Bluebeard has recorded his slayings of her predecessors and the location in his home of the ax with which he had killed them. Hearing Bluebeard approach, the wife returns the diary to its hiding place. She goes to the police at the first opportunity. Under the mere evidence rule, the police could get a search warrant for the ax, an instrumentality of the crime, but not for the diary, which is "mere evidence." If the police were to arrest Bluebeard with the diary on his person it could then be seized, but they could not search his house for it.*

Justice Brennan, speaking for the majority in *Warden,* said that the distinction between "mere evidence" and the fruits or instruments of a crime and contraband was "wholly irrational." He noted, however, that *Warden,* which involved the seizure of some clothing, did not require the court to consider whether "testimonial" or "communicative" items, such as a diary or letters, could be seized or whether their use as "mere evidence" violated the 5th Amendment's ban on self-incrimination.

Justice Douglas, the lone dissenter, said that a "mere evidence" search of personal effects, including clothing, constituted an unreasonable search within the meaning of the 4th Amendment.

Abridgment of the *Warden v. Hayden* decision (387 U.S. 294, May 29, 1967):

Justice Brennan delivering the opinion of the court:

---

*Two Studies in Constitutional Interpretation (Ohio State University Press, 1969).

We review in this case the validity of the proposition that there is under the 4th Amendment a "distinction between merely evidentiary materials, on the one hand, which may not be seized either under the authority of a search warrant or during the course of a search incident to arrest, and on the other hand, those objects which may validly be seized including the instrumentalities and means by which a crime is committed, the fruits of crime such as stolen property, weapons by which escape of the person arrested might be effected, and property the possession of which is a crime."

A Maryland court sitting without a jury convicted respondent of armed robbery. Items of his clothing, a cap, jacket, and trousers, among other things, were seized during a search of his home, and were admitted in evidence without objection....

About 8 a.m. on Mar. 17, 1962, an armed robber entered the business premises of the Diamond Cab Co. in Baltimore, Md. He took some $363 and ran. 2 cab drivers in the vicinity, attracted by shouts of "Holdup," followed the man to 2111 Cocoa Lane. One driver notified the company dispatcher by radio that the man was a Negro about 5'8" tall, wearing a light cap and dark jacket, and that he had entered the house on Cocoa Lane. The dispatcher relayed the information to police.... Within minutes, police arrived at the house.... An officer knocked and announced their presence. Mrs. Hayden answered, and the officers told her they believed that a robber had entered the house and asked to search the house. She offered no objection.

The officers spread out through the first and 2d floors and the cellar in search of the robber. Hayden was found in an upstairs bedroom feigning sleep. He was arrested when the officers on the first floor and in the cellar reported that no other man was in the house. Meanwhile an officer was attracted to an adjoining bathroom by the noise of running water and discovered a shotgun and a pistol in a flush tank; another officer who, according to the District Court, "was searching the cellar for a man or the money," found a jacket and trousers of the type the fleeing man was said to have worn in a washing machine. A clip of ammunition for the pistol and a cap were found under the mattress of Hayden's bed, and ammunition for the shotgun was found in a bureau drawer in Hayden's room. All these items of evidence were introduced against respondent at his trial. . . .

We come, then, to the question whether, even though the search was lawful, the Court of Appeals was correct in holding that the seizure and introduction of the items of clothing violated the 4th Amendment because they are "mere evidence." The distinction made by some of our cases between seizure of items of evidential value only and seizure of instrumentalities, fruits, or contraband has been criticized by courts and commentators. The Court of Appeals, however, felt "obligated to adhere to it." . . . We today reject the distinction as based on premises no longer accepted as rules governing the application of the 4th Amendment. . . .

Nothing in the language of the 4th Amendment supports the distinction between "mere evidence" and instrumentalities, fruits of crime or contraband. On its face, the provision assures the "right of the people to be secure in their persons, houses, papers, and effects . . . ," without regard to the use to which any of these things are applied. This "right of the people" is certainly unrelated to the "mere evidence" limitation. Privacy is disturbed no more by a search directed to a purely evidentiary object than it is by a search directed to an instrumentality, fruit or contraband. A magistrate can intervene in both situations, and the requirements of probable cause and specificity can be preserved intact. . . .

The items of clothing involved in this case are not "testimonial" or "communicative" in nature, and their introduction therefore did not compel respondent to become a witness against himself in violation of the 5th Amendment. . . .

Justice Fortas, whom Chief Justice Warren joined, concurring:

While I agree that the 4th Amendment should not be held to require exclusion from evidence of the clothing as well as the weapons and ammunition found by the officers during the search, I cannot join in the majority's broad—and in my judgment, totally unnecessary—repudiation of the so-called "mere evidence" rule. . . .

In the present case, the articles of clothing admitted into evidence are not within any of the traditional categories which describe what materials may be seized, either with or without a warrant. The restrictiveness of these categories has been subjected to telling criticism, and although I believe that we should approach expansion of these categories with the diffidence which their imposing provenance commands, I agree that the use of identifying clothing worn in the commission of a crime and seized during "hot pursuit" is within the spirit and intendment of the "hot pursuit" exception to the search-warrant requirement. That is because the clothing is pertinent to identification of the person hotly pursued as being, in fact, the person whose pursuit was justified by connection with the crime. I would frankly place the ruling on that basis. I would not drive an enormous and dangerous hole in the 4th Amendment to accommodate a specific and, I think, reasonable exception....

Justice Douglas dissenting:

The right of privacy protected by the 4th Amendment relates in part of course to the precincts of the home or the office. But it does not make them sanctuaries where the law can never reach.... We have no such sanctuaries here. A policeman in "hot pursuit" or an officer with a search warrant can enter any house, any room, any building, any office. The privacy of those *places* is of course protected against invasion except in limited situations. The full privacy protected by the 4th Amendment is, however, reached when we come to books, pamphlets, papers, letters, documents and other personal effects. Unless they are contraband or instruments of the crime, they may not be reached by any warrant nor may they be lawfully seized by the police who are in "hot pursuit." By reason of the 4th Amendment, the police may not rummage around among these personal effects, no matter how formally perfect their authority may appear to be. They may not seize them. If they do, those articles may not be used in evidence. Any invasion whatsoever of those personal effects is "unreasonable" within the meaning of the 4th Amendment....

The constitutional philosophy is, I think, clear. The personal effects and possessions of the individual (all contraband and the like excepted) are sacrosanct from prying eyes, from the long arm of the law, from any rummaging by police. Privacy involves the choice of the individual to disclose or to reveal what he believes, what he thinks, what he possesses. The article may be a nondescript work of art, a manuscript of a book, a personal account book, a diary, invoices, personal clothing, jewelry, or whatnot. Those who wrote the Bill of Rights believed that every individual needs both to communicate with others and to keep his affairs to himself. That dual aspect of privacy means that the individual should have the freedom to select for himself the time and circumstances when he will share his secrets with others and decide the extent of that sharing.... The Framers, who were as knowledgeable as we, knew what police surveillance meant and how the practice of rummaging through one's personal effects could destroy freedom.

It was in that tradition that we held in *Griswold v. Connecticut* [1965]... that lawmakers could not, as respects husband and wife at least, make the use of contraceptives a crime....

This right of privacy, sustained in *Griswold,* is kin to the right of privacy created by the 4th Amendment. That there is a zone that no police can enter—whether in "hot pursuit" or armed with a meticulously proper warrant—has been emphasized by *Boyd* and by *Gouled.* They have been consistently and continuously approved. I would adhere to them and leave with the individual the choice of opening his private effects (apart from contraband and the like) to the police or keeping their contents a secret and their integrity inviolate. The existence of that choice is the very essence of the right of privacy. Without it the 4th Amendment and the 5th are ready instruments for the police state that the Framers sought to avoid.

Wiretapping & Bugging

The Supreme Court ruled June 17, 1968, in *Lee v. Florida,* that evidence obtained from a telephone wiretap could not be used in state trials. A similar prohibition for federal trials had been in effect since 1937.

The underlying constitutional question was whether the 4th Amendment applied to "searches" conducted by electronic means such as wiretapping and eavesdropping. In 1928, in *Olmstead v. United States,* the court had held that the language of the 4th Amendment did not extend to electronic searches. Justice Louis Brandeis issued a famous dissent. "Time works changes, brings into existence new conditions and new purposes," he said. "Therefore, a principle to be vital must be capable of wider application than the mischief which gave it birth."

6 years after *Olmstead,* Congress passed the Federal Communications Act of 1934, establishing the Federal Communications Commission. Section 605 of this law held that "no person not being authorized by the sender shall intercept any communication and divulge...the existence, contents, substance, purport, effect, or meaning of such intercepted communication to any person." In 1937, in *Nardone v. United States,* the Supreme Court interpreted Section 605 to cover wiretapping; it ruled that the federal government could not introduce into a federal trial information obtained from a wiretap. In a 2d *Nardone* decision, in 1939, the court held inadmissible in federal trials information secured from leads obtained from wiretaps.

The federal government took the position, however, that Section 605 did not prohibit wiretapping *per se* but only the "divulgence" of information obtained from wiretapping. The Department of Justice and the FBI contended also that they were empowered to tap wires in matters relating to national security. This view was assailed by some on the ground that there was no constitutional basis for such actions. The states, meanwhile, continued not only to tap wires but to divulge the contents of wiretaps in state trials despite Section 605, and the

Supreme Court noted in *Lee v. Florida* that "research has failed to uncover a single reported prosecution of a law enforcement officer for violation of Section 605 since the statute was enacted."

In *Schwartz v. Texas* the Supreme Court had held in 1952 that even though "the introduction of the intercepted communications would itself be a violation" of federal law, states were not required to reject such evidence. Since state courts were free to accept evidence obtained in violation of the Constitution *(Wolf v. Colorado,* 1949), the court reasoned that the states should not be required to reject evidence obtained and divulged in violation of Section 605.

The *Mapp* decision (1961), forbidding the states to use evidence obtained in violation of the 4th Amendment, led to *Lee v. Florida,* a case in which the court applied the exclusionary rule to evidence obtained in violation of Section 605. Justice Potter Stewart, writing for the majority, said that the court was forced to conclude as it did in *Mapp* "that nothing short of mandatory exclusion will compel respect for the federal law." The 3 dissenters, Justices Hugo L. Black, John Marshall Harlan and Byron R. White, asserted that evidence obtained in violation of Section 605 should be admitted in state trials until Congress forbade this. *Lee v. Florida* was announced 2 days before the 1968 Omnibus Crime Control & Safe Streets Act of 1968 and its electronic-surveillance provisions were signed into law by Pres. Lyndon B. Johnson June 15, 1968.

The term "bugging" refers to electronic surveillance techniques other than wiretapping. Prior to the passage of the 1968 Omnibus Crime Control & Safe Streets Act, which authorized wiretapping and bugging under specified circumstances, the precise legal status of bugging was murky. In 1928, in *Olmstead v. United States,* the Supreme Court held that the 4th Amendment was applicable only when electronic eavesdropping was accompanied by a "trespass." Thus, in *Goldman v. United States,* the court in 1942 upheld the use by federal agents of a dictaphone that had been placed *against* the wall of a private office. In 1961, in *Silverman v. United States,* the court held that listening to conversations by means of a "spike-mike" inserted *into* the outside wall of a house amounted to an illegal search and seizure under the 4th Amendment.   Restrictions placed on wiretaps by Section 305 of the 1934 Federal Communications Act were not relevant in such cases since that law applied only to the over-hearing of phone, telegraph and radiotelegraph conversations.

A New York statute permitting judicially approved electronic eavesdropping was invalidated by a 5-4 Supreme Court decision June 12, 1967 in the case of *Berger v. New York.* In the view of many observers, the decision overruled *Olmstead* and the *Goldman-Silverman* distinction.

Writing for the majority, Justice Tom Clark declared the New York law a violation of the 4th Amendment. Under the 4th Amendment no search warrant "shall issue, but upon probable cause, supported by Oath, or affirmation, and particularly describing the place to be searched, and persons or things to be seized." The New York law was held defective because of its failure to require warrants to include "particularization." The New York law, Clark said, was unconstitutional since "it lays down no requirement for particularity in the warrant as to what specific crime has been or is being committed, nor 'the place to be searched,' or 'the persons or things to be seized' as specifically required by the 4th Amendment." According to Clark, these safeguards are especially important in cases of eavesdropping since, "by its very nature, eavesdropping involves an intrusion on privacy that is broad in scope."

The majority also considered the statute defective for permitting eavesdropping for a 2-month period on the basis of a single showing of probable cause. According to Clark, during such a period "the conversations of any and all persons coming into the area covered by the device will be seized indiscriminately and without regard to their connection with the crime under investigation." A 3d reason for the law being declared unconstitutional was its failure to provide for the automatic termination of the eavesdropping once the conversation sought was "seized." The majority also contended that the law was unconstitutional for its failure to permit bugging "without any showing of exigent circumstances." "In short," Clark asserted, "the statute's blanket grant of permission to eavesdrop is without adequate judicial supervision or protective procedures."

Clark noted that the majority of law enforcement officials were reported by the President's Commission on Law Enforcement & Justice to believe that electronic eavesdropping was an important technique of law enforcement, especially in the area of organized crime. According to Clark, however, "we have found no empirical statistics on the use of electronic devices (bugging) in the fight against organized crime. Indeed, there are even figures which indicate to the contrary." "In any event," Clark asserted, "we cannot forgive the requirements of the 4th Amendment in the name of law enforcement."

Justice William O. Douglas, in a concurring opinion, reiterated his long standing opposition to electronic eavesdropping. According to Douglas, "if a statute were to authorize placing a policeman in every home or office where it was shown that there was probable cause to believe that evidence of crime would be obtained, there is little doubt that it would be struck down as a bald invasion of privacy, far worse than the general warrants prohibited by the 4th Amendment. I can see no difference between such a statute and one authorizing electronic surveillance, which, in effect, places an invisible policeman in the home."

Justice Hugo L. Black, in the chief dissenting opinion, argued that the 4th Amendment does not prohibit the use in court of evidence seized in an unreasonable manner and that had the framers intended such a result, "they woluld have used plain appropriate language to do so." The language of the 4th Amendment, according to Black, "only bans searches and seizures of 'persons, houses, papers, and effects.'" "It simply requires an imaginative transformation of the English language to say that conversations can be searched and seized," he said.

Abridgment of the *Berger v. New York* decision (388 U.S. 41, June 12, 1967):

Justice Clark delivering the opinion of the court:

...[Ralph] Berger...was convicted on 2 counts of conspiracy to bribe the chairman of the New York State Liquor Authority. The case arose out of the complaint of one Ralph Pansini to the district attorney's office that agents of the State Liquor Authority had entered his bar and grill and without¹ cause seized his books and records. Pansini asserted that the raid was in reprisal for his failure to pay a bribe for a liquor license. Numerous complaints had been filed with the district attorney's office charging the payment of bribes by applicants for liquor licenses. On the direction of that office, Pansini, while equipped with a "minifon" recording device, interviewed an employe of the Authority. The employe advised Pansini that the price for a license was $10,000 and suggested that he contact attorney Harry Neyer. Neyer subsequently told Pansini that he worked with the Authority employe before and that the latter was aware of the going rate on liquor licenses downtown.

On the basis of this evidence an eavesdrop order was obtained from a Justice of the State Supreme Court, as provided by [N.Y. Code Criminal Procedure] § 813-a. The order permitted the installation, for a period of 60 days, of a recording device in Neyer's office. On the basis of leads obtained from this eavesdrop a 2d order permitting the installation, for a like period, of a recording device in the office of one Harry Steinman was obtained. After some 2 weeks of eavesdropping a conspiracy was uncovered involving the issuance of liquor licenses for the Playboy and Tenement Clubs, both of New York City. Petitioner was indicted as "a go-between" for the principal conspirators.... Relevant portions of the recordings were received in evidence at the trial and were played to the jury, all over the objection of the petitioner. The parties have stipulated that the district attorney "had no information upon which to proceed to present a case to the grand jury, or on the basis of which to prosecute" the petitioner except by the use of the eavesdrop evidence....

The 4th Amendment commands that a warrant issue not only upon probable cause supported by oath or affirmation, but also "particularly describing the place to be searched, and the persons or things to be seized." New York's statute lacks this particularization. It merely says that a warrant may issue on reasonable ground to believe that evidence of crime may be obtained by the eavesdrop. It lays down no requirement for particularity in the warrant as to what specific crime has been or is being committed, nor "the place to be searched," or "the persons or things to be seized" as specifically required by the 4th Amendment. The need for particularity and evidence of reliability in the showing required when judicial authorization

of a search is sought is especially great in the case of eavesdropping. By its very nature eavesdropping involves an intrusion on privacy that is broad in scope. As was said in *Osborn v.
United States*... (1966), the "indiscriminate use of such devices
in law enforcement raises grave constitutional questions under
the 4th and 5th Amendments," and imposes "a heavier responsibility on this court in its supervision of the fairness of
procedures...."...

We believe the statute here is equally offensive.
First,... eavesdropping is authorized without requiring belief
that any particular offense has been or is being committed; nor
that the "property" sought, the conversations, be particularly
described. The purpose of the probable-cause requirement of the
4th Amendment to keep the state out of constitutionally protected areas until it has reason to believe that a specific crime
has been or is being committed is thereby wholly aborted. Likewise, the statute's failure to describe with particularity the
conversations sought gives the officer a roving commission to
"seize" any and all conversations. It is true that the statute
requires the naming of "the person or persons whose
communications, conversations or discussions are to be
overheard or recorded...." But this does no more than identify
the person whose constitutionally protected area is to be invaded rather than "particularly describing" the communications, conversations, or discussions to be seized. As with general
warrants this leaves too much to the discretion of the officer
executing the order. Secondly, authorization of eavesdropping
for a 2-month period is the equivalent of a series of intrusions,
searches and seizures pursuant to a single showing of probable
cause. Prompt execution is also avoided. During such a long
and continuous (24 hours a day) period the conversations of any
and all persons coming into the area covered by the device will
be seized indiscriminately and without regard to their connection with the crime under investigation. Moreover, the statute
permits, and there were authorized here, extensions of the
original 2-month period—presumably for 2 months each—on a
mere showing that such extension is "in the public interest."
Apparently the original grounds on which the eavesdrop order
was initially issued also form the basis of the renewal. This we
believe insufficient without a showing of present probable cause
for the continuance of the eavesdrop. 3d, the statute places no

termination date on the eavesdrop once the conversation sought is seized. This is left entirely in the discretion of the officer. Finally, the statute's procedure, necessarily because its success depends on secrecy, has no requirement for notice as do conventional warrants, nor does it overcome this defect by requiring some showing of special facts. On the contrary, it permits unconsented entry without any showing of exigent circumstances. Such a showing of exigency, in order to avoid notice, would appear more important in eavesdropping, with its inherent dangers, than that required when conventional procedures of search and seizure are utilized. Nor does the statute provide for a return on the warrant thereby leaving full discretion in the officer as to the use of seized conversations of innocent as well as guilty parties. In short, the statute's blanket grant of permission to eavesdrop is without adequate judicial supervision or protective procedures....

It is said with fervor that electronic eavesdropping is a most important technique of law enforcement and that outlawing it will severely cripple crime detection. The monumental report of the President's Commission on Law Enforcement & Administration of Justice... informs us that the majority of law enforcement officials say that this is especially true in the detection of organized crime. As the commission reports, there can be no question about the serious proportions of professional criminal activity in this country. However, we have found no empirical statistics on the use of electronic devices (bugging) in the fight against organized crime. Indeed, there are even figures available in the wiretap category which indicate to the contrary.... As the commission points out, "[w]iretapping was the mainstay of the New York attack against organized crime until federal court decisions intervened. Recently, chief reliance in some offices has been placed on bugging, where the information is to be used in court. Law enforcement officials believe that the successes achieved in some parts of the state are attributable primarily to a combination of dedicated and competent personnel and adequate legal tools; and that the failure to do more in New York has resulted primarily from the failure to commit additional resources of time and men," rather than electronic devices....

... The President's commission also emphasizes... the need for wiretapping in the investigation of organized crime because of the telephone's "relatively free use" by those engaged in the business and the difficulty of infiltrating their organizations.... The Congress, though long importuned, has not amended the 1934 Act to permit it.

We are also advised by the solicitor general of the United States that the federal government has abandoned the use of electronic eavesdropping for "prosecutorial purposes."... Despite these actions of the federal government there has been no failure of law enforcement in that field....

...It is not asking too much that officers be required to comply with the basic command of the 4th Amendment before the innermost secrets of one's home or office are invaded. Few threats to liberty exist which are greater than that posed by the use of eavesdropping devices. Some may claim that without the use of such devices crime detection in certain areas may suffer some delays since eavesdropping is quicker, easier and more certain. However, techniques and practices may well be developed that will operate just as speedily and certainly—and what is more important—without attending illegality.

It is said that neither a warrant nor a statute authorizing eavesdropping can be drawn so as to meet the 4th Amendment's requirements. If that be true then the "fruits" of eavesdropping devices are barred under the Amendment. On the other hand this court has in the past, under specific conditions and circumstances, sustained the use of eavesdropping devices. See *Goldman v. United States* [1942]...; *On Lee v. United States* [1952]...; *Lopez v. United States*...; and *Osborn v. United States* [1966].... In the latter case the eavesdropping device was permitted where the "commission of a specific offense" was charged, its use was "under the most precise and discriminate circumstances" and the effective administration of justice in a federal court was at stake. The states are under no greater restrictions. The 4th Amendment does not make the "precincts of the home or the office...sanctuaries where the law can never reach." Douglas...dissenting in *Warden, Maryland Penitentiary v. Hayden* [1967]..., but it does prescribe a constitutional standard that must be met before official invasion is permissible. Our concern with the statute here is whether its language permits a trespassory invasion of the home, by general warrant, contrary to the command of the 4th Amendment. As it is written, we believe that it does.

Justice Douglas concurring:

I join the opinion of the court because at long last it over-rules *sub silentio Olmstead v. United States* [1928]... and its offspring and brings wiretapping and other electronic eaves-dropping fully within the purview of the 4th Amendment. I also join the opinion because it condemns electronic surveillance, for its similarity to the general warrants out of which our Revolu-tion sprang and allows a discreet surveillance only on a showing of "probable cause."...

Yet there persists my overriding objection to electronic surveillance, *viz.,* that it is a search for "mere evidence" which, as I have maintained on other occasions *(Osborn v. United States* [1966],... is a violation of the 4th and 5th Amendments, no matter the nicety and precision with which a warrant may be drawn....

A discreet selective wiretap or electronic "bugging" is of course not rummaging around, collecting everything in the particular time and space zone. But even though it is limited in time, it is the greatest of all invasions of privacy. It places a government agent in the bedroom, in the business conference, in the social hour, in the lawyer's office—everywhere and any-where a "bug" can be placed....

The traditional wiretap or electronic eavesdropping device constitutes a dragnet, sweeping in all conversations within its scope—without regard to the participants or the nature of the conversations. It intrudes upon the privacy of those not even suspected of crime and intercepts the most intimate of conver-sations....

It is, of course, possible for a statute to provide that wire-tap or electronic eavesdrop evidence is admissible only in a prosecution for the crime to which the showing of probable cause related.... But such a limitation would not alter the fact that the order authorizes a general search. Whether or not the evidence obtained is used at a trial for another crime, the privacy of the individual has been infringed by the interception of all of his conversations. And, even though the information is not introduced as evidence, it can and probably will be used as leads and background information. Again, a statute could provide that evidence developed from eavesdrop information could not be used at trial.... But, under a regime of total surveillance, where a multitude of conversations are recorded, it would be very difficult to show which aspects of the information had been used as investigative information.

As my brother White says in his dissent, this same vice inheres in any search for tangible evidence such as invoices, letters, diaries and the like. "In searching for seizable matters, the police must necessarily see or hear, and comprehend, items which do not relate to the purpose of the search." That is precisely why the 4th Amendment made any such rummaging around unconstitutional, even though supported by a formally adequate warrant....

With all respect, my brother Black misses the point of the 4th Amendment. It does not make every search constitutional provided there is a warrant that is technically adequate. The history of the 4th Amendment ... makes it plain that any search in the precincts of the home for personal items that are lawfully possessed and not articles of a crime is "unreasonable." That is the essence of the "mere evidence" rule that long obtained until overruled by *Hayden.*

The words that a man says consciously on a radio are public property. But I do not see how government using surreptitious methods can put a person on the radio and use his words to convict him. Under our regime a man stands mute if he chooses, or talks if he chooses. The test is whether he acts voluntarily. That is the essence of the face of privacy protected by the "mere evidence" rule. For the 4th Amendment and the 5th come into play when the accused is "the unwilling source of the evidence" *(Gouled v. United States* [1921]...), there being no difference "whether he be obliged to supply evidence against himself or whether such evidence be obtained by an illegal search of his premises and seizure of his private papers."...

That is the essence of my dissent in *Hayden.* In short, I do not see how any electronic surveillance that collects evidence or provides leads to evidence is or can be constitutional under the 4th and 5th Amendments. We could amend the Constitution and so provide—a step that would take us closer to the ideological group we profess to despise. Until the amending process ushers us into that kind of totalitarian regime, I would adhere to the protection of privacy which the 4th Amendment ... was designed to afford the individual. And unlike my brother Black, I would adhere to *Mapp v. Ohio* ... and apply the exclusionary rule in state as well as federal trials—a rule fashioned out of the 4th Amendment and constituting a high constitutional barricade against the intrusion of Big Brother into the lives of all of us.

Justice Stewart concurring in the result:

I fully agree with Mr. Justice Black, Mr. Justice Harlan, and Mr. Justice White that this New York law is entirely constitutional. In short, I think that "electronic eavesdropping, *as such* or as it is permitted by this statute, is not an unreasonable search and seizure." The statute contains many provisions more stringent than the 4th Amendment generally requires, as Mr. Justice Black has so forcefully pointed out. . . .

In order to hold this statute unconstitutional, therefore, we would have to either rewrite the statute or rewrite the Constitution. I can only conclude that the court today seems to have rewritten both.

The issue before us, as Mr. Justice White says, is "whether *this* search complied with 4th Amendment standards." For me that issue is an extremely close one in the circumstances of this case. It certainly cannot be resolved by incantation of ritual phrases like "general warrant." Its resolution involves "the unavoidable task in any search and seizure case: was the particular search and seizure reasonable or not?"

I would hold that the affidavits on which the judicial order issued in this case did not constitute a showing of probable cause adequate to justify the authorizing order. The need for particularity and evidence of reliability in the showing required when judicial authorization is sought for the kind of electronic eavesdropping involved in this case is especially great. The standard of reasonableness embodied in the 4th Amendment demands that the showing of justification match the degree of intrusion. By its very nature electronic eavesdropping for a 60-day period, even of a specified office, involves a broad invasion of a constitutionally protected area. Only the most precise and rigorous standard of probable cause should justify an intrusion of this sort. I think the affidavits presented to the judge who. authorized the electronic surveillance of the Steinman office failed to meet such a standard.

So far as the record shows, the only basis for the Steinman order consisted of 2 affidavits. One of them contained factual allegations supported only by bare, unexplained references to "evidence" in the district attorney's office and "evidence" obtained by the Neyer eavesdrop. No underlying facts were presented on the basis of which the judge could evaluate these general allegations. The 2d affidavit was no more than a statement of another assistant district attorney that he had read his associate's affidavit and was satisfied on that basis alone that proper grounds were presented for the issuance of an authorizing order.

This might be enough to satisfy the standards of the 4th Amendment for a conventional search or arrest.... But I think it was constitutionally insufficient to constitute probable cause to justify an intrusion of the scope and duration that was permitted in this case.

Accordingly, I would reverse the judgment.

Justice Black dissenting:

...The 5th Amendment's language forbids a court to hear evidence against a person that he has been compelled to give, without regard to reasonableness or anything else. Unlike [the]...5th Amendment provisions, the 4th Amendment relating to searches and seizures contains no...unequivocal commands. It provides: "The right of the people to be secure in their persons, houses, papers, and effects, against unreasonable searches and seizures, shall not be violated, and no Warrants shall issue, but upon probable cause, supported by Oath or affirmation, and particularly describing the place to be searched, and the persons or things to be seized."

Obviously, those who wrote this 4th Amendment knew from experience that searches and seizures were too valuable to law enforcement to prohibit them entirely, but also knew at the same time that while searches or seizures must not be stopped, they should be slowed down, and warrants should be issued only after studied caution. This accounts for use of the imprecise and flexible term, "unreasonable," the key word permeating this whole Amendment. Also it is noticeable that this Amendment contains no appropriate language, as does the 5th, to forbid the use and introduction of search and seizure evidence even though secured "unreasonably." Nor does this 4th Amendment attempt to describe with precision what was meant by its words, "probable cause"; nor by whom the "Oath or affirmation" should be taken; nor what it need contain. Although the Amendment does specifically say that the warrant should particularly describe "the place to be searched, and the persons or things to be seized," it does not impose any precise limits on the spatial or temporal extent of the search or the quantitative extent of the seizure. Thus this amendment, aimed against only "unreasonable" searches and seizures, seeks to guard against them by providing, as the court says, that a "neutral and detached authority be interposed between the police and the public, *Johnson v. United States* [1948].... And, as the court admits, the amendment itself provides no sanctions to enforce its standards of searches, seizures, and warrants. This was left for Congress to carry out if it chose to do so.

Had the framers of this amendment desired to prohibit the use in court of evidence secured by an unreasonable search or seizure, they would have used plain appropriate language to do so, just as they did in prohibiting the use of enforced self-incriminatory evidence in the 5th Amendment. Since the 4th Amendment contains no language forbidding the use of such evidence, I think there is no such constitutional rule. So I continue to believe that the exclusionary rule formulated to bar such evidence in the *Weeks* case [1914] is not rooted in the 4th Amendment but rests on the "supervisory power" of this court over the other federal courts.... For these reasons and others to be stated, I do not believe the 4th Amendment standing alone, even if applicable to electronic eavesdropping, commands exclusion of the overheard evidence in this case....

While the electronic eavesdropping here bears some analogy to the problems with which the 4th Amendment is concerned, I am by no means satisfied that the amendment controls the constitutionality of such eavesdropping. As pointed out, the amendment only bans searches and seizures of "persons, houses, papers and effects." This literal language imports tangible things, and it would require an expansion of the language used by the framers, in the interest of "privacy" or some equally vague judge-made goal, to hold that it applies to the spoken word. It simply requires an imaginative transformation of the English language to say that conversations can be searched and words seized. Referring to wiretapping, this court in *Olmstead v. United States* [1928],... refused to make that transformation.

Assuming, as the court holds, that the 4th Amendment applies to eavesdropping and that the evidence obtained by an eavesdrop which violates the 4th Amendment must be excluded in state courts, I disagree with the court's holding that the New York statute on its face fails to comport with the amendment. I also agree with my brother White that the statute as here applied did not violate any of petitioner's 4th Amendment rights ... and that he is not entitled to a reversal of his conviction merely because the statute might have been applied in some way that would not have accorded with the amendment. ...

As I see it, the differences between the court and me in this case rest on different basic beliefs as to our duty in interpreting the Constitution. This basic charter of our government was written in few words to define governmental powers generally on the one hand and to define governmental limitations on the other. I believe it is the court's duty to interpret these grants and limitations so as to carry out as nearly as possible the original intent of the framers. But I do not believe that it is our duty to go further than the framers did on the theory that the judges are charged with responsibility for keeping the Constitution "up to date." Of course, where the Constitution has stated a broad purpose to be accomplished under any circumstances, we must consider that modern science has made it necessary to use new means in accomplishing the framers' goal. A good illustration of this is the commerce clause which gives Congress power to regulate commerce between the states however it may be carried on, whether by ox wagons or jet planes. But the 4th Amendment gives no hint that it was designed to put an end to the age-old practice of using eavesdropping to combat crime. If changes in that amendment are necessary, due to contemporary human reaction to technological advances, I think those changes should be accomplished by amendments, as the Constitution itself provides. ...

Both the states and the national government are at present confronted with a crime problem that threatens the peace, order, and tranquility of the people. There are ... some constitutional commands that leave no room for doubt—certain procedures must be followed by courts regardless of how much more difficult they make it to convict and punish for crime. These commands we should enforce firmly and to the letter.

But my objection to what the court does today is the picking out of a broad general provision against unreasonable searches and seizures and the erecting out of it a constitutional obstacle against electronic eavesdropping that makes it impossible for lawmakers to overcome. Honest men may rightly differ on the potential dangers or benefits inherent in electronic eaves-dropping and wiretapping.... But that is the very reason that legislatures, like New York's, should be left free to pass laws about the subject, rather than be told that the Constitution forbids it on grounds no more forceful than the court has been able to muster in this case.

Justice White dissenting:

Today's majority does not, in so many words, hold that all wiretapping and eavesdropping are constitutionally impermis-sible. But by transparent indirection it achieves practically the same result by striking down the New York statute and im-posing a series of requirements for legalized electronic sur-veillance that will be almost impossible to satisfy.

In so doing, the court ignores or discounts the need for wiretapping authority and incredibly suggests that there has been no breakdown of federal law enforcement despite the unavailability of a federal statute legalizing electronic surveillance. The court thereby impliedly disagrees with the carefully documented reports of the Crime Commission which, contrary to the court's intimations, underline the serious proportions of professional criminal activity in this country, the failure of current national and state efforts to eliminate it, and the need for a statute permitting carefully controlled official use of electronic surveillance, particularly in dealing with organized crime and official corruption.... How the court can feel itself so much better qualified than the commission, which spent months on its study, to assess the needs of law enforcement is beyond my comprehension. We have only just decided that reasonableness of a search under the 4th Amend-ment must be determined by weighing the invasions of 4th Amendment interests which wiretapping and eavesdropping entail against the public need justifying such invasions. *Camara v. Municipal Court* [1967]...; *See v. City of Seattle* [1967].... In these terms, it would seem imperative that the court at least deal with facts of the real world. This the court utterly fails to do. In my view, its opinion is wholly unresponsive to the test of reasonableness under the 4th Amendment....

6 months after it had seemed to some observers that, in *Berger,* the Supreme Court had undercut the legitimate use of electronic eavesdropping, the court Dec. 18, 1967 appeared to invite state legislatures and Congress to enact eavesdropping legislation. The decision, in *Katz v. United States,* concerned the use of a listening and recording device that FBI agents had attached to the outside wall of a public phone booth used by Charles Katz, a bookmaker.

In seeking to avoid conflict with the 4th Amendment, as interpreted in *Olmstead,* FBI men had placed a listening device on the outside wall of the phone booth. In *Katz,* the court ruled, however, that *Olmstead* had been eroded by subsequent decisions to such an extent that it could no longer be considered controlling. Therefore, Justice Stewart said in the majority opinion, the fact that the bugging device "did not happen to penetrate the wall of the booth can have no constitutional significance." The government had also argued that a public phone booth was not a "constitutionally protected area." The court disagreed. "[T]he 4th Amendment protects people, not places," Stewart said. What an individual "seeks to preserve as private, even in an area accessible to the public, may be constitutionally protected," he held. "The government's activities ... violated the privacy upon which [Katz] justifiably relied."

The remaining issue thus was the constitutionality of the electronic bug. The FBI, in attempting to adhere to the 4th Amendment's requirement of probable cause, had not bugged the phone booth until it had established a strong probability that Katz was using the phone to conduct interstate gambling activities. In an effort to reconcile their activity with the 4th Amendment's ban on general warrants, the FBI agents took care to overhear only Katz' end of the conversations.

According to Stewart, "accepting this account of the government's actions as accurate, it is clear that this surveillance was so narrowly circumscribed that a duly authorized magistrate, properly notified of the need for such investigation, specifically informed of the basis on which it was to proceed, and clearly apprised of the precise intrusion it would entail, could constitutionally have authorized, with appropriate safeguards, the very limited search and seizure that the government asserts in fact took place."

Since there was no federal statute authorizing magistrates to issue warrants for eavesdropping, Stewart's statement was seen as a clear invitation for Congress to enact such a measure.

The court reversed Katz' conviction and $300 fine because of the lack of a warrant authorizing the particular electronic search.

In a footnote, Stewart left open the question of whether prior authorization by a magistrate was required in situations involving national security. In a separate concurring opinion, Justice White took issue with this footnote. "We should not require the warrant procedure and the magistrate's judgment if the President of the United States or his chief legal officer, the Attorney General, has considered the requirements of national security and authorized electronic surveillance as reasonable," he said.

The lone dissent in *Katz* was filed by Justice Black, who reiterated his view that electronic eavesdropping does not constitute a search under the 4th Amendment. Black, however, expressed approval of the result achieved in *Katz* wherein "what appeared to be insuperable obstacles" in *Berger* to the passage of constitutionally valid eavesdropping legislation were obviated.

Abridgment of the *Katz v. United States* decision (389 U.S. 347, Dec. 18, 1967):

Justice Stewart delivering the opinion of the court:

The petitioner was convicted in the District Court for the Southern District of California under an 8-count indictment charging him with transmitting wagering information by telephone from Los Angeles to Miami and Boston, in violation of a federal statute. At trial the government was permitted, over the petitioner's objection, to introduce evidence of the pe-titioner's end of telephone conversations, overheard by FBI agents who had attached an electronic listening and recording device to the outside of the public telephone booth from which he had placed his calls. In affirming his conviction, the Court of Appeals rejected the contention that the recordings had been obtained in violation of the 4th Amendment, because "[t]here was no physical entrance into the area occupied by [the peti-tioner]." We granted *certiorari* in order to consider the con-stitutional questions thus presented....

Because of the misleading way the issues have been formu-lated, the parties have attached great significance to the characterization of the telephone booth from which the petitioner placed his calls. The petitioner has strenuously argued that the booth was a "constitutionally protected area." The government has maintained with equal vigor that it was not. But this effort to decide whether or not a given "area," viewed in the abstract, is "constitutionally protected" deflects attention from the problem presented by this case. For the 4th Amendment protects people, not places. What a person knowingly exposes to the public, even in his own home or office, is not a subject of 4th Amendment protection.... What he seeks to preserve as private, even in an area accessible to the public, may be constitutionally protected....

The government stresses the fact that the telephone booth from which the petitioner made his calls was constructed partly of glass, so that he was as visible after he entered it as he would have been if he had remained outside. But what he sought to exclude when he entered the booth was not the intruding eye—it was the uninvited ear. He did not shed his right to do so simply because he made his calls from a place where he might be seen. No less than an individual in a business office, in a friend's apartment, or in a taxicab, a person in a telephone booth may rely upon the protection of the 4th Amendment....

The government contends, however, that the activities of its agents in this case should not be tested by 4th Amendment requirements, for the surveillance technique they employed involved no physical penetration of the telephone booth.... It is true that the absence of such penetration was at one time thought to foreclose further 4th Amendment inquiry, *Olmstead v. United States* [1928]...*Goldman v. United States* [1942]...for that amendment was thought to limit only searches and seizures of tangible property.... Thus, although a closely divided Court supposed in *Olmstead* that surveillance without any trespass and without the seizure of any material object fell outside the ambit of the Constitution, we have since departed from the narrow view on which that decision rested. Indeed, we have expressly held that the 4th Amendment governs not only the seizure of tangible items, but extends as well to the recording of oral statements, overheard without any "technical trespass under ... local property law." *Silverman v. United States,* [1961].... Once this much is acknowledged, and once it is recognized that the 4th Amendment protects people—and not simply "areas"—against unreasonable searches and seizures, it becomes clear that the reach of that amendment cannot turn upon the presence or absence of a physical intrusion into any given enclosure.

We conclude that the underpinnings of *Olmstead* and *Goldman* have been so eroded by our subsequent decisions that the "trespass" doctrine there enunciated can no longer be regarded as controlling. The government's activities in electronically listening to and recording the petitioner's words violated the privacy upon which he justifiably relied while using the telephone booth and thus constituted a "search and seizure" within the meaning of the 4th Amendment....

The question remaining for decision, then, is whether the search and seizure conducted in this case complied with constitutional standards. In that regard, the government's position is that its agents acted in an entirely defensible manner: They did not begin their electronic surveillance until investigation of the petitioner's activities had established a strong probability that he was using the telephone in question to transmit gambling information to persons in other states, in violation of federal law. Moreover, the surveillance was limited, both in scope and in duration, to the specific purpose of establishing the contents of the petitioner's unlawful telephonic communications. The agents confined their surveillance to the brief periods during which he used the telephone booth, and they took great care to overhear only the conversations of the petitioner himself.

Accepting this account of the government's actions as accurate, it is clear that this surveillance was so narrowly circumscribed that a duly authorized magistrate, properly notified of the need for such investigation, specifically informed of the basis on which it was to proceed, and clearly apprised of the precise intrusion it would entail, could constitutionally have authorized, with appropriate safeguards, the very limited search and seizure that the government asserts in fact took place. Only last term we sustained the validity of such an authorization, holding that, under sufficiently "precise and discriminate circumstances," a federal court may empower government agents to employ a concealed electronic device "for the narrow and particularized purpose of ascertaining the truth of the ... allegations" of a "detailed factual affidavit alleging the commission of a specific criminal offense." *Osborn v. United States....* Discussing that holding, the court in *Berger v. New York ...* said that "the order authorizing the use of the electronic device" in *Osborn* "afforded similar protections to those ... of conventional warrants authorizing the seizure of tangible evidence."...

The government urges that, because its agents relied upon the decisions in *Olmstead* and *Goldman,* and because they did no more here than they might properly have done with prior judicial sanction, we should retroactively validate their conduct. That we cannot do. It is apparent that the agents in this case acted with restraint. Yet the inescapable fact is that this restraint was imposed by the agents themselves, not by a judicial officer. They were not required, before commencing the search, to present their estimate of probable cause for detached scrutiny by a neutral magistrate. They were not compelled, during the conduct of the search itself, to observe precise limits established in advance by a specific court order. Nor were they directed, after the search had been completed, to notify the authorizing magistrate in detail of all that had been seized. In the absence of such safeguards, this court has never sustained a search upon the sole ground that officers reasonably expected to find evidence of a particular crime and voluntarily confined their activities to the least intrusive means consistent with that end. Searches conducted without warrants have been held unlawful "notwithstanding facts unquestionably showing probable cause."...

The government does not question these basic principles. Rather, it urges the creation of a new exception to cover this case. It argues that surveillance of a telephone booth should be exempted from the usual requirement of advance authorization by a magistrate upon a showing of probable cause. We cannot agree. Omission of such authorization "bypasses the safeguards provided by an objective predetermination of probable cause, and substitutes instead the far less reliable procedure of an after-the-event justification for the ... search, too likely to be subtly influenced by the familiar shortcomings of hindsight judgment." *Beck v. Ohio* [1964].... And bypassing a neutral predetermination of the scope of a search leaves individuals secure from 4th Amendment violations "only in the discretion of the police."...

These considerations do not vanish when the search in question is transferred from the setting of a home, an office, or a hotel room, to that of a telephone booth.... The government agents here ignored "the procedure of antecedent justification ... that is central to the 4th Amendment," a procedure that we hold to be a constitutional precondition of the kind of electronic surveillance involved in this case. Because the surveillance here failed to meet that condition, and because it led to the petitioner's conviction, the judgment must be reversed.

Justice Douglas, whom Brennan joined,

concurring:

...I feel compelled to reply to the separate concurring opinion of my brother White, which I view as a wholly unwarranted green light for the Executive Branch to resort to electronic eavesdropping without a warrant in cases which the Executive Branch itself labels "national security" matters.

Neither the President nor the Attorney General is a magistrate. In matters where they believe national security may be involved they are not detached, disinterested and neutral, as a court or magistrate must be. Under the separation of powers created by the Constitution, the Executive Branch is not supposed to be neutral and disinterested. Rather it should vigorously investigate and prevent breaches of national security and prosecute those who violate the pertinent federal laws. The President and Attorney General are properly interested parties, cast in the role of adversary, in national security cases. They may even be the intended victims of subversive action. Since spies and saboteurs are as entitled to the protection of the 4th Amendment as suspected gamblers like petitioner, I cannot agree that where spies and saboteurs are involved adequate protection of 4th Amendment rights is assured when the President and Attorney General assume both the position of adversary-and-prosecutor and disinterested, neutral magistrate.

There is, so far as I understand constitutional history, no distinction under the 4th Amendment between types of crimes. Article III, § 3, gives "treason" a very narrow definition and puts restrictions on its proof. But the 4th Amendment draws no lines between various substantive offenses. ...

I would respect the present lines of distinction and not improvise because a particular crime seems particularly heinous. When the framers took that step, as they did with treason, the worst crime of all, they made their purpose manifest.

Justice White concurring:

...I note the court's acknowledgment that there are circumstances in which it is reasonable to search without a warrant. In this connection, ... the court points out that today's decision does not reach national security cases. Wiretapping to protect the security of the nation has been authorized by successive Presidents. The present Administration would apparently save national security cases from restrictions against wiretapping.... We should not require the warrant procedure and the magistrate's judgment if the President of the United States or his chief legal officer, the Attorney General, has considered the requirements of national security and authorized electronic surveillance as reasonable.

Justice Black dissenting:

If I could agree with the court that eavesdropping carried on by electronic means (equivalent to wiretapping) constitutes a "search" or "seizure," I would be happy to join the court's opinion. For on that premise my brother Stewart sets out methods in accord with the 4th Amendment to guide states in the enactment and enforcement of laws passed to regulate wiretapping by government. In this respect today's opinion differs sharply from *Berger v. New York* ..., which held void on its face a New York statute authorizing wiretapping on warrants issued by magistrates on showings of probable causes. The *Berger* case also set up what appeared to be insuperable obstacles to the valid passage of such wiretapping laws by states. The court's opinion in this case, however, removes the doubts about state power in this field and abates to a large extent the confusion and near paralyzing effect of the *Berger* holding. Notwithstanding these good efforts of the Court, I am still unable to agree with its interpretation of the 4th Amendment.

My basic objection is 2-fold: (1) I do not believe that the words of the amendment will bear the meaning given them by today's decision, and (2) I do not believe that it is the proper role of this court to rewrite the amendment in order "to bring it into harmony with the times" and thus reach a result that many people believe to be desirable.

... For me the language of the amendment is the crucial place to look in construing a written document such as our Constitution. The 4th Amendment says that "The right of the people to be secure in their persons, houses, papers, and effects, against unreasonable searches and seizures, shall not be violated, and no Warrants shall issue, but upon probable cause, supported by Oath or affirmation, and particularly describing the place to be searched, and the persons or things to be seized."

The first clause protects "persons, houses, papers, and effects, against unreasonable searches and seizures...." These words connote the idea of tangible things with size, form and weight, things capable of being searched, seized, or both. The 2d clause of the amendment still further establishes its Framers' purpose to limit its protection to tangible things by providing that no warrants shall issue but those "particularly describing the place to be searched and the person or things to be seized." A conversation overheard by eavesdropping, whether by plain snooping or wiretapping, is not tangible and, under the normally accepted meanings of the words, can neither be searched nor seized. In addition the language of the 2d clause indicates that the amendment refers to something not only tangible so it can be seized but to something already in existence so it can be described. Yet the court's interpretation would have the amendment apply to overhearing future conversations which by their very nature are nonexistent until they take place. How can one "describe" a future conversation, and if not, how can a magistrate issue a warrant to eavesdrop one in the future? It is argued that information showing what is expected to be said is sufficient to limit the boundaries of what later can be admitted into evidence; but does such general information really meet the specific language of the amendment which says "particularly describing"? ... I must conclude that the 4th Amendment simply does not apply to eavesdropping.

Tapping telephone wires, of course, was an unknown possibility at the time the 4th Amendment was adopted. But eavesdropping (and wiretapping is nothing more than eavesdropping by telephone) was, as even the majority opinion in *Berger* ... recognized, "an ancient practice which at common law was condemned as a nuisance.... In those days the eavesdropper listened by naked ear under the eaves of houses or their windows, or beyond their walls seeking out private discourse."... There can be no doubt that the framers were aware of this practice, and if they had desired to outlaw or restrict the use of evidence obtained by eavesdropping, I believe that they would have used the appropriate language to do so in the 4th Amendment.... No one, it seems to me, can read the debates on the Bill of Rights without reaching the conclusion that its framers and critics well knew the meaning of the words they used, what they would be understood to mean by others, their scope and their limitations. Under these circumstances it strikes me as a charge against their scholarship, their commonsense and their candor to give to the 4th Amendment's language the eavesdropping meaning the court imputes to it today.

I do not deny that common sense requires and that this court often has said that the Bill of Rights' safeguards should be given a liberal construction. This principle, however, does not justify construing the search and seizure amendment as applying to eavesdropping or the "seizure" of conversations. The 4th Amendment was aimed directly at the abhorred practice of breaking in, ransacking and searching homes and other buildings and seizing peoples' personal belongings without warrants issued by magistrates. The amendment deserves, and this court has given it, a liberal construction in order to protect against warrantless searches of buildings and seizures of tangible personal effects. But until today this court has refused to say that eavesdropping comes within the ambit of 4th Amendment restrictions. . . .

The 4th Amendment protects privacy only to the extent that it prohibits unreasonable searches and seizures of "persons, houses, papers and effects." No general right is created by the amendment so as to give this court the unlimited power to hold unconstitutional everything which affects privacy. . . .

For these reasons I respectfully dissent.

6 months after *Katz* Congress passed the 1968 Omnibus Crime Control & Safe Streets Act, Title III of which dealt with wiretapping and bugging. It authorized the Justice Department to seek an order from a federal judge authorizing wiretapping and bugging to obtain evidence relating to: (a) Enforcement of the Atomic Energy Act of 1954, espionage, sabotage, treason and riots. (b) Illegal payments and loans to labor organizations, or any labor-related offense that involves murder, kidnapping, robbery or extortion. (c) Bribery of public officials and witnesses, bribery in sporting contests, transmission of wagering information. (d) Influencing or injuring an

officer, juror or witness generally. (e) Obstruction of criminal investigations. (f) Presidential assassinations, kidnapping and assault. (g) Interference with commerce by threats or violence. (h) Interstate and foreign travel or transportation in aid of racketeering. (i) An offer, acceptance or solicitation to influence operations of employe benefit plans. (j) Theft from interstate shipment. (k) Embezzlement from pension and welfare funds. (l) Interstate transportation of stolen property. (m) Offenses relating to counterfeiting and bankruptcy fraud. (n) Offenses involving the manufacture, importation, receiving, concealment, buying, selling or otherwise dealing in narcotic drugs, marihuana or other dangerous drugs punishable under any federal law. (o) Any conspiracy to commit any of these offenses.

Title III permits state, county and local prosecuting attorneys to seek from a state judge an order authorizing wiretapping and bugging to obtain evidence relating to "evidence of the commission of the offense of murder, kidnapping, gambling, robbery, bribery, extortion, or dealing in narcotic drugs, marihuana or other dangerous drugs, or other crime dangerous to life, limb, or property, and punishable by imprisonment for more than one year, designated in any applicable state statute authorizing such interception, or any conspiracy to commit any of the foregoing offenses."

Under Title III, each application for a court order permitting electronic surveillance must include: (a) "a full and complete statement of the facts and circumstances relied upon by the applicant, to justify his belief that an order should be issued"; (b) "a full and complete statement as to whether or not other investigative procedures have been tried and failed or why they reasonably appear to be unlikely to succeed if tried or to be too dangerous"; (c) "a statement of the period of time for which the interception is required to be maintained."

The judge may issue, as requested or modified, an order authorizing the interception of wire or oral communications if the judge determines that: (a) "There is probable cause for belief that an individual is committing, has committed, or is about to commit a particular offense [enumerated in Title III]"; (b) "there is probable cause for belief that particular communications concerning that offense will be obtained through such interception"; (c) "normal investigative procedures have been tried and have failed or reasonably appear to be unlikely to succeed if tried or to be too dangerous."

Title III permits state and federal authorities to wiretap and bug without a court order when "an emergency situation with respect to conspiratorial activities threatening the national security interest or to conspiratorial activities characteristic of organized crime that requires a wire or oral communications to be intercepted before an order authorizing such interception can with due diligence be obtained." And "if an application for an order approving the interception is made ... within 48 hours after the interception has occurred, or begin[s] to occur."

In *Alderman et al. v. United States,* the court held Mar. 10, 1969 that a criminal defendant must be permitted to review the transcripts of all illegally overheard conversations to which he was a party or which took place on "his premises." The purpose of the ruling was to enable the defense to determine whether any of the prosecution's evidence was

obtained as a result of illegal eavesdropping. Under
the 4th Amendment unconstitutionally obtained
evidence can not be admitted in evidence against a
person whose 4th Amendment rights were violated.
Under the so-called "fruit of the poisonous tree"
doctrine, this principle applies to evidence secured
from leads furnished by an illegal search.

In *Alderman,* the government contended that
the trial judge, and not the defense, should be permitted to review records of illegal eavesdropping to
determine whether the prosecution's case was based
on the illegal eavesdropping. The court rejected this
position on the ground that "the task is too complex
and the margin of error too great to rely wholly on
the *in camera* judgment of the trial court to identify
those records which might have contributed to the
government's case."

A related issue was whether unconstitutionally
seized evidence could be used in evidence against a 3d
party whose 4th Amendment rights were not
violated. For example, were the government to
illegally tap Mr. X's telephone and overhear a
conversation between Mr. X and Mr. Y that implicated Mr. Z, could that evidence be used against Mr.
Z? The majority answered that question in the
affirmative in holding that 4th Amendment rights
are "personal rights" and that unconstitutionally
seized evidence need not be excluded when prosecuting a person whose 4th Amendment rights were
not violated by the unconstitutional seizure.

In insisting that it was not deprecating 4th
Amendment rights, by encouraging illegal eavesdropping, the majority decision of Justice White
noted that under the 1968 Omnibus Crime Control &
Safe Streets Act, persons who violate its provisions

are subject to fines of up to $10,000 and imprisonment for up to 5 years and that the law also authorizes the recovery of civil damages by persons whose conversations were illegally overheard.

The *Alderman* decision subsumed 3 separate cases. One case involved 2 men convicted of conspiring to transmit murderous threats. The 2d and 3d cases concerned Igor A. Ivanov and John William Butenko, convicted of conspiring to transmit to the Soviet Union information relating to the national security. All 3 cases were referred to District Courts to determine whether the electronic surveillances in question violated the 4th Amendment.

Abridgment of the *Alderman et al. v. United States* decision (394 U.S. 165, Mar. 10, 1969):

Justice White delivering the opinion of the court:

...The exclusionary rule fashioned in *Weeks v. United States*, ... (1914), and *Mapp v. Ohio*, ... (1961), excludes from a criminal trial any evidence seized from the defendant in violation of his 4th Amendment rights. Fruits of such evidence are excluded as well. *Silverthorn Lumber Co. v. United States*, ... (1920). Because the amendment now affords protection against the uninvited ear, oral statements, if illegally overheard, and their fruits are also subject to suppression....

In *Mapp* and *Weeks*, the defendant against whom the evidence was held to be inadmissible was the victim of the search. However, in the cases before us each petitioner demands retrial if any of the evidence used to convict him was the product of unauthorized surveillance, regardless of whose 4th Amendment rights the surveillance violated. At the very least, it is urged that if evidence is inadmissible against one defendant or conspirator, because tainted by electronic surveillance illegal as to him, it is also inadmissible against his codefendant or coconspirator.

This expansive reading of the 4th Amendment and of the exclusionary rule fashioned to enforce it is admittedly inconsistent with prior cases, and we reject it. The established principle is that suppression of the product of a 4th Amendment violation can be successfully urged only by those whose rights were violated by the search itself, not by those who are aggrieved solely by the introduction of damaging evidence. Coconspirators and codefendants have been accorded no special standing.

Thus in *Goldstein v. United States,* ... (1942), testimony induced by disclosing to witnesses their own telephonic communications intercepted by the government contrary to 47 U.S.C. § 605 was held admissible against their coconspirators. The court equated the rule under § 605 with the exclusionary rule under the 4th Amendment. *Wong Sun v. United States,* ... (1963) came to like conclusions. There, 2 defendants were tried together; narcotics seized from a 3d party were held inadmissible against one defendant because they were the product of statements made by him at the time of his unlawful arrest. But the same narcotics were found to be admissible against the codefendant because "the seizure of this heroin invaded no right of privacy or person or premises which would entitle [him] to object to its use at his trial."

... This same principle was twice acknowledged last term. *Mancusi v. DeForte* ...; *Simmons v. United States.* ...

We adhere to these cases and to the general rule that 4th Amendment rights are personal rights which, like some other constitutional rights, may not be vicariously asserted.... There is no necessity to exclude evidence against one defendant in order to protect the rights of another. No rights of the victim of an illegal search are at stake when the evidence is offered against some other party....

What petitioners appear to assert is an independent constitutional right of their own to exclude relevant and probative evidence because it was seized from another in violation of the 4th Amendment. But we think there is a substantial difference for constitutional purposes between preventing the incrimination of a defendant through the very evidence illegally seized from him and suppressing evidence on the motion of a party who cannot claim this predicate for exclusion.

The necessity for that predicate was not eliminated by recognizing and acknowledging the deterrent aim of the rule. See *Linkletter v. Walker* ... (1965); *Elkins v. United States* ... (1960). Neither those cases nor any others hold that anything which deters illegal searches is thereby commanded by the 4th Amendment. The deterrent values of preventing the incrimination of those whose rights the police have violated have been considered sufficient to justify the suppression of probative evidence even though the case against the defendant is weakened or destroyed. We adhere to that judgment. But we are not convinced that the additional benefits of extending the exclusionary rule to other defendants would justify further encroachment upon the public interest in prosecuting those accused of crime and having them acquitted or convicted on the basis of all the evidence which exposes the truth.

We do not deprecate 4th Amendment rights. The security of persons and property remains a fundamental value which law enforcement officers must respect. Nor should those who flaunt the rules escape unscathed. In this respect we are mindful that there is now a comprehensive statute making unauthorized electronic surveillance a serious crime.* The general rule under the statute is that official eavesdropping and wiretapping are permitted only with probable cause and a warrant. Without experience showing the contrary, we should not assume that this new statute will be cavalierly disregarded or will not be enforced against transgressors.

Of course, Congress or state legislatures may extend the exclusionary rule and provide that illegally seized evidence is inadmissible against anyone for any purpose. But for constitutional purposes, we are not now inclined to depart from the existing rule that unlawful wiretapping or eavesdropping, whether deliberate or negligent, can produce nothing usable against the person aggrieved by the invasion....

In these cases, therefore, any petitioner would be entitled to the suppression of government evidence originating in electronic surveillance violative of his own 4th Amendment right to be free of unreasonable searches and seizures. Such

---

* 1968 Omnibus Crime Control & Safe Streets Act

violation would occur if the United States unlawfully overheard conversations of a petitioner himself or conversations occurring on his premises, whether or not he was present or participated in those conversations. The United States concedes this much and agrees that for purposes of a hearing to determine whether the government's evidence is tainted by illegal surveillance, the transcripts or recordings of the overheard conversations of any petitioner or of 3d persons on his premises must be duly and properly examined in the District Court.

Mr. Justice Harlan and Mr. Justice Stewart, who are in partial dissent on this phase of the case, object to our protecting the homeowner against the use of 3d-party conversations overheard on his premises by an unauthorized surveillance. Their position is that unless the conversational privacy of the homeowner himself is invaded, there is no basis in the 4th Amendment for excluding 3d-party conversations overhead on his premises. We cannot agree. If the police make an unwarranted search of a house and seize tangible property belonging to 3d parties—even a transcript of a 3d-party conversation—the homeowner may object to its use against him, not because he had any interest in the seized items as "effects" protected by the 4th Amendment, but because they were the fruits of an unauthorized search of his house, which is itself expressly protected by the 4th Amendment. Nothing seen or found on the premises may legally form the basis for an arrest or search warrant or for testimony at the homeowner's trial, since the prosecution would be using the fruits of a 4th Amendment violation....

The court has characteristically applied the same rule where an unauthorized electronic surveillance is carried out by physical invasion of the premises. This much the dissent frankly concedes. Like physical evidence which might be seized, overheard conversations are fruits of an illegal entry and are inadmissible in evidence.... When *Silverman* [*v. United States, 1961*] was decided, no right of conversational privacy had been recognized as such; the right vindicated in that case was the 4th Amendment right to be secure in one's own home. In *Wong Sun* [*v. United States*], the words spoken by Blackie Toy when the police illegally entered his house were not usable against him because they were the fruits of a physical invasion of his premises which violated the 4th Amendment.

Because the court has now decided that the 4th Amendment protects a person's private conversations as well as his private premises, ... the dissent would discard the concept that private conversations overheard through an illegal entry into a private place must be excluded as the fruits of a 4th Amendment violation. Although officers without a valid warrant may not search a house for physical evidence or incriminating information, whether the owner is present or away, the dissent would permit them to enter that house without consent and without a warrant, install a listening device and use any overheard 3d-party conversations against the owner in a criminal case, in spite of the obvious violation of his 4th Amendment right to be secure in his own dwelling. Even if the owner is present on his premises during the surveillance, he would have no complaint unless his own conversations were offered or used against him. Information from a telephone tap or from the microphone in the kitchen or in the rooms of guests or children would be freely usable as long as the homeowner's own conversations are not monitored and used against him. Indeed, if the police, instead of installing a device, secreted themselves on the premises, they could neither testify about nor use against the owner anything they saw or carried away but would be free to use against him everything they overheard except his own conversations. And should police overhear 3d parties describing narcotics which they have discovered in the owner's desk drawer, the police could not then open the drawer and seize the narcotics, but they could secure a warrant on the basis of what they had heard and forthwith seize the narcotics pursuant to that warrant.

These views we do not accept. We adhere to the established view in this court that the right to be secure in one's house against unauthorized intrusion is not limited to protection against a policeman viewing or seizing tangible property— "papers" and "effects." Otherwise, the express security for the home provided by the 4th Amendment would approach redundancy. The rights of the owner of the premises are as clearly invaded when the police enter and install a listening device in his house as they are when the entry is made to undertake a warrantless search for tangible property; and the prosecution as surely employs the fruits of an illegal search of the home when it offers overheard 3d-party conversations as it does when it introduces tangible evidence belonging not to the homeowner but to others. Nor do we believe that *Katz,* by holding that the 4th Amendment protects persons and their private conversations, was intended to withdraw any of the protection which the amendment extends to the home or to overrule the existing doctrine, recognized at least since *Silverman,* that conversations as well as property are excludable from the criminal trial when they are found to be the fruits of an illegal invasion of the home. It was noted in *Silverman* ... "this court has never held that a federal officer may without warrant and without consent physically entrench into a man's office or home, there secretly observe or listen, and relate at the man's subsequent criminal trial what was seen or heard." The court proceeded to hold quite the contrary. We take the same course here....

The remaining aspect of this case relates to the procedures to be followed by the District Court in resolving the ultimate issue which will be before it—whether the evidence against any petitioner grew out of his illegally overheard conversations or conversations occurring on his premises....

The government concedes that it must disclose to petitioners any surveillance records which are relevant to the decision of this ultimate issue. And it recognizes that this disclosure must be made even though attended by potential danger to the reputation or safety of 3d parties or to the national security—unless the United States would prefer dismissal of the case to disclosure of the information. However, the government contends that it need not be put to this disclose or dismiss option in the instant cases because none of the information obtained from its surveillance is "arguably relevant" to petitioners' convictions, in the sense that none of the overheard conversations arguably underlay any of the evidence offered in these cases. Although not now insisting that its own evaluation of relevance should be accepted automatically and without judicial scrutiny, the United States urges that the records of the specified conversations be first submitted to the trial judge for an *in camera* examination. Any record found arguably relevant by the judge would be turned over to the petitioner whose 4th Amendment rights have been violated, and that petitioner would then have the opportunity to use the disclosed information in his attempt to show that the government has used tainted evidence to convict him. Material not arguably relevant would not be disclosed to any petitioner.

... We conclude that surveillance records as to which any petitioner has standing to object should be turned over to him without being screened *in camera* by the trial judge. Admittedly, there may be much learned from an electronic surveillance which ultimately contributes nothing to probative evidence. But winnowing this material from those items which might have made a substantial contribution to the case against a petitioner is a task which should not be entrusted wholly to the court in the first instance.... An apparently innocent phrase, a chance remark, a reference to what appears to be a neutral person or event, the identity of a caller or the individual on the other end of a telephone, or even the manner of speaking or using words may have special significance to one who knows the more intimate facts of an accused's life. And yet that information may be wholly colorless and devoid of meaning to one less well acquainted with all relevant circumstances. Unavoidably, this is a matter of judgment, but in our view the task is too complex, and the margin for error too great, to rely wholly on the *in camera* judgment of the trial court to identify those records which might have contributed to the government's case.

The United States concedes that when an illegal search has come to light, it has the ultimate burden of persuasion to show that its evidence is untainted. But at the same time petitioners acknowledge that they must go forward with specific evidence demonstrating taint. "[T]he trial judge must give opportunity, however closely confined, to the accused to prove that a substantial portion of the case against him was the fruit of the poisonous tree. This leaves ample opportunity to the government to convince the trial court that its proof had an independent origin." *Nardone v. United States* ... (1939). With this task ahead of them, and if the hearings are to be more than a formality and petitioners not left entirely to reliance on government testimony, there should be turned over to them the records of those overheard conversations which the government was not entitled to use in building its case against them.

Adversary proceedings are a major aspect of our system of criminal justice. Their superiority as a means for attaining justice in a given case is nowhere more evident than in those cases, such as the ones at bar, where an issue must be decided on the basis of a large volume of factual materials, and after consideration of the many and subtle interrelationships which may exist among the facts reflected by these records. As the need for adversary inquiry is increased by the complexity of the issues presented for adjudication, and by the consequent inadequacy of *ex parte* procedures as a means for their accurate resolution, the displacement of well-informed advocacy necessarily becomes less justifiable.

Adversary proceedings will not magically eliminate all error, but they will substantially reduce its incidence by guarding against the possibility that the trial judge, through lack of time or unfamiliarity with the information contained in and suggested by the materials, will be unable to provide the scrutiny which the 4th Amendment exclusionary rule demands. It may be that the prospect of disclosure will compel the government to dismiss some prosecutions in deference to national security or 3d-party interests. But this is a choice the government concededly faces with respect to material which it has obtained illegally and which it admits, or which a judge would find, is arguably relevant to the evidence offered against the petitioner.*

We think this resolution will avoid an exorbitant expenditure of judicial time and energy and will not unduly prejudice others or the public interest. It must be remembered that dis-

---

* The dissenting opinions ... would require turnover of arguably relevant material, whatever its impact on national security might be. To this extent there is agreement that the defendant's interest in excluding the fruits of illegally obtained evidence entitles him to the product of the surveillance. Given this basic proposition, the matter comes down to a judgment as to whether *in camera* inspection would characteristically be sufficiently reliable when national security interests are at stake. On this issue, the majority and the dissenters part company.

closure will be limited to the transcripts of a petitioner's own conversations and of those which took place on his premises. It can be safely assumed that much of this he will already know, and disclosure should therefore involve a minimum hazard to others. In addition, the trial court can and should, where appropriate, place petitioner and his counsel under enforceable orders against unwarranted disclosure of the materials which they may be entitled to inspect. . . .

None of this means that any petitioner will have an unlimited license to rummage in the files of the Department of Justice. Armed with the specified records of overheard conversations and with the right to cross-examine the appropriate officials in regard to the connection between those records and the case made against him, a petitioner may need or be entitled to nothing else. Whether this is the case or not must be left to the informed discretion, good sense and fairness of the trial judge. . . .

Justice Harlan concurring in part and dissenting in part:

The court's careful opinion is, I think, constructed on a faulty premise, which substantially undermines the validity of its ultimate conclusions. The majority confronts this case as if each of the 2 major problems it raises can be solved in only one of 2 ways. The court seems to assume that *either* the traditional standing doctrine is to be expanded *or* that the traditional doctrine is to be maintained. Again, it is assumed that *either* an *in camera* decision is to be made by the judge in every case *or* that there is to be an automatic turnover of all conversations in every case. I do not believe, however, that the range of choice open to us on either issue is restricted to the 2 alternatives the court considers. On both issues, there is a 3d solution which would, in my view, more satisfactorily accommodate the competing interests at stake.

. . . I am in substantial agreement with the reasons the court has given for refusing to expand the traditional standing doctrine to permit a 4th Amendment challenge to be raised either by a co-defendant or a coconspirator. But it does not follow from this that we may apply the traditional standing rules without further analysis. The traditional rules, as the majority correctly understands them, would grant standing with regard to (1) conversations in which the accused himself participated and (2) *all* conversations occurring on the accused's "premises," regardless of whether he participated in the particular conversation in any way. As I hope to show, the traditional rationale for this 2d rule—granting standing to the property owner—does not fit a case involving the infringement of conversational privacy. Moreover, no other persuasive rationale can be developed in support of the property owner's right to make a 4th Amendment claim as to conversations in which he did not himself participate. Consequently, I would hold that, in the circumstances before us, standing should be granted only to those who actually participated in the conversation that has been illegally overheard.

... There is a very simple reason why the traditional law of standing permits the owner of the premises to exclude a tangible object illegally seized on his property, despite the fact that he does not own the particular object taken by the police. Even though he does not have title to the object, the owner of the premises is in possession of it—and we have held that a property interest of even less substance is a sufficient predicate for standing under the 4th Amendment. *Jones v. United States* ... (1960). This simple rationale does not, however, justify granting standing to the property owner with regard to 3d-party conversations. The absent property owner does not have a property interest of any sort in a conversation in which he did not participate. The words that were spoken are gone beyond recall.

Consequently, in order to justify the traditional rule, one must argue, as does the majority, that the owner of the premises should be granted standing because the bugged 3d-party conversations are "fruits" of the police's infringement of the owner's property rights. The "fruits" theory, however, does not necessarily fit when the police overhear private conversations in violation of the 4th Amendment. As *Katz v. United States* ... squarely holds, the right to the privacy of one's conversation does not hinge on whether the government has committed a technical trespass upon the premises on which the conversations took place. *Olmstead v. New York,* ... (1928), is no longer the law. If in fact there has been no trespass upon the premises, I do not understand how traditional theory permits the owner to complain if a conversation is overheard in which he did not participate. Certainly the owner cannot suppress records of such conversations on the ground that they are the "fruits" of an unconstitutional invasion of his property rights. . . .

It is true, of course, that the "fruits" theory would require a different result if the police used a listening device which did physically trespass upon the accused's premises. But the fact that this theory depends completely on the presence or absence of a technical trespass only serves to show that the entire theoretical basis of standing law must be reconsidered in the area of conversational privacy. For we have not buried *Olmstead,* so far as it dealt with the substance of 4th Amendment rights, only to give it new life in the law of standing. Instead, we should reject traditional property concepts entirely, and reinterpret standing law in the light of the substantive principles developed in *Katz.* Standing should be granted to every person who participates in a conversation he legitimately expects will remain private—for it is such persons that *Katz* protects. On the other hand, property owners should not be permitted to assert a 4th Amendment claim in this area if we are to respect the principle, whose vitality the court has now once again reaffirmed, which establishes "the general rule that 4th Amendment rights are personal rights which ... may not be vicariously asserted." ... For granting property owners standing does not permit them to vindicate intrusions upon their *own* privacy, but simply permits criminal defendants to intrude into the private lives of others.

The following hypothetical suggests the paradoxical quality of the court's rule. Imagine that I own an office building and permit a friend of mine, Smith, to use one of the vacant offices without charge. Smith uses the office to have a private talk with a 3d person, Jones. The next day, I ask my friend to tell me what Jones had said in the office I had given him. Smith replies that the conversation was private and that what was said was "none of your business." Can it be that I could properly feel aggrieved because the conversation occurred on my property? It would make no sense if I were to reply to Smith: *"My privacy* has been infringed if you do not tell me what was said, for I own the *property!"* It is precisely the other way around—Smith is telling me that when he and Jones had talked together, they had a legitimate expectation that their conversation would remain secret, even from me as the property owner.

Now suppose that I had placed a listening device in the office I had given to Smith, without telling him. Could anyone doubt that I would be guilty of an outrageous violation of the privacy of Smith and Jones if I then listened to what they had said? It would be ludicrous to defend my conduct on the ground that I, after all, was the owner of the office building. The case does not stand differently if I am accused of a crime and demand the right to hear the Smith-Jones conversation which the police had monitored. The government doubtless has violated the privacy of Smith and Jones, but their privacy would be violated *further* if the conversation were also made available to me.

In the field of conversational privacy, the 4th Amendment protects persons, not places. *See Katz v. United States....* And a man can only be in one place at one time. If the privacy of his conversation is respected at that place, he may engage in all those activities for which that privacy is an essential prerequisite. His *privacy* is not at all disturbed by the fact that other people in other places cannot speak without the fear of being overheard. That fact may be profoundly disturbing to the man whose privacy remains intact. But it remains a fact about *other* people's privacy. To permit a criminal defendant to complain about such intrusions is to permit the vicarious assertion of 4th Amendment rights—a step which I decline to take in relation to property owners for much the same reasons as those which have impelled the court to deny standing to co-conspirators.

In rejecting the "property" rule advanced by the court, I do not mean to suggest that standing may never properly be granted to permit the vicarious assertion of 4th Amendment rights. While it is arguable that an individual should be permitted to raise a constitutional claim when the privacy of members of his family has been violated, I need not reach this question on the facts of the cases before us. It must be noted, however, that even if this court recognized a man's right to protest whenever the privacy of his family was infringed, the lines the majority draws today would still seem extremely arbitrary. Under the prevailing "property" rule, for example, a husband generally cannot complain if the police overhear his wife talking at her office or in a public phone booth ... although he can complain when the police overhear her talking at home. Yet surely the husband's interest in his wife's privacy is equally worthy of respect in all 3 cases. If standing is to be extended to protect a person's interest in his family's privacy, an individual should be permitted to make a constitutional claim *whenever* a family member's reasonable expectation of privacy has been infringed, regardless of the place where his privacy was invaded. Indeed, the court's emphasis on property ownership could well mean that a husband, as owner of a particular property, is entitled to complain as to a violation of his wife's privacy, but that the wife could not complain as to the unlawful surveillance of her husband since she did not have a sufficiently substantial interest in the property on which the intrusion occurred. In contrast, if a perfect stranger is overheard on one's property, standing is established. ...

The court's lengthy discussion of my position loses sight of the basic justification for the narrower standing rule I have advanced. ...

The court's response seems to be that the 4th Amendment protects "houses" as well as "persons." But this is simply to treat private conversations as if they were pieces of tangible *property.* Since an individual cannot carry his possessions with him wherever he goes, the 4th Amendment protects a person's "house" so that his personal possessions may be kept out of the government's easy reach. In contrast, a man must necessarily carry his voice around with him, and cannot leave it at home even if he wished. When a man is not at home, he cannot converse there. There is thus no need to protect a man's "house" in order to protect *his* right to engage in private conversation. Consequently, the court has not increased the scope of an accused's *personal* privacy by holding that the police have unconstitutionally invaded his "house" by putting a "bug" there. Houses don't speak; only people do. The police only have violated the *privacy* of those persons whose conversations are overheard.

I entirely agree, however, that if the police see a person's tangible property while committing their trespass, they may not constitutionally use this knowledge either to obtain a search warrant or to gain a conviction. Since a man has no choice but to leave the bulk of his physical possessions in his "house," the

4th Amendment must protect his "house" in this way or else the immunity of his personal possessions from arbitrary search could not be assured. Thus if an individual's personal *possessions* are to be protected at all, they must be protected in his house; but a person's private *conversations* are protected as much as is possible when he can complain as to any conversation in which he personally participated. To go further and protect other conversations occurring on his property is simply to give the householder the right to complain as to the government's treatment of others.

... While the court grants special standing rights to property owners, it refuses to reach the question whether employes, business visitors, social guests and other persons with less substantial property interests are also entitled to special standing privileges. Yet this question will be presented to the District Court on remand in the *Alderisio* case, and it will doubtless be an issue in many of the other cases now on our docket which we will remand for reconsideration in the light of our decision today. While a definitive solution to this problem is obviously premature, the court's failure to give the lower courts any guidance whatever on this point will result in widespread confusion as trial judges throughout the land attempt to divine the rationale behind the property rule established today. Confusion will be compounded by our own past decisions which have decisively rejected the notion that the accused must necessarily have a possessory interest in the premises before he may assert a 4th Amendment claim. . . .

While I would hold that property owners have no right as such to hear conversations in which they were not participants, it appears to me that at a minimum the court should adopt the government's suggested judicial screening procedure with regard to 3d-party conversations. Property owners should not be permitted to intrude into the private lives of others unless a trial judge determines that the conversation at issue is at least arguably relevant to the pending prosecution.

On the other hand, I would agree that in the typical case, the prosecution should be required to hand over the records of all conversations in which the accused played a part. Since the other parties to these conversations knew they were talking to the accused, they can hardly have an important interest in concealing from him what they said to him. Whatever risk of unauthorized disclosure that is involved may generally be minimized even further by the issuance of appropriate protective orders. . . .

There is, however, at least one class of cases in which the standard considerations do not apply. I refer to the situations exemplified by *Ivanov* and *Butenko,* in which the defendant is charged, under one statute or another, with spying for a foreign power. In contrast to the typical situation, here the accused may learn important new information even if the turnover is limited to conversations in which he was a participant. For example, he may learn the location of a listening device—a fact that may be of crucial significance in espionage work. Moreover, he will be entitled to learn this fact even though a valid warrant has subsequently been issued authorizing electronic surveillance at the same location. Similarly, the accused may find out that the United States has obtained certain information that his foreign government believes is still secret, even when our government has also received this information from an independent source in a constitutional way. And he may learn that those in whom he has been reposing confidence are in fact American undercover agents.

Even more important, there is much less reason to believe that a protective court order will effectively deter the defendant in an espionage case from turning over the new information he has received to those who are not entitled to it. . . .

Moreover, apart from the sense of fair play of most judges, additional safeguards could be devised which would assure that an *in camera* procedure would be used only when an unauthorized disclosure presents a substantial risk to the national security. . . .

The court's failure to consider the special characteristics of the *Ivanov* and *Butenko* cases is particularly surprising in the light of the reasons it gives for creating an absolute rule in favor of an automatic turnover. For the majority properly recognizes that its preference for a full adversary hearing cannot be justified by an easy reference to an absolute principle condemning *in camera* judicial decisions in all situations. Indeed, this court has expressly authorized the use of such procedures in closely related areas involving the vindication of 4th Amendment rights. . . . If, as the court rightly states, the propriety of an *in camera* screening procedure is a "matter of judgment,"... depending on an informed consideration of all the competing factors, I do not understand why the trial judge should not be authorized to consider whether the accused simply cannot be trusted to keep the government's records confidential. Nor do I understand why the government must be confronted with the choice of dismissing the indictment or disclosing the information because the accused cannot be counted on to keep faith with the court. Moreover, it is not difficult to imagine cases in which the danger of unauthorized disclosure of important information would clearly outweigh the risk that an error may be made by the trial judge in determining whether a particular conversation is arguably relevant to the pending prosecution. ... Though the court itself recognizes that "the need for adversary inquiry is increased by the complexity of the issues presented for adjudication," ... it nevertheless leaves no room for an informed decision by the trial judge that the risk of error on the facts of a given case is insubstantial. Since the number of espionage cases is small, there is no change whatever that these decisions will be made in a hurried fashion or that they will not be subjected to the most searching scrutiny on appeal....

In sum, I would require the government to turn over to Alderman and Alderisio only the records of those conversations in which each defendant participated, and I would leave the way open for a preliminary *in camera* screening procedure in the *Ivanov* and *Butenko* cases.

Justice Fortas concurring in part and dissenting in part:

In the present cases, the court holds (1) that the government may use evidence it obtains by unlawful electronic surveillance against any defendant who does not have "standing" to complain; (2) that a defendant has standing only if he was a party to the overheard conversation or if it took place on "his premises"; and (3) that all illegally obtained surveillance records as to which a defendant has standing (including national security information) must be submitted to the defendant or his counsel, subject to appropriate protective orders, and their relevance to the defendant's trial must be determined in adversary proceedings. The defendant is entitled to suppression or exclusion from his trial of such illegally obtained information and its fruits.

I find it necessary to file this separate opinion because I believe (1) that a person concerning whom an investigation involving illegal electronic surveillance has been conducted, as well as the persons given "standing" in the majority opinion, has the right to suppression of the illegally obtained material and its fruits; and (2) that it is permissible for the trial judge, subject to suitable specifications, to order that information vital to the national security shall be examined only *in camera* to determine its relevance or materiality, although I agree that all other information that may be the subject of a motion to suppress must be shown to the defendant or his counsel so that its materiality can be determined in an adversary hearing....

The effect of the court's decision, bluntly acknowledged, is to add another to the long list of cases in which the courts have tolerated governmental conduct that violates the 4th Amendment. The courts have done this by resort to the legalism of "standing."...

It is a fundamental principle of our constitutional scheme that government, like the individual, is bound by the law. We do not subscribe to the totalitarian principle that the government ... may disregard the law even in pursuit of the lawbreaker. As this court said in *Mapp v. Ohio...*, "Nothing can destroy a government more quickly than its failure to observe its own laws, or worse, its disregard of the charter of its own existence."...

It is disquieting when an individual policeman, through carelessness or ignorance or in response to the pressure of events, seizes a person or conducts a search without compliance with the standards prescribed by law. It is even more disturbing when law enforcement officers engage in unconstitutional conduct not because of their individual error but pursuant to a calculated institutional policy and directive.

Surreptitious electronic surveillance ... is a "search and seizure" within the ambit of the 4th Amendment. *Silverman v. United States ...; Katz v. United States....* It is usually the product of calculated, official decision rather than the error of an individual agent of the state. And because by nature it is hidden, unlawful electronic surveillance is even more offensive to a free society than the unlawful search and seizure of tangible material.

In recognition of the principle that lawlessness on the part of the government must be stoutly condemned, this court has ruled that when such lawless conduct occurs, the government may not profit from its fruits. *Weeks v. United States* ... held that in a federal prosecution the government may not use evidence secured through an illegal search and seizure. In *Mapp v. Ohio,* ... the exclusionary rule was applied to the states. In that case the court expressly recognized that only a prohibition of the use of unlawfully seized material could properly implement the constitutional prohibition. It acknowledged that other remedies were not effective sanctions.... As this court said in *Walder v. United States* ... (1954), "the government cannot violate the 4th Amendment ... and use the fruits of such unlawful conduct to secure a conviction. ... [T]hese methods are outlawed and convictions obtained by means of them are invalidated, because they encourage the kind of society that is obnoxious to free men."

But for reasons which many commentators charge are related more to convenience and judicial prudence than to constitutional principles, courts of all states except California and of the federal system, including this court, have allowed in evidence material obtained by police agents in direct and acknowledged violation of the 4th Amendment. They have allowed this evidence except in those cases where a defendant who moves for suppression of the material can show that his personal right of privacy was violated by the unlawful search or seizure. This restriction on persons who can suppress illegally acquired evidence has been attributed by some commentators to the fact that the constitutional right to suppress was at one time considered to stem in part from the 5th Amendment's privilege against self-incrimination. ... But if the exclusionary rule follows from the 4th Amendment itself, there is no basis for confining its invocation to persons whose right of privacy has been violated by an illegal search. The 4th Amendment, unlike the 5th, is couched in terms of a guarantee that the government will not engage in unreasonable searches and seizures. It is a general prohibition, a fundamental part of the constitutional compact, the observance of which is essential to the welfare of all persons. Accordingly, commentators have urged that the necessary implication of the 4th Amendment is that any defendant against whom illegally acquired evidence is offered, whether or not it was obtained in violation of his right to privacy, may have the evidence excluded. It is also contended that this is the only means to secure the observance of the 4th Amendment.

I find these arguments cogent and appealing. The 4th Amendment is not merely a privilege accorded to him whose domain has been lawlessly invaded. It grants the individual a personal right, not to privacy, but to insist that the state utilize only lawful means of proceeding against him. And it is an assurance to all that the government will exercise its formidable powers to arrest and to investigate only subject to the rule of law. . . .

I do not agree with the court's decision that sensitive national security material that may not be relevant to defendant's prosecution must be turned over to the defendant or his counsel for their scrutiny. By the term "national security material," I mean to refer to a rigid and limited category. It would not include material relating to any activities except those specifically directed to acts of sabotage, espionage, or aggression by or on behalf of foreign states.

Because the court believes that no distinction can be made with respect to the defendant's right to suppress relevant evidence on the basis of the sensitivity of the material, it has concluded that no distinction can be made as to the method of determining whether the material is relevant. I agree that an *in camera* inspection of the records of unlawful surveillance should not be the usual method of determining relevance. I agree with all that the court says about the inadequacy of an inspection in which the defendant cannot participate and the burden that it places upon the trial judge. But in cases where the trial court explicitly determines, in written findings, sealed and available for examination by reviewing courts, that disclosure would substantially injure national security interests, I do not think that disclosure to the defendant is necessary in order for the government to proceed with a prosecution. . . .

Let me emphasize that the defendant's right to suppress is the same whether the charge is espionage, sabotage, or another kind of crime: Relevant material that has been illegally seized may be suppressed if the defendant has standing, but the existence of nonrelevant illegal evidence will not prevent a prosecution. . . .

I agree with the majority that the possibility of error in determining relevance is much greater if there is only *in camera* examination. But I also agree with my brother Harlan that disclosure of some of the material may pose a serious danger to the national interest. I therefore reach the conclusion that a differentiation may properly be made between the method of handling materials the disclosure of which would endanger the national security and other illegally obtained materials. Skepticism as to the court's ability to detect and turn over to the defendant all relevant material may be well-founded, but *in camera* inspection does not so clearly threaten to deprive defendants of their constitutional rights that it justifies endangering the national security. Accordingly, I would hold that after certification by the Attorney General that specific portions of unlawfully obtained materials are sensitive, the trial judge may find that their disclosure to the defendant or his counsel would substantially injure national security interests, and he may determine *in camera* whether the materials are arguably relevant to the defendant's prosecution.

Solicitor Gen. Erwin Griswold, in a rare Justice Department petition for rehearing, asked the Supreme Court Mar. 19, 1969 to rule that wiretapping and other electronic eavesdropping without a warrant or other 4th Amendment safeguards was not unconstitutional when used to gather "foreign intelligence information." According to Griswold, "that which has long been practiced by all nations, in the interests of self-preservation, cannot easily be regarded as unreasonable." In representing the Justice Department and the Administration, Griswold urged that conversations of criminal defendants overheard in the course of such eavesdropping need not be disclosed in court. If the court disagreed, Griswold warned, the Justice Department might stop telling the court about eavesdropping that it considered irrelevant to any criminal case. The Justice

Department had begun informing the court of all eavesdropping, he said, because it assumed that the court would not require disclosures that would have an adverse "impact upon the gathering of foreign intelligence information."

The government petition for a rehearing was denied by the Supreme Court Mar. 24. That day, in *Giordano v. United States,* the court ordered a number of cases referred to the District Courts to determine whether government eavesdropping was unlawful and therefore required the disclosure called for by *Alderman.* Justice Stewart issued a concurring opinion that chided the Justice Department for misreading *Alderman.* Stewart pointed out that the court had specifically limited its disclosure requirement to interceptions that violated the 4th Amendment. He emphasized that the court had not ruled on the constitutionality of electronic surveillance relating to the gathering of "foreign intelligence information."

The court's order did not include a written opinion.

Justice Stewart concurring:

... As we made explicit in *Alderman, Butenko* and *Ivanov,* the requirement that certain products of governmental electronic surveillance be turned over to defense counsel was expressly limited to situations where the surveillance had violated the 4th Amendment. We did not decide in those cases, and we do not decide in these, that any of the surveillances *did* violate the 4th Amendment. Instead, we have left that threshold question for the District Courts to decide in all these cases.

Moreover, we did not in *Alderman, Butenko* or *Ivanov,* and we do not today, specify the procedure that the District Courts are to follow in making this preliminary determination. We have nowhere indicated that this determination cannot appropriately be made in *ex parte, in camera* proceedings. ...

Finally, the court has not in any of these cases addressed itself to the standards governing the constitutionality of electronic surveillance relating to the gathering of foreign intelligence information—necessary for the conduct of international affairs and for the protection of national defense secrets and installations from foreign espionage and sabotage.

Mr. Justice White has elsewhere made clear his view that such surveillance does not violate the 4th Amendment, "if the President of the United States or his chief legal officer, the Attorney General, has considered the requirements of national security and authorized electronic surveillance as reasonable." While 2 members of the court have indicated disagreement with that view, the issue remains open. . . .

Court Curbs Eavesdropping on Radicals

In an 8-0 decision June 19, 1972, the Supreme Court ordered the government not to employ electronic eavesdropping devices against radicals without a court order. The case, *United States v. United States District Court for the Eastern District of Michigan,* involved the government's use of a warrantless wiretap, or taps, to overhear the conversations of Lawrence "Pun" Plamondon, a member of the White Panthers, who was subsequently charged with bombing a CIA (Central Intelligence Agency) office in Ann Arbor, Mich.

During pretrial proceedings, Plamondon's attorneys moved to review the records of any illegal wiretaps used to monitor Plamondon's conversations. Although conceding that Plamondon had been overheard on a warrantless wiretap, the government contended that its activities were legal since they had been carried out under the President's power to protect the national security. In such cases, the Justice Department contended, it was not necessary for the government to obtain a warrant pursuant to the 1968 law authorizing court-approved eavesdropping. In its brief the government noted that the 1968 law contained a provision stating that nothing in the law was meant to limit the power of the President "to protect the United States against the overthrow of the government by force or other unlawful means, or against any other clear and present danger to the structure of the government."

Writing for the majority, Justice Powell contended, however, that the clause sought only "to make clear that the Act simply did not legislate with respect to national security surveillances." It did not, therefore, alter the basic 4th Amendment requirement that a search be carried out pursuant to a court-issued warrant, Powell held. 4th Amendment "freedoms cannot properly be guaranteed if domestic security surveillances may be conducted solely within the discretion of the executive branch." The court also rejected the government's claims that "special circumstances," characteristic of domestic security investigations, justified the use of warrantless eavesdrops. Since such surveillances are directed primarily at collecting intelligence with respect to subversive forces, and not for evidence for use in criminal prosecutions, it would not be appropriate to require the government to demonstrate "probable cause" as required by the 4th Amendment, the Justice Department told the court. The Justice Department also asserted that judges would not be in a position to know whether the national security required a particular surveillance and that disclosing such information to magistrates "would create serious potential dangers to the national security and to the lives of informants and agents."

While noting the force of these arguments, the court contended, however, that it was not sufficient to nullify the 4th Amendment requirement for court-issued warrants. Because of the special

circumstances involved in national security
investigations, Powell said, Congress might wish to
pass legislation that establishes special, and possibly
less stringent, requirements for national security
surveillances.

The majority decision emphasized that it did not
touch on the President's right to wiretap foreign
spies and that it was limited to domestic groups with
"no significant connection with a foreign power, its
agents or agencies."

Justice Douglas, in a concurring opinion,
claimed that the nation was in the "throes of another
national seizure of paranoia, resembling the hysteria
which surrounded the Alien & Sedition Acts, the
Palmer raids and the McCarthy era." "Those who
register dissent or who petition their governments
for redress are subjected to scrutiny by grand juries,
by the FBI or even by the military," Douglas
charged. "Their associates are interrogated. Their
homes are bugged and their telephones are wiretapped. They are befriended by secret government
informers. Their patriotism and loyalty are questioned."

Justice White argued in a concurring opinion
that the case should have been decided wholly on the
narrower issue of the scope of the 1968 law and not
on the larger issue of the President's right to
authorize warrantless electronic surveillance. Justice
Rehnquist, who as a member of the Justice Department, before coming to the court, had spoken out in
favor of warrantless wiretapping and bugging, did
not participate in the decision.

The immediate effect of the decision was to
require the government to permit Plamondon's
attorneys to review the records of what the court

declared to be an illegal wiretap to determine whether any of the evidence introduced against Plamondon was based on the illegal wiretapping.

(10 days after the decision was handed down, the Justice Department told Congress that it was currently conducting 27 wiretaps without warrants and that "less than 3" of them involved domestic groups, all of which were said to be linked with foreign organizations. The Justice Department had reported that it had conducted 113 executive-ordered, warrantless electronic surveillances in 1970.)

Abridgment of the decision in the case of *United States v. United States District Court for the Eastern District of Michigan* (June 19, 1972):

Justice Powell delivering the opinion of the court:

The issue before us is an important one for the people of our country and their government. It involves the delicate question of the President's power, acting through the Attorney General, to authorize electronic surveillance in internal security matters without prior judicial approval. Successive Presidents for more than one-quarter of a century have authorized such surveillance in varying degrees, without guidance from the Congress or a definitive decision of this court. This case brings the issue here for the first time. Its resolution is a matter of national concern, requiring sensitivity both to the government's right to protect itself from unlawful subversion and attack and to the citizen's right to be secure in his privacy against unreasonable government intrusion.

This case arises from a criminal proceeding ... in which the United States charged 3 defendants with conspiracy to destroy government property in violation of 18 U.S.C. § 371. One of the defendants, Plamondon, was charged with the dynamite bombing of an office of the Central Intelligence Agency in Ann Arbor, Michigan.

During pretrial proceedings, the defendants moved to compel the United States to disclose certain electronic surveillance information and to conduct a hearing to determine whether this information "tainted" the evidence on which the indictment was based or which the government intended to offer at trial. In response, the government filed an affidavit of the Attorney General acknowledging that its agents had overheard conversations in which Plamondon had participated. The affidavit also stated that the Attorney General approved the wiretaps "to gather intelligence information deemed necessary to protect the nation from attempts of domestic organizations to attack and subvert the existing structure of the government." The affidavit, together with the logs of the surveillance, were filed in a sealed exhibit for *in camera* inspection by the District Court.

On the basis of the Attorney General's affidavit and the sealed exhibit, the government asserted that the surveillances were lawful, though conducted without prior judicial approval, as a reasonable exercise of the President's power (exercised through the Attorney General) to protect the national security. The district court held that the surveillance violated the 4th Amendment and ordered the government to make full disclosure to Plamondon of his overheard conversations.

The government then filed in the Court of Appeals for the 6th Circuit a petition for a writ of *mandamus* to set aside the district court order, which was stayed pending final disposition of the case. After concluding that it had jurisdiction, that court held that the surveillances were unlawful and that the district court had properly required disclosure of the overheard conversations....

Title III of the [1968] Omnibus Crime Control & Safe Streets Act authorizes the use of electronic surveillance for classes of crimes carefully specified [therein].... Such surveillance is subject to prior court order. Section 2518 sets forth the detailed and particularized application necessary to obtain such an order as well as carefully circumscribed conditions for its use. The act represents a comprehensive attempt by Congress to promote more effective control of crime while protecting the privacy of individual thought and expression. Much of Title III was drawn to meet the constitutional requirements for electronic surveillance enunciated by this court in *Berger v. New York* ... (1967) and *Katz v. United States* ... (1967).

Together with the elaborate surveillance requirements in Title III, there is the following proviso, 18 U.S.C. § 2511 (3): "Nothing contained in this chapter or in section 605 of the Communications Act of 1934 (48 Stat. 1103; 47 U.S.C. § 605) shall limit the constitutional power of the President to take such measures as he deems necessary to protect the nation against actual or potential attack or other hostile acts of a foreign power, to obtain foreign intelligence information deemed essential to the security of the United States, or to protect national security information against foreign intelligence activities. *Nor shall anything contained in this chapter be deemed to limit the constitutional power of the President to take such measures as he deems necessary to protect the United States against the overthrow of the government by force or other unlawful means, or against any other clear and present danger to the structure or existence of the government.* The contents of any wire or oral communication intercepted by authority of the President in the exercise of the foregoing powers may be received in evidence in any trial, hearing, or other proceeding only where such interception was reasonable, and shall not be otherwise used or disclosed except as is necessary to implement that power." (Emphasis supplied.)

The government relies on § 2511 (3). It argues that "in excepting national security surveillances from the act's warrant requirement Congress recognized the President's authority to conduct such surveillances without prior judicial approval." ... The section thus is viewed as a recognition or affirmance of a constitutional authority in the President to conduct warrantless domestic security surveillance such as that involved in this case.

We think the language of § 2511 (3), as well as the legislative history of the statute, refutes this interpretation. The relevant language is that: "Nothing contained in this chapter ... shall limit the constitutional power of the President to take such measures as he deems necessary to protect ..." against the dangers specified. At most, this is an implicit recognition that the President does have certain powers in the specified areas. Few would doubt this, as the section refers—among other things—to protection "against actual or potential attack or other hostile acts of a foreign power." But so far as the use of the President's electronic surveillance power is concerned, the language is essentially neutral. ...

It is important at the outset to emphasize the limited nature of the question before the court. This case raises no constitutional challenge to electronic surveillance as specifically authorized by Title III of the Omnibus Crime Control & Safe Streets Act of 1968. Nor is there any question or doubt as to the necessity of obtaining a warrant in the surveillance of crimes unrelated to the national security interest.... Further, the instant case requires no judgment on the scope of the President's surveillance power with respect to the activities of foreign powers, within or without this country. The Attorney General's affidavit in this case states that the surveillances were "deemed necessary to protect the nation from attempts of *domestic organizations* to attack and subvert the existing structure of government" (emphasis supplied). There is no evidence of any involvement, directly or indirectly, of a foreign power.

Our present inquiry, though important, is therefore a narrow one. It addresses a question left open by *Katz* ...: "Whether safeguards other than prior authorization by a magistrate would satisfy the 4th Amendment in a situation involving the national security...." The determination of this question requires the essential 4th Amendment inquiry into the "reasonableness" of the search and seizure in question, and the way in which that "reasonableness" derives content and meaning through reference to the warrant clause....

We begin the inquiry by noting that the President of the United States has the fundamental duty, under Art. II, § 1, of the Constitution, "to preserve, protect, and defend the Constitution of the United States." Implicit in that duty is the power to protect our government against those who would subvert or overthrow it by unlawful means. In the discharge of this duty, the President—through the Attorney General—may find it necessary to employ electronic surveillance to obtain intelligence information on the plans of those who plot unlawful acts against the government. The use of such surveillance in internal security cases has been sanctioned more or less continuously by various Presidents and Attorneys General since July 1946....

Though the government and respondents debate their seriousness and magnitude, threats and acts of sabotage against the government exist in sufficient number to justify investigative powers with respect to them. The covertness and complexity of potential unlawful conduct against the government and the necessary dependency of many conspirators upon the telephone make electronic surveillance an effective investigatory instrument in certain circumstances. The marked acceleration in technological developments and sophistication in their use have resulted in new techniques for the planning, commission and concealment of criminal activities. It would be contrary to the public interest for government to deny to itself the prudent and lawful employment of those very techniques which are employed against the government and its law abiding citizens.

It has been said that "the most basic function of any government is to provide for the security of the individual and of his property." *Miranda v. Arizona* ... (1966) (WHITE, J., dissenting). And unless government safeguards its own capacity to function and to preserve the security of its people, society itself could become so disordered that all rights and liberties would be endangered. As Chief Justice Hughes reminded us in *Cox v. New Hampshire* ... (1940): "Civil liberties, as guaranteed by the Constitution, imply the existence of an organized society maintaining public order without which liberty itself would be lost in the excesses of unrestrained abuses."

But a recognition of these elementary truths does not make the employment by government of electronic surveillance a welcome development—even when employed with restraint and under judicial supervision. There is, understandably, a deep-seated uneasiness and apprehension that this capability will be used to intrude upon cherished privacy of law-abiding citizens. We look to the Bill of Rights to safeguard this privacy....

National security cases, moreover, often reflect a convergence of First and 4th Amendment values not present in cases of "ordinary" crime. Though the investigative duty of the executive may be stronger in such cases, so also is there greater jeopardy to constitutionally protected speech. "Historically the struggle for freedom of speech and press in England was bound up with the issue of the scope of the search and seizure power." *Marcus v. Search Warrant* ... (1961). History abundantly documents the tendency of government—however benevolent and benign its motives—to view with suspicion those who most fervently dispute its policies. 4th Amendment protections become the more necessary when the targets of official surveillance may be those suspected of unorthodoxy in their political beliefs. The danger to political dissent is acute where the government attempts to act under so vague a concept as the power to protect "domestic security."...

As the 4th Amendment is not absolute in its terms, our task is to examine and balance the basic values at stake in this case: the duty of government to protect the domestic security, and the potential danger posed by unreasonable surveillance to individual privacy and free expression. If the legitimate need of government to safeguard domestic security requires the use of electronic surveillance, the question is whether the needs of citizens for privacy and free expression may not be better protected by requiring a warrant before such surveillance is undertaken. We must also ask whether a warrant requirement would unduly frustrate the efforts of government to protect itself from acts of subversion and overthrow directed against it....

...4th Amendment freedoms cannot properly be guaranteed if domestic security surveillances may be conducted solely within the discretion of the executive branch. The 4th Amendment does not contemplate the executive officers of government as neutral and disinterested magistrates. Their duty and responsibility is to enforce the laws, to investigate and to prosecute. *Katz v. United States* ... (DOUGLAS, J., concurring). But those charged with this investigative and prosecutorial duty should not be the sole judges of when to utilize constitutionally sensitive means in pursuing their tasks. The historical judgment, which the 4th Amendment accepts, is that unreviewed executive discretion may yield too readily to pressures to obtain incriminating evidence and overlook potential invasions of privacy and protected speech.

It may well be that, in the instant case, the government's surveillance of Plamondon's conversations was a reasonable one which readily would have gained prior judicial approval. But this court "has never sustained a search upon the sole ground that officers reasonably expected to find evidence of a particular crime and voluntarily confined their activities to the least intrusive means consistent with that end." *Katz* .... The 4th Amendment contemplates a prior judicial judgment, not the risk that executive discretion may be reasonably exercised. This judicial role accords with our basic constitutional doctrine that individual freedoms will best be preserved through a separation of powers and division of functions among the different branches and levels of government.... The independent check upon executive discretion is not satisfied, as the government argues, by "extremely limited" post-surveillance judicial review. Indeed, post-surveillance review would never reach the surveillances which failed to result in prosecutions. Prior review by a neutral and detached magistrate is the time-tested means of effectuating 4th Amendment rights....

The government argues that the special circumstances applicable to domestic security surveillances necessitate a further exception to the warrant requirement. It is urged that the requirement of prior judicial review would obstruct the President in the discharge of his constitutional duty to protect domestic security. We are told further that these surveillances are directed primarily to the collecting and maintaining of intelligence with respect to subversive forces and are not an attempt to gather evidence for specific criminal prosecutions. It is said that this type of surveillance should not be subject to traditional warrant requirements which were established to govern investigation of criminal activity, not on-going intelligence gathering....

The government further insists that courts "as a practical matter would have neither the knowledge nor the techniques necessary to determine whether there was probable cause to believe that surveillance was necessary to protect national security." These security problems, the government contends, involve "a large number of complex and subtle factors" beyond the competence of courts to evaluate....

As a final reason for exemption from a warrant requirement, the government believes that disclosure to a magistrate of all or even a significant portion of the information involved in domestic security surveillances "would create serious potential dangers to the national security and to the lives of informants and agents.... Secrecy is the essential ingredient in intelligence gathering; requiring prior judicial authorization would create a greater 'danger of leaks ..., because in addition to the judge, you have the clerk, the stenographer and some other official like a law assistant or bailiff who may be apprised of the nature' of the surveillance."...

These contentions in behalf of a complete exemption from the warrant requirement, when urged on behalf of the President and the national security in its domestic implications, merit the most careful consideration. We certainly do not reject them lightly, especially at a time of worldwide ferment and when civil disorders in this country are more prevalent than in the less turbulent periods of our history. . . .

But we do not think a case has been made for the requested departure from 4th Amendment standards. The circumstances described do not justify complete exemption of domestic security surveillance from prior judicial scrutiny. Official surveillance, whether its purpose be criminal investigation or on-going intelligence gathering, risks infringement of constitutionally protected privacy of speech. Security surveillances are especially sensitive because of the inherent vagueness of the domestic security concept, the necessarily broad and continuing nature of intelligence gathering, and the temptation to utilize such surveillances to oversee political dissent. We recognize, as we have before, the constitutional basis of the President's domestic security role, but we think it must be exercised in a manner compatible with the 4th Amendment. In this case we hold that this requires an appropriate prior warrant procedure.

We cannot accept the government's argument that internal security matters are too subtle and complex for judicial evaluation. . . . If the threat is too subtle or complex for our senior law enforcement officers to convey its significance to a court, one may question whether there is probable cause for surveillance.

Nor do we believe prior judicial approval will fracture the secrecy essential to official intelligence gathering. . . . Moreover, a warrant application involves no public or adversary proceedings: it is an *ex parte* request before a magistrate or judge. Whatever security dangers clerical and secretarial personnel may pose can be minimized by proper administrative measures, possibly to the point of allowing the government itself to provide the necessary clerical assistance.

Thus, we conclude that the government's concerns do not justify departure in this case from the customary 4th Amendment requirement of judicial approval prior to initiation of a search or surveillance. Although some added burden will be imposed upon the Attorney General, this inconvenience is justified in a free society to protect constitutional values. Nor do we think the government's domestic surveillance powers will be impaired to any significant degree.... By no means of least importance will be the reassurance of the public generally that indiscriminate wiretapping and bugging of law-abiding citizens cannot occur.

... We emphasize, before concluding this opinion, the scope of our decision. As stated at the outset, this case involves only the domestic aspects of national security. We have not addressed, and express no opinion as to, the issues which may be involved with respect to activities of foreign powers or their agents. Nor does our decision rest on the language of § 2511 (3) or any other section of Title III of the Omnibus Crime Control & Safe Streets Act of 1968. That Act does not attempt to define or delineate the powers of the President to meet domestic threats to the national security.

Moreover, we do not hold that the same type of standards and procedures prescribed by Title III are necessarily applicable to this case. We recognize that domestic security surveillance may involve different policy and practical considerations from the surveillance of "ordinary crime." The gathering of security intelligence is often long range and in-volves the interrelation of various sources and types of information. The exact targets of such surveillance may be more difficult to identify than in surveillance operations against many types of crime specified in Title III. Often, too, the emphasis of domestic intelligence gathering is on the prevention of unlawful activity or the enhancement of the government's preparedness for some possible future crisis or emergency. Thus, the focus of domestic surveillance may be less precise than that directed against more conventional types of crime.

Given these potential distinctions between Title III criminal surveillances and those involving the domestic security, Congress may wish to consider protective standards for the latter which differ from those already prescribed for specified crimes in Title III. Different standards may be compatible with the 4th Amendment if they are reasonable both in relation to the legitimate need of government for intelligence information and the protected rights of our citizens. For the warrant application may vary according to the governmental interest to be enforced and the nature of citizen rights deserving protection....

...We do not attempt to detail the precise standards for domestic security warrants any more than our decision in *Katz* sought to set the refined requirements for the specified criminal surveillances which now constitute Title III. We do hold, however, that prior judicial approval is required for the type of domestic security surveillance involved in this case and that such approval may be made in accordance with such reasonable standards as the Congress may prescribe....

Justice Douglas concurring:

... This is an important phase in the campaign of the police and intelligence agencies to obtain exemptions from the warrant clause of the 4th Amendment. For, due to the clandestine nature of electronic eavesdropping, the need is acute for placing on the government the heavy burden to show that "exigencies of the situation [make its] course imperative" [*Coolidge v. New Hampshire,* 1971]. Other abuses such as the search incident to arrest, have been partly deterred by the threat of damage actions against offending officers, the risk of adverse publicity, or the possibility of reform through the political process. These latter safeguards, however, are ineffective against lawless wiretapping and "bugging" of which their victims are totally unaware. Moreover, even the risk of exclusion of tainted evidence would here appear to be of negligible deterrent value inasmuch as the United States frankly concedes that the primary purpose of these searches is to fortify its intelligence collage rather than to accumulate evidence to support indictments and convictions. If the warrant clause were held inapplicable here, then the federal intelligence machine would literally enjoy unchecked discretion.

Here federal agents wish to rummage for months on end through every conversation, no matter how intimate or personal, carried over selected telephone lines simply to seize those few utterances which may add to their sense of the pulse of a domestic underground.

We are told that one national security wiretap lasted for 14 months and monitored over 900 conversations. Sen. Edward Kennedy found recently that "warrantless devices accounted for an average of 78 to 209 days of listening per device, as compared with a 13-day per device average for those devices installed under court order." He concluded that the government's revelations posed "the frightening possibility that the conversations of untold thousands of citizens of this country are being monitored on secret devices which no judge has authorized and which may remain in operation for months and perhaps years at a time." Even the most innocent and random caller who uses or telephones into a tapped line can become a flagged number in the government's data bank....

...[W]e are currently in the throes of another national seizure of paranoia, resembling the hysteria which surrounded the Alien & Sedition Acts, the Palmer raids, and the McCarthy era. Those who register dissent or who petition their governments for redress are subjected to scrutiny by grand juries, by the FBI or even by the military. Their associates are interrogated. Their homes are bugged and their telephones are wiretapped. They are befriended by secret government informers. Their patriotism and loyalty are questioned. Sen. Sam Ervin, who has chaired hearings on military surveillance of civilian dissidents, warns that "it is not an exaggeration to talk in terms of hundreds of thousands of ... dossiers." Sen. Kennedy ... found "the frightening possibility that the conversations of untold thousands are being monitored on secret devices." More than our privacy is implicated. Also at stake is the reach of the government's power to intimidate its critics.

When the Executive attempts to excuse these tactics as essential to its defense against internal subversion, we are obliged to remind it, without apology, of this court's long commitment to the preservation of the Bill of Rights from the corrosive environment of precisely such expedients. As Justice [Louis] Brandeis said, concurring in *Whitney v. California,* "those who won our independence by revolution were not cowards. They did not fear political change. They did not exalt order at the cost of liberty."

Justice White concurring:

... The threshold statutory question is simply put: Was the electronic surveillance undertaken by the government in this case a measure deemed necessary by the President to implement either the first or 2d branch of the exception carved out by § 2511 (3) to the general requirement of a warrant?

The answer, it seems to me, must turn on the affidavit of the Attorney General offered by the United States in opposition to defendants' motion to disclose surveillance records. It is apparent that there is nothing whatsoever in this affidavit suggesting that the surveillance was undertaken within the first branch of the § 2511 (3) exception, that is, to protect against foreign attack, to gather foreign intelligence or to protect national security information. The sole assertion was that the monitoring at issue was employed to gather intelligence information "deemed necessary to protect the nation from attempts of domestic organizations to attack and subvert the existing structure of the government." ...

Neither can I conclude from this characterization that the wiretap employed here fell within the exception recognized by the 2d sentence of § 2511 (3); for it utterly fails to assume responsibility for the judgment that Congress demanded: that the surveillance was necessary to prevent overthrow by force or other unlawful means or that there was any other clear and present danger to the structure or existence of the government. The affidavit speaks only of attempts to attack or subvert; it makes no reference to force or unlawfulness; it articulates no conclusion that the attempts involved any clear and present danger to the existence or structure of the government.

The shortcomings of the affidavit when measured against § 2511 (3) are patent. Indeed, the United States in oral argument conceded no less. The specific inquiry put to government counsel was: "[D]o you think the affidavit, standing alone, satisfies the Safe Streets Act?" The Assistant Attorney General answered "No sir, we do not rely upon the affidavit itself ...." ...

Government counsel, however, seek to save their case by reference to the *in camera* exhibit submitted to the district court to supplement the Attorney General's affidavit. It is said that the exhibit includes the request for wiretap approval submitted to the Attorney General, that the request asserted the need to avert a clear and present danger to the structure and existence of the government, and that the Attorney General endorsed his approval on the request. But I am unconvinced the mere endorsement of the Attorney General on the request for approval submitted to him must be taken as the Attorney General's own opinion that the wiretap was necessary to avert a clear and present danger to the existence or structure of the government when in an affidavit later filed in court and specifically characterizing the purposes of the interception and at least impliedly the grounds for his prior approval, the Attorney General said only that the tap was undertaken to secure intelligence thought necessary to protect against attempts to attack and subvert the structure of government. If the Attorney General's approval of the interception is to be given a judicially cognizable meaning different from the meaning he seems to have ascribed to it in his affidavit filed in court, there obviously must be further proceedings in the district court.

Moreover, I am reluctant myself to proceed in the first instance to examine the *in camera* material and either sustain or reject the surveillance as a necessary measure to avert the dangers referred to in § 2511 (3). What Congress excepted from the warrant requirement was a surveillance which *the President* would assume responsibility for deeming an essential measure to protect against clear and present danger. No judge can satisfy this congressional requirement.

Without the necessary threshold determination, the interception is, in my opinion, contrary to the terms of the statute and subject therefore to the prohibition contained in § 2515 against the use of the fruits of the warrantless electronic surveillance as evidence at any trial....

Government Informers

The Supreme Court ruled Dec. 12, 1966 that courts could accept evidence given by government informers against defendants.

The case involved James Hoffa, president of the International Brotherhood of Teamsters, who had been convicted Mar. 14, 1964 and sent to prison for attempting to bribe members of a jury in a previous trial. A major portion of the evidence used to convict Hoffa was furnished by Edward Partin, a government informer. The use of electronic eavesdropping was not an issue.

In appealing his conviction, Hoffa contended that information furnished the government by Partin should not have been admitted into evidence. Partin, it was claimed, was equivalent to an electronic eavesdropping device. Since at that time, prior to the 1968 Omnibus Crime Control & Safe Streets Act, evidence from a listening device planted in a home, office or hotel room could not be used as evidence, Hoffa's attorneys argued that information obtained from Partin likewise should not have been admitted into evidence.

The court rejected this analogy. "Neither this court nor any member of it has ever expressed the view that the 4th Amendment protects a wrong-doer's misplaced belief that a person to whom he voluntarily confides his wrongdoing will not reveal it," Justice Stewart said in the majority opinion.

Chief Justice Warren dissented. According to Warren, the circumstances surrounding Hoffa's conviction required the conviction's reversal by the Supreme Court in keeping with the court's re-sponsibility for supervising the fairness of federal trials. Warren took issue with the government's reliance on testimony furnished by Partin, who was then under state and federal indictments for a variety of crimes, including perjury, manslaughter and kidnapping. Warren emphasized that Partin had yet to be prosecuted for any of the charges brought against him in the 4 years since he had volunteered to inform against Hoffa. "This type of informer and the uses to which he was put in this case evidence a serious potential for undermining the integrity of the truth-finding process in the federal courts," Warren asserted. "Given the incentives and background of Partin, no conviction should be allowed to stand when based heavily on his testimony."

Abridgment of the *Hoffa v. United States* decision (385 U.S. 293, Dec. 12, 1966):

Justice Stewart delivering the opinion of the court:

Over a period of several weeks in the late autumn of 1962 there took place in a federal court in Nashville, Tennessee, a trial by jury in which James Hoffa was charged with violating a provision of the Taft-Hartley Act. That trial, known in the present record as the Test Fleet trial, ended with a hung jury. The petitioners now before us—James Hoffa, Thomas Parks, Larry Campbell, and Ewing King—were tried and convicted in 1964 for endeavoring to bribe members of that jury. The convictions were affirmed by the Court of Appeals. A substantial element in the government's proof that led to the convictions of these petitioners was contributed by a witness named Edward Partin, who testified to several incriminating statements which he said petitioners Hoffa and King had made in his presence during the course of the Test Fleet trial. Our grant of *certiorari* was limited to the single issue of whether the government's use in this case of evidence supplied by Partin operated to invalidate these convictions....

The specific question before us, as framed by counsel for the petitioners, is this: "Whether evidence obtained by the government by means of deceptively placing a secret informer in the quarters and councils of the defendant during one criminal trial so violates the defendant's 4th, 5th and 6th Amendment rights that suppression of such evidence is required in a subsequent trial of the same defendant on a different charge."...

... During the course of the [Test Fleet] trial ... [Hoffa] occupied a 3-room suite in the Andrew Jackson Hotel in Nashville. One of his constant companions throughout the trial was the petitioner King, president of the Nashville local of the Teamsters Union. Edward Partin, a resident of Baton Rouge, Louisiana, and a local Teamsters Union official there, made repeated visits to Nashville during the period of the trial. On these visits he frequented the Hoffa hotel suite and was continually in the company of Hoffa and his associates, including King, in and around the hotel suite, the hotel lobby, the courthouse and elsewhere in Nashville. During this period Partin made frequent reports to a federal agent named Sheridan concerning conversations he said Hoffa and King had had with him and with each other, disclosing endeavors to bribe members of the Test Fleet jury. Partin's reports and his subsequent testimony at the petitioners' trial unquestionably contributed, directly or indirectly, to the convictions of all 4 of the petitioners.

The chain of circumstances which led Partin to be in Nashville during the Test Fleet trial extended back at least to September of 1962. At that time Partin was in jail in Baton Rouge on a state criminal charge. He was also under a federal indictment for embezzling union funds, and other indictments for state offenses were pending against him. Between that time and Partin's initial visit to Nashville on Oct. 22 he was released on bail on the state criminal charge, and proceedings under the federal indictment were postponed. On Oct. 8 Partin telephoned Hoffa in Washington, D.C. ... Partin asked if he could see Hoffa ..., and Hoffa acquiesced. Partin again called Hoffa on Oct. 18 and arranged to meet him in Nashville. During this period Partin also consulted on several occasions with federal law enforcement agents, who told him that Hoffa might attempt to tamper with the Test Fleet jury and asked him to be on the lookout in Nashville for such attempts and to report to the federal authorities any evidence of wrongdoing that he discovered. Partin agreed to do so.

After the Test Fleet trial was completed, Partin's wife received 4 monthly installment payments of $300 from government funds, and the state and federal charges against Partin were either dropped or not actively pursued.

... The government insists the fair inference is that Partin went to Nashville on his own initiative to discuss union business and his own problems with Hoffa, that Partin ultimately cooperated closely with federal authorities only after he discovered evidence of jury tampering in the Test Fleet trial, that the payments to Partin's wife were simply in partial reimbursement of Partin's subsequent out-of-pocket expenses, and that the failure to prosecute Partin on the state and federal charges had no necessary connection with his services as an informer. The findings of the trial court support this version of the facts, and these findings were accepted by the Court of Appeals as "supported by substantial evidence.".... We proceed upon the premise that Partin was a government informer from the time he first arrived in Nashville on Oct. 22, and that the government compensated him for his services as such....

It is contended that only by violating the petitioner's rights under the 4th Amendment was Partin able to hear the petitioner's incriminating statements in the hotel suite, and that Partin's testimony was therefore inadmissible under the exclusionary rule of *Weeks v. United States* [1914].... The argument is that Partin's failure to disclose his role as a government informer vitiated the consent that the petitioner gave to Partin's repeated entries into the suite, and that by listening to the petitioner's statements Partin conducted an illegal "search" for verbal evidence....

Where the argument falls is in its misapprehension of the fundamental nature and scope of 4th Amendment protection. What the 4th Amendment protects is the security a man relies upon when he places himself or his property within a constitutionally protected area, be it his home or his office, his hotel room or his automobile. There he is protected from unwarranted governmental intrusion. And when he puts something in his filing cabinet, in his desk drawer, or in his pocket, he has the right to know it will be secure from an unreasonable search or an unreasonable seizure....

In the present case, however, it is evident that no interest legitimately protected by the 4th Amendment is involved. It is obvious that the petitioner was not relying on the security of his hotel suite when he made the incriminating statements to Partin or in Partin's presence. Partin did not enter the suite by force or by stealth. He was not a surreptitious eavesdropper. Partin was in the suite by invitation, and every conversation which he heard was either directed to him or knowingly carried on in his presence. The petitioner, in a word, was not relying on the security of the hotel room; he was relying upon his misplaced confidence that Partin would not reveal his wrongdoing. As counsel for the petitioner himself points out, some of the communications with Partin did not take place in the suite at all but in the "hall of the hotel," in the "Andrew Jackson Hotel lobby," and "at the courthouse."

Neither this court nor any member of it has ever expressed the view that the 4th Amendment protects a wrongdoer's misplaced belief that a person to whom he voluntarily confides his wrongdoing will not reveal it. Indeed, the court unanimously rejected that very contention less than 4 years ago in *Lopez v. United States* [1963]. . . . In that case the petitioner had been convicted of attempted bribery of an internal revenue agent named Davis. The court was divided with regard to the admissibility in evidence of a surreptitious electronic recording of an incriminating conversation Lopez had had in his private office with Davis. But there was no dissent to the view that testimony about the conversation by Davis himself was clearly admissible.

As the court put it, "Davis was not guilty of an unlawful invasion of petitioner's office simply because his apparent willingness to accept a bribe was not real. . . . He was in the office with petitioner's consent, and while there he did not violate the privacy of the office by seizing something surreptitiously without petitioner's knowledge. . . . The only evidence obtained consisted of statements made by Lopez to Davis, statements which Lopez knew full well could be used against him by Davis if he wished. . . ." . . . In the words of the dissenting opinion in *Lopez,* "The risk of being overheard by an eavesdropper or betrayed by an informer or deceived as to the identity of one with whom one deals is probably inherent in the conditions of human society. It is the kind of risk we necessarily assume whenever we speak.". . .

Adhering to these views, we hold that no right protected by the 4th Amendment was violated in the present case.

Chief Justice Warren dissenting:

. . . At this late date in the annals of law enforcement, it seems to me that we cannot say either that every use of informers and undercover agents is proper or, on the other hand, that no uses are. There are some situations where the law could not adequately be enforced without the employment of some guile or misrepresentation of identity. A law enforcement officer performing his official duties cannot be required always to be in uniform or to wear his badge of authority on the lapel of his civilian clothing. Nor need he be required in all situations to proclaim himself an arm of the law. It blinks the realities of sophisticated, modern-day criminal activity and legitimate law enforcement practices to argue the contrary. However, one of the important duties of this court is to give careful scrutiny to practices of government agents when they are challenged in cases before us, in order to insure that the protections of the Constitution are respected and to maintain the integrity of federal law enforcement....

In the *Osborn* case, the petitioner employed Robert Vick, a police officer of Nashville, Tennessee, to investigate persons who were members of a panel from which a federal criminal jury was to be selected in a prior trial of James Hoffa in that city. Although he knew Vick's loyalty was due the police department, when he learned that Vick had a cousin on the panel he urged Vick to offer the cousin $10,000 in return for the latter's promise to vote for acquittal if selected to sit on the petit jury. Vick informed federal authorities of this proposal and made an affidavit to that effect for the judge who was to preside at the Hoffa trial. The judge, in order to determine the truthfulness of the affidavit and to protect the integrity of the trial, authorized the equipping of Vick with a recording device to be used in further conversations with petitioner. I see nothing wrong with the government thus verifying the truthfulness of the informer and protecting his credibility in this fashion. *Lopez v. United States* ... (1963). This decision in no sense supports a conclusion that unbridled use of electronic recording equipment is to be permitted in searching out crime. And it does not lend judicial sanction to wiretapping, electronic "bugging" or any of the other questionable spying practices that are used to invade privacy.... .

But I consider ... *Osborn* to be materially, even fundamentally, different from this *Hoffa* case. Here, Edward Partin, a jailbird languishing in a Louisiana jail under indictments for such state and federal crimes as embezzlement, kidnapping and manslaughter (and soon to be charged with perjury and assault), contacted federal authorities and told them he was willing to become, and would be useful as, an informer against Hoffa who was then about to be tried in the Test Fleet case. A motive for his doing this is immediately apparent—namely, his strong desire to work his way out of jail and out of his various legal entanglements with the state and federal governments. And it is interesting to note that, if this was his motive, he has been uniquely successful in satisfying it. In the 4 years since he first volunteered to be an informer against Hoffa he has not been prosecuted on any of the serious federal charges for which he was at that time jailed, and the state charges have apparently vanished into thin air.

Shortly after Partin made contact with the federal authorities and told them of his position in the Baton Rouge Local of the Teamster's Union and of his acquaintance with Hoffa, his bail was suddenly reduced from $50,000 to $5,000 and he was released from jail. He immediately telephoned Hoffa, who was then in New Jersey, and, by collaborating with a state law enforcement official, surreptitiously made a tape recording of the conversation. A copy of the recording was furnished to federal authorities.... Partin telephoned Hoffa a few weeks later and succeeded in making a date to meet in Nashville where Hoffa and his attorneys were then preparing for the Test Fleet trial. Unknown to Hoffa, this call was also recorded and again federal authorities were informed as to the details.

Upon his arrival in Nashville, Partin manifested his "friendship" and made himself useful to Hoffa, thereby worming his way into Hoffa's hotel suite and becoming part and parcel of Hoffa's entourage. As the "faithful" servant and factotum of the defense camp which he became, he was in a position to overhear conversations not directed to him, many of which were between attorneys and either their client or prospective defense witnesses. Pursuant to the general instructions he received from federal authorities to report "any attempts at witness intimidation or tampering with the jury," "anything illegal," or even "anything of interest," Partin became the equivalent of a bugging device which moved with Hoffa wherever he went. Everything Partin saw or heard was reported to federal authorities and much of it was ultimately the subject matter of his testimony in this case. For his services he was well paid by the government, both through devious and secret alimony payments to his divorced wife and, it may be inferred, by executed promises not to pursue the indictments under which he was charged at the time he became an informer.

This type of informer and the uses to which he was put in this case evidence a serious potential for undermining the integrity of the truth-finding process in the federal courts. Given the incentives and background of Partin, no conviction should be allowed to stand when based heavily on his testimony. And that is exactly the quicksand upon which these convictions rest, because without Partin, who was the principal government witness, there would probably have been no convictions here. Thus, although petitioners make their main arguments on constitutional grounds and raise serious 4th and 6th Amendment questions, it should not even be necessary for the court to reach those questions. For the affront to the quality and fairness of federal law enforcement which this case presents is sufficient to require an exercise of our supervisory powers....

I do not say that the government may never use as a witness a person of dubious or even bad character. In performing its duty to prosecute crime the government must take the witnesses as it finds them. They may be persons of good, bad or doubtful credibility, but their testimony may be the only way to establish the facts, leaving it to the jury to determine their credibility. In this case, however, we have a totally different situation. Here the government reaches into the jailhouse to employ a man who was himself facing indictments far more serious (and later including one for perjury) than the one confronting the man against whom he offered to inform. It employed him not for the purpose of testifying to something that had already happened, but rather for the purpose of infiltration to see if crimes would in the future be committed. The government in its zeal even assisted him in gaining a position from which he could be a witness to the confidential relationship of attorney and client engaged in the preparation of a criminal defense. And, for the dubious evidence thus obtained, the government paid an enormous price. Certainly if a criminal defendant insinuated his informer into the prosecution's camp in this manner he would be guilty of obstructing justice. I cannot agree that what happened in this case is in keeping with the standards of justice in our federal system and I must, therefore, dissent.

The Supreme Court Apr. 5, 1971, in a 5-4 decision, upheld the unrestricted use of electronic devices by government agents or informers for the purpose of recording or transmitting conversations to which they are a party. The case was *United States v. White.* Chief Justice Warren Earl Burger and Justices Byron R. White, Potter Stewart, Hugo L. Black and Harry A. Blackmun formed the majority. The dissenters were Justices William J. Brennan Jr., William O. Douglas, John Marshall Harlan and Thurgood Marshall.

The case involved James A. White, a narcotics dealer, 8 of whose conversations with Harvey Jackson, a government informer, were recorded on a listening device hidden on Jackson and relayed to a government agent. On 4 of these occasions, the government agent was hiding in a closet in the informer's home.

In a previous case, *On Lee v. United States,* the Supreme Court in 1952 had upheld the government's use of a recording device hidden on an informer who engaged a friend, a narcotics suspect, in an incriminating conversation. In *Lopez v. United States,* the court in 1963 upheld the government's use of a recording device hidden on an Internal Revenue agent; the device was used to record a taxpayer's attempt to bribe the agent. At that time, however, court interpretations had applied the 4th Amendment only to searches involving a physical trespass. Since then, however, the court in *Katz v. United States* (1967) had dropped the trespass requirement in reading the 4th Amendment to require a warrant based on a showing of probable cause regardless of whether a physical trespass was involved. The Court of Appeals interpreted *Katz* to require a warrant in instances in which the police or a police informer is wired for sound.

Justice White, speaking for the Supreme Court, rejected the Court of Appeals' contention. He relied

instead on the *Hoffa v. United States* holding that
the 4th Amendment affords no protection to "a
wrongdoer's misplaced belief that a person to whom
he voluntarily confides his wrongdoing will not
reveal it." White, therefore, concluded that the
normal warrant requirement was not needed to wire
a government agent or informer. According to
White, there was no constitutional difference
between a situation in which an undercover police
officer or informant engages a defendant in an
incriminating conversation that he later writes down
and a situation in which the same conversation is
recorded on a listening device hidden on the officer
or informant. "If the law gives no protection to the
wrongdoer whose trusted accomplice is or becomes a
police agent, neither should it protect him when that
same agent has recorded or transmitted the
conversations which are later offered in evidence,"
White said.

The 4 dissenting justices agreed with the lower
court decision that a warrant should have been obtained. Justice Brennan added that a warrant should
be required not only in cases of 3d-party electronic
monitoring but also in instances in which the
monitoring is done by a government official as in
Lopez.

Justices Harlan and Douglas emphasized what
they held to be the dangers of electronic surveillance.
Douglas called it "the greatest leveler of human
privacy ever known." Harlan asserted that electronic
monitoring by government informers serves "to
undermine that confidence and sense of security in
dealing with one another that is characteristic of
individual relationships between citizens in a free
society." Harlan stressed that he was not seeking to

prevent such monitoring but only "to interpose a search warrant procedure between law enforcement agencies engaging in electronic eavesdropping and the public generally."

Abridgment of the *United States v. White* decision (28 U.S. 453, Apr. 5, 1971):

Justice White announcing the judgment of the court:

In 1966, respondent James A. White was tried and convicted under 2 consolidated indictments charging various illegal transactions in narcotics.... He was fined and sentenced as a 2d offender to 25-year concurrent sentences. The issue before us is whether the 4th Amendment bars from evidence the testimony of governmental agents who related certain conversations which had occurred between defendant White and a government informant, Harvey Jackson, and which the agents overheard by monitoring the frequency of a radio transmitter carried by Jackson and concealed on his person. On 4 occasions the conversations took place in Jackson's home; each of these conversations was overheard by an agent concealed in a kitchen closet with Jackson's consent and by a 2d agent outside the house using a radio receiver. 4 other conversations—one in respondent's home, one in a restaurant and 2 in Jackson's car—were overheard by the use of radio equipment. The prosecution was unable to locate and produce Jackson at the trial, and the trial court overruled objections to the testimony of the agents who conducted the electronic surveillance. The jury returned a guilty verdict and defendant appealed.

The Court of Appeals read *Katz v. United States,* ... (1967), as overruling *On Lee v. United States,* ... (1952), and interpreting the 4th Amendment to forbid the introduction of the agents' testimony in the circumstances of this case. Accordingly, the court reversed but without adverting to the fact that the transactions at issue here had occurred before *Katz* was decided in this Court. In our view, the Court of Appeals misinterpreted both the *Katz* case and the 4th Amendment and in any event erred in applying the *Katz* case to events which occurred before that decision was rendered by this court....

Until *Katz v. United States,* neither wiretapping nor electronic eavesdropping violated a defendant's 4th amendment rights "unless there has been an official search and seizure of his person, or such a seizure of his papers or his tangible material effects, or an actual physical invasion of his house 'or curtilage' for the purpose of making a seizure." *Olmstead v. United States ...* (1928); *Goldman v. United States ...* (1942). But where "eavesdropping was accomplished by means of an unauthorized physical penetration into the premises occupied" by the defendant, although falling short of a "technical trespass under the local property law," the 4th Amendment was violated and any evidence of what was seen and heard, as well as tangible objects seized, were considered inadmissible fruits of an unlawful invasion....

Katz v. United States, however, finally swept away doctrines that electronic eavesdropping is permissible under the 4th Amendment unless physical invasion of a constitutionally protected area produced the challenged evidence....

The Court of Appeals understood *Katz* to render inadmissible against White the agents' testimony concerning conversations which Jackson broadcast to them. We cannot agree. *Katz* involved no revelation to the government by a party to conversations with the defendant nor did the court indicate in any way that a defendant has a justifiable and constitutionally protected expectation that a person with whom he is conversing will not then or later reveal the conversation to the police.

Hoffa v. United States ..., which was left undisturbed by *Katz,* held that however strongly a defendant may trust an apparent colleague, his expectations in this respect are not protected by the 4th Amendment when it turns out that the colleague is a government agent regularly communicating with the authorities. In these circumstances, "no interest legitimately protected by the 4th Amendment is involved." ... No warrant to "search and seize" is required in such circumstances, nor is it when the government sends to defendant's home a secret agent who conceals his identity and makes a purchase of narcotics from the accused, *Lewis v. United States...* (1966), or when the same agent, unbeknown to the defendant, carries electronic equipment to record the defendant's words and the evidence so gathered is later offered in evidence. *Lopez v. United States....*

Conceding that *Hoffa, Lewis* and *Lopez* remained unaffected by *Katz,* the Court of Appeals nevertheless read both *Katz* and the 4th Amendment to require a different result if the agent not only records his conversations with the defendant but instantaneously transmits them electronically to other agents equipped with radio receivers. Where this occurs, the Court of Appeals held, the 4th Amendment is violated and the testimony of the listening agents must be excluded from evidence.

To reach this result it was necessary for the Court of Appeals to hold that *On Lee v. United States* was no longer good law. In that case, which involved facts very similar to the case before us, the court first rejected claims of a 4th Amendment violation because the informer had not trespassed when he entered the defendant's premises and conversed with him. To this extent the court's rationale cannot survive *Katz....* But the court announced a 2d and independent ground for its decision; for it went on to say that overruling *Olmstead* and *Goldman* would be of no aid to *On Lee* since he "was talking confidentially and indiscreetly with one he trusted, and he was overheard.... It would be a dubious service to the genuine liberties protected by the 4th Amendment to make them bedfellows with spurious liberties improvised by farfetched analogies which would liken eavesdropping on a conversation, with the connivance of one of the parties, to an unreasonable search or seizure. We find no violation of the 4th Amendment here."... We see no indication in *Katz* that the court meant to disturb that understanding of the 4th Amendment or to disturb the result reached in the *On Lee* case, nor are we now inclined to overturn this view of the 4th Amendment.

Concededly a police agent who conceals his police connections may write down for official use his conversations with a defendant and testify concerning them, without a warrant authorizing his encounters with the defendant and without otherwise violating the latter's 4th Amendment rights. *Hoffa v. United States....* For constitutional purposes, no different result is required if the agent instead of immediately reporting and transcribing his conversations with defendant, either (1) simultaneously records them with electronic equipment which he is carrying on his person, *Lopez v. United States...* ; (2) or carries radio equipment which simultaneously transmits the conversations either to recording equipment located elsewhere or to other agents monitoring the transmitting frequency. *On Lee v. United States....* If the conduct and revelations of an agent operating without electronic equipment do not invade the defendant's constitutionally justifiable expectations of privacy, neither does a simultaneous recording of the same conversations made by the agent or by others from transmissions received from the agent to whom the defendant is talking and whose trustworthiness the defendant necessarily risks.

Our problem is not what the privacy expectations of particular defendants in particular situations may be or the extent to which they may in fact have relied on the discretion of their companions.... Our problem, in terms of the principles announced in *Katz,* is what expectations of privacy are constitutionally "justifiable"—what expectations the 4th Amendment will protect in the absence of a warrant. So far, the law permits the frustration of actual expectations of privacy by permitting authorities to use the testimony of those associates who for one reason or another have determined to turn to the police, as well as by authorizing the use of informants in the manner exemplified by *Hoffa* and *Lewis.* If the law gives no protection to the wrongdoer whose trusted accomplice is or becomes a police agent, neither should it protect him when that same agent has recorded or transmitted the conversations which are later offered in evidence to prove the state's case....

Inescapably, one contemplating illegal activities must realize and risk that his companions may be reporting to the police.... Given the possibility or probability that one of his colleagues is cooperating with the police, it is only speculation to assert that the defendant's utterances would be substantially different or his sense of security any less if he also thought it possible that the suspected colleague is wired for sound. At least there is no persuasive evidence that the difference in this respect between the electronically equipped and the unequipped agent is substantial enough to require discrete constitutional recognition, particularly under the 4th Amendment which is ruled by fluid concepts of "reasonableness."

Nor should we be too ready to erect constitutional barriers to relevant and probative evidence which is also accurate and reliable. An electronic recording will many times produce a more reliable rendition of what a defendant has said than will the unaided memory of a police agent. It may also be that with the recording in existence it is less likely that the informant will change his mind, less chance that threat or injury will suppress unfavorable evidence and less chance that cross-examination will confound the testimony.... We are not prepared to hold that a defendant who has no constitutional right to exclude the informer's unaided testimony nevertheless has a 4th Amendment privilege against a more accurate version of the events in question.

It is thus untenable to consider the activities and reports of the police agent himself, though acting without a warrant, to be a "reasonable" investigative effort and lawful under the 4th Amendment but to view the same agent with a recorder or transmitter as conducting an "unreasonable" and unconstitutional search and seizure....

No different result should obtain where, as in *On Lee* and the instant case, the informer disappears and is unavailable at trial; for the issue of whether specified events on a certain day violate the 4th Amendment should not be determined by what later happens to the informer. His unavailability at trial and proffering the testimony of other agents ... do not appear critical to deciding whether prior events invaded the defendant's 4th Amendment rights.

The Court of Appeals was in error for another reason. In *Desist v. United States* ... (1969), we held that our decision in *Katz v. United States* applied only to those electronic surveillances which occurred subsequent to the date of that decision. Here the events in question took place in the late 1965 and early 1966, long prior to *Katz.* We adhere to the rationale of *Desist,* see *Williams v. United States* [1971].... It was error for the Court of Appeals to dispose of this case based on its understanding of the principles announced in the *Katz* case. The court should have judged this case by the pre-*Katz* law and under that law, as *On Lee* clearly holds, the electronic surveillance here involved did not violate White's rights to be free from unreasonable searches and seizures.

The judgment of the Court of Appeals is reversed.

Justice Brennan concurring in the result:

I agree that *Desist v. United States* ... requires reversal of the judgment of the Court of Appeals. Therefore, a majority of the court supports disposition of this case on that ground. However, my brothers Douglas, Harlan and White also debate the question whether *On Lee v. United States* ... may any longer be regarded as sound law. My brother White argues that *On Lee* is still sound law. My brothers Douglas and Harlan argue that it is not. Neither position commands the support of a majority of the court. For myself, I agree with my brothers Douglas and Harlan. But I go further. It is my view that the reasoning of both my brothers Douglas and Harlan compels the conclusion that *Lopez v. United States* ... is also no longer sound law. In other words, it is my view that current 4th Amendment jurisprudence interposes a warrant requirement not only in cases of 3d-party electronic monitoring (the situation in *On Lee* and in this case) but also in cases of electronic recording by a government agent of a face-to-face conversation with a criminal suspect, which was the situation in *Lopez*. For I adhere to the [Harlan] dissent in *Lopez* ... in which ... "the doctrinal basis of our subsequent 14th Amendment decisions may be said to have had its genesis." *Katz v. United States* ... adopted that "doctrinal basis" and thus, it seems to me, agreed with the argument in that dissent that "subsequent decisions and subsequent experience have sapped whatever vitality *On Lee* may once have had; that it should now be regarded as overruled" and that the situation in *Lopez* "is rationally indistinguishable."... I remain of the view that the 4th Amendment imposes the warrant requirement in both the *On Lee* and *Lopez* situations.

Justice Douglas dissenting:

... The issue in this case is clouded and concealed by the very discussion of it in legalistic terms. What the ancients knew as "eavesdropping," we now call "electronic surveillance"; but to equate the 2 is to treat man's first gunpowder on the same level as the nuclear bomb. Electronic surveillance is the greatest leveler of human privacy ever known. How most forms of it can be held "reasonable" within the meaning of the 4th Amendment is a mystery. To be sure the Constitution and Bill of Rights are not to be read as covering only the technology known in the 18th century. Otherwise its concept of "commerce" would be hopeless when it comes to the management of modern affairs. At the same time the concepts of privacy which the Founders enshrined in the 4th Amendment vanish completely when we slavishly allow an all-powerful government, proclaiming law and order, efficiency and other benign purposes, to penetrate all the walls and doors which men need to shield them from the pressures of a turbulent life around them and give them the health and strength to carry on.

That is why a "strict construction" of the 4th Amendment is necessary if every man's liberty and privacy are to be constitutionally honored.

When Franklin D. Roosevelt on May 21, 1940, authorized wiretapping in cases of "5th column" activities and sabotage and limited "so far as possible to aliens," he said that "under ordinary and normal circumstances wire-tapping by government agents should not be carried on for the excellent reason that it is almost bound to lead to abuse of civil rights.". . .

Today no one perhaps notices because only a small, obscure criminal is the victim. But every person is the victim, for the technology we exalt today is everyman's master. Any doubters should read Arthur R. Miller's *The Assault On Privacy* (1971). After describing the monitoring of conversations and their storage in data banks, Prof. Miller goes on to describe "human monitoring," which he calls the "ultimate step in mechanical snooping"—a device for spotting unorthodox or aberrational behavior across a wide spectrum. "Given the advancing state of both the remote sensory art and the capacity of computors to handle an uninterrupted and synoptic data flow, there seems to be no physical barriers left to shield us from intrusion.". . .

When one reads what is going on in this area today, our judicial treatment of the subject seems as remote from reality as the well-known Baron Parke was remote from the social problems of his day. . . .

We held in *Berger v. New York* . . . that wiretapping is a search and seizure within the meaning of the 4th Amendment and therefore must meet its requirements, *viz.:* there must be a prior showing of probable cause, the warrant authorizing the wiretap must particularly describe "the place to be searched and the persons or things to be seized," and that it may not have the breadth, generality and long life of the general warrant against which the 4th Amendment was aimed.

In *Katz v. United States* . . . we held that an electronic device, used without trespass onto any given enclosure (there a telephone booth), was a search for which a 4th Amendment warrant was needed. Mr. Justice Stewart, speaking for the court, said: "Wherever a man may be, he is entitled to know that he will remain free from unreasonable searches, and seizures.". . .

As a result of *Berger* and of *Katz,* both wiretapping and electronic surveillance through a "bug" or other device are now covered by the 4th Amendment.

There were prior decisions representing an opposed view. In *On Lee v. United States* . . ., [an] undercover agent with a radio transmitter concealed on his person interviewed the defendant whose words were heard over a radio receiver by another agent down the street. The idea, discredited by *Katz,* that there was no violation of the 4th Amendment because there was no trespass, was the core of the *On Lee* decision. . . .

Lopez v. United States . . . was also pre-*Berger* and pre-*Katz.* The government agent there involved carried a pocket wire recorder which the court said "was not planted by means of an unlawful physical invasion of petitioner's premises under circumstances which would violate the 4th Amendment.". . .

It is urged by the Department of Justice that *On Lee* be established as the controlling decision in this field. I would stand by *Berger* and *Katz* and reaffirm the need for judicial supervision under the 4th Amendment of the use of electronic surveillance which, uncontrolled, promises to lead us into a police state.

These were wholly pre-arranged episodes of surveillance. The first was in the informant's home to which respondent had been invited. The 2d was also in the informer's home, the next day. The 3d was 4 days later at the home of the respondent. The 4th was in the informer's car 2 days later. 12 days after that a meeting in the informer's home was intruded upon. The 6th occurred at a street rendezvous. The 7th was in the informer's home and the 8th in a restaurant owned by respondent's mother-in-law. So far as time is concerned there is no excuse for not seeking a warrant. And while there is always an effort involved in preparing affidavits or other evidence in support of a showing of probable cause, that burden was given constitutional sanction in the 4th Amendment against the activities of the agents of George III. It was designed not to protect criminals but to protect everyone's privacy.

On Lee and *Lopez* are of a vintage opposed to *Berger* and *Katz.* However they may be explained, they are products of the old common-law notions of trespass. *Katz,* on the other hand, emphasized that with few exceptions "searches conducted outside the judicial process, without prior approval by judge or magistrate, are *per se* unreasonable under the 4th Amendment...." ...*Camara v. Municipal Court* [1967] ... put administrative searches under the 4th Amendment. We held that administrative actions, like other searches, implicated officials in an invasion of privacy and that the 4th Amendment was meant to guard against the arbitrariness of any such invasion....

In *Chimel v. California* ..., in considering the constitutionality of a search incident to an arrest we held that, while the area in the immediate reach of an arrestee is "reasonable" though made without a warrant, a search beyond that zone may generally be made "only under the authority of a search warrant.".... And in 2 "stop and frisk" cases, *Terry v. Ohio* ... and *Davis v. Mississippi* ... , we held that any restraint of the person, however brief, was subject to judicial inquiry on "reasonableness" ... and that "the 4th Amendment governs all intrusions by agents of the public upon personal security...."
...

We have moved far away from the rationale of *On Lee* and *Lopez* and only a retrogressive step of large dimensions would bring us back to it.

The threads of thought running through our recent decisions are that these extensive intrusions into privacy made by electronic surveillance make self-restraint by law enforcement officials an inadequate protection, that the requirement of warrants under the 4th Amendment is essential to a free society.

Monitoring, if prevalent, certainly kills free discourse and spontaneous utterances. Free discourse—a First Amendment value—may be frivolous or serious, humble or defiant, reactionary or revolutionary, profane or in good taste; but it is not free if there is surveillance. Free discourse liberates the spirit, though it may produce only froth. The individual must keep some facts concerning his thoughts within a small zone of people. At the same time he must be free to pour out his woes or inspirations or dreams to others. He remains the sole judge as to what must be said and what must remain unspoken. This is the essence of the idea of privacy implicit in the First and 5th Amendments as well as in the 4th....

Now that the discredited decisions in *On Lee* and *Lopez* are resuscitated and revived, must everyone live in fear that every word he speaks may be transmitted or recorded and later repeated to the entire world? I can imagine nothing that has a more chilling effect on people speaking their minds and expressing their views on important matters. The advocates of that regime should spend some time in totalitarian countries and learn firsthand the kind of regime they are creating here....

The decision not to make *Katz* retroactive to any electronic surveillance which occurred prior to Dec. 18, 1967 (the day we decided *Katz),* is not, in my view, a tenable one....

Justice Harlan dissenting:

The uncontested facts of this case squarely challenge the continuing viability of *On Lee v. United States....* As the plurality opinion of Mr. Justice White itself makes clear, important constitutional developments since *On Lee* mandate that we reassess that case, which has continued to govern official behavior of this sort in spite of the subsequent erosion of its doctrinal foundations. With all respect, my agreement with the majority ends at that point.

I think that a perception of the scope and role of the 4th Amendment, as elucidated by this court since *On Lee* was decided, and full comprehension of the precise issue at stake leads to the conclusion that *On Lee* can no longer be regarded as sound law. Nor do I think the date we decided *Katz v. United States* ... (1967) can be deemed controlling both for the reasons discussed in my dissent in *Desist v. United States* ... and my separate opinion in *Williams v. United States* ... and because, in my view, it requires no discussion of the holding in *Katz,* as distinguished from its underlying rationale as to the reach of the 4th Amendment, to comprehend the constitutional infirmity of *On Lee....*

...We deal here with the constitutional validity of instantaneous 3d-party electronic eavesdropping, conducted by federal law enforcement officers, without any prior judicial approval of the technique utilized, but with the consent and cooperation of a participant in the conversation, and where the substance of the matter electronically overheard is related in a federal criminal trial by those who eavesdropped as direct, not merely corroborative, evidence of the guilt of the non-consenting party. The magnitude of the issue at hand is evidenced not simply by the obvious doctrinal difficulty of weighing such activity in the 4th Amendment balance, but also, and more importantly, by the prevalence of police utilization of this technique. Prof. Westin has documented in careful detail the numerous devices that make technologically feasible the Orwellian Big Brother. Of immediate relevance is his observation that "participant recording, in which one participant in a conversation or meeting, either a police officer or a cooperating party, wears a concealed device that records or broadcasts to others nearby ..., is used tens of thousands of times each year, particularly in cases involving extortion, conspiracy, narcotics, gambling, prostitution, corruption by police officials, ... and similar crimes."

Moreover, ... the factors that must be reckoned with in reaching constitutional conclusions respecting the use of electronic eavesdropping as a tool of law enforcement are exceedingly subtle and complex. They have provoked sharp differences of opinion both within and without the judiciary, and the entire problem has been the subject of continuing study by various governmental and nongovernmental bodies.

Finally, given the importance of electronic eavesdropping as a technique for coping with the more deep-seated kinds of criminal activity, and the complexities that are encountered in striking a workable constitutional balance between the public and private interests at stake, I believe that the courts should proceed with specially measured steps in this field. More particularly, I think this court should not foreclose itself from reconsidering doctrines that would prevent the states from seeking, independently of the niceties of federal restrictions as they may develop, solutions to such vexing problems, see *Mapp v. Ohio* ... and *Ker v. California* ... and see also *Berger v. New York* ...; *Baldwin v. New York* ... (1970) (dissenting opinion); *California v. Green* ... (1970) (concurring opinion). I also think that in the adjudication of federal cases, the court should leave ample room for Congressional developments....

... The decisions of this court since *On Lee* do more than demonstrate that the doctrine of that case is wholly open for reconsideration and has been since well before *Katz*   was decided. They also establish sound general principles for application of the 4th Amendment that were either dimly perceived or not fully worked out at the time of *On Lee.* . . . [T]hat verbal communication is protected by the 4th Amendment, that the reasonableness of a search does not depend on the presence or absence of a trespass and that the 4th Amendment is principally concerned with protecting interests of privacy, rather than property rights.

Especially when other recent 4th Amendment decisions, not otherwise so immediately relevant, are read with those already discussed, the primacy of an additional general principle becomes equally evident: official investigatory action that impinges on privacy must typically, in order to be constitutionally permissible, be subjected to the warrant requirement. . . .

In *Camara [v. Municipal Court* (1967)] the court brought under the 4th Amendment administrative searches that had once been thought to be without its sweep. In doing so the opinion emphasized the desirability of establishing in advance those circumstances that justified the intrusion into a home and submitting them for review to an independent assessor, principles that this Court has always deemed to be at the core of 4th Amendment protections. . . .

Since it is the task of the law to form and project, as well as mirror and reflect, we should not, as judges, merely recite the expectations and risks without examining the desirability of saddling them upon society. The critical question, therefore, is whether under our system of government, as reflected in the Constitution, we should impose on our citizens the risks of the electronic listener or observer without at least the protection of a warrant requirement.

This question must, in my view, be answered by assessing the nature of a particular practice and the likely extent of its impact on the individual's sense of security balanced against the utility of the conduct as a technique of law enforcement. For those more extensive intrusions that significantly jeopardize the sense of security which is the paramount concern of 4th Amendment liberties, I am of the view that more than self-restraint by law enforcement officials is required and at the least warrants should be necessary. . . .

The impact of the practice of 3d-party bugging, must, I think, be considered such as to undermine that confidence and sense of security in dealing with one another that is characteristic of individual relationships between citizens in a free society. It goes beyond the impact on privacy occasioned by the ordinary type of "informer" investigation upheld in *Lewis* and *Hoffa.* The argument of the plurality opinion, to the effect that it is irrelevant whether secrets are revealed by the mere tattle-tale or the transistor, ignores the differences occasioned by 3d-party monitoring and recording which insures full and accurate disclosure of all that is said, free of the possibility of error and oversight that inheres in human reporting.

... Were 3d-party bugging a prevalent practice, it might well smother that spontaneity—reflected in frivolous, impetuous, sacrilegious and defiant discourse—that liberates daily life....

Finally, it is too easy to forget—and, hence, too often forgotten—that the issue here is whether to interpose a search warrant procedure between law enforcement agencies engaging in electronic eavesdropping and the public generally. By casting its "risk analysis" solely in terms of the expectations and risks that "wrongdoers" or "one contemplating illegal activities" ought to bear, the plurality opinion, I think, misses the mark entirely. *On Lee* does not simply mandate that criminals must daily run the risk of unknown eavesdroppers prying on their private affairs; it subjects each and every law-abiding member of society to that risk. The very purpose of interposing the 4th Amendment warrant requirement is to redistribute the privacy risks throughout society in a way that produces the results the plurality opinion ascribes to the *On Lee* rule. Abolition of *On Lee* would not end electronic eavesdropping. It would prevent public officials from engaging in that practice unless they first had probable cause to suspect an individual of involvement in illegal activities and had tested their version of the facts before a detached judicial officer. The interest *On Lee* fails to protect is the expectation of the ordinary citizen, who has never engaged in illegal conduct in his life, that he may carry on his private discourse freely, openly and spontaneously without measuring his every word against the connotations it might carry when instantaneously heard by others unknown to him and unfamiliar with his situation or analyzed in a cold, formal record played days, months or years after the conversation. Interposition of a warrant requirement is designed not to shield "wrongdoers" but to secure a measure of privacy and a sense of personal security throughout our society.

The 4th Amendment does, of course, leave room for the employment of modern technology in criminal law enforcement, but in the stream of current developments in 4th Amendment law I think it must be held that 3d-party electronic monitoring, subject only to the self-restraint of law enforcement officials, has no place in our society. . . .

Justice Marshall dissenting:

I am convinced that the correct view of the 4th Amendment in the area of electronic surveillance is one that brings the safeguards of the warrant requirement to bear on the investigatory activity involved in this case. In this regard I agree with the dissents of Mr. Justice Douglas and Mr. Justice Harlan. In short, I believe that *On Lee v. United States* . . . cannot be considered viable in light of the constitutional principles articulated in *Katz v. United States* . . . and other cases. And for reasons expressed by Mr. Justice Fortas in dissent in *Desist v. United States* . . ., I do not think we should feel constrained to employ a discarded theory of the 4th Amendment in evaluating the governmental intrusions challenged here.

POLICING THE POLICE

Police Largely Escape Penalty for Misconduct

Bullying tactics by the police are criminal offenses in most instances. Since 1921, for example, it has been a crime for a federal official to participate in an illegal search. Yet it is generally agreed that the law has seldom been enforced. An 1866 Reconstruction statute makes it a criminal offense for any person, acting "under color of any law, statute, ordinance, regulation, or custom," to violate a citizen's rights. Occasionally the Justice Department prosecutes policemen on charges of violating this law, as in its unsuccessful action against 8 Chicago policemen after the 1968 Democratic National Convention. A policeman who strikes a citizen violates state law. The threat of federal or state prosecution is so remote, however, that it is not considered a deterrent to police lawlessness.

In only 8 states can an individual sue the state for damages in cases of alleged police misconduct, and the federal government is immune from such suits. The lack of effective sanctions against police misconduct has contributed to an increase in private damage suits filed against individual police officers. Such suits are rarely successful. A study in Los Angeles found that 91% of those who sued policemen lost while those who "won" collected, on average, $\frac{1}{20}$

of 1% of their claimed damages. A further difficulty in dealing with police misconduct is that department disciplinary proceedings are usually suspended when a suit is brought against a policeman so as not to prejudice the suit.

Paul Chevigny, a police expert at the New York City Civil Liberties Union, maintained in his book *Police Power: Police Abuses in New York City,* that New York police officers routinely charge persons whom they mistreat, and whom they feel may seek redress, with such crimes as disorderly conduct, resisting arrest or assault in order to protect themselves and the police department. Such charges can then be dropped or reduced if the victim agrees not to sue. The practice is reportedly so common that, according to Chevigny, an arresting officer in one case of alleged police brutality told the judge: "We never laid a hand on him. You can tell that. If we had, he would have been charged with resisting arrest, isn't that right?"

A 1954 Supreme Court case, *Barr v. Mateo,* has been interpreted by some lower court judges as granting all federal officials, including law officers, immunity from damage suits that "might appreciably inhibit the fearless, vigorous and effective administration of policies of government." The case arose out of a libel suit against the acting Director of Rent Stabilization for statements made in a press release. Some observers have held, however, that the court was seeking only to protect high-level federal officials from libel suits.

In *Bivens v. 6 Unknown Named Agents,* the Supreme Court June 21, 1971 passed over an opportunity to rule whether federal law enforcement officials are immune from private damage suits.

Webster Bivens, a New York Negro, ex-convict and narcotics dealer, had sought to bring suit in federal court after 6 agents of the Federal Bureau of Narcotics had entered his apartment at 6:30 one morning and had arrested him for alleged narcotics violations. The agents had neither an arrest warrant nor a search warrant. They handcuffed Bivens in front of his wife and children, threatened to arrest the entire family and searched the apartment. Bivens was then taken to a federal courthouse, where he was interrogated and booked. Thereafter, Bivens sought to sue each agent for $15,000 for what he described as great humiliation, embarrassment and mental suffering as a result of the agents' conduct.

In refusing to decide whether an individual can sue a federal law officer, the court limited itself to the narrower issue of whether Bivens could bring suit in a federal court for the violation of his 4th Amendment rights. The Justice Department had argued that such suits should be entered in state court and that they should be decided wholly on the basis of state law as between 2 private individuals. The court decided the issue in favor of Bivens. Chief Justice Burger, in dissent, accused the majority of constructing a "remedy of its own" to compensate for the failure of the "exclusionary rule" to deter unconstitutional police behavior. His dissenting opinion contains a lengthy review of the exclusionary rule, which holds that illegally seized evidence cannot be used in court. Rather than facilitating suit against law officers, Burger suggested that Congress establish a special tribunal to award damages "to the completely innocent persons who are sometimes the victims of illegal [federal] police conduct." That law would permit the use in court of evidence seized in violation of the 4th Amendment.

Abridgment of the *Bivens v. 6 Unknown Named Agents* decision (403 U.S. 388, June 21, 1971):

Justice Brennan delivering the opinion of the court:

Respondents do not argue that petitioner should be entirely without remedy for an unconstitutional invasion of his rights by federal agents. In respondents' view, however, the rights which petitioner asserts—primarily rights of privacy—are creations of state and not of federal law. Accordingly, they argue, petitioner may obtain money damages to redress invasion of these rights only by an action in tort, under state law, in the state courts. In this scheme the 4th Amendment would serve merely to limit the extent to which the agents could defend the state law tort suit by asserting that their actions were a valid exercise of federal power: if the agents were shown to have violated the 4th Amendment, such a defense would be lost to them and they would stand before the state law merely as private individuals. Candidly admitting that it is the policy of the Department of Justice to remove all such suits from the state to the federal courts for decision, respondents nevertheless urge that we uphold dismissal of petitioner's complaint in federal court and remit him to filing an action in the state courts in order that the case may properly be removed to the federal court for decision on the basis of state law.

We think that respondents' thesis rests upon an unduly restrictive view of the 4th Amendment's protection against unreasonable searches and seizures by federal agents, a view that has consistently been rejected by this court. Respondents seek to treat the relationship between a citizen and a federal agent unconstitutionally exercising his authority as no different from the relationship between 2 private citizens. In so doing, they ignore the fact that power, once granted, does not disappear like a magic gift when it is wrongfully used. An agent acting—albeit unconstitutionally—in the name of the United States possesses a far greater capacity for harm than an individual trespasser exercising no authority other than his own.... The

4th Amendment operates as a limitation upon the exercise of federal power regardless of whether the state in whose jurisdiction that power is exercised would prohibit or penalize the identical act if engaged in by a private citizen. It guarantees to citizens of the United States the absolute right to be free from unreasonable searches and seizures carried out by virtue of federal authority.

And I think it is clear that Bivens advances a claim of the sort that, if proved, would be properly compensable in damages. The personal interests protected by the 4th Amendment are those we attempt to capture by the notion of "privacy"; while the court today [in *Coolidge v. New Hampshire*] properly points out that the type of harm which officials can inflict when they invade protected zones of an individual's life are different from the types of harm private citizens inflict on one another, the experience of judges in dealing with private trespass and false imprisonment claims supports the conclusion that courts of law are capable of making the types of judgment concerning causation and magnitude of injury necessary to accord meaningful compensation for invasion of 4th Amendment rights.

On the other hand, the limitations on state remedies for violation of common law rights by private citizens argue in favor of a federal damage remedy. The injuries inflicted by officials acting under color of law, while no less compensable in damages than those inflicted by private parties, are substantially different in kind, as the court's opinion today discusses in detail....

Putting aside the desirability of leaving the problem of federal official liability to the vagaries of common law actions, it is apparent that damages in some form is the only possible remedy for someone in Bivens' alleged position. It will be a rare case indeed in which an individual in Bivens' position will be able to obviate the harm by securing injunctive relief from any court. However desirable a direct remedy against the government might be as a substitute for individual official liability, the sovereign still remains immune to suit. Finally, assuming Bivens' innocence of the crime charged, the "exclusionary rule" is simply irrelevant. For people in Bivens' shoes, it is damages or nothing.

The only substantial policy consideration advanced against recognition of a federal cause of action for violation of 4th Amendment rights by federal officials is the incremental expenditure of judicial resources that will be necessitated by this class of litigation. There is, however, something ultimately self-defeating about this argument. For if, as the government contends, damages will rarely be realized by plaintiffs in these cases because of jury hostility, the limited resources of the official concerned, etc., then I am not ready to assume that there will be a significant increase in the expenditure of judicial resources on these claims. Few responsible lawyers and plaintiffs are likely to choose the course of litigation if the statistical chances of success are truly *de minimis.* And I simply cannot agree with my brother Black that the possibility of "frivolous" claims—if defined simply as claims with no legal merits—warrants closing the courthouse doors to people in Bivens' situation. There are other ways, short of that, of coping with frivolous lawsuits....

...While I express no view on the immunity defense offered in the instant case, I deem it proper to venture the thought that at the very least such a remedy would be available for the most flagrant and patently unjustified sorts of police conduct. Although litigants may not often choose to seek relief, it is important, in a civilized society, that the judicial branch of the nation's government stand ready to afford a remedy in these circumstances. It goes without saying that I intimate no view on the merits of petitioner's underlying claim....

Chief Justice Burger dissenting:

I dissent from today's holding which judicially creates a damage remedy not provided for by the Constitution and not enacted by Congress. We would more surely preserve the important values of the doctrine of separation of powers—and perhaps get a better result—by recommending a solution to the Congress as the branch of government in which the Constitution has vested the legislative power, Legislation is the business of the Congress, and it has the facilities and competence for that task—as we do not....

This case has significance far beyond its facts and its holding. For more than 55 years this court has enforced a rule under which evidence of undoubted reliability and probative value has been suppressed and excluded from criminal cases whenever it was obtained in violation of the 4th Amendment. *Weeks v. United States* ... (1914).... This rule was extended to the States in *Mapp v. Ohio*.... The rule has rested on a theory that suppression of evidence in these circumstances was imperative to deter law enforcement authorities from using improper methods to obtain evidence.

The deterrence theory underlying the suppression doctrine, or exclusionary rule, has a certain appeal in spite of the high price society pays for such a drastic remedy. Notwithstanding its plausibility many judges and lawyers and some of our most distinguished legal scholars have never quite been able to escape the force of Cardozo's statement of the doctrine's anomalous result: "The criminal is to go free because the constable has blundered.... A room is searched against the law, and the body of a murdered man is found.... The privacy of the home has been infringed, and the murderer goes free." *People v. DeFore....*

The plurality opinion in *Irvine v. California* ... (1954) catalogued the doctrine's defects: "Rejection of the evidence does nothing to punish the wrongdoing official, while it may, and likely will, release the wrongdoing defendant. It deprives society of its remedy against one lawbreaker because he has been pursued by another. It protects one against whom incriminating evidence is discovered, but does nothing to protect innocent persons who are the victims of illegal but fruitless searches."

From time to time members of the court, recognizing the validity of these protests, have articulated varying alternative justifications for the suppression of important evidence in a criminal trial. Under one of these alternative theories the rule's foundation is shifted to the "sporting contest" thesis that the government must "play the game fairly" and cannot be allowed to profit from its own illegal acts. *Olmstead v. United States* ... (1928) (dissenting opinions).... But the exclusionary rule does not ineluctably flow from a desire to ensure that government plays the "game" according to the rules. If an effective alternative remedy is available, concern for official observance of the law does not require adherence to the exclusionary rule. Nor is it easy to understand how a court can be thought to endorse a violation of the 4th Amendment by allowing illegally seized evidence to be introduced against a defendant if an effective remedy is provided against the government.

The exclusionary rule has also been justified on the theory that the relationship between the self-incrimination clause of the 5th Amendment and the 4th Amendment requires the suppression of evidence seized in violation of the latter....

Even ignoring, however, the decisions of this court which have held that the 5th Amendment applies only to "testimonial" disclosures, *United States v. Wade* ... (1967); *Schmerber v. California* ... (1966), it seems clear that the self-incrimination clause does not protect a person from the seizure of evidence that is incriminating. It protects a person only from being the conduit by which the police acquire evidence. Mr. Justice Holmes once put it succinctly, "A party is privileged from producing the evidence but not from its production." *Johnson v. United States* ... (1913).

It is clear, however, that neither of these theories under-girds the decided cases in this court. Rather the exclusionary rule has rested on the deterrent rationale—the hope that law enforcement officials would be deterred from unlawful searches and seizures if the illegally seized, albeit trustworthy, evidence was suppressed often enough and the courts persistently enough deprived them of any benefits they might have gained from their illegal conduct.

This evidentiary rule is unique to American jurisprudence. Although the English and Canadian legal systems are highly regarded, neither has adopted our rule.

I do not question the need for some remedy to give meaning and teeth to the constitutional guarantees against unlawful conduct by government officials.... But the hope that this objective could be accomplished by the exclusion of reliable evidence from criminal trials was hardly more than a wistful dream. Although I would hesitate to abandon it until some meaningful substitute is developed, the history of the suppression doctrine demonstrates that it is both conceptually sterile and practically ineffective in accomplishing its stated objective. This is illustrated by the paradox that an unlawful act against a totally innocent person—such as petitioner claims to be—has been left without an effective remedy, and hence the court finds it necessary now—55 years later—to construct a remedy of its own.

Some clear demonstration of the benefits and effectiveness of the exclusionary rule is required to justify it in view of the high price it extracts from society—the release of countless guilty criminals.... But there is no empirical evidence to support the claim that the rule actually deters illegal conduct of law enforcement officials....

There are several reasons for this failure. The rule does not apply any direct sanction to the individual official whose illegal conduct results in the exclusion of evidence in a criminal trial. With rare exceptions law enforcement agencies do not impose direct sanctions on the individual officer responsible for a particular judicial application of the suppression doctrine.... Thus there is virtually nothing done to bring about a change in his practices. The immediate sanction triggered by the application of the rule is visited upon the prosecutor whose case against a criminal is either weakened or destroyed. The doctrine deprives the police in no real sense....

The suppression doctrine vaguely assumes that law enforcement is a monolithic governmental enterprise. For example, the dissenters in *Wolf v. Colorado* ... argued that "Only by exclusion can we impress upon the zealous *prosecutor* that violation of the Constitution will do him no good. And only when that point is driven home can the *prosecutor* be expected to emphasize the importance of observing the constitutional demands in *his instructions to the police.*" (Emphasis added.) But the prosecutor who loses his case because of police misconduct is not an official in the police department; he can rarely set in motion any corrective action or administrative penalties. Moreover, he does not have control or direction over police procedures or police action that lead to the exclusion of evidence....

Whatever educational effect the rule conceivably might have in theory is greatly diminished in fact by the realities of law enforcement work. Policemen do not have the time, inclination or training to read and grasp the nuances of the appellate opinions that ultimately define the standards of conduct they are to follow....

The presumed educational effect of judicial opinions is also reduced by the long time lapse—often several years—between the original police action and its final judicial evaluation. Given a policeman's pressing responsibilities, it would be surprising if he ever becomes aware of the final result after such a delay. Finally the exclusionary rule's deterrrent impact is diluted by the fact that there are large areas of police activity which do not result in criminal prosecutions—hence the rule has virtually no applicability and no effect in such situations. . . .

Today's holding seeks to fill one of the gaps of the suppression doctrine—at the price of impinging on the legislative and policy functions which the Constitution vests in Congress. Nevertheless, the holding serves the useful purpose of exposing the fundamental weaknesses of the suppression doctrine. Suppressing unchallenged truth has set guilty criminals free but demonstrably has neither deterred deliberate violations of the 4th Amendment nor decreased those errors in judgment which will inevitably occur given the pressures inherent in police work having to do with serious crimes.

Although unfortunately ineffective, the exlusionary rule has increasingly been characterized by a single, monolithic and drastic judicial response to all official violations of legal norms. Inadvertent errors of judgment that do not work any grave injustice will inevitably occur under the pressure of police work. These honest mistakes have been treated in the same way as deliberate and flagrant *Irvine*-type violations of the 4th Amendment. For example, in *Miller v. United States* . . . (1958), reliable evidence was suppressed because of a police officer's failure to say a "few more words" during the arrest and search of a known narcotics peddler.

This court's decision announced today in *Coolidge v. New Hampshire* dramatically illustrates the extent to which the doctrine represents a mechanically inflexible response to widely varying degrees of police error and the resulting high price which society pays. I dissented in *Coolidge* primarily because I do not believe the 4th Amendment had been violated. Even on the court's contrary premise, however, whatever violation occurred was surely insufficient in nature and extent to justify the drastic result dictated by the suppression doctrine. A fair trial by jury has resolved doubts as to Coolidge's guilt. But now his conviction on retrial is placed in serious question by the remand for a new trial—years after the crime—in which evidence which the New Hampshire courts found relevant and reliable will be withheld from the jury's consideration. . . .

Freeing either a tiger or a mouse in a schoolroom is an illegal act, but no rational person would suggest that these acts should be punished in the same way. From time to time judges have occasion to pass on regulations governing police procedures. I wonder what would be the judicial response to a police order authorizing "shoot-to-kill" with respect to every fugitive. It is easy to predict our collective wrath and outrage. We, in common with all rational minds, would say that the police response must relate to the gravity and need; that a "shoot" order might conceivably be tolerable to prevent the escape of a convicted killer but surely not for a car thief, a pickpocket or a shoplifter.

I submit that society has at least as much right to expect rationally graded responses from judges in place of the universal "capital punishment" we inflict on all evidence when police error is shown in its acquisition.... Yet for over 55 years, and with increasing scope and intensity as today's *Coolidge* holding shows, our legal system has treated vastly dissimilar cases as if they were the same....

Instead of continuing to enforce the suppression doctrine, inflexibly, rigidly, and mechanically, we should view it as one of the experimental steps in the great tradition of the common law and acknowledge its shortcomings. But in the same spirit we should be prepared to discontinue what the experience of over half a century has shown neither deters errant officers nor affords a remedy to the totally innocent victims of official misconduct.

I do not propose, however, that we abandon the suppression doctrine until some meaningful alternative can be developed. In a sense our legal system has become the captive of its own creation. To overrule *Weeks* and *Mapp,* even assuming the court was now prepared to take that step, could raise yet new problems. Obviously the public interest would be poorly served if law enforcement officials were suddenly to gain the impression, however erroneous, that all constitutional restraints on police had somehow been removed—that an open season on "criminals" had been declared....

Reasonable and effective substitutes [for the suppression doctrine] can be formulated if Congress would take the lead.... I see no insuperable obstacle to the elimination of the suppression doctrine if Congress would provide some meaningful and effective remedy against unlawful conduct by government officials.

The problems of both error and deliberate misconduct by law enforcement officials call for a workable remedy. Private damage actions against individual police officers concededly have not adequately met this requirement, and it would be fallacious to assume today's work of the court in creating a remedy will really accomplish its stated objective. There is some validity to the claims that juries will not return verdicts against individual officers except in those unusual cases where the violation has been flagrant or where the error has been complete, as in the arrest of the wrong person or the search of the wrong house.... Jurors may well refuse to penalize a police officer at the behest of a person they believe to be a "criminal" and probably will not punish an officer for honest errors of judgment....

I conclude, therefore, that an entirely different remedy is necessary but it is one that in my view is as much beyond judicial power as the step the court takes today. Congress should develop an administrative or quasi-judicial remedy against the government itself to afford compensation and restitution for persons whose 4th Amendment rights have been violated....

A simple structure would suffice. For example, Congress could enact a statute along the following lines: (a) a waiver of sovereign immunity as to the illegal acts of law enforcement officials committed in the performance of assigned duties; (b) the creation of a cause of action for damages sustained by any person aggrieved by conduct of governmental agents in violation of the 4th Amendment or statutes regulating official conduct; (c) the creation of a tribunal ... to adjudicate all claims under the statute; (d) a provision that this statutory remedy is in lieu of the exclusion of evidence secured for use in criminal cases in violation of the 4th Amendment; and (e) a provision directing that no evidence, otherwise admissible, shall be excluded from any criminal proceeding because of violation of the 4th Amendment.

... Finally, appellate judicial review could be made available on much the same basis that it is now provided as to district courts and regulatory agencies. This would leave to the courts the ultimate responsibility for determining and articulating standards.

Once the constitutional validity of such a statute is established, it can reasonably be assumed that the states would develop their own remedial systems on the federal model. Indeed there is nothing to prevent a state from enacting a comparable statutory scheme without waiting on the Congress. Steps along these lines would move our system toward more responsible law enforcement on the one hand and away from the irrational and drastic results of the suppression doctrine on the other. Independent of the alternative embraced in this dissenting opinion, I believe the time has come to re-examine the scope of the exclusionary rule and consider at least some narrowing of its thrust so as to eliminate the anomalies it has produced.

... I can only hope now that the Congress will manifest a willingness to view realistically the hard evidence of the half-century history of the suppression doctrine revealing thousands of cases in which the criminal was set free because the constable blundered and virtually no evidence that innocent victims of police error ... have been afforded meaningful redress.

Enjoining the Police

In a few instances victims of illegal police practices have obtained federal court injunctions ordering a halt to unlawful police actions.

A recently revitalized Reconstruction law, the 1871 Ku Klux Act, Sec. 1983, authorizes injunctions to bar state and local officials from denying any person "any rights, privileges or immunities secured by the Constitution and [federal] laws." A permanent injunction secured in 1966, for example, barred Baltimore police from searching homes without warrants on the basis of anonymous tips. It was obtained after Baltimore police had searched more than 300 Negro homes without warrants in a 19-day period in an unsuccessful effort to apprehend 2 men suspected of murdering a policeman. Such searches, although routine in the black community, were not undertaken in white sections of the city.

In a more recent case, a federal court issued an injunction ordering the Charlotte, N.C. police department to refrain from harassing persons under color of a vagrancy statute and from conducting illegal searches and seizures. This injunction was issued on the complaint of members of a local "hippie house" that had been searched by the police on 14 separate occasions in a 2-month period without proper search warrants.

EYEWITNESS IDENTIFICATION

Lawyers for Suspects at Lineups

In an effort to lessen the chances of a mistaken identification at police lineups, the Supreme Court ruled June 12, 1967 that a suspect has the right to have a lawyer witness any lineup in which he is forced to participate after he has been indicted. A courtroom identification associated with a post-indictment lineup in which the defendant's right to counsel was not observed cannot be used in evidence against him, the court ruled. This requirement was imposed on federal and state authorities in the companion cases of *U.S. v. Wade* and *Gilbert v. California.* In *Stovall v. Denno,* decided the same day, the court ruled that *Wade* and *Gilbert* would not be applied retroactively and that they affected only future lineups.

In the majority opinion in *Wade,* Justice William J. Brennan said that the history of criminal law was "rife" with instances of mistaken identifications. He held that improperly conducted lineups were "a major factor contributing to the high incidence of miscarriage of justice from mistaken identification...." The integrity of a lineup can be compromised by many factors, he noted, as, for example, if a black-haired suspect is placed in a lineup among a group of light-haired persons or if a suspect is required to wear distinctive clothing similar to that worn by the perpetrator of the crime. Eyewitnesses are also more apt to focus on a particular suspect if they have seen him in the custody of the police prior to the lineup, as was the case in *Wade.* If done intentionally, such tactics result in what police sometimes call an "Oklahoma show-up."

In upholding a suspect's right to have a lawyer witness a lineup in which he is required to participate, the court sought to enable defense counsel to point out, in the ensuing trial, any irregularities in the lineup.

Justice Byron R. White objected to the new constitutional rule in what he claimed was the absence of evidence of a "widespread" use of improper lineups. White suggested, moreover, that cases of mistaken identification were more apt to result from the difficulties inherent in all eyewitness testimony and not from the convening of improperly conducted lineups.

Chief Justice Earl Warren and Justices Hugo L. Black, Abe Fortas and William O. Douglas asserted in *Wade* that a defendant's 5th Amendment right not to testify against himself is violated when he is forced at a lineup to utter the words of the person who committed the crime. The majority did not share this view.

Section II of the 1968 Omnibus Crime Control & Safe Streets Act sought to repeal *Wade* on the federal level by encouraging the admissibility of eyewitness testimony in federal prosecutions. It declared: "The testimony of a witness that he saw the accused commit or participate in the commission of the crime for which the accused is being tried shall be admissible in evidence in a criminal prosecution...."

Ex-U.S. Atty. Gen. Ramsey Clark, however, ordered federal authorities not to introduce evidence that conflicted with *Wade* and other Supreme Court decisions. His immediate successor, John Mitchell, announced shortly after taking office in 1969 that although lawyers should be present at lineups, the Justice Department was nevertheless prepared to "salvage some cases which otherwise might be lost" by introducing evidence that could not be justified under *Wade* and other decisions.

Abridgment of the *United States v. Wade* decision (388 U.S. 218, June 12, 1967):

Justice Brennan delivering the court's opinion:

The question here is whether courtroom identifications of an accused at trial are to be excluded from evidence because the accused was exhibited to the witnesses before trial at a post-indictment lineup conducted for identification purposes without notice to and in the absence of the accused's appointed counsel.

The federally insured bank in Eustace, Texas, was robbed on Sept. 21, 1964. A man with a small strip of tape on each side of his face entered the bank, pointed a pistol at the female cashier and the vice president, the only persons in the bank at the time, and forced them to fill a pillowcase with the bank's money. The man then drove away with an accomplice waiting in a stolen car outside the bank. On Mar. 23, 1965, an indictment was returned against respondent Wade and 2 others for conspiring to rob the bank, and against Wade and the accomplice for the robbery itself. Wade was arrested on Apr. 2, and counsel was appointed to represent him on Apr. 26. 15 days later an FBI agent, without notice to Wade's lawyer, arranged to have the 2 bank employees observe a lineup made up of Wade and 5 or 6 other prisoners and conducted in a courtroom of the local county courthouse. Each person in the line wore strips of tape such as allegedly worn by the robber and upon direction each said something like "put the money in the bag," the words allegedly uttered by the robber. Both bank employes identified Wade in the lineup as the bank robber.

At trial, the 2 employes, when asked on direct examination if the robber was in the courtroom, pointed to Wade. The prior lineup identification was then elicited from both employes on cross-examination. At the close of testimony, Wade's counsel moved for a judgment of acquittal or, alternatively, to strike the bank officials' courtroom identifications on the ground that conduct of the lineup, without notice to and in the absence of his appointed counsel, violated his 5th Amendment privilege against self-incrimination and his 6th Amendment right to the assistance of counsel. The motion was denied, and Wade was convicted....

Neither the lineup itself nor anything shown by this record that Wade was required to do in the lineup violated his privilege against self-incrimination. We have only recently reaffirmed that the privilege "protects an accused only from being compelled to testify against himself, or otherwise provide the state with evidence of a testimonial or communicative nature...." *Schmerber v. California* [1966].... We there held that compelling a suspect to submit to a withdrawal of a sample of his blood for analysis for alcohol content and the admission in evidence of the analysis report was not compulsion to those ends....

The fact that the lineup involved no violation of Wade's privilege against self-incrimination does not, however, dispose of his contention that the courtroom identifications should have been excluded because the lineup was conducted without notice to and in the absence of his counsel....

... [I]n this case it is urged that the assistance of counsel at the lineup was indispensable to protect Wade's most basic right as a criminal defendant—his right to a fair trial at which the witnesses against him might be meaningfully cross-examined....

... [T]he confrontation compelled by the state between the accused and the victim or witnesses to a crime to elicit identification evidence is peculiarly riddled with innumerable dangers and variable factors which might seriously, even crucially, derogate from a fair trial. The vagaries of eyewitness identification are well known; the annals of criminal law are rife with instances of mistaken identification.... A major factor contributing to the high incidence of miscarriage of justice from mistaken identification has been the degree of suggestion inherent in the manner in which the prosecution presents the suspect to witnesses for pretrial identification. A commentator has observed that "the influence of improper suggestion upon identifying witnesses probably accounts for more miscarriages of justice than any other single factor—perhaps it is responsible for more such errors than all other factors combined." Wall, Eyewitness Identification in Criminal Cases 26. Suggestion can be created intentionally or unintentionally in many subtle ways. And the dangers for the suspect are particularly grave when the witness' opportunity for observation was insubstantial, and thus his susceptibility to suggestion the greatest.

Moreover, "it is a matter of common experience that, once a witness has picked out the accused at the lineup, he is not likely to go back on his word later on, so that in practice the issue of identity may (in the absence of other relevant evidence) for all practical purposes be determined there and then, before the trial."*...

What facts have been disclosed in specific cases about the conduct of pretrial confrontations for identification illustrate both the potential for substantial prejudice to the accused at that stage and the need for its revelation at trial. A commentator provides some striking examples: "In a Canadian case ... the defendant had been picked out of a lineup of 6 men, of which he was the only Oriental. In other cases, a black-haired suspect was placed upon a group of light-haired persons, tall suspects have been made to stand with short non-suspects, and, in a case where the perpetrator of the crime was known to be a youth, a suspect under 20 was placed in a lineup with 5 other persons, all of whom were 40 or over."†

Similarly, state reports, in the course of describing prior identifications admitted as evidence of guilt, reveal numerous instances of suggestive procedures, for example, that all in the lineup but the suspect were known to the identifying witness, that the other participants in a lineup were grossly dissimilar in appearance from the suspect, that only the suspect was required to wear distinctive clothing which the culprit allegedly wore,

---

* Williams & Hammelmann, Identification Parades, Part I, [1963] Crim. L. Rev. 479, 482.

† Wall, *Eyewitness Identification in Criminal Cases.*

that the witness is told by the police that they have caught the culprit after which the defendant is brought before the witness alone or is viewed in jail, that the suspect is pointed out before or during a lineup, and that the participants in the lineup are asked to try on an article of clothing which fits only the suspect....

...[W]e do not assume that these risks are the result of police procedures intentionally designed to prejudice an accused. Rather, we assume they derive from the dangers inherent in eyewitness identification and the suggestibility inherent in the context of the pretrial identification....

Since it appears that there is grave potential for prejudice, intentional or not, in the pretrial lineup, which may not be capable of reconstruction at trial, and since presence of counsel itself can often avert prejudice and assure a meaningful confrontation at trial, there can be little doubt that for Wade the post-indictment lineup was a critical stage of the prosecution at which he was "as much entitled to such aid [of counsel] ... as at the trial itself." *Powell v. Alabama....* Thus both Wade and his counsel should have been notified of the impending lineup, and counsel's presence should have been a requisite to conduct of the lineup, absent an "intelligent waiver."... No substantial countervailing policy considerations have been advanced against the requirement of the presence of counsel. Concern is expressed that the requirement will forestall prompt identifications and result in obstruction of the confrontations. As for the first, we note that in the 2 cases in which the right to counsel is today held to apply, counsel had already been appointed and no argument is made in either case that notice to counsel would have prejudicially delayed the confrontations. Moreover, we leave open the question whether the presence of substitute counsel might not suffice where notification and presence of the suspect's own counsel would result in prejudicial delay.... In our view counsel can hardly impede legitimate law enforcement; on the contrary, ... law enforcement may be assisted by preventing the infiltration of taint in the prosecution's identification evidence. That result cannot help the guilty avoid conviction but can only help assure that the right man has been brought to justice.

Legislative or other regulations, such as those of local police departments, which eliminate the risks of abuse and unintentional suggestion at lineup proceedings and the impediments to meaningful confrontation at trial may also remove the basis for regarding the stage as "critical." But neither Congress nor the federal authorities has seen fit to provide a solution....

Justice Black, dissenting in part and concurring in part:

...[Wade] contended that by forcing him to participate in the lineup, wear strips of tape on his face and repeat the words used by the robber, all without counsel, the government had (1) compelled him to be a witness against himself in violation of the 5th Amendment, and (2) deprived him of the assistance of counsel for his defense in violation of the 6th Amendment.

The court ... rejects Wade's 5th Amendment contention. From that I dissent. ...The court sustains Wade's claim of denial of right to counsel in the out-of-court lineup, and in that I concur.... The court remands the case to the district court to consider whether the courtroom identification of Wade was the fruit of the illegal lineup, and if it were, to grant him a new trial unless the court concludes that the courtroom identification was harmless error. I would reverse the Court of Appeals' reversal of Wade's conviction, but I would not remand for further proceedings. Since the prosecution did not use the out-of-court lineup identification against Wade at his trial, I believe the conviction should be affirmed.

Justice White, joined by Harlan and Stewart, dissenting in part and concurring in part:

...The court's opinion is far reaching. It proceeds first by creating a new *per se* rule of constitutional law: a criminal suspect cannot be subjected to a pretrial identification process in the absence of his counsel without violating the 6th Amendment. If he is, the state may not buttress a later courtroom identification of the witness by any reference to the previous identification. Furthermore, the courtroom identification is not admissible at all unless the state can establish by clear and convincing proof that the testimony is not the fruit of the earlier identification made in the absence of defendant's counsel—admittedly a heavy burden for the state and probably an impossible one. For all intents and purposes, courtroom identifications are barred if pretrial identifications have occurred without counsel being present.

The premise for the court's rule is not the general unreliability of eyewitness identifications nor the difficulties inherent in observation, recall and recognition. The court assumes a narrower evil as the basis for its rule—improper police suggestion which contributes to erroneous identifications. The court apparently believes that improper police procedures are so widespread that a broad prophylactic rule must be laid down, requiring the presence of counsel at all pretrial identifications, in order to detect recurring instances of police misconduct. I do not share this pervasive distrust of all official investigations. None of the materials the court relies upon supports it. Certainly, I would bow to solid fact, but the court quite obviously does not have before it any reliable, comprehensive survey of current police practices on which to base its new rule. Until it does, the court should avoid excluding relevant evidence from state criminal trials. . . .

The court goes beyond assuming that a great majority of the country's police departments are following improper practices at pretrial identifications. To find the lineup a "critical" stage of the proceeding and to exclude identifications made in the absence of counsel, the court must also assume that police "suggestion," if it occurs at all, leads to erroneous rather than accurate identifications and that reprehensible police conduct will have an unavoidable and largely undiscoverable impact on the trial. This in turn assumes that there is now no adequate source from which defense counsel can learn about the circumstances of the pretrial identification in order to place before the jury all of the considerations which should enter into an appraisal of courtroom identification evidence. But these are treacherous and unsupported assumptions, resting as they do on the notion that the defendant will not be aware, that the police and the witnesses will forget or prevaricate, that defense counsel will be unable to bring out the truth and that neither jury, judge nor appellate court is a sufficient safeguard against unacceptable police conduct occurring at a pretrial identification procedure. I am unable to share the court's view of the willingness of the police and the ordinary citizen-witness to dissemble, either with respect to the identification of the defendant or with respect to the circumstances surrounding a pretrial identification.

There are several striking aspects to the court's holding.

First, the rule does not bar courtroom identifications where there have been no previous identifications in the presence of the police, although when identified in the courtroom, the defendant is known to be in custody and charged with the commission of a crime.

2d, the court seems to say that if suitable legislative standards were adopted for the conduct of pretrial identifications, thereby lessening the hazards in such confrontations, it would not insist on the presence of counsel. But if this is true, why does not the court simply fashion what it deems to be constitutionally acceptable procedures for the authorities to follow? Certainly the court is correct in suggesting that the new rule will be wholly inapplicable where police departments themselves have established suitable safeguards.

3d, courtroom identification may be barred, absent counsel at a prior identification, regardless of the extent of counsel's information concerning the circumstances of the previous confrontation between witness and defendant—apparently even if there were recordings or sound-movies of the events as they occurred. But if the rule is premised on the defendant's right to have his counsel know, there seems little basis for not accepting other means to inform. A disinterested observer, recordings, photographs—any one of them would seem adequate to furnish the basis for a meaningful cross-examination of the eyewitness who identifies the defendant in the courtroom.

I share the court's view that the criminal trial, at the very least, should aim at truthful factfinding, including accurate eyewitness identifications. I doubt, however, on the basis of our present information, that the tragic mistakes which have occurred in criminal trials are as much the product of improper police conduct as they are the consequence of the difficulties inherent in eyewitness testimony and in resolving evidentiary conflicts by court or jury. I doubt that the court's new rule will obviate these difficulties, or that the situation will be measurably improved by inserting defense counsel into the investigative processes of police departments everywhere. . . .

Beyond this, however, requiring counsel at pretrial identifications as an invariable rule trenches on other valid state interests. One of them is its concern with the prompt and efficient enforcement of its criminal laws. Identifications frequently take place after arrest but before indictment or information is filed. The police may have arrested a suspect on probable cause but may still have the wrong man. Both the suspect and the state have every interest in a prompt identification at that stage, the suspect in order to secure his immediate release and the state because prompt and early identification enhances *accurate* identification and because it must know whether it is on the right investigative track. Unavoidably, however, the absolute rule requiring the presence of counsel will cause significant delay and it may very well result in no pretrial identification at all. . . .

Nor do I think the witnesses themselves can be ignored. They will now be required to be present at the convenience of counsel rather than their own. Many may be much less willing to participate if the identification stage is transformed into an adversary proceeding not under the control of a judge. Others may fear for their own safety if their identity is known at an early date, especially when there is no way of knowing until the lineup occurs whether or not the police really have the right man.

Finally, I think the court's new rule is vulnerable in terms of its own unimpeachable purpose of increasing the reliability of identification testimony.

Law enforcement officers have the obligation to convict the guilty and to make sure they do not convict the innocent. They must be dedicated to making the criminal trial a procedure for the ascertainment of the true facts surrounding the commission of the crime. To this extent, our so-called adversary system is not adversary at all; nor should it be. But defense counsel has no comparable obligation to ascertain or present the truth. Our system assigns him a different mission. He must be and is interested in not convicting the innocent, but, absent a voluntary plea of guilty, we also insist that he defend his client whether he is innocent or guilty. The state has the obligation to present the evidence. Defense counsel need present nothing, even if he knows what the truth is. . . . If he can confuse a witness, even a truthful one, or make him appear at a disadvantage, unsure or indecisive, that will be his normal course. Our interest in not convicting the innocent permits counsel to put the state to its proof, to put the state's case in the worst possible light, regardless of what he thinks or knows to be the truth.... More often that not, defense counsel will cross-examine a prosecution witness and impeach him if he can, even if he thinks the witness is telling the truth, just as he will attempt to destroy a witness who he thinks is lying. In this respect, as part of our modified adversary system and as part of the duty imposed on the most honorable defense counsel, we countenance or require conduct which in many instances has little, if any, relation to the search for truth.

I would not extend this system, at least as it presently operates, to police investigations and would not require counsel's presence at pretrial identification procedures. Counsel's interest is in not having his client placed at the scene of the crime, regardless of his whereabouts. Some counsel may advise their clients to refuse to make any movements or to speak any words in a lineup or even to appear in one.... Others will not only observe what occurs and develop possibilities for later cross-examination but will hover over witnesses and begin their cross-examination then, menacing truthful fact finding as thoroughly as the court fears the police now do. Certainly there is an implicit invitation to counsel to suggest rules for the line-up and to manage and produce it as best he can. I therefore doubt that the court's new rule, at least absent some clearly defined limits on counsel's role, will measurably contribute to more reliable pretrial identifications. My fears are that it will have precisely the opposite result.... In my view, the state is entitled to investigate and develop its case outside the presence of defense counsel. This includes the right to have private conversations with identification witnesses, just as defense counsel may have his own consultations with these and other witnesses without having the prosecutor present....

Justice Fortas, whom Warren and Douglas joined, concurring in part and dissenting in part:

1. I agree with the court that the exhibition of the person of the accused at a lineup is not itself a violation of the privilege against self-incrimination. In itself, it is no more subject to constitutional objection than the exhibition of the person of the

accused in the courtroom for identification purposes. It is an incident of the state's power to arrest, and a reasonable and justifiable aspect of the state's custody resulting from arrest. It does not require that the accused take affirmative, volitional action but only that, having been duly arrested, he may be seen for identification purposes. It is, however, a "critical stage" in the prosecution, and I agree with the court that the opportunity to have counsel present must be made available.

2. In my view, however, the accused may not be compelled in a lineup to speak the words uttered by the person who committed the crime. I am confident that it could not be compelled in court. It cannot be compelled in a lineup. It is more than passive, mute assistance to the eyes of the victim or of witnesses. It is the kind of volitional act—the kind of forced cooperation by the accused—which is within the historical perimeter of the privilege against compelled self-incrimination.

Our history and tradition teach and command that an accused may stand mute. The privilege means just that; not less than that. According to the court, an accused may be jailed—indefinitely—until he is willing to say, for an identifying audience, whatever was said in the course of the commission of the crime.... This is intolerable under our constitutional system.

I completely agree that the accused must be advised of and given the right to counsel before a lineup—and I join in that part of the court's opinion; but this is an empty right unless we mean to insist upon the accused's fundamental constitutional immunities. One of these is that the accused may not be compelled to speak. To compel him to speak would violate the privilege against self-incrimination, which is incorporated in the 5th Amendment.

This great privilege is not merely a shield for the accused. It is also a prescription of technique designed to guide the state's investigation. History teaches us that self-accusation is an unreliable instrument of detection, apt to inculpate the innocent-but-weak and to enable the guilty to escape. But this is not the end of the story. The privilege historically goes to the roots of democratic and religious principle. It prevents the debasement of the citizen which would result from compelling him to "accuse" himself before the power of the state....

An accused cannot be compelled to utter the words spoken by the criminal in the course of the crime. I thoroughly disagree with the court's statement that such compulsion does not violate the 5th Amendment. The court relies upon *Schmerber v. California* ... (1966) to support this.... *Schmerber,* which authorized the forced extraction of blood from the veins of an unwilling human being, did not compel the person actively to cooperate—to accuse himself by a volitional act which differs only in degree from compelling him to act out the crime, which, I assume, would be rebuffed by the court. It is the latter feature which places the compelled utterance by the accused squarely within the history and noble purpose of the 5th Amendment's commandment.

To permit *Schmerber* to apply in any respect beyond its holding is, in my opinion, indefensible. To permit its insidious doctrine to extend beyond the invasion of the body, which it permits, to compulsion of the will of a man, is to deny and defy a precious part of our historical faith and to discard one of the most profoundly cherished instruments by which we have established the freedom and dignity of the individual. We should not so alter the balance between the rights of the individual and of the state, achieved over centuries of conflict.

3. While the court holds that the accused must be advised of and given the right to counsel at the lineup, it makes the privilege meaningless in this important respect. Unless counsel has been waived or, being present, has not objected to the accused's utterance of words used in the course of committing the crime, to compel such an utterance is constitutional error.

Accordingly, while I join the court in requiring vacating of the judgment below for a determination as to whether the identification of respondent was based upon factors independent of the lineup, I would do so not only because of the failure to offer counsel before the lineup but also because of the violation of respondent's 5th Amendment rights.

In *Stovall v. Denno,* the court ruled June 12, 1967 that the right to counsel at lineups set forth in *Wade* was not retroactive. In *Stovall,* this requirement was limited to lineups carried out after *Wade.* Justice Brennan, speaking for the majority, said that *Wade* would not be applied retroactively because of the increased workload that such a ruling would impose on the courts.

Although the right to counsel at trial established in *Gideon v. Wainwright* (1963) was retroactive, Brennan distinguished that precedent from the current case on the ground that the lack of counsel at a trial would almost "invariably" lead to a denial of a fair trial. In contrast, according to Brennan, many lineups devoid of counsel had been conducted fairly and thus did not jeopardize the defendant's right to a fair trial. Brennan said however, that defendants prior to *Wade* who had been forced to participate in lineups without an attorney could obtain relief by proving that the particular lineup was so unfair as to violate due process.

In the current case, Stovall had argued that the one-man lineup in which he had been forced to participate represented a denial of due process. Stovall had been taken to a hospital room of a woman who had been stabbed 11 times and whose husband had been stabbed to death by the same intruder. The woman identified Stovall as the assailant. Because it was not certain that the woman would survive, the court ruled that it was constitutional for the police to bring Stovall to the hospital room despite the higher risk of mis-identification associated with one-man lineups.

Justice Black, in dissent, argued in favor of retroactivity: "Once the court determines what the Constitution says, I do not believe it has the power, by weighing 'countervailing interests,' to legislate a timetable by which the Constitution's provisions shall become effective."

Abridgment of the *Stovall v. Denno* decision

(388 U.S. 293, June 12, 1967):

Justice Brennan delivering the opinion of the court:

... This case ... provides a vehicle for deciding the extent to which the rules announced in *Wade* and *Gilbert*—requiring the exclusion of identification evidence which is tainted by exhibiting the accused to identifying witnesses before trial in the absence of his counsel—are to be applied retroactively.... A further question is whether in any event, on the facts of the particular confrontation involved in this case, petitioner was denied due process of law in violation of the 14th Amendment....

Dr. Paul Behrendt was stabbed to death in the kitchen of his home in Garden City, Long Island, about midnight Aug. 23, 1961. Dr. Behrendt's wife, also a physician, had followed her husband to the kitchen and jumped at the assailant. He knocked her to the floor and stabbed her 11 times. The police found a shirt on the kitchen floor and keys in a pocket which they traced to petitioner. They arrested him on the afternoon of Aug. 24. An arraignment was promptly held but was postponed until petitioner could retain counsel.

Mrs. Behrendt was hospitalized for major surgery to save her life. The police, without affording petitioner time to retain counsel, arranged with her surgeon to permit them to bring petitioner to her hospital room about noon of Aug. 25, the day after the surgery. Petitioner was handcuffed to one of 5 police officers who, with 2 members of the staff of the district attorney, brought him to the hospital room. Petitioner was the only Negro in the room. Mrs. Behrendt identified him from her hospital bed after being asked by an officer whether he "was the man" and after petitioner repeated at the direction of an officer a "few words for voice identification." None of the witnesses could recall the words that were used. Mrs. Behrendt and the officers testified at the trial to her identification of the petitioner in the hospital room, and she also made an in-court identification of petitioner in the courtroom.

Petitioner was convicted and sentenced to death. The New York Court of Appeals affirmed without opinion.... Petitioner *pro se* sought federal *habeas corpus* in the District Court for the Southern District of New York. He claimed that among other constitutional rights allegedly denied him at his trial, the admission of Mrs. Behrendt's identification testimony violated his rights under the 5th, 6th, and 14th Amendments because he had been compelled to submit to the hospital room confrontation without the help of counsel and under circumstances which unfairly focussed the witness' attention on him as the man believed by the police to be the guilty person....

... We hold that *Wade* and *Gilbert* affect only those cases and all future cases which involve confrontations for identification purposes conducted in the absence of counsel after this date. The rulings of *Wade* and *Gilbert* are therefore inapplicable in the present case. We think also that on the facts of this case petitioner was not deprived of due process of law in violation of the 14th Amendment. The judgment of the Court of Appeals is, therefore, affirmed.

Our recent discussions of the retroactivity of other constitutional rules of criminal procedure made unnecessary any detailed treatment of that question here.... "These cases establish the principle that in criminal litigation concerning constitutional claims, 'the court may in the interest of justice make the rule prospective ... where the exigencies of the situation require such an application'...." *Johnson v. New Jersey* [1966].... The criteria guiding resolution of the question implicate (a) the purpose to be served by the new standards, (b) the extent of the reliance by law enforcement authorities on the old standards, and (c) the effect on the administration of justice of a retroactive application of the new standards. "[T]he retroactivity or nonretroactivity of a rule is not automatically determined by the provision of the Constitution on which the dictate is based. Each constitutional rule of criminal procedure has its own distinct functions, its own background of precedent, and its own impact on the administration of justice, and the way in which these factors combine must inevitably vary with the dictate involved." *Johnson [v. New Jersey]....*

Wade and *Gilbert* fashion exclusionary rules to deter law enforcement authorities from exhibiting an accused to witnesses before trial for identification purposes without notice to and in the absence of counsel. A conviction which rests on a mistaken identification is a gross miscarriage of justice. The *Wade* and *Gilbert* rules are aimed at minimizing that possibility by preventing the unfairness at the pretrial confrontation that experience has proved can occur and assuring meaningful examination of the identification witness' testimony at trial. Does it follow that the rules should be applied retroactively? We do not think so.

It is true that the right to the assistance of counsel has been applied retroactively at stages of the prosecution where denial of the right must almost invariably deny a fair trial, for example, at the trial itself, *Gideon v. Wainwright* [1963], ... or at some forms of arraignment, *Hamilton v. Alabama* [1961], ... or on appeal, *Douglas v. California* [1963]. ... "The basic purpose of a trial is the determination of truth, and it is self-evident that to deny a lawyer's help through the technical intricacies of a criminal trial or to deny a full opportunity to appeal a conviction because the accused is poor is to impede that purpose and to infect a criminal proceeding with the clear danger of convicting the innocent." *Tehan v. Shott* [1966]. ...

We have outlined in *Wade* the dangers and unfairness inherent in confrontations for identification. The possibility of unfairness at that point is great, both because of the manner in which confrontations are frequently conducted, and because of the likelihood that the accused will often be precluded from reconstructing what occurred and thereby from obtaining a full hearing on the identification issue at trial. The presence of counsel will significantly promote fairness at the confrontation and a full hearing at trial on the issue of identification. We have, therefore, concluded that the confrontation is a "critical stage" and that counsel is required at all confrontations. It must be recognized, however, that, unlike cases in which counsel is absent at trial or on appeal, it may confidently be assumed that confrontations for identification can be and often have been conducted in the absence of counsel with scrupulous fairness and without prejudice to the accused at trial. Therefore, while we feel that the exclusionary rules set forth in *Wade* and *Gilbert* are justified by the need to assure the integrity and reliability of our system of justice, they undoubtedly will affect cases in which no unfairness will be present. Of course, we should also assume there have been injustices in the past which could have been averted by having counsel present at the confrontation for identification, just as there are injustices when counsel is absent at trial. But the certainty and frequency with which we can say in the confrontation cases that no injustice occurred differ greatly enough from the cases involving absence of counsel at trial or on appeal to justify treating the situations as different in kind for the purpose of retroactive application, especially in light of the strong countervailing interests outlined below, and because it remains open to all persons to allege and prove, as Stovall attempts to do in this case, that the confrontation resulted in such unfairness that it infringed his right to due process of law....

The unusual force of the countervailing considerations strengthens our conclusion in favor of prospective application. The law enforcement officials of the federal government and of all 50 states have heretofore proceeded on the premise that the Constitution did not require the presence of counsel at pretrial confrontations for identification. Today's rulings were not foreshadowed in our cases; no court announced such a requirement until *Wade* was decided by the Court of Appeals for the 5th Circuit.... The overwhelming majority of American courts have always treated the evidence question not as one of admissibility but as one of credibility for the jury.... Law enforcement authorities fairly relied on this virtually unanimous weight of authority, now no longer valid, in conducting pretrial confrontations in the absence of counsel. It is, therefore, very clear that retroactive application of *Wade* and *Gilbert* "would seriously disrupt the administration of our criminal laws." *Johnson v. New Jersey....* In *Tehan v. Shott* ... we thought it persuasive against retroactive application of the no-comment rule of *Griffin v. California* [1965] ... that such application would have a serious impact on the 6 states that allowed comment on an accused's failure to take the stand. We said, "To require all of those states now to void the conviction of every person who did not testify at his trial would have an impact upon the administration of their criminal law so devastating as to need no elaboration."... That impact is insignificant compared to the impact to be expected from retroactivity of the *Wade* and *Gilbert* rules. At the very least, the processing of current criminal calendars would be disrupted while hearings were conducted to determine taint, if any, in identification evidence, and whether in any event the admission of the evidence was harmless error. Doubtless, too, inquiry would be handicapped by the unavailability of witnesses and dim memories. We conclude, therefore, that the *Wade* and *Gilbert* rules should not be made retroactive.

We also conclude that, for these purposes, no distinction is justified between convictions now final, as in the instant case, and convictions at various stages of trial and direct review. We regard the factors of reliance and burden on the administration of justice as entitled to such overriding significance as to make that distinction unsupportable. We recognize that Wade and Gilbert are, therefore, the only victims of pretrial confrontations in the absence of their counsel to have the benefit of the rules established in their cases. That they must be given that benefit is, however, an unavoidable consequence of the necessity that constitutional adjudications not stand as mere dictum. Sound policies of decision-making, rooted in the command of Article III of the Constitution that we resolve issues solely in concrete cases or controversies, and in the possible effect upon the incentive of counsel to advance contentions requiring a change in the law, militate against denying Wade and Gilbert the benefit of today's decisions. Inequity arguably results from according the benefit of a new rule to the parties in the case in which it is announced but not to other litigants similarly situated in the trial or appellate process who have raised the same issue. But we regard the fact that the parties involved are chance beneficiaries as an insignificant cost for adherence to sound principles of decision-making....

We turn now to the question whether petitioner, although not entitled to the application of *Wade* and *Gilbert* to his case, is entitled to relief on his claim that in any event the confrontation conducted in this case was so unnecessarily suggestive and conducive to irreparable mistaken identification that he was denied due process of law.... The practice of showing suspects singly to persons for the purpose of identification, and not as part of a lineup, has been widely condemned. However, a claimed violation of due process of law in the conduct of a confrontation depends on the totality of the circumstances surrounding it, and the record in the present case reveals that the showing of Stovall to Mrs. Behrendt in an immediate hospital confrontation was imperative. The Court of Appeals ... stated ...: "Here was the only person in the world who could possibly exonerate Stovall. Her words and only her words 'He is not the man' could have resulted in freedom for Stovall. The hospital was not far distant from the courthouse and jail. No one knew how long Mrs. Behrendt might live. Faced with the responsibility of identifying the attacker, with the need for immediate action and with the knowledge that Mrs. Behrendt could not visit the jail, the police followed the only feasible procedure and took Stovall to the hospital room. Under these circumstances, the usual police station lineup, which Stovall now argues he should have had, was out of the question."

The judgment of the Court of Appeals is affirmed.

Justice Douglas indicated his belief that *U.S. v. Wade* should be made retroactive.

Justice Black dissenting:

... The first question in this case is whether other defendants, already in prison on such unconstitutional evidence, shall be accorded the benefit of the rule. In this case the court holds that the petitioner here, convicted on such unconstitutional evidence, must remain in prison, and that besides Wade and Gilbert, who are "chance beneficiaries," no one can invoke the rule except defendants exhibited in lineups in the future. I dissent from that holding. It keeps people serving sentences who were convicted through the use of unconstitutional evidence. This is sought to be justified on the ground that retroactive application of the holding in *Gilbert* and *Wade* would somehow work a "burden on the administration of justice" and would not serve the court's purpose "to deter law enforcement authorities." It seems to me that to deny this petitioner and others like him the benefit of the new rule deprives them of a constitutional trial and perpetrates a rank discrimination against them. Once the court determines what the Constitution says, I do not believe it has the power, by weighing "countervailing interests," to legislate a timetable by which the Constitution's provisions shall become effective. For reasons stated in my dissent in *Linkletter v. Walker* [1965] ... I would hold that the petitioner here and every other person in jail under convictions based on unconstitutional evidence should be given the advantage of today's newly announced constitutional rules. ...

A defendant's right to an attorney during a police lineup was sharply limited by the Supreme

Court in *Kirby v. Illinois,* decided June 7, 1972. This was the first case in which Pres. Richard M. Nixon's first 4 appointees to the court, Chief Justice Warren Earl Burger and Justices Harry A. Blackmun, Lewis F. Powell Jr. and William H. Rehnquist, had an opportunity to review one of the Warren Court's controversial criminal law decisions. Justice Potter Stewart, who had dissented in the court's 1967 rulings that extended the right of counsel to lineups, joined the newer justices to form a 5-man majority. They held that the right of counsel did not extend to lineups conducted prior to the placing of formal charges against the defendant.

The result of the decision was to permit the police to conduct lineups in the absence of defense counsel prior to bringing formal charges against the suspect. In effect, this eliminated the requirement of defense counsel at virtually all lineups since the police could postpone indictment until after the lineup. The decision eliminated the potential problem, however, of an innocent suspect, who under the old requirements, might have been required to spend several hours in a police station waiting for a lawyer before he could be shown to eyewitnesses and cleared.

According to the majority, the right of counsel did not commence until the suspect was formally charged, "for it is only then that the government has committed itself to prosecute, and only then that the adverse positions of the government and defendant have solidified." The majority, therefore, said it refused "to import into a routine police investigation" the 6th Amendment right of counsel. The majority acknowledged the right of the defense to have excluded from evidence identifications obtained from a lineup shown to have been conducted unfairly.

Justice Brennan, joined by Douglas and Marshall, asserted in a minority opinion that the need for a lawyer was consistent throughout the entire criminal procedure. In permitting the police to conduct lineups in the absence of defense counsel in the interval between an arrest and the bringing of formal charges, Brennan asserted the majority had resorted to "mere formalism." Justice White, in a one-sentence dissent, asserted that the court's previous rulings on the subject extended to all lineups.

Abridgement of the *Kirby v. Illinois* decision (406 U.S. 682, June 7, 1972):

Justice Stewart, whom Chief Justice Burger and Justices Blackmun and Rehnquist joined, delivering the judgment of the court:

In *United States v. Wade* ... and *Gilbert v. California* ... this court held "that a post-indictment pretrial lineup at which the accused is exhibited to identifying witnesses is a critical stage of the criminal prosecution; that police conduct of such a lineup without notice to and in the absence of his counsel denies the accused his 6th [and 14th] Amendment right to counsel and calls in question the admissibility at trial of the in-court identifications of the accused by witnesses who attended the lineup." ... Those cases further held that no "in-court identifications" are admissible in evidence if their "source" is a lineup conducted in violation of this constitutional standard. "Only a *per se* exclusionary rule as to such testimony can be an effective sanction," the court said, "to assure that law enforcement officers will respect the accused's constitutional right to the presence of his counsel at the critical lineup." ... In the present case we are asked to extend the *Wade-Gilbert per se* exclusionary rule to identification testimony based upon a police station showup that took place *before* the defendant had been indicted or otherwise formally charged with any criminal offense.

On Feb. 21, 1968, a man named Willie Shard reported to the Chicago police that the previous day 2 men had robbed him on a Chicago street of a wallet containing, among other things, travellers checks and a Social Security card. On Feb. 22, 2 police officers stopped the petitioner and a companion, Ralph Bean, on West Madison Street in Chicago. When asked for identification, the petitioner produced a wallet that contained 3 travellers checks and a Social Security card, all bearing the name of Willie Shard. Papers with Shard's name on them were also found in Bean's possession. When asked to explain his possession of Shard's property, the petitioner first said that the travellers checks were "play money" and then told the officers that he had won them in a crap game. The officers then arrested the petitioner and Bean and took them to a police station.

Only after arriving at the police station, and checking the records there, did the arresting officers learn of the Shard robbery. A police car was then dispatched to Shard's place of employment, where it picked up Shard and brought him to the police station. Immediately upon entering the room in the police station where the petitioner and Bean were seated at a table, Shard positively identified them as the men who had robbed him 2 days earlier. No lawyer was present in the room, and neither the petitioner nor Bean had asked for legal assistance or been advised of any right to the presence of counsel.

More than 6 weeks later, the petitioner and Bean were indicted for the robbery of Willie Shard. Upon arraignment, counsel was appointed to represent them, and they pleaded not guilty. A pretrial motion to suppress Shard's identification testimony was denied, and at the trial Shard testified as a witness for the prosecution. In his testimony he described his identification of the 2 men at the police station on Feb. 22 and identified them again in the courtroom as the men who had robbed him on Feb. 20. He was cross-examined at length regarding the circumstances of his identification of the 2 defendants.... The jury found both defendants guilty, and the petitioner's conviction was affirmed on appeal....

We note at the outset that the constitutional privilege against compulsory self-incrimination is in no way implicated here....

...[T]he doctrine of *Miranda v. Arizona* ... has no applicability whatever to the issue before us. For the *Miranda* decision was based exclusively upon the 5th and 14th Amendment privilege against compulsory self-incrimination, upon the theory that custodial *interrogation* is inherently coercive.

The *Wade-Gilbert* exclusionary rule, by contrast, stems from a quite different constitutional guarantee—the guarantee of the right to counsel contained in the 6th and 14th Amendments. Unless all semblance of principled constitutional adjudication is to be abandoned, therefore, it is to the decisions construing that guarantee that we must look in determining the present controversy.

In a line of constitutional cases in this court stemming back to the court's landmark opinion in *Powell v. Alabama* [1932]..., it has been firmly established that a person's 6th and 14th Amendment right to counsel attaches only at or after the time that adversary judicial proceedings have been initiated against him....

This is not to say that a defendant in a criminal case has a constitutional right to counsel only at the trial itself. The *Powell* case makes clear that the right attaches at the time of arraignment, and the court has recently held that it exists also at the time of a preliminary hearing. *Coleman v. Alabama* [1970].... But the point is that, while members of the court have differed as to existence of the right to counsel in the contexts of some of the above cases, *all* of those cases have involved points of time at or after the initiation of adversary judicial criminal proceedings—whether by way of formal charge, preliminary hearing, indictment, information, or arraignment....

The initiation of judicial criminal proceedings is far from a mere formalism. It is the starting point of our whole system of adversary criminal justice. For it is only then that the government has committed itself to prosecute, and only then that the adverse positions of government and defendant have solidified. It is then that a defendant finds himself faced with the prosecutorial forces of organized society, and immersed in the intricacies of substantive and procedural criminal law. It is this point, therefore, that marks the commencement of the "criminal prosecutions" to which alone the explicit guarantees of the 6th Amendment are applicable. . . .

In this case we are asked to import into a routine police investigation an absolute constitutional guarantee historically and rationally applicable only after the onset of formal prosecutorial proceedings. We decline to do so. Less than a year after *Wade* and *Gilbert* were decided, the court explained the rule of those decisions as follows: "The rationale of those cases was that an accused is entitled to counsel at any 'critical stage of the *prosecution,'* and that a post-indictment lineup is such a 'critical stage.' " (Emphasis supplied.) *Simmons v. United States.* . . . We decline to depart from that rationale today by imposing a *per se* exclusionary rule upon testimony concerning an identification that took place long before the commencement of any prosecution whatever.

. . . What has been said is not to suggest that there may not be occasions during the course of a criminal investigation when the police do abuse identification procedures. Such abuses are not beyond the reach of the Constitution. As the court pointed out in *Wade* itself, it is always necessary to "scrutinize *any* pretrial confrontation. . . ." . . . The due process clause of the 5th and 14th Amendments forbids a lineup that is unnecessarily suggestive and conducive to irreparable mistaken identification. *Stovall v. Denno* (1967). . . . When a person has not been formally charged with a criminal offense, *Stovall* strikes the appropriate constitutional balance between the right of a suspect to be protected from prejudicial procedures and the interest of society in the prompt and purposeful investigation of an unsolved crime.

Justice Brennan, whom Douglas and Marshall joined, dissenting:

. . . In *Wade,* after concluding that the lineup conducted in that case did not violate the accused's right against self-incrimination, . . . the court addressed the argument "that the assistance of counsel at the lineup was indispensable to protect Wade's most basic right as a criminal defendant—his right to a fair trial at which the witnesses against him might be meaningfully cross-examined." . . . The court began by emphasizing that the 6th Amendment guarantee "encompasses counsel's assistance whenever necessary to assure a meaningful 'defence.' " ...

It was that constitutional principle that the court applied in *Wade* to pretrial confrontations for identification purposes. The court first met the government's contention that a confrontation for identification is "a mere preparatory step in the gathering of the prosecution's evidence," much like the scientific examination of fingerprints and blood samples. The court responded that in the latter instances "the accused has the opportunity for a meaningful confrontation of the government's case at trial through the ordinary processes of cross-examination of the government's expert witnesses and the presentation of the evidence of his own experts." The accused thus has no right to have counsel present at such examinations: "they are not critical stages since there is minimal risk that his counsel's absence at such stages might derogate from his right to a fair trial." ...

In contrast, the court said, "the confrontation compelled by the state between the accused and the victim or witnesses to a crime to elicit identification evidence is peculiarly riddled with innumerable dangers and variable factors which might seriously, even crucially, derogate from a fair trial." ... Most importantly, "the accused's inability effectively to reconstruct at trial any unfairness that occurred at the lineup may deprive him of his only opportunity meaningfully to attack the credibility of the witness' courtroom identification." ...

In view of *Wade,* it is plain, and the plurality today does not attempt to dispute it, that there inhere in a confrontation for identification conducted after arrest the identical hazards to a fair trial that inhere in such a confrontation conducted "after the onset of formal prosecutorial proceedings." ... The plurality apparently considers an arrest, which for present purposes we must assume to be based upon probable cause, to be nothing more than part of "a routine police investigation" ... and thus not "the starting point of our whole system of adversary criminal justice." ... An arrest, according to the plurality, does not face the accused "with the prosecutorial forces of organized society," nor immerse him "in the intricacies of substantive and procedural criminal law." Those consequences ensue, says the plurality, only with "[t]he initiation of judicial criminal proceedings," "[f]or it is only then that the government has committed itself to prosecute, and only then that the adverse positions of government and defendant have solidified."... If these propositions do not amount to "mere formalism," ... it is difficult to know how to characterize them. An arrest evidences the belief of the police that the perpetrator of a crime has been caught. A post-arrest confrontation for identification is not "a mere preparatory step in the gathering of the prosecution's evidence." *Wade.*... A primary, and frequently sole, purpose of the confrontation for identification at that stage is to accumulate proof to buttress the conclusion of the police that they have the offender in hand. The plurality offers no reason ... for concluding that a post-arrest confrontation for identification, unlike a post-charge confrontation, is not among those "critical confrontations of the accused by the prosecution at pretrial proceedings where the results might well settle the accused's fate and reduce the trial itself to a mere formality." ...

The highly suggestive form of confrontation employed in this case underscores the point. This showup was particularly fraught with the peril of mistaken identification. In the setting of a police station squad room where all present except petitioner and Bean were police officers, the danger was quite real that Shard's understandable resentment might lead him too readily to agree with the police that the pair under arrest, and the only persons exhibited to him, were indeed the robbers. "It is hard to imagine a situation more clearly conveying the suggestion to the witness that the one presented is believed guilty by the police." *Id....* The state had no case without Shard's identification testimony,* and safeguards against that consequence were therefore of critical importance. Shard's testimony itself demonstrates the necessity for such safeguards. On direct examination, Shard identified petitioner and Bean not as the alleged robbers on trial in the courtroom but as the pair he saw at the police station. His testimony thus lends strong support to the observation, quoted by the court in *Wade,* ... that "[i]t is a matter of common experience that, once a witness has picked out the accused at the line-up, he is not likely to go back on his

---

* Bean took the stand and testified that he and petitioner found Shard's travelers checks and social security card two hours before their arrest strewn upon the ground in an alley.

word later on, so that in practice the issue of identity may (in the absence of other relevant evidence) for all practical purposes be determined there and then, before the trial."...

Wade and *Gilbert,* of course, happened to involve post-indictment confrontations. Yet even a cursory perusal of the opinions in those cases reveals that nothing at all turned upon that particular circumstance. In short, it is fair to conclude that rather than "declin[ing] to depart from [the] rationale" of *Wade* and *Gilbert,* ... the plurality today, albeit purporting to be engaged in "principled constitutional adjudication," ... refuses even to recognize that "rationale." For my part, I do not agree that we "extend" *Wade* and *Gilbert* ... by holding that the principles of those cases apply to confrontations for identification conducted after arrest. Because Shard testified at trial about his identification of petitioner at the police station showup, the exclusionary rule of *Gilbert* ... requires reversal.

Justice White dissenting:

United States v. Wade ... and *Gilbert v. California* ... govern this case and compel reversal of the judgment of the Illinois Supreme Court.

Identification by Photographs

In *Simmons v. United States,* the court held Mar. 18, 1968 that it was constitutional for the police to show eyewitnesses photos of a suspect.

Justice Harlan, speaking for the court, conceded that photographic identifications are subject to the same abuses as lineups and that eyewitnesses subsequently tend to keep in mind the image of the photo rather than that of the person actually seen, thus reducing the trustworthiness of later lineups or courtroom identifications. The possibility of a mistaken identification notwithstanding, Harlan pointed out that the procedure was used "widely" and "effectively" in "apprehending offenders" and "sparing innocent suspects the ignominy of arrest by allowing eyewitnesses to exonerate them through the scrutiny of photographs." For this reason the court refused to prohibit photographic identifications, preferring instead to overrule any conviction in which the "photographic identification procedure was so impermissibly suggestive as to give rise to a very substantial likelihood of irreparable misidentification."

Abridgment of the *Simmons v. United States* decision (390 U.S. 377, Mar. 18, 1968):

Justice Harlan delivering the opinion of the court:

The evidence at trial showed that at about 1:45 p.m. on Feb. 27, 1964, 2 men entered a Chicago savings and loan association. One of them pointed a gun at a teller and ordered her to put money into a sack which the gunman supplied. The men remained in the bank about 5 minutes. After they left, a bank employe rushed to the street and saw one of the men sitting on the passenger side of a departing white 1960 Thunderbird automobile with a large scrape on the right door. Within an hour police located in the vicinity a car matching this description. They discovered that it belonged to a Mrs. Rey, sister-in-law of petitioner Simmons. She told the police that she had loaned the car for the afternoon to her brother, William Andrews.

At about 5:15 p.m. the same day, 2 FBI agents came to the house of Mrs. Mahon, Andrews' mother, about half a block from the place where the car was then parked. The agents had no warrant, and at trial it was disputed whether Mrs. Mahon gave them permission to search the house. They did search, and in the basement they found 2 suitcases, of which Mrs. Mahon disclaimed any knowledge. One suitcase contained, among other items, a gun holster, a sack similar to the one used in the robbery, and several coin cards and bill wrappers from the bank which had been robbed.

The following morning the FBI obtained from another of Andrews' sisters some snapshots of Andrews and of petitioner Simmons, who was said by the sister to have been with

Andrews the previous afternoon. These snapshots were shown to the 5 bank employes who had witnessed the robbery. Each witness identified pictures of Simmons as representing one of the robbers. A week or 2 later, 3 of these employes identified photographs of petitioner Garrett as depicting the other robber, the other 2 witnesses stating that they did not have a clear view of the second robber. . . .

During the trial, all 5 bank employe witnesses identified Simmons as one of the robbers. 3 of them identified Garrett as the 2d robber, the other 2 testifying that they did not get a good look at the 2d robber. . . .

The jury found Simmons and Garrett, as well as Andrews, guilty as charged. On appeal, the Court of Appeals for the 7th Circuit affirmed as to Simmons and Garrett, but reversed the conviction of Andrews on the ground that there was insufficient evidence to connect him with the robbery. . . .

[Now] Simmons asserts that his pretrial identification by means of photographs was in the circumstances so unnecessarily suggestive and conducive to misidentification as to deny him due process of law, or at least to require reversal of his conviction in the exercise of our supervisory power over the lower federal courts. . . .

The facts as to the identification claim are these. . . . FBI agents on the day following the robbery obtained from Andrews' sister a number of snapshots of Andrews and Simmons. There seem to have been at least 6 of these pictures, consisting mostly of group photographs of Andrews, Simmons and others. Later the same day, these were shown to the 5 bank employes who had witnessed the robbery . . . , the photographs being exhibited to each employe separately. Each of the 5 employes identified Simmons from the photographs. At later dates, some of these witnesses were again interviewed by the FBI and shown indeterminate numbers of pictures. Again, all identified Simmons. At trial, the government did not introduce any of the photographs but relied upon in-court identification by the 5 eyewitnesses, each of whom swore that Simmons was one of the robbers.

In support of his argument, Simmons looks to last term's "lineup" decisions—*United States v. Wade*. . . and *Gilbert v. California* . . .—in which this court first departed from the rule that the manner of an extra-judicial identification affects only the weight, not the admissibility, of identification testimony at trial. The rationale of those cases was that an accused is entitled to counsel at any "critical stage of the prosecution" and that a post-indictment lineup is such a "critical stage." ... Simmons, however, does not contend that he was entitled to counsel at the time the pictures were shown to the witnesses. Rather, he asserts simply that in the circumstances the identification procedure was so unduly prejudicial as fatally to taint his conviction. This is a claim which must be evaluated in light of the totality of surrounding circumstances.... Viewed in that context, we find the claim untenable.

It must be recognized that improper employment of photographs by police may sometimes cause witnesses to err in identifying criminals. A witness may have obtained only a brief glimpse of a criminal, or may have seen him under poor conditions. Even if the police subsequently follow the most correct photographic identification procedures and show him the pictures of a number of individuals without indicating whom they suspect, there is some danger that the witness may make an incorrect identification. This danger will be increased if the police display to the witness only the picture of a single individual who generally resembles the person he saw, or if they show him the pictures of several persons among which the photograph of a single such individual recurs or is in some way emphasized. The chance of misidentification is also heightened if the police indicate to the witness that they have other evidence that one of the persons pictured committed the crime. Regardless of how the initial misidentification comes about, the witness thereafter is apt to retain in his memory the image of the photograph rather than of the person actually seen, reducing the trustworthiness of subsequent lineup or courtroom identification.

Despite the hazards of initial identification by photograph, this procedure has been used widely and effectively in criminal law enforcement, from the standpoint both of apprehending offenders and of sparing innocent suspects the ignominy of arrest by allowing eyewitnesses to exonerate them through scrutiny of photographs. The danger that use of the technique may result in convictions based on misidentification may be substantially lessened by a course of cross-examination at trial which exposes to the jury the method's potential for error. We are unwilling to prohibit its employment, either in the exercise of our supervisory power or, still less, as a matter of constitutional requirement. Instead, we hold that each case must be considered on its own facts, and that convictions based on eyewitness identification at trial following a pretrial identification by photograph will be set aside on that ground only if the photographic identification procedure was so impermissibly suggestive as to give rise to a very substantial likelihood of irreparable misidentification. This standard accords with our resolution of a similar issue in *Stovall v. Denno* [1967] ... and with decisions of other courts on the question of identification by photograph.

Applying the standard to this case, we conclude that petitioner Simmons' claim on this score must fail. In the first place, it is not suggested that it was unnecessary for the FBI to resort to photographic identification in this instance. A serious felony had been committed. The perpetrators were still at large. The inconclusive clues which law enforcement officials possessed led to Andrews and Simmons. It was essential for the FBI agents swiftly to determine whether they were on the right track, so that they could properly deploy their forces in Chicago and, if necessary, alert officials in other cities. The justification for this method of procedure was hardly less compelling than that which we found to justify the "one-man lineup" in *Stovall v. Denno*....

In the 2d place, there was in the circumstances of this case little chance that the procedure utilized led to misidentification of Simmons. The robbery took place in the afternoon in a well-lighted bank. The robbers wore no masks. 5 bank employes had been able to see the robber later identified as Simmons for periods ranging up to 5 minutes. Those witnesses were shown the photographs only a day later, while their memories were still fresh. At least 6 photographs were displayed to each witness. Apparently, these consisted primarily of group photographs, with Simmons and Andrews each appearing several times in the series. Each witness was alone when he or she saw the photographs. There is no evidence to indicate that the witnesses were told anything about the progress of the investigation or that the FBI agents in any other way suggested which persons in the pictures were under suspicion.

Under these conditions, all 5 eyewitnesses identified Simmons as one of the robbers. None identified Andrews, who apparently was as prominent in the photographs as Simmons. These initial identifications were confirmed by all 5 witnesses in subsequent viewings of photographs and at trial, where each witness identified Simmons in person. Notwithstanding cross-examination, none of the witnesses displayed any doubt about their respective identifications of Simmons. Taken together, these circumstances leave little room for doubt that the identification of Simmons was correct, even though the identification procedure employed may have in some respects fallen short of the ideal. We hold that in the factual surroundings of this case the identification procedure used was not such as to deny Simmons due process of law or to call for reversal under our supervisory authority....

CAPITAL PUNISHMENT

Death Penalty Invalid as Currently Imposed

In a 5-4 decision June 29, 1972, the Supreme Court declared capital punishment, as currently administered in the U.S., a "cruel and unusual punishment" of the type proscribed by the 8th Amendment. The decision, in the case of *Furman v. Georgia,* saved from execution some 645 persons on death rows throughout the U.S. and overruled the death penalty provisions of 40 states, the District of Columbia and the federal government.

Each of 9 justices issued a separate opinion, which together totalled 243 pages. The majority was formed by the 5 survivors of the Warren Court, Justices William O. Douglas, William J. Brennan Jr., Thurgood Marshall, Byron R. White and Potter Stewart.

The justices in the majority were of 2 views. Brennan and Marshall held that capital punishment in and of itself constituted a cruel and unusual punishment.

In conceding that the framers of the Bill of Rights did not intend to outlaw legal executions when they passed the 8th Amendment, Brennan noted that the court had held in 1958 that the 8th Amendment "must draw its meaning from the evolving standards of decency that mark the progress of a maturing society." Accordingly, Brennan said, a punishment is "cruel and unusual" if "it does not comport with human dignity." He held that the principles on which such a determination should be made depend on whether a particular punishment is unnecessarily severe, arbitrary and excessive and on whether it is unacceptable to contemporary society. According to Brennan, the death penalty was deficient on all 4 criteria, most notably in the frequency in which it was imposed— fewer than 50 times a year in a nation of more than 200 million people in which thousands of murders and rapes are committed annually. "When the punishment of death is inflicted in a trivial number of cases in which it is legally available, the conclusion is virtually inescapable that it is being inflicted arbitrarily," he said. Moreover, the death penalty was unnecessarily severe, he asserted, since he saw no evidence that it served any purpose that could not be served as well by imprisonment. Brennan described as "implausible" the notion that a potential criminal would fail to commit a capital crime for fear of the death penalty.

Marshall used similar arguments, adding that the death penalty was "morally unacceptable" if for no other reason than that it most frequently was imposed on blacks, "the poor, the ignorant and the underprivileged members of society." Marshall noted that of the 3,859 persons executed in the U.S. since 1930, 1,751 were white and 2,066 black. Of the 455 persons executed for rape during that period, 48 were white and 405 black.

White, Stewart and Douglas, while not holding capital punishment unconstitutional *per se,* argued that it was unconstitutional as currently administered because of the relatively rare and arbitrary manner in which it was imposed. Stewart compared the imposition of the death penalty with the chance of being struck by lightning. The Constitution, he said, cannot tolerate a system that permits the death penalty to be so "wantonly and so freakishly imposed."

The 4 dissenters were the 4 Nixon appointees— Chief Justice Warren Earl Burger and Justices Lewis F. Powell Jr., Harry A. Blackmun and William H. Rehnquist. They emphasized in their separate dissents what they considered the proper role of the Supreme Court. In their view, public policy, to the extent possible, should be determined by legislators rather than judges. While "over-reaching" by the Legislative and Executive Branches might jeopardize individual rights, Justice Rehnquist said, "judicial overruling may result in sacrifice of the equally important right of the people to govern themselves."

Blackmun, in his dissent, expressed the "excruciating agony of the spirit" faced by a justice whose deep-seated personal views cannot be reconciled with his reading of the Constitution. "I yield to no one in the depth of my distaste, antipathy, and, indeed abhorrence, for the death penalty," he said. "That distaste is buttressed by a belief that capital punishment serves no useful purpose that can be demonstrated. Were I a legislator, I would vote against the death penalty." Yet, he said, "we should not allow our personal preferences as to the wisdom of legislative and congressional action, or our distaste for such action, to guide our judicial decision in cases such as these."

Burger, in his long dissent, agreed that the 8th Amendment should be interpreted with reference to society's "evolving standards of decency," but to Burger the crucial element in such a determination was the attitude of Congress and the state legislatures, which overwhelmingly favored some form of capital punishment. In "a democracy, the legislative judgment is presumed to embody the basic standards of decency prevailing in the society," he asserted. Burger, furthermore, did not accept the majority's contention that capital punishment was unconstitutional because of the relatively small number of instances in which it was imposed. That view, he said, "suggests that capital punishment can be made to satisfy the 8th Amendment values if its rate of imposition is somehow multiplied." The majority opinions, he said, suggest that the flexible sentencing system created by the legislatures and carried out by judges and juries "has yielded more mercy than the 8th Amendment can stand." One result of the majority ruling, Burger predicted, might be to encourage legislatures that want to maintain the death penalty to establish a mandatory death penalty for certain crimes. "I could more easily be persuaded that mandatory systems of death, without the intervening and ameliorating impact of lay jurors, are so arbitrary and doctrinaire that they violate the Constitution," he said.

Although the decision applied to all persons currently awaiting execution, it involved the appeals of 3 Southern blacks who had been sentenced to death. In one case the crime was murder; in the other 2 cases the crime was rape.

Abridgment of the *Furman v. Georgia* decision

(408 U.S. 238, June 29, 1972):

Justice Douglas concurring:

... In each [of the 3 cases] the determination of whether the penalty should be death or a lighter punishment was left by the state to the discretion of the judge or of the jury. In each of the 3 cases the trial was to a jury. They are here on petitions for *certiorari* which we granted limited to the question whether the imposition and execution of the death penalty constitutes "cruel and unusual punishments" within the meaning of the 8th Amendment as applied to the states by the 14th. I vote to vacate each judgment, believing that the exaction of the death penalty does violate the 8th and 14th Amendments....

There is increasing recognition of the fact that the basic theme of equal protection is implicit in "cruel and unusual" punishments. "A penalty ... should be considered 'unusually' imposed if it is administered arbitrarily or discriminatorily."* The same authors add that "the extreme rarity with which applicable death penalty provisions are put to use raises a strong inference of arbitrariness." The President's Commission on Law Enforcement & Administration of Justice recently concluded: "Finally there is evidence that the imposition of the death sentence and the exercise of dispensing power by the courts and the executive follow discriminatory patterns. The death sentence is disproportionately imposed and carried out on the poor, the Negro, and the members of unpopular groups."

A study of capital cases in Texas from 1924 to 1968 reached the following conclusions: "Application of the death penalty is unequal: most of those executed were poor, young, and ignorant. 75 of the 460 cases involved codefendants, who, under Texas law, were given separate trials. In several instances, where a white and a Negro were codefendants, the white was sentenced to life imprisonment or a term of years, and the Negro was given the death penalty. Another ethnic disparity is found in the type of sentence imposed for rape. The Negro convicted of rape is far more likely to get the death penalty than a term sentence, whereas whites and Latins are far more likely to get a term sentence than the death penalty."

---

* Goldberg & Dershowitz, Declaring the Death Penalty Unconstitutional, 83 Harv. L. Rev. 1773, 1790.

Warden Lewis E. Lawes of Sing Sing said: "Not only does capital punishment fail in its justification, but no punishment could be invented with so many inherent defects. It is an unequal punishment in the way it is applied to the rich and to the poor. The defendant of wealth and position never goes to the electric chair or to the gallows. Juries do not intentionally favor the rich, the law is theoretically impartial, but the defendant with ample means is able to have his case presented with every favorable aspect, while the poor defendant often has a lawyer assigned by the court. Sometimes such assignment is considered part of political patronage; usually the lawyer assigned has had no experience whatever in a capital case."

Former Attorney General Ramsey Clark has said, "It is the poor, the sick, the ignorant, the powerless and the hated who are executed." One searches our chronicles in vain for the execution of any member of the affluent strata of this society. The Leopolds and Loebs are given prison terms, not sentenced to death.

Jackson, a black, convicted of the rape of a white woman, was 21 years old. A court-appointed psychiatrist said that Jackson was of average education and average intelligence, that he was not an imbecile or schizophrenic or psychotic, that his traits were the product of environmental influences, and that he was competent to stand trial. Jackson had entered the house after the husband left for work. He held scissors against the neck of the wife, demanding money. She could find none, and a struggle ensued for the scissors, a battle which she lost; and she was then raped, Jackson keeping the scissors pressed against her neck. While there did not appear to be any long-term traumatic impact on the victim, she was bruised and abrased in the struggle but was not hospitalized. Jackson was a convict who had escaped from a work gang in the area, a result of a 3-year sentence for auto theft. He was at large for 3 days and during that time had committed several other offenses— burglary, auto theft, and assault and battery.

Furman, a black, killed a householder while seeking to enter the home at night. Furman shot the deceased through a closed door. He was 26 years old and had finished the 6th grade in school. Pending trial, he was committed to the Georgia Central State Hospital for a psychiatric examination on his plea of insanity tendered by court-appointed counsel. The

superintendent reported: that a unanimous staff diagnostic conference on the same date had concluded "that this patient
should retain his present diagnosis of Mental Deficiency, Mild
to Moderate, with Psychotic Episodes associated with Convulsive Disorder." The physicians agreed that "at present the
patient is not psychotic, but he is not capable of cooperating
with his counsel in the preparation of his defense"; and the staff
believed "that he is in need of further psychiatric hospitaliza-
tion and treatment."

Later he reported that the staff diagnosis was Mental Deficiency, Mild to Moderate, with Psychotic Episodes associated
with Convulsive Disorder. He concluded, however, that Furman was "not psychotic at present, knows right from wrong
and is able to cooperate with his counsel in preparing his
defense."

Branch, a black, entered the rural home of a 65-year-old
widow, a white, while she slept and raped her, holding his arm
against her throat. Thereupon he demanded money and for 30
minutes or more the widow searched for money, finding little.
As he left, Jackson said if the widow told anyone what happened, he would return and kill her. The record is barren of any
medical or psychiatric evidence showing injury to her as a
result of Branch's attack.

He had previously been convicted of felony theft and
found to be a borderline mentally deficient and well below the
average IQ of Texas prison inmates. He had the equivalent of
5½ years of grade school education. He had a "dull
intelligence" and was in the lower 4 percentile of his class.

We cannot say from facts disclosed in these records that
these defendants were sentenced to death because they were
black. Yet our task is not restricted to an effort to divine what
motives impelled these death penalties. Rather we deal with a
system of law and of justice that leaves to the uncontrolled
discretion of judges or juries the determination whether
defendants committing these crimes should die or be imprisoned. Under these laws no standards govern the selection of
the penalty. People live or die, dependent on the whim of one
man or of 12. . . .

The high service rendered by the "cruel and unusual"
punishment clause of the 8th Amendment is to require
legislatures to write penal laws that are evenhanded,

nonselective and nonarbitrary and to require judges to see to it that general laws are not applied sparsely, selectively and spottily to unpopular groups.

A law that stated that anyone making more than $50,000 would be exempt from the death penalty would plainly fall, as would a law that in terms said that blacks, those who never went beyond the 5th grade in school, or those who made less than $3,000 a year, or those who were unpopular or unstable should be the only people executed. A law which in the overall view reaches that result in practice has no more sanctity than a law which in terms provides the same.

Thus, these discretionary statutes are unconstitutional in their operation. They are pregnant with discrimination, and discrimination is an ingredient not compatible with the idea of equal protection of the laws that is implicit in the ban on "cruel and unusual" punishments.

Any law which is nondiscriminatory on its face may be applied in such a way as to violate the equal protection clause of the 14th Amendment.... Such conceivably might be the fate of a mandatory death penalty, where equal or lesser sentences were imposed on the elite, a harsher one on the minorities or members of the lower castes. Whether a mandatory death penalty would otherwise be constitutional is a question I do not reach....

Justice Brennan concurring:

... Ours would indeed be a simple task were we required merely to measure a challenged punishment against those that history has long condemned. That narrow and unwarranted view of the clause, however, was left behind with the 19th century. Our task today is more complex. We know "that the words of the [clause] are not precise and that their scope is not static." We know, therefore, that the clause "must draw its meaning from the evolving standards of decency that mark the progress of a maturing society." *Trop v. Dulles* (1958).... That knowledge, of course, is but the beginning of the inquiry.

In *Trop v. Dulles* ... it was said that "[t]he question is whether [a] penalty subjects the individual to a fate forbidden by the principle of civilized treatment guaranteed by the [clause]." It was also said that a challenged punishment must be examined "in light of the basic prohibition against inhuman treatment" embodied in the clause.... It was said, finally, that: "The basic concept underlying the [clause] is nothing less than the dignity of man. While the state has power to punish, the [clause] stands to assure that this power be exercised within the limits of civilized standards."... At bottom, then, the cruel and unusual punishments clause prohibits the infliction of uncivilized and inhuman punishments. The state, even as it punishes, must treat its members with respect for their intrinsic worth as human beings. A punishment is "cruel and unusual," therefore, if it does not comport with human dignity.

This formulation, of course, does not of itself yield principles for assessing the constitutional validity of particular punishments. Nevertheless, even though "[t]his court has had little occasion to give precise content to the [clause]," *ibid.,* there are principles recognized in our cases and inherent in the clause sufficient to permit a judicial determination whether a challenged punishment comports with human dignity.

The primary principle is that a punishment must not be so severe as to be degrading to the dignity of human beings. Pain, certainly, may be a factor in the judgment. The infliction of an extremely severe punishment will often entail physical suffering. See *Weems v. United States* [1910].... Yet the Framers also know "that there could be exercises of cruelty by laws other than those which inflicted bodily pain or mutilation" *id.* Even though "[t]here may be involved no physical mistreatment, no primitive torture," *Trop v. Dulles,* ... severe mental pain may be inherent in the infliction of a particular punishment. See *Weems v. United States....* That, indeed, was one of the conclusions underlying the holding of the plurality in *Trop v. Dulles* that the punishment of expatriation violates the clause....

More than the presence of pain, however, is comprehended in the judgment that the extreme severity of a punishment makes it degrading to the dignity of human beings. The barbaric punishments condemned by history, "punishments which inflict torture, such as the rack, the thumbscrew, the iron boot, the stretching of limbs and the like," are, of course, "attended with acute pain and suffering." *O'Neil v. Vermont...* (1892) (Field, J., dissenting). When we consider why they have been condemned, however, we realize that the pain involved is not the only reason. The true significance of these punishments is that they treat members of the human race as nonhumans, as objects to be toyed with and discarded. They are thus inconsistent with the fundamental premise of the clause that even the vilest criminal remains a human being possessed of common human dignity....

In determining whether a punishment comports with human dignity, we are aided also by a 2d principle inherent in the clause—that the state must not arbitrarily inflict a severe punishment. This principle derives from the notion that the state does not respect human dignity when, without reason, it inflicts upon some people a severe punishment that it does not inflict upon others. Indeed, the very words "cruel and unusual punishments" imply condemnation of the arbitrary infliction of severe punishments....

A 3d principle inherent in the clause is that a severe punishment must not be unacceptable to contemporary society. Rejection by society, of course, is a strong indication that a severe punishment does not comport with human dignity. In applying this principle, however, we must make certain that the judicial determination is as objective as possible....

The final principle inherent in the clause is that a severe punishment must not be excessive. A punishment is excessive under this principle if it is unnecessary: The indication of a severe punishment by the state cannot comport with human dignity when it is nothing more than the pointless infliction of suffering if there is a significantly less severe punishment adequate to achieve the purposes for which the punishment is inflicted....

The question, then, is whether the deliberate infliction of death is today consistent with the command of the clause that the state may not inflict punishments that do not comport with human dignity. I will analyze the punishment of death in terms of the principles set out above and the cumulative test to which they lead: It is a denial of human dignity for the state arbitrarily to subject a person to an unusually severe punishment that society has indicated it does not regard as acceptable and that cannot be shown to serve any penal purpose more effectively than a significantly less drastic punishment. Under these principles and this test, death is today a "cruel and unusual" punishment....

... Death is today an unusually severe punishment, unusual in its pain, in its finality and in its enormity. No other existing punishment is comparable to death in terms of physical and mental suffering. Although our information is not conclusive, it appears that there is no method available that guarantees an immediate and painless death. Since the discontinuance of flogging as a constitutionally permissible punishment, ... death remains as the only punishment that may involve the conscious infliction of physical pain. In addition, we know that mental pain is an inseparable part of our practice of punishing criminals by death, for the prospect of pending execution exacts a frightful toll during the inevitable long wait between the imposition of sentence and the actual infliction of death....

In comparison to all other punishments today, the deliberate extinguishment of human life by the state is uniquely degrading to human dignity. I would not hesitate to hold, on that ground alone, that death is today a "cruel and unusual" punishment, were it not that death is a punishment of long-standing usage and acceptance in this country. I therefore turn to the 3d principle that the state may not arbitrarily inflict an unusually severe punishment.

The outstanding characteristic of our present practice of punishing criminals by death is the infrequency with which we resort to it. The evidence is conclusive that death is not the ordinary punishment for any crime.

There has been a steady decline in the infliction of this punishment in every decade since the 1930s, the earliest period for which accurate statistics are available. In the 1930s, executions averaged 167 per year; in the 1940s, the average was 128; in the 1950s, it was 72; and in the years 1960-1962, it was 48. There have been a total of 46 executions since then, 36 of them in 1963-1964. Yet our population and the numbers of capital crimes committed have increased greatly over the past 4 decades....

When a country of over 200 million people inflicts an unusually severe punishment no more than 50 times a year, the inference is strong that the punishment is not being regularly and fairly applied. To dispel it would indeed require a clear showing of nonarbitrary infliction.

Although there are no exact figures available, we know that thousands of murders and rapes are committed annually in states where death is an authorized punishment for those crimes. However, the rate of infliction is characterized—as "freakishly" or "spectacularly" rare, or simply as rare—it would take the purest sophistry to deny that death is inflicted in only a minute fraction of these cases. How much rarer, after all, could the infliction of death be?

When the punishment of death is inflicted in a trivial number of the cases in which it is legally available, the conclusion is virtually inescapable that it is being inflicted arbitrarily. Indeed, it smacks of little more than a lottery system....

...When the rate of infliction is at this low level, it is highly implausible that only the worst criminals or the criminals who commit the worst crimes are selected for this punishment. No one has yet suggested a rational basis that could differentiate in those terms the few who die from the many who go to prison....

The states' primary claim is that death is a necessary punishment because it prevents the commission of capital crimes more effectively than any less severe punishment. The first part of this claim is that the infliction of death is necessary to stop the individuals executed from committing further crimes. The sufficient answer to this is that if a criminal convicted of a capital crime poses a danger to society, effective administration of the state's pardon and parole laws can delay or deny his release from prison, and techniques of isolation can eliminate or minimize the danger while he remains confined.

The more significant argument is that the threat of death prevents the commission of capital crimes because it deters potential criminals who would not be deterred by the threat of imprisonment....

It is important to focus upon the precise import of this argument. It is not denied that many, and probably most, capital crimes cannot be deterred by the threat of punishment. Thus the argument can apply only to those who think rationally about the commission of capital crimes. Particularly is that true when the potential criminal, under this argument, must not only consider the risk of punishment but also distinguish between 2 possible punishments. The concern, then, is with a particular type of potential criminal, the rational person who will commit a capital crime knowing that the punishment is long-term imprisonment, which may well be for the rest of his life, but will not commit the crime knowing that the punishment is death. On the face of it, the assumption that such persons exist is implausible. . . .

In sum, the punishment of death is inconsistent with all 4 principles: Death is an unusually severe and degrading punishment; there is a strong probability that it is inflicted arbitrarily; its rejection by contemporary society is virtually total; and there is no reason to believe that it serves any penal purpose more effectively than the less severe punishment of imprisonment. The function of these principles is to enable a court to determine whether a punishment comports with human dignity. . . . Death, quite simply, does not. . . .

Justice Stewart concurring:

. . . These death sentences are cruel and unusual in the same way that being struck by lightning is cruel and unusual. For, of all the people convicted of rapes and murders in 1967 and 1968, many just as reprehensible as these, the petitioners are among a capriciously selected random handful upon whom the sentence of death has in fact been imposed. . . . I simply conclude that the 8th and 14th Amendments cannot tolerate the infliction of a sentence of death under legal systems that permit this unique penalty to be so wantonly and so freakishly imposed.

Justice White concurring:

. . . I do not at all intimate that the death penalty is unconstitutional per se or that 'there is no system of capital punishment that would comport with the 8th Amendment. That question . . . is not presented by these cases and need not be decided. . . .

The narrower question to which I address myself concerns the constitutionality of capital punishment statutes under which (1) the legislature authorizes the imposition of the death penalty for murder or rape; (2) the legislature does not itself mandate the penalty. . . .

The imposition and execution of the death penalty are obviously cruel in the dictionary sense. But the penalty has not been considered cruel and unusual punishment in the constitutional sense because it was thought justified by the social ends it was deemed to serve. At the moment that it ceases realistically to further these purposes, however, the emerging question is whether its imposition in such circumstances would violate the 8th Amendment. It is my view that it would, for its imposition would then be the pointless and needless extinction of life with only marginal contributions to any discernible social or public purposes. A penalty with such negligible returns to the state would be patently excessive and cruel and unusual punishment violative of the 8th Amendment.

It is also my judgment that this point has been reached with respect to capital punishment as it is presently administered under the statutes involved in these cases. Concededly, it is difficult to prove as a general proposition that capital punishment, however administered, more effectively serves the ends of the criminal law than does imprisonment. But however that may be, I cannot avoid the conclusion that as the statutes before us are now administered, the penalty is so infrequently imposed that the threat of execution is too attenuated to be of substantial service to criminal justice.

... I can do no more than state a conclusion based on 10 years of almost daily exposure to the facts and circumstances of hundreds and hundreds of federal and state criminal cases involving crimes for which death is the authorized penalty. That conclusion... is that the death penalty is exacted with great infrequency even for the most atrocious crimes and that there is no meaningful basis for distinguishing the few cases in which it is imposed from the many cases in which it is not. The short of it is that the policy of vesting sentencing authority primarily in juries—a decision largely motivated by the desire to mitigate the harshness of the law and to bring community judgment to bear on the sentence as well as guilt or innocence—has so effectively achieved its aim that capital punishment within the confines of the statutes now before us has for all practical purposes run its course....

Justice Marshall concurring:

... [E]ven if capital punishment is not excessive, it nonetheless violates the 8th Amendment because it is morally unacceptable to the people of the United States at this time in their history.

In judging whether or not a given penalty is morally acceptable, most courts have said that the punishment is valid unless "it shocks the conscience and sense of justice of the people."

Judge Frank once noted the problems inherent in the use of such a measuring stick: "[The court,] before it reduces a sentence as 'cruel and unusual,' must have reasonably good assurances that the sentence offends the 'common conscience.' And, in any context, such a standard—the community's attitude—is usually an unknowable. It resembles a slithery shadow, since one can seldom learn, at all accurately, what the community, or a majority, actually feels. Even a carefully-taken 'public opinion poll' would be inconclusive in a case like this." While a public opinion poll obviously is of some assistance in indicating public acceptance or rejection of a specific penalty, its utility cannot be very great. This is because whether or not a punishment is cruel and unusual depends, not on whether its mere mention "shocks the conscience and sense of justice of the people," but on whether people who were fully informed as to the purposes of the penalty and its liabilities would find the penalty shocking, unjust, and unacceptable.

In other words, the question with which we must deal is not whether a substantial proportion of American citizens would today, if polled, opine that capital punishment is barbarously cruel, but whether they would find it to be so in the light of all information presently available.

This is not to suggest that with respect to this test of unconstitutionality people are required to act rationally; they are not. With respect to this judgment, a violation of the 8th Amendment is totally dependent on the predictable subjective, emotional reactions of informed citizens.

It has often been noted that American citizens know almost nothing about capital punishment. Some of the conclusions arrived at in the preceding section and the supporting evidence would be critical to an informed judgment on the morality of the death penalty: *e.g.,* that the death penalty is no more effective a deterrent than life imprisonment, that convicted murderers are rarely executed but are usually sentenced to a term in prison; that convicted murderers usually are model prisoners and that they almost always become law-abiding citizens upon their release from prison; that the costs of executing a capital offender exceed the costs of imprisoning him for life; that while in prison, a convict under sentence of death performs none of the useful functions that life prisoners perform; that no attempt is made in the sentencing process to ferret out likely recidivists for execution; and that the death penalty may actually stimulate criminal activity.

This information would almost surely convince the average citizen that the death penalty was unwise, but a problem arises as to whether it would convince him that the penalty was morally reprehensible. This problem arises from the fact that the public's desire for retribution, even though this is a goal which the legislature cannot constitutionally pursue as its sole justification for capital punishment, might influence the citizenry's view of the morality of capital punishment. The solution to the problem lies in the fact that no one has ever seriously advanced retribution as a legitimate goal of our society. Defenses of capital punishment are always mounted on deterrent or other similar theories. This should not be surprising. It is the people of this country who have urged in the past that prisons rehabilitate as well as isolate offenders, and it is the people who have injected a sense of purpose into our penology. I cannot believe that at this stage in our history, the American people would ever knowingly support purposeless vengeance. Thus, I believe that the great mass of citizens would conclude on the basis of the material already considered that the death penalty is immoral and therefore unconstitutional.

But, if this information needs supplementing, I believe that the following facts would serve to convince even the most hesitant of citizens to condemn death as a sanction: capital punishment is imposed discriminatorily against certain identifiable classes of people; there is evidence that innocent people have been executed before their innocence can be proved; and the death penalty wreaks havoc with our entire criminal justice system....

Regarding discrimination, it has been said that "[i]t is usually the poor, the illiterate, the underprivileged, the member of the minority group—the man who, because he is without means, and is defended by a court appointed attorney—who becomes society's sacrificial lamb...." Indeed, a look at the bare statistics regarding executions is enough to betray much of the discrimination. A total of 3,859 persons have been executed since 1930, of which 1,751 were white and 2,066 were Negro.... 1,664 of the executed murderers were white, and

1,630 were Negro.... 48 whites and 405 Negroes were executed for rape.... Negroes were executed far more often than whites in proportion to their percentage of the population. Studies indicate that while the higher rate of execution among Negroes is partially due to a higher rate of crime, there is evidence of racial discrimination....

There is also overwhelming evidence that the death penalty is employed against men and not women. Only 32 women have been executed since 1930, while 3,827 men have met a similar fate....

It also is evident that the burden of capital punishment falls upon the poor, the ignorant and the underprivileged members of society. It is the poor and the members of minority groups who are least able to voice their complaints against capital punishment. Their impotence leaves them victims of a sanction which the wealthier, better-represented, just-as-guilty person can escape. So long as the capital sanction is used only against the forlorn, easily forgotten members of society, legislators are content to maintain the *status quo,* because change would draw attention to the problem and concern might develop. Ignorance is perpetuated and apathy soon becomes its mate, and we have today's situation.

...[Americans] are unaware of the potential dangers of executing an innocent man. Our "beyond-a-reasonable-doubt" burden of proof in criminal cases is intended to protect the innocent, but we know it is not foolproof. Various studies have shown that people whose innocence is later convincingly established are convicted and sentenced to death.

Proving one's innocence after a jury finding of guilt is almost impossible. While reviewing courts are willing to entertain all kinds of collateral attacks where a sentence of death is involved, they very rarely dispute the jury's interpretation of the evidence.... If an innocent man has been found guilty, he must then depend on the good faith of the prosecutor's office to help him establish his innocence. There is evidence, however, that prosecutors do not welcome the idea of having convictions, which they labored hard to secure, overturned, and that their cooperation is highly unlikely.

No matter how careful courts are, the possibility of perjured testimony, mistaken honest testimony, and human error remain all too real. We have no way of judging how many innocent persons have been executed, but we can be certain that there were some.... Surely there will be more as long as capital punishment remains part of our penal law.

While it is difficult to ascertain with certainty the degree to which the death penalty is discriminatorily imposed or the number of innocent persons sentenced to die, there is one conclusion about the penalty that is universally accepted—*i.e.,* it "tends to distort the course of the criminal law." As Mr. Justice Frankfurter said: "I am strongly against capital punishment.... When life is at hazard in a trial, it sensationalizes the whole thing almost unwittingly; the effect on juries, the bar, the public, the judiciary, I regard as very bad. I think scientifically the claim of deterrence is not worth much. Whatever proof there may be in my judgment does not outweigh the social loss due to the inherent sensationalism of a trial for life." The deleterious effects of the death penalty are also felt otherwise than at trial. For example, its very existence "inevitably sabotages a social or institutional program of reformation." In short "[t]he presence of the death penalty, as the keystone of our penal system bedevils the administration of criminal justice all the way down the line and is the stumbling block in the path of general reform and of the treatment of crime and criminal."*

Assuming knowledge of all the facts presently available regarding capital punishment, the average citizen would, in my opinion, find it shocking to his conscience and sense of justice. For this reason alone capital punishment cannot stand....

At a time in our history when the streets of the nation's cities inspire fear and dispair, rather than pride and hope, it is difficult to maintain objectivity and concern for our fellow citizens. But the measure of a country's greatness is its ability to retain compassion in time of crisis....

In striking down capital punishment, this court does not malign our system of government. On the contrary, it pays homage to it. Only in a free society could right triumph in difficult times and could civilization record its magnificent advancement. In recognizing the humanity of our fellow beings, we pay ourselves the highest tribute. We achieve "a major milestone in the long road up from barbarism" and join the approximately 70 other jurisdictions in the world which

---

* Dr. S. Glueck of Harvard University.

celebrate their regard for civilization and humanity by shunning capital punishment....

Chief Justice Burger, whom Blackmun, Powell and Rehnquist joined, dissenting:

... If we were possessed of legislative power, I would either join with Mr. Justice Brennan and Mr. Justice Marshall or, at the very least, restrict the use of capital punishment to a small category of the most heinous crimes. Our constitutional inquiry, however, must be divorced from personal feelings as to the morality and efficacy of the death penalty and be confined to the meaning and applicability of the uncertain language of the 8th Amendment. There is no novelty in being called upon to interpret a constitutional provision that is less than self-defining, but of all our fundamental guarantees, the ban on "cruel and unusual punishments" is one of the most difficult to translate into judicially manageable terms. The widely divergent views of the amendment expressed in today's opinions reveal the haze that surrounds this constitutional command. Yet it is essential to our role as a court that we not seize upon the enigmatic character of the guarantee as an invitation to enact our personal predilections into law.

Although the 8th Amendment literally reads as prohibiting only those punishments that are both "cruel" and "unusual," history compels the conclusion that the Constitution prohibits all punishments of extreme and barbarous cruelty, regardless of how frequently or infrequently imposed....

Counsel for petitioners properly concede that capital punishment was not impermissibly cruel at the time of the adoption of the 8th Amendment. Not only do the records of the debates indicate that the founding fathers were limited in their concern to the prevention of torture, but it is also clear from the language of the Constitution itself that there was no thought whatever of the elimination of capital punishment. The opening sentence of the 5th Amendment is a guarantee that the death penalty not be imposed "unless on a presentment or indictment of a grand jury." The double jeopardy clause of the 5th Amendment is a prohibition against being "twice put in jeopardy of life" for the same offense. Similarly, the due process clause commands "due process of law" before an accused can be "deprived of life, liberty or property." Thus the explicit language of the Constitution affirmatively acknowledges the legal power to impose capital punishment; it does not expressly or by implication acknowledge the legal power to impose any of the various punishments that have been banned as cruel since 1791. Since the 8th Amendment was adopted on the same day in 1791 as the 5th Amendment, it hardly needs more to establish that the death penalty was not "cruel" in the constitutional sense at that time.

In the 181 years since the enactment of the 8th Amendment, not a single decision of this court has cast the slightest shadow of a doubt on the constitutionality of capital punishment. In rejecting 8th Amendment attacks on particular modes of execution, the court has more than once implicitly denied that capital punishment is impermissibly "cruel" in the constitutional sense....

However, the inquiry cannot end here. For reasons unrelated to any change in intrinsic cruelty, the 8th Amendment prohibition cannot fairly be limited to those punishments thought excessively cruel and barbarous at the time of the adoption of the 8th Amendment. A punishment is inordinately cruel, in the sense we must deal with it in these cases, chiefly as perceived by the society so characterizing it. The standard of extreme cruelty is not merely descriptive but necessarily embodies a moral judgment. The standard itself remains the same, but its applicability must change as the basic mores of society change.... Nevertheless, the court up to now has never actually held that a punishment has become impermissibly cruel due to a shift in the weight of accepted social values; nor has the court suggested judicially manageable criteria for measuring such a shift in moral consensus.

The court's quiescence in this area can be attributed to the fact that in a democratic society, legislatures, not courts, are constituted to respond to the will and consequently the moral values of the people.... Accordingly, punishments such as branding and the cutting off of ears, which were commonplace at the time of the adoption of the Constitution, passed from the penal scene without judicial intervention because they became basically offensive to the people and the legislatures responded to this sentiment.

Beyond any doubt if we were today called upon to review such punishments, we would find them excessively cruel because we could say with complete assurance that contemporary society universally rejects such bizarre penalties.... The critical fact is that this court has never had to hold that a mode of punishment authorized by a domestic legislature was so cruel as to be fundamentally at odds with our basic notions of decency.... Judicial findings of impermissible cruelty have been limited, for the most part, to offensive punishments devised without specific authority by prison officials, not by legislatures.... The paucity of judicial decisions invalidating legislatively prescribed punishments is powerful evidence that in this country legislatures have in fact been responsive—albeit belatedly at times—to changes in social attitudes and moral values.

I do not suggest that the validity of legislatively authorized punishments presents no justiciable issue under the 8th Amendment but rather that the primacy of the legislative role narrowly confines the scope of judicial inquiry. Whether or not provable, and whether or not true at all times, in a democracy the legislative judgment is presumed to embody the basic standards of decency prevailing in the society. This presumption can only be negated by unambiguous and compelling evidence of legislative default.

... There are no obvious indications that capital punishment offends the conscience of society to such a degree that our traditional deference to the legislative judgment must be abandoned. It is not a punishment such as burning at the stake that everyone would ineffably find to be repugnant to all civilized standards. Nor is it a punishment so roundly condemned that only a few aberrant legislatures have retained it on the statute books. Capital punishment is authorized by statute in 40 states, the District of Columbia and in the federal courts for the commission of certain crimes. On 4 occasions in the last 11 years Congress has added to the list of federal crimes punishable by death. In looking for reliable *indicia* of contemporary attitude, none more trustworthy has been advanced.

One conceivable source of evidence that legislatures have abdicated their essentially barometric role with respect to community values would be public opinion polls, of which there have been many in the past decade addressed to the question of capital punishment. Without assessing the reliability of such polls, or intimating that any judicial reliance could ever be placed on them, it need only be noted that the reported results have shown nothing approximating the universal condemnation of capital punishment that might lead us to suspect that the legislatures in general have lost touch with current social values.

Counsel for petitioners rely on a different body of empirical evidence. They argue, in effect, that the number of cases in which the death penalty is imposed, as compared with the number of cases in which it is statutorily available, reflects a general revulsion toward the penalty that would lead to its repeal if only it were more generally and widely enforced. It cannot be gainsaid that by the choice of juries—and sometimes judges—the death penalty is imposed in far fewer than half the cases in which it is available. To go further and characterize the rate of imposition as "freakishly rare," as petitioners insist, is unwarranted hyperbole.... The rate of imposition does not impel the conclusion that capital punishment is now regarded as intolerably cruel or uncivilized.

It is argued that in those capital cases where juries have recommended mercy, they have given expression to civilized values and effectively renounced the legislative authorization for capital punishment. At the same time it is argued that where juries have made the awesome decision to send men to their deaths, they have acted arbitrarily and without sensitivity to prevailing standards of decency. This explanation for the infrequency of imposition of capital punishment is unsupported by known facts and is inconsistent in principle with everything this court has ever said about the functioning of juries in capital cases....

It would, of course, be unrealistic to assume that juries have been perfectly consistent in choosing the cases where the death penalty is to be imposed, for no human institution performs with perfect consistency. There are doubtless prisoners on death row who would not be there had they been tried before a different jury or in a different state. In this sense their fate has been controlled by a fortuitous circumstance. However, this element of fortuity does not stand as an indictment either of the general functioning of juries in capital cases or of the integrity of jury decisions in individual cases. There is no empirical basis for concluding that juries have generally failed to discharge in good faith the responsibility described in

Witherspoon [v. Illinois, 1968]—that of choosing between life and death in individual cases according to the dictates of community values.

The rate of imposition of death sentences falls far short of providing the requisite unambiguous evidence that the legislatures of 40 states and the Congress have turned their backs on current or evolving standards of decency in continuing to make the death penalty available. For if selective imposition evidences a rejection of capital punishment in those cases where it is not imposed, it surely evidences a correlative affirmation of the penalty in those cases where it is imposed. Absent some clear indication that the continued imposition of the death penalty on a selective basis is violative of prevailing standards of civilized conduct, the 8th Amendment cannot be said to interdict its use . . . .

Today the court has not ruled that capital punishment is *per se* violative of the 8th Amendment; nor has it ruled that the punishment is barred for any particular class or classes of crimes. The substantially similar concurring opinions of Mr. Justice Stewart and Mr. Justice White, which are necessary to support the judgment setting aside petitioners' sentences, stop short of reaching the ultimate question. The actual scope of the court's ruling, which I take to be embodied in these concurring opinions, is not entirely clear. This much, however, seems apparent: if the legislatures are to continue to authorize capital punishment for some crimes, juries and judges can no longer be permitted to make the sentencing determination in the same manner they have in the past. This approach—not urged in oral arguments or briefs—misconceives the nature of the constitutional command against "cruel and unusual punishments," disregards controlling case law and demands a rigidity in capital cases which, if possible of achievement, cannot be regarded as a welcome change. Indeed the contrary seems to be the case. . . .

The critical factor in the concurring opinions of both Mr. Justice Stewart and Mr. Justice White is the infrequency with which the penalty is imposed. This factor is taken not as evidence of society's abhorrence of capital punishment—the inference that petitioners would have the court draw—but as the earmark of a deteriorated system of sentencing. It is concluded that petitioners' sentences must be set aside, not because the punishment is impermissibly cruel, but because juries and judges have failed to exercise their sentencing discretion in acceptable fashion.

To be sure, there is a recitation cast in 8th Amendment terms: petitioners' sentences are "cruel" because they exceed that which the legislatures have deemed necessary for all cases; petitioners' sentences are "unusual" because they exceed that which is imposed in most cases. This application of the words of the 8th Amendment suggests that capital punishment can be made to satisfy 8th Amendment values if its rate of imposition is somehow multiplied; it seemingly follows that the flexible sentencing system created by the legislatures, and carried out by juries and judges, has yielded more mercy than the 8th Amendment can stand. The implications of this approach are mildly ironical....

Justice Blackmun dissenting:

... Cases such as these provide for me an excruciating agony of the spirit. I yield to no one in the depth of my distaste, antipathy and, indeed, abhorrence, for the death penalty, with all its aspects of physical distress and fear and of moral judgment exercised by finite minds. That distaste is buttressed by a belief that capital punishment serves no useful purpose that can be demonstrated. For me, it violates childhood's training and life's experiences, and is not compatible with the philosophical convictions I have been able to develop. It is antagonistic to any sense of "reverence for life." Were I a legislator, I would vote against the death penalty for the policy reasons argued by counsel for the respective petitioners and expressed and adopted in the several opinions filed by the justices who vote to reverse these convictions....

I do not sit on these cases, however, as a legislator responsive, at least in part, to the will of constituents. Our task here, as must so frequently be emphasized and re-emphasized, is to pass upon the constitutionality of legislation that has been enacted and that is challenged. This is the sole task for judges. We should not allow our personal preferences as to the wisdom of legislative and congressional action, or our distaste for such action, to guide our judicial decision in cases such as these. The temptations to cross that policy line are very great. In fact, as today's decision reveals, they are almost irresistible....

Although personally I may rejoice at the court's result, I find it difficult to accept or to justify as a matter of history, of law, or of constitutional pronouncement. I fear the court has overstepped. It has sought and has achieved an end.

Justice Powell dissenting:

... I now return to the overriding question in these cases: whether this court, acting in conformity with the Constitution, can justify its judgment to abolish capital punishment as heretofore known in this country. It is important to keep in focus the enormity of the step undertaken by the court today. Not only does it invalidate hundreds of state and federal laws, it deprives those jurisdictions of the power to legislate with respect to capital punishment in the future, except in a manner consistent with the cloudily outlined views of those justices who do not purport to undertake total abolition. Nothing short of an amendment to the United States Constitution can reverse the court's judgment. Meanwhile, all flexibility is foreclosed. The normal democratic process, as well as the opportunities for the several states to respond to the will of their people expressed through ballot referenda (as in Massachusetts, Illinois, and Colorado), is now shut off.

The sobering disadvantage of constitutional adjudication of this magnitude is the universality and permanence of the judgment. The enduring merit of legislative action is its responsiveness to the democratic process, and to revision and change: mistaken judgments may be corrected and refinements perfected. In England and Canada, critical choices were made after studies canvassing all competing views, and in those countries revisions may be made in light of experience....

... This is a classic case for the exercise of our oft-announced allegiance to judicial restraint. I know of no case in which greater gravity and delicacy have attached to the duty that this court is called on to perform whenever legislation—state or federal—is challenged on constitutional grounds. It seems to me that the sweeping judicial action undertaken today reflects a basic lack of faith and confidence in the democratic process. Many may regret, as I do, the failure of some legislative bodies to address the capital punishment issue with greater frankness or effectiveness. Many might decry their failure either to abolish the penalty entirely or selectively, or to

establish standards for its enforcement. But impatience with
the slowness, and even the unresponsiveness, of legislatures is
no justification for judicial intrusion upon their historic
powers....

Justice Rehnquist dissenting:

The court's judgment today strikes down a penalty that
our nation's legislators have thought necessary since our
country was founded. My brothers Douglas, Brennan and
Marshall would at one fell swoop invalidate laws enacted by
Congress and 40 of the 50 state legislatures and would consign
to the limbo of unconstitutionality under a single rubric
penalties for offenses as varied and unique as murder, piracy,
mutiny, highjacking and desertion in the face of the enemy. My
brothers Stewart and White, asserting reliance on a more
limited rationale—the reluctance of judges and juries actually
to impose the death penalty in the majority of capital cases—
join in the judgment in these cases. Whatever its precise
rationale, today's holding necessarily brings into sharp relief
the fundamental question of the role of judicial review in a
democratic society. How can government by the elected representatives of the people coexist with the power of the federal
judiciary, whose members are constitutionally insulated from
responsiveness to the popular will, to declare invalid laws duly
enacted by the popular branches of government?

The answer, of course, is found in Hamilton's Federalist
Paper No. 78 and in Chief Justice Marshall's classic opinion in
Marbury v. Madison...(1803). An oft told story since then, it
bears summarization once more. Sovereignty resides ultimately
in the people as a whole, and by adopting through their states a
written Constitution for the nation, and subsequently adding
amendments to that instrument, they have both granted certain
powers to the national government and denied other powers to
the national and the state governments. Courts are exercising
no more than the judicial function conferred upon them by Art.
III of the Constitution when they assess, in a case before them,
whether or not a particular legislative enactment is within the
authority granted by the Constitution to the enacting body, and
whether it runs afoul of some limitation placed by the Constitution on the authority of that body. For the theory is that the
people themselves have spoken in the Constitution, and there-

fore its commands are superior to the commands of the legislature, which is merely an agent of the people.

The founding fathers thus wisely sought to have the best of
both worlds, the undeniable benefits of both democratic self-
government and individual rights protected against possible
excesses of that form of government.

The courts in cases properly before them have been
entrusted under the Constitution with the last word, short of
constitutional amendment, as to whether a law passed by the
legislature conforms to the Constitution. But just because
courts in general, and this court in particular, do have the last
word, the admonition of Mr. Justice Stone in *United States v.
Butler* [1936] must be constantly borne in mind: "[W]hile unconstitutional exercise of power by the executive and legislative
branches of the government is subject to judicial restraint, the
only check upon our own exercise of power is our own sense of
self-restraint."...

Rigorous attention to the limits of this court's authority is
likewise enjoined because of the natural desire that beguiles
judges along with other human beings into imposing their own
views of goodness, truth and justice upon others. Judges differ
only in that they have the power, if not the authority, to
enforce their desires. This is doubtless why nearly 2 centuries of
judicial precedent from this court counsel the sparing use of
that power. The most expansive reading of the leading constitutional cases does not remotely suggest that this court has
been granted a roving commission, either by the founding
fathers or by the framers of the 14th Amendment, to strike
down laws that are based upon notions of policy or morality
suddenly found unacceptable by a majority of this court....

If there can be said to be one dominant theme in the
Constitution, perhaps more fully articulated in The Federalist
Papers than in the instrument itself, it is the notion of checks
and balances. The framers were well aware of the natural desire
of office holders as well as others to seek to expand the scope
and authority of their particular office at the expense of others.
They sought to provide against success in such efforts by
erecting adequate checks and balances in the form of grants of
authority to each branch of the government in order to
counteract and prevent usurpation on the part of the others.

This philosophy of the framers is best described by one of the ablest and greatest of their number, James Madison, in Federalist No. 51: "In framing a government which is to be administered by men over men, the great difficulty lies in this: you must first enable the government to control the governed; and in the next place oblige it to control itself."

Madison's observation applies to the Judicial Branch with at least as much force as to the Legislative and Executive Branches. While overreaching by the Legislative and Executive Branches may result in the sacrifice of individual protections that the Constitution was designed to secure against action of the state, judicial overreaching may result in sacrifice of the equally important right of the people to govern themselves. The due process and equal protection clauses of the 14th Amendment were "never intended to destroy the states' power to govern themselves." Black, J., in *Oregon v. Mitchell*...(1970).

The very nature of judicial review, as pointed out by Justice Stone in his dissent in the *Butler* case, makes the courts the least subject to Madisonian check in the event that they shall, for the best of motives, expand judicial authority beyond the limits contemplated by the framers. It is for this reason that judicial self-restraint is surely an implied, if not an expressed, condition of the grant of authority of judicial review. The court's holding these cases has been reached, I believe, in complete disregard of that implied condition.

Cruel & Unusual Punishment

Prior to the June 29, 1972 decision *(Furman v. Georgia),* the 8th Amendment's ban on "cruel and unusual punishments" had been taken up by the Supreme Court in only 10 cases. In *Francis v. Resweber,* decided in 1947, the court had ruled, 5-4, that it was not unconstitutional to execute a man whom the executioner had failed, because of malfunction of the electric chair, to kill in 2 prior attempts. According to an eyewitness, "the electro-

cutioner turned on the switch, and when he did
Willie Francis' lips puffed out and he groaned and
jumped so that the chair came off the floor. Apparently the switch was turned on twice, and then
the condemned man yelled, 'Take it off. Let me
breathe.' "

Francis appealed to the Supreme Court arguing
that it would be "cruel and unusual" to execute him
because he had once gone through the difficult
preparation for execution and had once received
through his body a current of electricity intended to
cause his death. The court ruled, however, that "the
fact that an unforeseeable accident prevented the
prompt consummation of the sentence cannot ... add
an element of cruelty to a subsequent execution.
There is no purpose to inflict unnecessary pain nor is
any unnecessary pain involved in the proposed
execution."

In protesting "death by installments," Justice
Harold H. Burton, dissenting, contended that the
impact on Francis, not the intent of the executioner,
should be the crucial factor.

Other 8th Amendment cases did not involve
capital punishment, although the rulings on them
had a bearing on the issue.

Prior to the 1972 *Furman* decision, the Supreme
Court had only once reversed a criminal penalty for
being "cruel and unusual." This was in *Robinson v.
California,* decided June 25, 1962, when the court
ruled, 7-1, that it was unconstitutional for a state to
make it a criminal offense for one to "be addicted to
the use of narcotics." Justice Potter Stewart, in the
majority opinion, described narcotic addiction as an
"illness." Therefore, he said, a state law "which
imprisons a person thus afflicted as a criminal, even

though he has never touched any narcotic drug within the state or been guilty of any irregular behavior there, inflicts a cruel and unusual punishment." "Even one day in prison would be a cruel and unusual punishment for the 'crime' of having a common cold," Stewart held. The court, however, took pains to recognize the government's right to regulate the sale and use of "dangerous drugs" and its right to establish compulsory treatment programs requiring involuntary confinement for addicts.

The court had ruled in an 8th Amendment case in 1958 that expatriation constitutes a cruel and unusual punishment. The majority in *Trop v. Dulles* held that "the amendment must draw its meaning from the evolving standards of decency that mark the progress of a maturing society."

Abridgment of the *Robinson v. California* decision (371 U.S. 905, June 25, 1962):

Justice Stewart announcing the decision of the court:

A California statute makes it a criminal offense for a person to "be addicted to the use of narcotics." This appeal draws into question the constitutionality of that provision of the state law, as construed by the California courts in the present case.

The appellant was convicted after a jury trial in the Municipal Court of Los Angeles. The evidence against him was given by 2 Los Angeles police officers. Officer Brown testified that he had had occasion to examine the appellant's arms one evening on a street in Los Angeles some 4 months before the trial. The officer testified that at that time he had observed "scar tissue and discoloration on the inside" of the appellant's right arm, and "what appeared to be numerous needle marks and a scab which was approximately 3 inches below the crook of the elbow" on the appellant's left arm. The officer also testified that the appellant under questioning had admitted to the occasional use of narcotics.

Officer Lindquist testified that he had examined the appellant the following morning in the Central Jail in Los Angeles. The officer stated that at that time he had observed discolorations and scabs on the appellant's arms, and he identified photographs which had been taken of the appellant's arms shortly after his arrest the night before. Based upon more than 10 years of experience as a member of the Narcotic Division of the Los Angeles Police Department, the witness gave his opinion that "these marks and the discoloration were the result of the injection of hypodermic needles into the tissue into the vein that was not sterile." He stated that the scabs were several days old at the time of his examination and that the appellant was neither under the influence of narcotics nor suffering withdrawal symptoms at the time he saw him. This witness also testified that the appellant had admitted using narcotics in the past.

The appellant testified in his own behalf, denying the alleged conversations with the police officers and denying that he had ever used narcotics or been addicted to their use. He explained the marks on his arms as resulting from an allergic condition contracted during his military service. His testimony was corroborated by 2 witnesses.

The trial judge instructed the jury that the statute made it a misdemeanor for a person "either to use narcotics, or to be addicted to the use of narcotics...."...

The judge further instructed the jury that the appellant could be convicted under a general verdict if the jury agreed *either* that he was of the "status" *or* had committed the "act" denounced by the statute. "All that the people must show is either that the defendant did use a narcotic in Los Angeles County or that while in the City of Los Angeles he was addicted to the use of narcotics...."

Under these instructions the jury returned a verdict finding the appellant "guilty of the offense charged."...

The broad power of a state to regulate the narcotic drugs traffic within its borders is not here in issue. More than 40 years ago, in *Whipple v. Martinson* [1921]..., this court explicitly recognized the validity of that power: "There can be no question of the authority of the state in the exercise of its police power to regulate the administration, sale, prescription and use of dangerous and habit-forming drugs.... The right to exercise this power is so manifest in the interest of the public health and welfare that it is unnecessary to enter upon a discussion of it beyond saying that it is too firmly established to be successfully called in question."...

Such regulation, it can be assumed, could take a variety of valid forms. A state might impose criminal sanctions, for example, against the unauthorized manufacture, prescription, sale, purchase or possession of narcotics within its borders. In the interest of discouraging the violation of such laws, or in the interest of the general health or welfare of its inhabitants, a state might establish a program of compulsory treatment for those addicted to narcotics. Such a program of treatment might require periods of involuntary confinement. And penal sanctions might be imposed for failure to comply with established compulsory treatment procedures.... Or a state might choose to attack the evils of narcotics traffic on broader fronts also—through public health education, for example.... In short, the range of valid choice which a state might make in this area is undoubtedly a wide one, and the wisdom of any particular choice within the allowable spectrum is not for us to decide....

It would be possible to construe the statute under which the appellant was convicted as one which is operative only upon proof of the actual use of narcotics within the state's jurisdiction. But the California courts have not so construed this law. Although there was evidence in the present case that the appellant had used narcotics in Los Angeles, the jury were instructed that they could convict him even if they disbelieved that evidence. The appellant could be convicted, they were told, if they found simply that the appellant's "status" or "chronic condition" was that of being "addicted to the use of narcotics." And it is impossible to know from the jury's verdict that the defendant was not convicted upon precisely such a finding....

This statute, therefore, is not one which punishes a person for the use of narcotics, for their purchase, sale or possession, or for antisocial or disorderly behavior resulting from their administration. It is not a law which even purports to provide or require medical treatment. Rather, we deal with a statute which makes the "status" of narcotic addiction a criminal offense, for which the offender may be prosecuted "at any time before he reforms." California has said that a person can be continuously guilty of this offense, whether or not he has ever used or possessed any narcotics within the state and whether or not he has been guilty of any antisocial behavior there.

It is unlikely that any state at this moment in history would attempt to make it a criminal offense for a person to be mentally ill, or a leper, or to be afflicted with a venereal disease. A state might determine that the general health and welfare require that the victims of these and other human afflictions be dealt with by compulsory treatment, involving quarantine, confinement or sequestration. But, in the light of contemporary human knowledge, a law which made a criminal offense of such a disease would doubtless be universally thought to be an infliction of cruel and unusual punishment in violation of the 8th and 14th Amendments. See *Francis v. Resweber....*

We cannot but consider the statute before us as of the same category. In this court counsel for the state recognized that narcotic addiction is an illness.... We hold that a state law which imprisons a person thus afflicted as a criminal, even though he has never touched any narcotic drug within the state or been guilty of any irregular behavior there, inflicts a cruel and unusual punishment in violation of the 14th Amendment. To be sure, imprisonment for 90 days is not, in the abstract, a punishment which is either cruel or unusual. But the question cannot be considered in the abstract. Even one day in prison would be a cruel and unusual punishment for the "crime" of having a common cold.

We are not unmindful that the vicious evils of the narcotics traffic have occasioned the grave concern of government. There are, as we have said, countless fronts on which those evils may be legitimately attacked. We deal in this case only with an individual provision of a particularized local law as it has so far been interpreted by the California courts.

Justices William O. Douglas and John Marshall Harlan issued separate concurring opinions.

Justice Thomas C. Clark dissenting:

...I deem this application of "cruel and unusual punishment" so novel that I suspect the court was hard put to find a way to ascribe to the framers of the Constitution the result reached today rather than to its own notions of ordered liberty. If this case involved economic regulation, the present court's allergy to substantive due process would surely save the statute and prevent the court from imposing its own philosophical predilections upon state legislatures or Congress. I fail to see why the court deems it more appropriate to write into the Constitution its own abstract notions of how best to handle the narcotics problem, for it obviously cannot match either the states or Congress in expert understanding....

In *Powell v. Texas,* however, the court June 17, 1968 rejected, 5-4, a claim that it was "cruel and unusual" to convict a chronic alcoholic for being drunk in a public place even though he may not have disturbed anyone. Justice Thurgood Marshall, speaking for the majority, said that there was as yet no generally effective method of treating the vast number of alcoholics. Further, he said, there were insufficient facilities to treat them and thus it would "be tragic to return large numbers of helpless, some-times dangerous and frequently unsanitary in-ebriates to the streets of our cities without even the opportunity to sober up adequately which a brief jail term provides."

Were the court to rule that a compulsive drinker cannot be convicted of public intoxication, Marshall added, "it is difficult to see how a state can convict an individual for murder, if that individual, while exhibiting normal behavior in all other respects, suffers a 'compulsion' to kill."

Justice Abe Fortas, in dissent, cited *Robinson.* Basing his opinion on "medical and sociological data," he said that it was "cruel and unusual" to inflict a criminal penalty on a "chronic alcoholic," who, in being drunk in public, did not do so "by his own volition but under a 'compulsion' which is part of his condition." The issue, he said, did not involve the responsibility of an alcoholic for criminal acts.

Abridgment of the *Powell v. Texas* decision (392 U.S. 514, June 17, 1968):

Justice Marshall delivering the judgment of the court:

In late Dec. 1966, appellant [Leroy Powell, who had been convicted of public intoxication about 100 times] was arrested and charged with being found in a state of intoxication in a public place, in violation of Texas Penal Code, Art. 477 (1952), which reads as follows: "Whoever shall get drunk or be found in a state of intoxication in any public place, or at any private house except his own, shall be fined not exceeding one hundred dollars."

Appellant was tried in the Corporation Court of Austin, Texas, found guilty and fined $20. He appealed to the County Court at Law No. 1 of Travis County, Texas, where a trial *de novo* was held. His counsel urged that appellant was "afflicted with the disease of chronic alcoholism," that "his appearance in public [while drunk was]... not of his own volition" and therefore that to punish him criminally for that conduct would be cruel and unusual, in violation of the 8th and 14th Amendments to the United States Constitution.

The trial judge in the county court, sitting without a jury, made certain findings of fact... but ruled as a matter of law that chronic alcoholism was not a defense to the charge. He found appellant guilty and fined him $50. There being no further right to appeal within the Texas judicial system, appellant appealed to this Court; we noted probable jurisdiction....

The principal testimony was that of Dr. David Wade, a fellow of the American Medical Association, duly certificated in psychiatry.... Dr. Wade sketched the outlines of the "disease" concept of alcoholism; noted that there is no generally accepted definition of "alcoholism"; alluded to the ongoing debate within the medical profession over whether alcohol is actually physically "addicting" or merely psychologically "habituating"; and concluded that in either case a "chronic alcoholic" is an "involuntary drinker," who is "powerless not to drink" and who "loses his self-control over his drinking." He testified that he had examined appellant, and that appellant is a "chronic alcoholic," who "by the time he has reached [the state of intoxication]... is not able to control his behavior, and

[who]... has reached this point because he has an uncontrollable compulsion to drink." Dr. Wade also responded in the negative to the question whether appellant has "the willpower to resist the constant excessive consumption of alcohol." He added that in his opinion jailing appellant without medical attention would operate neither to rehabilitate him nor to lessen his desire for alcohol.

On cross-examination, Dr. Wade admitted that when appellant was sober he knew the difference between right and wrong, and he responded affirmatively to the question whether appellant's act of taking the first drink in any given instance when he was sober was a "voluntary exercise of his will." Qualifying his answer, Dr. Wade stated that "these individuals have a compulsion, and this compulsion, while not completely overpowering, is... an exceedingly strong influence, and this compulsion coupled with the firm belief in their mind that they are going to be able to handle it from now on causes their judgment to be somewhat clouded."

Appellant testified concerning the history of his drinking problem. He... testified that he was unable to stop drinking; stated that when he was intoxicated he had no control over his actions and could not remember them later but that he did not become violent; and admitted that he did not remember his arrest on the occasion for which he was being tried....

... The state made no effort to obtain expert psychiatric testimony of its own or even to explore with appellant's witness the question of appellant's power to control the frequency, timing, and location of his drinking bouts or the substantial disagreement within the medical profession concerning the nature of the disease, the efficacy of treatment and the prerequisites for effective treatment. It did nothing to examine or illuminate what Dr. Wade might have meant by his reference to a "compulsion" which was "not completely overpowering" but which was "an exceedingly strong influence" or to inquire into the question of the proper role of such a "compulsion" in constitutional adjudication. Instead, the state contented itself with a brief argument that appellant had no defense to the charge because he "is legally sane and knows the difference between right and wrong."

... The trial court indicated its intention to disallow appellant's claimed defense of "chronic alcoholism." Thereupon defense counsel submitted, and the trial court entered, the following "findings of fact": "(1) That chronic alcoholism is a disease which destroys the afflicted person's willpower to resist the constant, excessive consumption of alcohol. (2) That a chronic alcoholic does not appear in public by his own volition but under a compulsion symptomatic of the disease of chronic alcoholism. (3) That Leroy Powell, defendant herein, is a chronic alcoholic who is afflicted with the disease of chronic alcoholism."

... Those are not "findings of fact" in any recognizable, traditional sense in which that term has been used in a court of law; they are the premises of a syllogism transparently designed to bring this case within the scope of this court's opinion in *Robinson v. California....* Nonetheless, the dissent would have us adopt these "findings" without critical examination; it would use them as the basis for a constitutional holding that "a person may not be punished if the condition essential to constitute the defined crime is part of the pattern of his disease and is occasioned by a compulsion symptomatic of the disease."...

The difficulty with that position ... is that it goes much too far on the basis of too little knowledge. In the first place, the record in this case is utterly inadequate to permit the sort of informed and responsible adjudication which alone can support the announcement of an important and wide-ranging new constitutional principle. We know very little about the circumstances surrounding the drinking bout which resulted in this conviction or about Leroy Powell's drinking problem, or indeed about alcoholism itself. The trial hardly reflects the sharp legal and evidentiary clash between fully prepared adversary litigants which is traditionally expected in major constitutional cases. The state put on only one witness, the arresting officer. The defense put on 3—a policeman who testified to appellant's long history of arrests for public drunkenness, the psychiatrist and appellant himself....

... Most psychiatrists are apparently of the opinion that alcoholism is far more difficult to treat than other forms of behavioral disorders, and some believe it is impossible to cure by means of psychotherapy.... Thus it is entirely possible that, even were the manpower and facilities available for a full-scale attack upon chronic alcoholism, we would find ourselves unable to help the vast bulk of our "visible"—let alone our "invisible"—alcoholic population.

However, facilities for the attempted treatment of indigent alcoholics are woefully lacking throughout the country. It would be tragic to return large numbers of helpless, sometimes dangerous and frequently unsanitary inebriates to the streets of our cities without even the opportunity to sober up adequately which a brief jail term provides. Presumably no state or city will tolerate such a state of affairs. Yet the medical profession cannot, and does not, tell us with any assurance that, even if the buildings, equipment and trained personnel were made available, it could provide anything more than slightly higher-class jails for our indigent habitual inebriates. Thus we run the grave risk that nothing will be accomplished beyond the hanging of a new sign—reading "hospital"—over one wing of the jailhouse.

One virtue of the criminal process is, at least, that the duration of penal incarceration typically has some outside statutory limit; this is universally true in the case of petty offenses, such as public drunkenness, where jail terms are quite short on the whole. "Therapeutic civil commitment" lacks this feature; one is typically committed until one is "cured." ...[This] might subject indigent alcoholics to the risk that they may be locked up for an indefinite period of time under the same conditions as before, with no more hope than before of receiving effective treatment and no prospect of periodic "freedom."

Faced with this unpleasant reality, we are unable to assert that the use of the criminal process as a means of dealing with the public aspects of problem drinking can ever be defended as rational. The picture of the penniless drunk propelled aimlessly and endlessly through the law's "revolving door" of arrest, incarceration, release and re-arrest is not a pretty one. But before we condemn the present practice across-the-board, perhaps we ought to be able to point to some clear promise of a better world for these unfortunate people. Unfortunately, no such promise has yet been forthcoming. If, in addition to the absence of a coherent approach to the problem of treatment, we consider the almost complete absence of facilities and manpower for the implementation of a rehabilitation program, it is difficult to say in the present context that the criminal process is utterly lacking in social value. This court has never held that anything in the Constitution requires that penal sanctions be designed solely to achieve therapeutic or rehabilitative effects, and it can hardly be said with assurance that incarceration serves such purposes any better for the general run of criminals than it does for public drunks.

Ignorance likewise impedes our assessment of the deterrent effect of criminal sanctions for public drunkenness. The fact that a high percentage of American alcoholics conceal their drinking problems, not merely by avoiding public displays of intoxication but also by shunning all forms of treatment, is indicative that some powerful deterrent operates to inhibit the public revelation of the existence of alcoholism.... Criminal conviction represents the degrading public revelation of what Anglo-American society has long condemned as a moral defect, and the existence of criminal sanctions may serve to reinforce this cultural taboo, just as we presume it serves to reinforce other, stronger feelings against murder, rape, theft and other forms of antisocial conduct.

Obviously, chronic alcoholics have not been deterred from drinking to excess by the existence of criminal sanctions against public drunkenness. But all those who violate penal laws of any kind are by definition undeterred. The long-standing and still raging debate over the validity of the deterrence justification for penal sanctions has not reached any sufficiently clear conclusions to permit it to be said that such sanctions are ineffective in any particular context or for any particular group of people who are able to appreciate the consequences of their acts. Certainly no effort was made at the trial of this case, beyond a monosyllabic answer to a perfunctory one-line question, to determine the effectiveness of penal sanctions in deterring Leroy Powell in particular or chronic alcoholics in general from drinking at all or from getting drunk in particular places or at particular times....

Appellant claims that his conviction on the facts of this case would violate the cruel and unusual punishment clause of the 8th Amendment as applied to the states through the 14th Amendment. The primary purpose of that clause has always been considered, and properly so, to be directed at the method or kind of punishment imposed for the violation of criminal statutes; the nature of the conduct made criminal is ordinarily relevant only to the fitness of the punishment imposed.... Appellant, however, seeks to come within the application of the cruel and unusual punishment clause announced in *Robinson v. California* ... which involved a state statute making it a crime to "be addicted to the use of narcotics." This court held there that "a state law which imprisons a person thus afflicted [with narcotic addiction] as a criminal, even though he has never touched any narcotic drug within the state or been guilty of any irregular behavior there, inflicts a cruel and unusual punishment...."

On its face the present case does not fall within that holding, since appellant was convicted not for being a chronic alcoholic but for being in public while drunk on a particular occasion. The State of Texas thus has not sought to punish a mere status, as California did in *Robinson;* nor has it attempted to regulate appellant's behavior in the privacy of his own home. Rather, it has imposed upon appellant a criminal sanction for public behavior which may create substantial health and safety hazards, both for appellant and for members of the general public, and which offends the moral and esthetic sensibilities of a large segment of the community. This seems a far cry from convicting one for being an addict, being a chronic alcoholic, being "mentally ill, or a leper...." ...

... If Leroy Powell cannot be convicted of public intoxication, it is difficult to see how a state can convict an individual for murder, if that individual, while exhibiting normal behavior in all other respects, suffers from a "compulsion" to kill, which is an "exceedingly strong influence," but "not completely overpowering." Even if we limit our consideration to chronic alcoholics, it would seem impossible to confine the principle within the arbitrary bounds which the dissent seems to envision.

It is not difficult to imagine a case involving psychiatric testimony to the effect that an individual suffers from some aggressive neurosis which he is able to control when sober; that very little alcohol suffices to remove the inhibitions which normally contain these aggressions, with the result that the individual engages in assaultive behavior without becoming actually intoxicated; and that the individual suffers from a very strong desire to drink, which is an "exceedingly strong influence" but "not completely overpowering." Without being untrue to the rationale of this case, should the principles advanced in dissent be accepted here, the court could not avoid holding such an individual constitutionally unaccountable for his assaultive behavior....

...It is simply not yet the time to write into the Constitution formulas cast in terms whose meaning, let alone relevance, is not yet clear either to doctors or to lawyers.

Justice Hugo L. Black, whom John Marshall Harlan joined, concurred in the judgment. Byron R. White issued a separate concurring opinion.

Justice Abe Fortas, whom Douglas, Brennan and Stewart joined, dissenting:

...At the trial in the county court, the arresting officer testified that he had observed appellant in the 2000 block of Hamilton Street in Austin; that appellant staggered when he walked; that his speech was slurred; and that he smelled strongly of alcohol. He was not loud or boisterous; he did not resist arrest; he was cooperative with the officer.

The defense established that appellant had been convicted of public intoxication approximately 100 times since 1949, primarily in Travis County, Texas. The circumstances were always the same: the "subject smelled strongly of alcoholic beverages, staggered when walking, speech incoherent." At the end of the proceedings, he would be fined.... Appellant was usually unable to pay the fines imposed for these offenses and therefore usually has been obliged to work the fines off in jail....

Appellant took the stand. He testified that he works at a tavern shining shoes. He makes about $12 a week which he uses to buy wine. He has a family, but he does not contribute to its support. He drinks wine every day. He gets drunk about once a week. When he gets drunk, he usually goes to sleep, "mostly" in public places such as the sidewalk. He does not disturb the peace or interfere with others....

The issue posed in this case is a narrow one. There is no challenge here to the validity of public intoxication statutes in general or to the Texas public intoxication statute in particular. This case does not concern the infliction of punishment upon the "social" drinker—or upon anyone other than a "chronic alcoholic" who, as the trier of fact here found, cannot "resist the constant, excessive consumption of alcohol." Nor does it relate to any offense other than the crime of public intoxication.

The sole question presented is whether a criminal penalty may be imposed upon a person suffering the disease of "chronic alcoholism" for a condition—being "in a state of intoxication" in public—which is a characteristic part of the pattern of his disease and which, the trial court found, was not the consequence of appellant's volition but of "a compulsion symptomatic of the disease of chronic alcoholism." We must consider whether the 8th Amendment, made applicable to the states through the 14th Amendment, prohibits the imposition of this penalty in these rather special circumstances as "cruel and unusual punishment." This case does not raise any question as to the right of the police to stop and detain those who are intoxicated in public, whether as a result of the disease or otherwise; or as to the state's power to commit chronic alcoholics for treatment. Nor does it concern the responsibility of an alcoholic for criminal *acts*. We deal here with the mere *condition* of being intoxicated in public.

... Consideration of the 8th Amendment issue in this case requires an understanding of "the disease of chronic alcoholism" with which, as the trial court found, appellant is afflicted, which has destroyed his "will power to resist the constant, excessive consumption of alcohol" and which leads him to "appear in public [not] by his own volition but under a compulsion symptomatic of the disease of chronic alcoholism." ... Although many aspects of the disease remain obscure, there are some hard facts—medical and, especially, legal facts—that are accessible to us and that provide a context in which the instant case may be analyzed. We are similarly woefully deficient in our medical, diagnostic, and therapeutic knowledge of mental disease and the problem of insanity; but few would urge that, because of this, we should totally reject the legal significance of what we do know about these phenomena. ...

It is entirely clear that the jailing of chronic alcoholics is punishment. It is not defended as therapeutic, nor is there any basis for claiming that it is therapeutic (or indeed a deterrent). The alcoholic offender is caught in a "revolving door"—leading from arrest on the street through a brief, unprofitable sojourn in jail, back to the street and, eventually, another arrest. The

jails, overcrowded and put to a use for which they are not suitable, have a destructive effect upon alcoholic inmates.

Finally, most commentators, as well as experienced judges,
are in agreement that "there is probably no drearier example of
the futility of using penal sanctions to solve a psychiatric
problem than the enforcement of the laws against drunkenness."* ...

Robinson stands upon a principle which, despite its
subtlety, must be simply stated and respectfully applied because
it is the foundation of individual liberty and the cornerstone of
the relations between a civilized state and its citizens: Criminal
penalties may not be inflicted upon a person for being in a
condition he is powerless to change. In all probability,
Robinson at some time before his conviction elected to take
narcotics. But the crime as defined did not punish this conduct.
The statute imposed a penalty for the offense of "addiction"—a
condition which Robinson could not control. Once Robinson
had become an addict, he was utterly powerless to avoid
criminal guilt. He was powerless to choose not to violate the
law.

In the present case, appellant is charged with a crime composed of 2 elements—being intoxicated and being found in a
public place while in that condition. The crime, so defined,
differs from that in *Robinson.* The statute covers more than a
mere status. But the essential constitutional defect here is the
same as in *Robinson,* for in both cases the particular defendant
was accused of being in a condition which he had no capacity to
change or avoid.. ...

Article 477 of the Texas Penal Code is specifically directed
to the accused's presence while in a state of intoxication "in any
public place, or at any private house except his own." This is the
essence of the crime. Ordinarily when the state proves such
presence in a state of intoxication, this will be sufficient for
conviction, and the punishment prescribed by the state may, of
course, be validly imposed. But here the findings of the trial
judge call into play the principle that a person may not be
punished if the condition essential to constitute the defined
crime is part of the pattern of his disease and is occasioned by a

---

* M. Guttmacher and H. Weihofen, *Psychiatry and the Law*
(1952).

compulsion symptomatic of the disease. This principle, narrow in scope and applicability, is implemented by the 8th Amendment's prohibition of "cruel and unusual punishment," as we construed that command in *Robinson*. It is true that the command of the 8th Amendment and its antecedent provision in the Bill of Rights of 1689 were initially directed to the type and degree of punishment inflicted. But in *Robinson* we recognized that "the principle that would deny power to exact capital punishment for a petty crime would also deny power to punish a person by fine or imprisonment for being sick.". . .

The findings in this case, read against the background of the medical and sociological data to which I have referred, compel the conclusion that the infliction upon appellant of a criminal penalty for being intoxicated in a public place would be "cruel and inhuman punishment" within the prohibition of the 8th Amendment. This conclusion follows because appellant is a "chronic alcoholic" who, according to the trier of fact, cannot resist the "constant excessive consumption of alcohol" and does not appear in public by his own volition but under a "compulsion" which is part of his condition. . . .

Discretion of the Jury

Only 14 months before invalidating capital punishment as currently administered, the Supreme Court had apparently cleared away 2 of the barriers against the death penalty. In *McGautha v. California* and *Crampton v. Ohio,* decided May 3, 1971, the Supreme Court had rejected, 6-3, 2 of the constitutional arguments that had been instrumental in blocking executions in the U.S. for nearly 4 years.

In *McGautha,* the court ruled that a defendant's constitutional rights were not infringed when a state failed to establish guidelines for juries in capital cases. In *Crampton,* the court upheld a procedure wherein a jury, having found a defendant guilty of a capital crime, immediately determined whether to impose the death penalty without hearing additional evidence. An alternative system, used in 6 states, permitted a defendant found guilty of a capital offense to plead his case before sentencing.

James Crampton had pleaded not guilty and not guilty by reason of insanity to the charge of premeditated murder of his wife. During his trial, Crampton, exercising his 5th Amendment rights, chose not to testify. The jury found Crampton guilty with no recommendation for mercy. Under a one-step system, such as that used in Ohio, Crampton was unable to explain his actions or plead for mercy before being sentenced to death. Given the opportunity, Crampton could have told the jury about his history of mental instability, alcoholism and drug addiction. Had he chosen to testify in his own behalf during the trial, however, he would have been subject to cross-examination by the prosecution. The precise constitutional issue, therefore, was whether Crampton's constitutional rights were denied by a procedure whereby he could remain silent on the issue of guilt only by forfeiting a chance to plead his case on the issue of punishment.

Justice John Marshall Harlan, in the majority opinion, acknowledged that under such a system a defendant could be sent to death "by a jury which never heard the sound of his voice." Although that may not be an ideal arrangement, Harlan conceded, there was nothing in the Constitution to preclude it.

McGautha involved Dennis G. McGautha, sentenced to death for murdering a storekeeper. Since the death penalty was imposed on far fewer than half the defendants found guilty of capital crimes, McGautha argued that the state and federal legislatures had in effect determined that the greater percentage of those convicted of capital crimes should be permitted to live. But having made that determination, McGautha contended, the legislatures failed to establish standards for juries to use in deciding who should live and who should die. In the majority opinion, Harlan stressed the difficulty of establishing a reasonably full set of criteria to be used by juries in exercising their discretion concerning the imposition of the death penalty. "In light of history, experience and the present limitations of human knowledge, we find it quite impossible to say that committing to the untramelled discretion of the jury the power to pronounce life or death in capital cases is offensive to anything in the Constitution," Harlan wrote.

In both cases Harlan's major concern was judicial restraint: "Our function is not to impose on the states... what might seem to be a better system for dealing with capital cases. Rather it is to decide whether the federal Constitution proscribes the present procedures of these 2 states in such cases." While conceding that it "may well be" that 2-step trials and criteria for jury sentencing discretion "are superior means of dealing with capital cases if the death penalty is to be retained," Harlan held that neither was required by the Constitution: The Constitution, "which marks the limits of our authority in these cases, does not guarantee trial procedures that are the best of all worlds or that accord with the most enlightened ideas of students of the infant science of criminology or even those that measure up to the individual predilections of members of this court. The Constitution requires no more than that trials be fairly conducted and that guaranteed rights of defendants be scrupulously respected."

The dissenting opinion in *Crampton* was written by Justice William O. Douglas, who argued for an expensive and evolving concept of due process: "The wooden position of the court, reflected in today's decision, cannot be reconciled with the evolving gloss of civilized standards which this court, long before the time of those who now sit here, have been reading into the protective procedural due process safeguards of the Bill of Rights. It is as though a dam had suddenly been placed across the stream of the law on procedural due process, a stream which has grown larger with the passing of years."

Justice William J. Brennan Jr., who wrote the dissent in *McGautha,* argued for the establishment of criteria to guide jurors in determining whether to impose the death penalty. In describing the lack of such standards as "nothing more than government by whim," Brennan contended that there was no reason to suppose that standards could not be written so that capital sentencing could "be surrounded with the protections ordinarily available to check arbitrary and lawless action."

Abridgment of the *McGautha v. California* and *Crampton v. Ohio* decision (401 U.S. 183, May 3, 1971):

Justice Harlan delivering the opinion of the court:

Petitioners McGautha and Crampton were convicted of murder in the first degree in the courts of California and Ohio respectively and sentenced to death pursuant to the statutes of those states. In each case the decision whether the defendant should live or die was left to the absolute discretion of the jury. In McGautha's case, the jury, in accordance with California

law, determined punishment in a separate proceeding following
the trial on the issue of guilt. In Crampton's case, in accordance
with Ohio law, the jury determined guilt and punishment after
a single trial and in a single verdict. We granted *certiorari* in
the *McGautha* case limited to the question whether petitioner's
constitutional rights were infringed by permitting the jury to
impose the death penalty without any governing standards....
We granted *certiorari* in the *Crampton* case limited to that
same question and to the further question whether the jury's imposition of the death sentence in the same proceeding and
verdict as determined the issue of guilt was constitutionally
permissible....

McGautha and his codefendant Wilkinson were charged
with committing 2 armed robberies and a murder on Feb. 14,
1967. In accordance with California procedure in capital cases,
the trial was in 2 stages, a guilt stage and a punishment stage.
At the guilt trial, the evidence tended to show that the defendants, armed with pistols, entered the market of Mrs. Pon
Lock early in the afternoon of the murder. While Wilkinson
kept a customer under guard, McGautha trained his gun on
Mrs. Lock and took almost $300. Roughly 3 hours later,
McGautha and Wilkinson held up another store, this one owned
by Mrs. Benjamin Smetana and operated by her with her
husband's assistance. While one defendant forcibly restrained a
customer, the other struck Mrs. Smetana on the head. A shot
was fired, fatally wounding Mr. Smetana. Wilkinson's former
girl friend testified that shortly after the robbery McGautha
told her he had shot a man and showed her an empty cartridge
in the chamber of his gun. Other evidence at the guilt stage was
inconclusive on the issue as to who fired the fatal shot. The jury
found both defendants guilty of 2 counts of armed robbery and
one count of first-degree murder as charged....

At the penalty trial, which took place on the following day
but before the same jury, the state waived its opening,
presented evidence of McGautha's prior felony convictions and
sentences ... and then rested. Wilkinson testified in his own
behalf, relating his unhappy childhood in Mississippi as the son
of a white father and a Negro mother, his honorable discharge
from the Army on the score of his low intelligence, his regular
attendance at church and his good record for holding jobs and
supporting his mother and siblings up to the time he was shot in

the back in an unprovoked assault by a street gang. Thereafter, he testified, he had difficulty obtaining or holding employment. About a year later he fell in with McGautha and his companions, and when they found themselves short of funds, one of the group suggested that they "knock over somebody." ... He admitted participating in the 2 robberies but said he had not known that the stores were to be held up until McGautha drew his gun. He testified that it had been McGautha who struck Mrs. Smetana and shot Mr. Smetana.

Wilkinson called several witnesses in his behalf. An undercover narcotics agent testified that he had seen the murder weapon in McGautha's possession and had seen McGautha demonstrating his quick draw.....

McGautha also testified in his own behalf at the penalty hearing. He admitted that the murder weapon was his but testified that he and Wilkinson had traded guns and that it was Wilkinson who had struck Mrs. Smetana and killed her husband. McGautha testified that he came from a broken home and that he had been wounded during World War II. He related his employment record, medical condition and remorse. He admitted his criminal record ... but testified that he had been a mere accomplice in 2 of those robberies and that his prior conviction for murder had resulted from a slaying in self-defense.... He called no witnesses in his behalf.

The jury was instructed in the following language:

"in this part of the trial the law does not forbid you from being influenced by pity for the defendants and you may be governed by mere sentiment and sympathy for the defendants in arriving at a proper penalty in this case; however, the law does forbid you from being governed by mere conjecture, prejudice, public opinion or public feeling.

"The defendants in this case have been found guilty of the offense of murder in the first degree, and it is now your duty to determine which of the penalties provided by law should be imposed on each defendant for that offense. Now in arriving at this determination you should consider all of the evidence received here in court ... throughout the trial before this jury. You may also consider all of the evidence of the circumstances surrounding the crime, of each defendant's background and history, and of the facts in aggravation or mitigation of the penalty which have been received here in court. However, it is not essential to your decision that you find mitigating circumstances on the one hand or evidence in aggravation of the offense on the other hand. . . .

"...Notwithstanding facts, if any, proved in mitigation or aggravation, in determining which punishment shall be inflicted, you are entirely free to act according to your own judgment, conscience, and absolute discretion. That verdict must express the individual opinion of each juror.

"Now, beyond prescribing the 2 alternative penalties, the law itself provides no standard for the guidance of the jury in the selection of the penalty, but, rather, commits the whole matter of determining which of the 2 penalties shall be fixed to the judgment, conscience and absolute discretion of the jury. In the determination of that matter, if the jury does agree, it must be unanimous as to which of the two penalties is imposed."...

...[T]he jury [later] returned verdicts fixing Wilkinson's punishment at life imprisonment and McGautha's punishment at death. . . .

Petitioner Crampton was indicted for the murder of his wife, Wilma Jean, purposely and with premeditated malice. He pleaded not guilty and not guilty by reason of insanity. In accordance with the Ohio practice which he challenges, his guilt and punishment were determined in a single unitary proceeding.

At trial the state's case was as follows. The Cramptons had been married about 4 months at the time of the murder. 2 months before the slaying Crampton was allowed to leave the state mental hospital, where he was undergoing observation and treatment for alcoholism and drug addiction, to attend the funeral of his wife's father. On this occasion he stole a knife from the house of his late father-in-law and ran away. He called the house several times and talked to his wife, greatly upsetting her. When she pleaded with him to return to the hospital and stated that she would have to call the police, he threatened to kill her if she did. Wilma and her brother nevertheless did notify the authorities, who picked Crampton up later the same evening. There was testimony of other threats Crampton had made on his wife's life, and it was revealed that about 10 days before the murder Mrs. Crampton's fear of her husband had caused her to request and receive police protection.

The state's main witness to the facts surrounding the murder was one William Collins, a convicted felon who had first met Crampton when they, along with Crampton's brother Jack, were in the state prison in Michigan. On Jan. 14, 1967, 3 days before the murder, Collins and Crampton met at Jack Crampton's house in Pontiac, Michigan. During those 3 days Collins and Crampton roamed the upper Midwest, committing a series of petty thefts and obtaining amphetamines, to which both were addicted, by theft and forged prescriptions.

About 9 o'clock on the evening of Jan. 16, Crampton called his wife from St. Joseph, Michigan; after the call he told Collins that he had to get back to Toledo, where his wife was, as fast as possible. They arrived in the early morning hours of Jan. 17. After Crampton had stopped by his wife's home and sent Collins to the door with a purported message for her, the 2 went to the home of Crampton's mother-in-law, which Crampton knew to be empty, to obtain some guns. They broke in and stole a rifle, ammunition and some handguns, including the .45 automatic which was later identified as the murder weapon. Crampton kept this gun with him. He indicated to Collins that he believed his wife was having an affair. He fired the .45 in the air, with a remark to the effect that "a slug of that type would do quite a bit of damage," and said that if he found his wife with the man he suspected he would kill them both.

That evening Crampton called his wife's home and learned that she was present. He quickly drove out to the house, and told Collins, "Leave me off right here in front of the house and you take the car and go back to the parking lot and if I'm not there by 6 o'clock in the morning you're on your own."

About 11:20 that evening Crampton was arrested for driving a stolen car. The murder weapon was found between the seats of the car.

Mrs. Crampton's body was found the next morning. She had been shot in the face at close range while she was using the toilet. A .45-caliber shell casing was near the body.... The coroner, who examined the body at 11:30 p.m. on Jan. 18, testified that in his opinion death had occurred 24 hours earlier, plus or minus 4 hours.

The defense called Crampton's mother as a witness. She testified about Crampton's background, including a serious concussion received at age 9, his good grades in junior high school, his stepfather's jealousy of him, his leaving home at age 14 to live with various relatives, his enlistment in the Navy at age 17, his marriage to a girl named Sandra, the birth of a son, a divorce, then a remarriage to Sandra and another divorce shortly after, and finally his marriage to Wilma. Mrs. Crampton also testified to Crampton's drug addiction, to his brushes with the law as a youth and as an adult and to his undesirable discharge from the Navy.

Crampton's attorney also introduced into evidence a series of hospital reports which contained further information on Crampton's background, including his criminal record, which was substantial, his court-martial conviction and undesirable discharge from the Navy, and the absence of any significant employment record. They also contained his claim that the shooting was accidental; that he had been gathering up guns around the house and had just removed the clip from an automatic when his wife asked to see it; that as he handed it to her it went off accidentally and killed her. All the reports concluded that Crampton was sane in both the legal and the medical senses. He was diagnosed as having a sociopathic personality disorder, along with alcohol and drug addiction. Crampton himself did not testify.

The jury was instructed that "If you find the defendant guilty of murder in the first degree, the punishment is death, unless you recommend mercy, in which event the punishment is imprisonment in the penitentiary during life." ... The jury was given no other instructions specifically addressed to the decision whether to recommend mercy....

The jury deliberated for over 4 hours and returned a verdict of guilty, with no recommendation for mercy....

Before proceeding to a consideration of the issues before us, it is important to recognize and underscore the nature of our responsibilities in judging them. Our function is not to impose on the states, *ex cathedra,* what might seem to us a better system for dealing with capital cases. Rather it is to decide whether the federal Constitution proscribes the present procedures of these 2 states in such cases. In assessing the validity of the conclusions reached in this opinion, that basic factor should be kept constantly in mind....

... [Petitioners contend] that jury sentencing discretion in capital cases was introduced as a mechanism for dispensing mercy—a means for dealing with the rare case in which the death penalty was thought to be unjustified. Now, they assert, the death penalty is imposed on far fewer than half the defendants found guilty of capital crimes. The state and federal legislatures which provide for jury discretion in capital sentencing have, it is said, implicitly determined that some— indeed, the greater portion—of those guilty of capital crimes should be permitted to live. But having made that determination, petitioners argue, they have stopped short—the legislatures have not only failed to provide a rational basis for distinguishing the one group from the other, ... but they have failed even to suggest any basis at all. Whatever the merits of providing such a mechanism to take account of the unforeseeable case calling for mercy, as was the original purpose, petitioners contend the mechanism is constitutionally intolerable as a means of selecting the extraordinary cases calling for the death penalty, which is its present-day function.

In our view, such force as this argument has derives largely from its generality.... To identify before the fact those characteristics of criminal homicides and their perpetrators which call for the death penalty, and to express these characteristics in language which can be fairly understood and applied by the sentencing authority, appear to be tasks which are beyond present human ability....

The final report of the National Commission on Reform of Federal Criminal Laws (1971) recommended entire abolition of the death penalty in federal cases. In a provisional chapter, prepared for the contingency that Congress might decide to retain the death penalty, the report contains a set of criteria virtually identical with the aggravating and mitigating circumstances listed by the Model Penal Code. With respect to the use to be made of the criteria, the report provides that: "[i]n deciding whether a sentence of death should be imposed, the court and the jury, if any, may consider the mitigating and aggravating circumstances set forth in the subsections below." ...

It is apparent that such criteria do not purport to provide more than the most minimal control over the sentencing authority's exercise of discretion. They do not purport to give an exhaustive list of the relevant considerations or the way in which they may be affected by the presence or absence of other circumstances. They do not even undertake to exclude constitutionally impermissible considerations. And, of course, they provide no protection against the jury determined to decide on whimsy or caprice. In short, they do no more than suggest some subjects for the jury to consider during its deliberations, and they bear witness to the intractable nature of the problem of "standards" which the history of capital punishment has from the beginning reflected. Thus they indeed caution against this court's undertaking to establish such standards itself or to pronounce at large that standards in this realm are constitutionally required.

In light of history, experience and the present limitations of human knowledge, we find it quite impossible to say that committing to the untrammelled discretion of the jury the power to pronounce life or death in capital cases is offensive to anything in the Constitution. The states are entitled to assume that jurors confronted with the truly awesome responsibility of decreeing death for a fellow human will act with due regard for the consequences of their decision and will consider a variety of factors, many of which will have been suggested by the evidence or by the arguments of defense counsel. For a court to attempt to catalog the appropriate factors in this elusive area could inhibit rather than expand the scope of consideration, for no list of circumstances would ever be really complete. The infinite variety of cases and facets to each case would make general standards either meaningless "boiler plate" or a statement of the obvious that no jury would need....

Crampton's argument for bifurcation runs as follows: Under *Malloy v. Hogan* ... (1964) and *Griffin v. California* ... (1965), he enjoyed a constitutional right not to be compelled to be a witness against himself. Yet under the Ohio single-trial procedure, he could remain silent on the issue of guilt only at the cost of surrendering any chance to plead his case on the issue of punishment. He contends that under the due process clause of the 14th Amendment ... he had a right to be heard on the issue of punishment and a right not to have his sentence fixed without the benefit of all the relevant evidence....

The criminal process, like the rest of the legal system, is replete with situations requiring "the making of difficult judgments" as to which course to follow. *McMann v. Richardson* ... (1970). Although a defendant may have a right, even of constitutional dimensions, to follow whichever course he chooses, the Constitution does not by that token always forbid requiring him to choose. The threshold question is whether compelling the election impairs to an appreciable extent any of the policies behind the rights involved. Analysis of this case in such terms leads to the conclusion that petitioner has failed to make out his claim of a constitutional violation in requiring him to undergo a unitary trial.

...We turn first to the privilege against compelled self-incrimination. The contention is that where guilt and punishment are to be determined by a jury at a single trial, the desire to address the jury on punishment unduly encourages waiver of the defendant's privilege to remain silent on the issue of guilt, or, to put the matter another way, that the single-verdict procedure unlawfully compels the defendant to become a witness against himself on the issue of guilt by the threat of sentencing him to death without having heard from him....

While we recognize the truth of Mr. Justice [Felix] Frankfurter's insight in *Green v. United States...* (1961) (plurality opinion) as to the peculiar immediacy of a personal plea by the defendant for leniency in sentencing, it is also true that the testimony of an accused denying the case against him has considerably more force than counsel's argument that the prosecution's case has not been proven. The relevant differences between sentencing and determination of guilt or innocence are not so great as to call for a difference in constitutional result. Nor does the fact that capital, as opposed to any other, sentencing is in issue seem to us to distinguish this case.... Even in noncapital sentencing, the sciences of penology, sociology, and psychology have not advanced to the point that sentencing is wholly a matter of scientific calculation from objectively verifiable facts.

We conclude that the policies of the privilege against compelled self-incrimination are not offended when a defendant in a capital case yields to the pressure to testify on the issue of punishment at the risk of damaging his case on guilt. We therefore turn to the converse situation, in which a defendant remains silent on the issue of guilt and thereby loses any opportunity to address the jury personally on punishment....

...This court has not directly determined whether or to what extent the concept of due process of law requires that a criminal defendant wishing to present evidence or argument presumably relevant to the issues involved in sentencing should be permitted to do so. Assuming, without deciding, that the Constitution does require such an opportunity, there was no denial of such a right in Crampton's case. The Ohio Constitution guarantees defendants the right to have their counsel argue in summation for mercy as well as for acquittal....

Before we conclude this opinion, it is appropriate for us to make a broader observation than the issues raised by these cases strictly call for. It may well be, as the American Law Institute and the National Commission on Reform of Federal Criminal Laws have concluded, that bifurcated trials and criteria for jury sentencing discretion are superior means of dealing with capital cases if the death penalty is to be retained at all. But the federal Constitution, which marks the limits of our authority in these cases, does not guarantee trial procedures that are the best of all worlds, or that accord with the most enlightened ideas of students of the infant science of criminology, or even those that measure up to the individual predilections of members of this court.... The Constitution requires no more than that trials be fairly conducted and that guaranteed rights of defendants be scrupulously respected. From a constitutional standpoint, we cannot conclude that it is impermissible for a state to consider that the compassionate purposes of jury sentencing in capital cases are better served by having the issues of guilt and punishment determined in a single trial than by focusing the jury's attention solely on punishment after the issue of guilt has been determined.

Certainly the facts of these gruesome murders bespeak no miscarriage of justice. The ability of juries, unassisted by standards, to distinguish between those defendants for whom the death penalty is appropriate punishment and those for whom imprisonment is sufficient is indeed illustrated by the discriminating verdict of the jury in McGautha's case, finding Wilkinson the less culpable of the 2 defendants and sparing his life.

The procedures which petitioners challenge are those by which most capital trials in this country are conducted, and by which all were conducted until a few years ago. We have determined that these procedures are consistent with the rights to which petitioners were constitutionally entitled and that their trials were entirely fair. Having reached these conclusions, we have performed our task of measuring the states' process by federal constitutional standards, and accordingly the judgment in each of these cases is *affirmed.*

Justice Douglas, joined by Brennan and Marshall, dissenting:

... [In Ohio] if a defendant wishes to testify in support of the defense of insanity or in mitigation of what he is charged with doing, he can do so only if he surrenders his right to be free from self-incrimination. Once he takes the stand he can be cross-examined not only as respects the crime charged but also on other misdeeds. . . .

If exaction of a constitutional right may not be made for assertion of a statutory right (such as the right to a hearing on parole revocation or the right to appeal), it follows *a fortiori* that the constitutional right to be free from the compulsion of self-incrimination may not be exacted as a condition to the constitutional right to be heard.

The truth is, as Mr. Justice Brennan points out in his dissent in these cases, that the wooden position of the court, reflected in today's decision, cannot be reconciled with the evolving gloss of civilized standards which this court, long before the time of those who now sit here, have been reading into the protective procedural due process safeguards of the Bill of Rights. It is as though a dam had suddenly been placed across the stream of the law on procedural due process, a stream which has grown larger with the passing years.

The court has history on its side—but history alone. Though nations have been killing men for centuries, felony crimes increase. The vestiges of law enshrined today have roots in barbaric procedures. Barbaric procedures such as ordeal by battle that became imbedded in the law were difficult to dislodge. Though torture was used to exact confessions, felonies mounted. Once it was thought that "sanity" was determined by ascertaining whether a person knew the difference between "right" and "wrong." Once it was a capital offense to steal from the person something "above the value of a shilling."

Insight and understanding have increased with the years, though the springes of crime remain in large part unknown.

But our own Federal Bureau of Investigation teaches that brains, not muscle, solve crimes. Coerced confessions are not only offensive to civilized standards but not responsive to the modern needs of criminal investigation. Psychiatry has shown that blind faith in rightness and wrongness is no reliable measure of human responsibility. The convergence of new technology for criminal investigation and of new insight into mental disorders has made many ancient legal procedures seem utterly unfair.

Who today would say it was not "cruel and unusual punishment" within the meaning of the 8th Amendment to impose the death sentence on a man who stole a loaf of bread, or in modern parlance, a sheet of food stamps? Who today would say that trial by battle satisfies the requirements of procedural due process?

We need not read procedural due process as designed to satisfy man's deepseated sadistic instincts. We need not in deference to those sadistic instincts say we are bound by history from defining procedural due process so as to deny men fair trials. Yet that is what the court does today. The whole evolution of procedural due process has been in the direction of insisting on fair procedures....

Justice Brennan, joined by Douglas and Marshall, dissenting:

These cases test the viability of principles whose roots draw strength from the very core of the due process clause. The question which petitioners present for our decision is whether the rule of law, basic to our society and binding upon the states by virtue of the due process clause of the 14th Amendment, is fundamentally inconsistent with capital sentencing procedures that are purposely constructed to allow the maximum possible variation from one case to the next and provide no mechanism to prevent that consciously maximized variation from reflecting merely random or arbitrary choice. The court does not, however, come to grips with that fundamental question. Instead, the court misapprehends petitioners' argument and deals with the cases as if petitioners contend that due process requires capital sentencing to be carried out under predetermined standards so precise as to be capable of purely mechanical application, entirely eliminating any vestiges of flexibility or discretion in their use. This misapprehended question is then treated in the context of the court's assumption that the legislatures of Ohio and California are incompetent to express with clarity the bases upon which they have determined that some persons guilty of some crimes should be killed, while others should live—an assumption that, significantly, finds no support in the arguments made by those states in these cases. With the issue so polarized, the court is lead to conclude that the rule of law and the power of the states to kill are in irreconcilable conflict. This conflict the court resolves in favor of the states' power to kill.

In my view the court errs at all points from its premises to its conclusions. Unlike the court, I do not believe that the legislatures of the 50 states are so devoid of wisdom and the power of rational thought that they are unable to face the problem of capital punishment directly and to determine for themselves the criteria under which convicted capital felons should be chosen to live or die. We are thus not, in my view, faced by the dilemma perceived by the court, for cases in this court have for almost a century and a half approved a multiplicity of imaginative procedures designed by the state and federal legislatures to assure even-handed treatment and ultimate legislative control regarding matters which the legislatures have deemed either too complex or otherwise inapposite for regulation under predetermined rules capable of automatic application in every case. Finally, even if I shared the court's view that the rule of law and the power of the states to kill are in irreconcilable conflict, I would have no hesitation in concluding that the rule of law must prevail.

Except where it incorporates specific substantive constitutional guarantees against state infringement, the due process clause of the 14th Amendment does not limit the power of the states to choose among competing social and economic theories in the ordering of life within their respective jurisdictions. But it does require that, if state power is to be exerted, these choices must be made by a responsible organ of state government. For if they are not, the very best that may be hoped for is that state power will be exercised not upon the basis of any social choice made by the people of the state but instead merely on the basis of social choices made at the whim of the particular state official wielding the power. If there is no effective supervision of this process to insure consistency of decision, it can amount to nothing more than government by whim. But ours has been "termed a government of laws, not of men." *Marbury v. Madison* . . . (1803). Government by whim is the very antithesis of due process.

It is not a mere historical accident that "[t]he history of liberty has largely been the history of observance of procedural safeguards." *McNabb v. United States* . . . (1943) (Frankfurter, J.). The range of permissible state choice among competing social and economic theories is so broad that almost any arbitrary or otherwise impermissible discrimination among individuals may mask itself as nothing more than such a permissible exercise of choice unless procedures are devised which adequately insure that the relevant choice is actually made. Such procedures may take a variety of forms. The decision-maker may be provided with a set of guidelines to apply in rendering judgment. His decision may be required to rest upon the presence or absence of specific factors. If the legislature concludes that the range of variation to be dealt with precludes adequate treatment under inflexible, predetermined standards, it may adopt more imaginative procedures. The specificity of standards may be relaxed, directing the decision-maker's attention to the basic policy determinations underlying the statute without binding his action with regard to matters of important but unforeseen detail. He may be instructed to consider a list of factors—either illustrative or exhaustive—intended to illuminate the question presented without setting a fixed balance. The process may draw upon the genius of the common law and direct itself towards the refinement of understanding through case-by-case development. In such cases decision may be left almost entirely in the hands of the body to which it is delegated, with ultimate legislative supervision on questions of basic policy afforded by requiring the decision-makers to explain their actions, and even-handed treatment enhanced by requiring disputed factual issues to be resolved and providing for some form of subsequent review. Creative legislatures may devise yet other procedures. . . .

It is of critical importance in the present cases to emphasize that we are not called upon to determine the adequacy or inadequacy of any particular legislative procedure designed to give rationality to the capital sentencing process.

For the plain fact is that the legislatures of California and Ohio, whence come these cases, have sought no solution at all. We are not presented with a state's attempt to provide standards, attacked as impermissible or inadequate. We are not presented with a legislative attempt to draw wisdom from experience through a process looking towards growth in understanding through the accumulation of a variety of experiences. We are not presented with the slightest attempt to bring the power of reason to bear on the considerations relevant to capital sentencing. We are faced with nothing more than stark legislative abdication. Not once in the history of this court, until today, have we sustained against a due process challenge such an unguided, unbridled, unreviewable exercise of naked power. Almost a century ago, we found an almost identical California procedure constitutionally inadequate to license a laundry. *Yick Wo v. Hopkins*...(1886). Today we hold it adequate to license a life. I would reverse petitioners' sentences of death....

Right to Impartial Jury

An earlier Supreme Court barrier to executions had been imposed in 1968.

The 6th Amendment guarantees the right of trial "by an impartial jury." In *Witherspoon v. Illinois,* decided June 3, 1968, the Supreme Court had ruled, 6-3, that a death sentence could not be carried out if the jury that imposed or recommended the sentence was chosen after prospective jurors were excluded "simply because they voiced general objections to the death penalty or expressed conscientious or religious scruples against its infliction." Writing for the majority, Justice Potter Stewart accused Illinois of having "stacked the deck" against William C. Witherspoon, accused of murdering a policeman, by excusing 47 of 96 prospective jurors who acknowledged having "scruples" about capital punishment.

The issue, according to the court, was "a narrow one." It did not involve a state's right to eliminate prospective jurors who said that their opposition to the death penalty would prevent them from making an impartial decision as to the defendant's guilt. Nor did it concern those unalterably opposed to considering the death penalty in the case at hand. For Illinois to have eliminated prospective jurors who said that they would not consider imposing the death penalty would have been one thing, Stewart said. "But when it swept from the jury all who expressed conscientious or religious scruples against capital punishment and all who opposed it in principle, the state crossed the line of neutrality. In its quest for a jury capable of imposing the death penalty, the state produced a jury uncommonly willing to condemn a man to die."

The court, however, did not overturn Witherspoon's conviction, as urged by his attorneys. Therefore, although a death sentence imposed by a jury "biased" in favor of capital punishment could not be carried out even in June 1968, a decision by such a jury as to the defendant's guilt remained valid under *Witherspoon*.

In a concurring opinion, Justice William O. Douglas said he could see no constitutional basis for excluding prospective jurors who were totally opposed to capital punishment. The exclusion of such persons, he said, deprives the accused of a jury representative of the community at large.

Justice Hugo L. Black, dissenting, accused the majority of forcing the states to use jurors with a bias against capital punishment. "If this court is to hold capital punishment unconstitutional," he said, "I think it should do so forthrightly, not be making it impossible for states to get juries that will enforce the death penalty."

An important aspect of *Witherspoon* was the contention that juries consisting wholly of persons with no scruples against capital punishment were biased against a defendant to the extent that such persons tended to be more punitive, authoritarian and less able to weigh evidence impartially than those who said they had reservations about capital punishment. Defense counsel presented what it said was "competent scientific evidence" that jurors unopposed to the death penalty "are partial to the prosecution on the issue of guilt or innocence." The court described these studies as "tentative" and "fragmentary," but it did suggest that it might reconsider the matter if less tenuous findings were produced later.

Abridgment of the *Witherspoon v. Illinois* decision (391 U.S. 510, June 3, 1968):

Justice Stewart delivering the opinion of the court:

The petitioner was brought to trial in 1960 in Cook County, Illinois, upon a charge of murder. The jury found him guilty and fixed his penalty at death. At the time of his trial an Illinois statute provided: "In trials for murder it shall be a cause for challenge of any juror who shall, on being examined, state that he has conscientious scruples against capital punishment, or that he is opposed to the same." Through this provision the State of Illinois armed the prosecution with unlimited challenges for cause in order to exclude those jurors who, in the words of the state's highest court, "might hesitate to return a verdict inflicting [death]." At the petitioner's trial, the prosecution eliminated nearly half the venire of prospective jurors by challenging, under the authority of this statute, any venireman

who expressed qualms about capital punishment. From those
who remained were chosen the jurors who ultimately found the
petitioner guilty and sentenced him to death. The Supreme
Court of Illinois denied post-conviction relief, and we granted
certiorari to decide whether the Constitution permits a state to
execute a man pursuant to the verdict of a jury so composed.

... The issue before us is a narrow one. It does not involve
the right of the prosecution to challenge for cause those
prospective jurors who state what their reservations about
capital punishment would prevent them from making an impartial decision as to the defendant's guilt. Nor does it involve
the state's assertion of a right to exclude from the jury in a
capital case those who say that they could never vote to impose
the death penalty or that they would refuse even to consider its
imposition in the case before them. For the State of Illinois did
not stop there but authorized the prosecution to exclude as well
all who said that they were opposed to capital punishment and
all who indicated that they had conscientious scruples against
inflicting it.

In the present case the tone was set when the trial judge
said early in the *voir dire,* "Let's get these conscientious
objectors out of the way, without wasting any time on them."
In rapid succession, 47 veniremen were successfully challenged
for cause on the basis of their attitudes toward the death
penalty. Only 5 of the 47 explicitly stated that under no circumstances would they vote to impose capital punishment. 6 said
that they did not "believe in the death penalty" and were excused without any attempt to determine whether they could
nonetheless return a verdict of death. 39 veniremen, including 4
of the 6 who indicated that they did not believe in capital
punishment, acknowledged having "conscientious or religious
scruples against the infliction of the death penalty" or against
its infliction "in a proper case" and were excluded without any
effort to find out whether their scruples would invariably
compel them to vote against capital punishment.

Only one venireman who admitted to "a religious or
conscientious scruple against the infliction of the death penalty
in a proper case" was examined at any length. She was asked:
"You don't believe in the death penalty?" She replied: "No. It's
just I wouldn't want to be responsible." The judge admonished
her not to forget her "duty as a citizen" and again asked her

whether she had "a religious or conscientious scruple" against capital punishment. This time, she replied in the negative. Moments later, however, she repeated that she would not "like to be responsible for... deciding somebody should be put to death." Evidently satisfied that this elaboration of the prospective juror's views disqualified her under the Illinois statute, the judge told her to "step aside."

... The petitioner contends that a state cannot confer upon a jury selected in this manner the power to determine guilt. He maintains that such a jury, unlike one chosen at random from a cross-section of the community, must necessarily be biased in favor of conviction, for the kind of juror who would be unperturbed by the prospect of sending a man to his death, he contends, is the kind of juror who would too readily ignore the presumption of the defendant's innocence, accept the prosecution's version of the facts, and return a verdict of guilt. To support this view, the petitioner refers to what he describes as "competent scientific evidence that death-qualified jurors are partial to the prosecution on the issue of guilt or innocence."

The data adduced by the petitioner, however, are too tentative and fragmentary to establish that jurors not opposed to the death penalty tend to favor the prosecution in the determination of guilt. We simply cannot conclude, either on the basis of the record now before us or as a matter of judicial notice, that the exclusion of jurors opposed to capital punishment results in an unrepresentative jury on the issue of guilt or substantially increases the risk of conviction. In light of the presently available information, we are not prepared to announce a *per se* constitutional rule requiring the reversal of every conviction returned by a jury selected as this one was.

It does not follow, however, that the petitioner is entitled to no relief. For in this case the jury was entrusted with 2 distinct responsibilities: first, to determine whether the petitioner was innocent or guilty; and 2d, if guilty, to determine whether his sentence should be imprisonment or death. It has not been shown that this jury was biased with respect to the petitioner's guilt. But it is self-evident that, in its role as arbiter of the punishment to be imposed, this jury fell woefully short of that impartiality to which the petitioner was entitled under the 6th and 14th Amendments....

The only justification the state has offered for the jury-selection technique it employed here is that individuals who express serious reservations about capital punishment cannot be relied upon to vote for it even when the laws of the state and the instructions of the trial judge would make death the proper penalty. But in Illinois, as in other states, the jury is given broad discretion to decide whether or not death *is* "the proper penalty" in a given case, and a juror's general views about capital punishment play an inevitable role in any such decision.

A man who opposes the death penalty, no less than one who favors it, can make the discretionary judgment entrusted to him by the state and can thus obey the oath he takes as a juror. But a jury from which all such men have been excluded cannot perform the task demanded of it. Guided by neither rule nor standard, "free to select or reject as it [sees] fit," a jury that must choose between life imprisonment and capital punishment can do little more—and must do nothing less—than express the conscience of the community on the ultimate question of life or death. Yet, in a nation less than half of whose people believe in the death penalty, a jury composed exclusively of such people cannot speak for the community. Culled of all who harbor doubts about the wisdom of capital punishment—of all who would be reluctant to pronounce the extreme penalty—such a jury can speak only for a distinct and dwindling minority.

If the state had excluded only those prospective jurors who stated in advance of trial that they would not even consider returning a verdict of death, it could argue that the resulting jury was simply "neutral" with respect to penalty. But when it swept from the jury all who expressed conscientious or religious scruples against capital punishment and all who opposed it in principle, the state crossed the line of neutrality. In its quest for a jury capable of imposing the death penalty, the state produced a jury uncommonly willing to condemn a man to die.

It is, of course, settled that a state may not entrust the determination of whether a man is innocent or guilty to a tribunal "organized to convict." *Fay v. New York* [1947]. . . . It requires but a short step from that principle to hold, as we do today, that a state may not entrust the determination of whether a man should live or die to a tribunal organized to return a verdict of death. Specifically, we hold that a sentence of death cannot be carried out if the jury that imposed or recommended it was chosen by excluding veniremen for cause simply because they voiced general objections to the death penalty or expressed conscientious or religious scruples against its infliction. No defendant can constitutionally be put to death at the hands of a tribunal so selected.

Whatever else might be said of capital punishment, it is at least clear that its imposition by a hanging jury cannot be squared with the Constitution. The state of Illinois has stacked the deck against the petitioner. To execute this death sentence would deprive him of his life without due process of law.

Justice Black, joined by John Marshall Harlan and Byron R. White, dissenting:

...If this court is to hold capital punishment unconstitutional, I think it should do so forthrightly, not by making it impossible for states to get juries that will enforce the death penalty....

On Apr. 29, 1959, *more than 9 years ago,* petitioner shot and killed a policeman in order to escape arrest. Petitioner had been struggling with a woman on the street whom he had met in a tavern when a police patrol car assigned to the vicinity stopped at a nearby traffic light. The woman was able to free herself from petitioner's grasp and rushed to the patrol car where she told the two policemen in it that petitioner was carrying a gun. Petitioner overheard this conversation and fled to a nearby parking lot and hid in one of the many parked trailers and tractors. It was while one of the policemen was searching this trailer that petitioner shot him. There is no doubt that petitioner killed the policeman....

At his trial for murder petitioner was represented by 3 appointed counsel, the chief of whom was the then chairman of the Chicago Bar Association Committee for the Defense of the Indigent. It is important to note that when those persons who acknowledged having "conscientious or religious scruples against the infliction of the death penalty" were excluded from the jury, defense counsel made no attempt to show that they were nonetheless competent jurors. In fact, when the jurors finally were accepted by defense counsel, the defense still had 3 peremptory challenges left to exercise. In the past this has frequently been taken as an indication that the jurors who were impaneled were impartial.... And it certainly amounts to a clear showing that in this case petitioner's able and distinguished counsel did not believe petitioner was being tried by a biased, much less a "hanging" jury.

After petitioner's conviction, another very distinguished attorney was appointed to prosecute his appeal, and an extensive brief alleging some 15 separate trial errors was filed in the Supreme Court of Illinois. Again, however, there was no indication that anyone thought petitioner had been convicted by a biased jury.... [In] Feb. 1965 petitioner filed a petition in the state courts requesting whatever form of remedy is "provided for by Illinois law." Among other claims now appeared the contention that petitioner's constitutional rights were violated when the trial court excused for cause prospective jurors having scruples against capital punishment. The state trial judge dismissed the petition on the ground that it failed to set forth facts sufficient to entitle the petitioner to relief. Petitioner then appealed to the Illinois Supreme Court where he was appearing for the 3d time in this case and where, more than 6 years after his trial, he argued that the disqualification for cause of jurors having conscientious or religious scruples against capital punishment was unconstitutional......

At the time of petitioner's trial, § 743 of the Illinois Criminal Code provided: "In trials for murder it shall be a cause for challenge of any juror, who shall on being examined state that he has conscientious scruples against capital punishment or that he is opposed to the same." The obvious purpose of this section is to insure, as well as laws can insure such a thing, that there be an impartial jury in cases in Illinois where the death sentence may be imposed. And this statute recognizes that the people as a whole, or as they are usually called, "society" or "the state," have as much right to an impartial jury as to criminal defendants....

As I see the issue in this case, it is a question of plain bias. A person who has conscientious or religious scruples against capital punishment will seldom if ever vote to impose the death penalty. This is just human nature, and no amount of semantic camouflage can cover it up. In the same manner, I would not dream of foisting on a criminal defendant a juror who admitted that he had conscientious or religious scruples against not inflicting the death sentence on any person convicted of murder (a juror who claims, for example, that he adheres literally to the

Biblical admonition of "an eye for an eye"). Yet the logical result of the majority's holding is that such persons must be allowed so that the "conscience of the community" will be fully represented when it decides "the ultimate question of life or death." While I have always advocated that the jury be as fully representative of the community as possible, I would never carry this so far as to require that those biased against one of the critical issues in a trial should be represented on a jury....

The majority opinion attempts to equate those who have conscientious or religious scruples against the death penalty with those who do not in such a way as to balance the allegedly conflicting viewpoints in order that a truly representative jury can be established to exercise the community's discretion in deciding on punishment. But for this purpose I do not believe that those who have conscientious or religious scruples against the death penalty and those who have no feelings either way are in any sense comparable. Scruples against the death penalty are commonly the result of a deep religious conviction or a profound philosophical commitment developed after much soul searching. The holders of such scruples must necessarily recoil from the prospect of making possible what they regard as immoral. On the other hand, I cannot accept the proposition that persons who do not have conscientious scruples against the death penalty are "prosecution prone." With regard to this group, I would agree with the following statement of the Court of Appeals for the District of Columbia:

"No proof is available, so far as we know, and we can imagine none, to indicate that, generally speaking, persons not opposed to capital punishment are as bent in their hostility to criminals as to be incapable of rendering impartial verdicts on the law and the evidence in a capital case. Being not opposed to capital punishment is not synonymous with favoring it. Individuals may indeed be so prejudiced in respect to serious crimes that they cannot be impartial arbiters, but that extreme is not indicated by mere lack of opposition to capital punishment. The 2 antipathies can readily coexist; contrariwise either can exist without the other; and indeed, neither may exist in a person. It seems clear enough to us that a person or a group of persons may not be opposed to capital punishment and at the same time may have no particular bias against any one criminal or, indeed, against criminals as a class; people, it seems to us, may be completely without a controlling conviction one way or the other on either subject...." *Tuberville v. United States*... (1962)....

It seems to me that the court's opinion today must be read as holding just the opposite from what has been stated above. For no matter how the court might try to hide it, the implication is inevitably in its opinion that people who do not have conscientious scruples against the death penalty are somehow callous to suffering and are, as some of the commentators cited by the court called them, "prosecution prone." This conclusion represents a psychological foray into the human mind that I have considerable doubt about my ability to make, and I must confess that the 2 or 3 so-called "studies" cited by the court on this subject are not persuasive to me.

Finally, I want to point out that the *real* holding in this case is, at least to me, very ambiguous. If we are to take the opinion literally, then I submit the court today has decided nothing of substance, but has merely indulged itself in a semantic exercise. For as I read the opinion, the new requirement placed upon the states is that they cease asking prospective jurors whether they have "conscientious or religious scruples against the infliction of the death penalty" but instead ask whether "they would *automatically* vote against the imposition of capital punishment without regard to any evidence that might be developed at the trial of the case before them."... I believe that this fine line the court attempts to draw is based on a semantic illusion and that the practical effect of the court's new formulation of the question to be asked state juries will not produce a significantly different kind of jury from the one chosen in this case. And I might add that the states will have been put to a great deal of trouble for nothing. Yet, as I stated above, it is not clear that this is all the court is holding. For the majority opinion goes out of its way to state that in some future case a defendant might well establish that a jury selected in the way the Illinois statute here provides is "less than neutral with respect to *guilt.*" ... This seems to me to be but a thinly veiled warning to the states that they had better change their jury selection procedures or face a decision by this court that their murder convictions have been obtained unconstitutionally.

I believe that the court's decision today goes a long way in destroying the concept of an impartial jury as we have known it. . . .

Justice White dissenting:

All Illinois citizens, including those who oppose the death penalty, are assured by the Constitution a fair opportunity to influence the Legislature's determinations about criminal sentences. *Reynolds v. Sims,* (1964) and succeeding cases. Those opposing the death penalty have not prevailed in that forum, however. The representatives of the people of Illinois have determined that the death penalty decision should be made in individual cases by a group of those citizens without conscientious scruples about one of the sentencing alternatives provided by the Legislature. This method of implementing the majority's will was presumably related to a desire to preserve the traditional policy of requiring that jury verdicts be unanimous. The Legislature undoubtedly felt that if all citizens could serve on the jury, and if one citizen with especially pronounced "scruples" could prevent a decision to impose death, the penalty would almost never be imposed. . . .

The court may have a strong dislike for this particular sentence, and it may desire to meet . . . standards of charity. Those are laudable motives, but hardly a substitute for the usual processes of reasoned analysis. If the court can offer no better constitutional grounds for today's decision than those provided in the opinion, it should restrain its dislike for the death penalty and leave the decision about appropriate penalties to branches of government whose members, selected by popular vote, have an authority not extended to this court.

RIGHTS OF JUVENILES IN COURT

Only Some Guarantees Extended to Children

In recent years the Supreme Court has been pressed to consider the extent to which constitutional rights are applicable in state juvenile court proceedings. The court responded by ruling that some constitutional rights must be observed in such proceedings while others may be ignored.

In the case of *In Re Gault,* the Supreme Court ruled May 15, 1967 that in juvenile proceedings that may result in a child being placed in an institution: (1) The child and his parents or guardians must be given sufficient notice of the charges in time to prepare a defense. (2) They must be notified of their right to counsel and be supplied with counsel if unable to afford counsel. (3) The child must be accorded the right not to testify against himself. (4) The defense must be allowed to cross-examine witnesses.

In the case of *In the Matter of Winship,* the court held May 31, 1970 that "proof beyond a reasonable doubt is among the 'essentials of due process and fair treatment' required during the adjudicatory stage when a juvenile is charged with an act which would constitute a crime if committed by an adult."

406

Approximately half of the children confined in large institutions for juvenile delinquents have not been convicted of any crime. They are there because they are runaways or truants or have destructive home situations. Yet half of the arrests for serious crime in the U.S. is of young people under the age 18. Recidivism among institutionalized delinquents is the highest of any group—74%.

Going against the trend toward more formal juvenile proceedings, akin to those provided adults, the Supreme Court ruled in *McKeiver et al. v. Pennsylvania* June 21, 1971 that trial by jury is not required in juvenile proceedings.

Some observers hold that *Gault* typified much that is wrong with state juvenile proceedings. Gerald Francis Gault, 15, on probation for being in the company of a boy who had stolen a wallet, was ordered to a state-run children's home until his 21st birthday "unless sooner discharged by due process of law." This followed the complaint of a neighbor who claimed to have received an obscene phone call. An adult guilty of this offense could be fined $5 to $50 or imprisoned for up to 2 months.

In extending certain procedural rights to juvenile proceedings, Justice Abe Fortas, speaking for the majority in *In Re Gault,* pointed out that juvenile courts were set up originally to determine what is best for the child as opposed to the mere consideration of guilt or innocence. To accomplish this goal, 19th-century reformers abandoned the regular criminal procedure in hope of substituting a more flexible, informal system designed to "treat" or "rehabilitate" the child by "clinical" rather than punitive measures. Fortas asserted, however, that departures from due process have often resulted "not in enlightened procedure, but in arbitrariness." "Under our Constitution, the condition of being a boy does not justify a kangaroo court," he said.

Justice Potter Stewart, in his dissent, acknowledged the failure of juvenile courts but insisted that improvement cannot be made by converting "a juvenile proceeding into a criminal prosecution." He noted the 19th-century case of a 12-year-old boy: "A jury found him guilty of murder, and he was sentenced to death by hanging. The sentence was executed. It was all very constitutional."

Abridgment of the *In Re Gault* decision (387 U.S. 1, May 15, 1967):

Justice Fortas delivering the opinion of the court:

... On Monday, June 8, 1964, at about 10 a.m., Gerald Francis Gault and a friend, Ronald Lewis, were taken into custody by the Sheriff of Gila County. Gerald was then still subject to a 6 months' probation order which had been entered on Feb. 25, 1964, as a result of his having been in the company of another boy who had stolen a wallet from a lady's purse. The police action on June 8 was taken as the result of a verbal complaint by a neighbor of the boys, Mrs. Cook, about a telephone call made to her in which the caller or callers made lewd or indecent remarks....

On June 9, Gerald, his mother, his older brother, and Probation Officers Flagg and Henderson appeared before the juvenile [court] judge in chambers. Gerald's father was not there. He was at work out of the city. Mrs. Cook, the complainant, was not there. No one was sworn at this hearing. No transcript or recording was made. No memorandum or record of the substance of the proceedings was prepared. Our information about the proceedings and the subsequent hearing on June 15 derives entirely from the testimony of the juvenile court judge, Mr. and Mrs. Gault and [Deputy Probation] Officer Flagg at the *habeas corpus* proceeding conducted 2 months later. From this, it appears that at the July 9 hearing Gerald was questioned by the judge about the telephone call. There was conflict as to what he said. His mother recalled that Gerald said he only dialed Mrs. Cook's number and handed the telephone to his friend, Ronald. Officer Flagg recalled that Gerald had admitted making the lewd remarks. Judge McGhee testified that Gerald "admitted making one of these [lewd] statements." At the conclusion of the hearing, the judge said he would "think about it." Gerald was taken back to the detention home. He was not sent to his own home with his parents. On June 11 or 12, after having been detained since June 8, Gerald was released and driven home. There is no explanation in the record as to why he was kept in the detention home or why he was released. At 5 p.m. on the day of Gerald's release, Mrs. Gault received a note signed by Officer Flagg.... Its entire text was as follows: "Mrs. Gault: Judge McGhee has set Monday June 15, 1964 at 11:00 A.M. as the date and time for further hearings on Gerald's delinquency. /s/ Flagg"

At the appointed time on Monday, June 15, Gerald, his father and mother, Ronald Lewis and his father, and Officers Flagg and Henderson were present before Judge McGhee. Witnesses at the *habeas corpus* proceeding differed in their recollections of Gerald's testimony at the June 15 hearing. Mr. and Mrs. Gault recalled that Gerald again testified that he had only dialed the number and that the other boy had made the remarks. Officer Flagg agreed that at this hearing Gerald did not admit making the lewd remarks. But Judge McGhee recalled that "there was some admission again of some of the lewd statements. He—he didn't admit any of the more serious lewd statements." Again, the complainant, Mrs. Cook, was not present. Mrs. Gault asked that Mrs. Cook be present "so she could see which boy had done the talking, the dirty talking over the phone." The juvenile [court] judge said "she didn't have to be present at that hearing." The judge did not speak to Mrs. Cook or communicate with her at any time. Probation Officer Flagg had talked to her once—over the telephone on June 9.

... At the conclusion of the hearing, the judge committed Gerald as a juvenile delinquent to the State Industrial School "for the period of his minority [that is, until 21], unless sooner discharged by due process of law." An order to that effect was entered. It recites that "after a full hearing and due deliberation the court finds that said minor is a delinquent child and that said minor is of the age of 15 years."

No appeal is permitted by Arizona law in juvenile cases. On Aug. 3, 1964, a petition for a writ of *habeas corpus* was filed with the Supreme Court of Arizona and referred by it to the Superior Court for hearing.

At the *habeas corpus* hearing on Aug. 17, Judge McGhee was vigorously cross-examined as to the basis for his actions. He testified that he had taken into account the fact that Gerald was on probation. He was asked "under what section of . . . the code you found the boy delinquent?"

. . . In substance, he concluded that Gerald came within ARS § 8-201-6(a), which specifies that a "delinquent child" includes one "who has violated a law of the state or an ordinance or regulation of a political subdivision thereof." The law which Gerald was found to have violated is ARS § 13-377. This section of the Arizona Criminal Code provides that a person who "in the presence of or hearing of any woman or child . . . uses vulgar, abusive or obscene language, is guilty of a misdemeanor . . . ." The penalty specified in the Criminal Code, which would apply to an adult, is $5 to $50, or imprisonment for not more than 2 months. The judge also testified that he acted under ARS § 8-201-6(d) which includes in the definition of a "delinquent child" one who, as the judge phrased it, is "habitually involved in immoral matters."

Asked about the basis for his conclusion that Gerald was "habitually involved in immoral matters," the judge testified, somewhat vaguely, that 2 years earlier, on July 2, 1962, a "referral" was made concerning Gerald, "where the boy had stolen a baseball glove from another boy and lied to the Police Department about it." The judge said there was "no hearing" and "no accusation" relating to this incident "because of lack of material foundation." But it seems to have remained in his mind as a relevant factor. The judge also testified that Gerald had admitted making other nuisance phone calls in the past which, as the judge recalled the boy's testimony, were "silly calls, or funny calls, or something like that . " . . .

. . . Appellants urge that we hold the Juvenile Code of Arizona invalid on its face or as applied in this case because, contrary to the due process clause of the 14th Amendment, the juvenile is taken from the custody of his parents and committed to a state institution pursuant to proceedings in which the juvenile court has virtually unlimited discretion, and in which the following basic rights are denied: 1. Notice of the charges; 2. Right to counsel; 3. Right to confrontation and cross-examination; 4. Privilege against self-incrimination; 5. Right to a transcript of the proceedings; and 6. Right to appellate review....

...In *Kent v. United States*...(1966), we considered the requirements for a valid waiver of the "exclusive" jurisdiction of the Juvenile Court of the District of Columbia so that a juvenile could be tried in the adult criminal court of the district. Although our decision turned upon the language of the statute, we emphasized the necessity that "the basic requirements of due process and fairness" be satisfied in such proceedings. *Haley v. Ohio*...(1948), involved the admissibility, in a state criminal court of general jurisdiction, of a confession by a 15-year-old boy. The court held that the 14th Amendment applied to prohibit the use of the coerced confession. Mr. Justice Douglas said, "Neither man nor child can be allowed to stand condemned by methods which flout constitutional requirements of due process of law." To the same effect is *Gallegos v. Colorado*...(1962). Accordingly, while these cases relate only to restricted aspects of the subject, they unmistakably indicate that, whatever may be their precise impact, neither the 14th Amendment nor the Bill of Rights is for adults alone.

We do not in this opinion consider the impact of these constitutional provisions upon the totality of the relationship of the juvenile and the state. We do not even consider the entire process relating to juvenile "delinquents."... We consider only the problems presented to us by this case. These relate to the proceedings by which a determination is made as to whether a juvenile is a "delinquent" as a result of alleged misconduct on his part, with the consequence that he may be committed to a state institution. As to these proceedings, there appears to be little current dissent from the proposition that the due process clause has a role to play. The problem is to ascertain the precise impact of the due process requirement upon such proceedings.

From the inception of the juvenile court system, wide differences have been tolerated—indeed insisted upon—between the procedural rights accorded to adults and those of juveniles. In practically all jurisdictions, there are rights granted to adults which are withheld from juveniles. In addition to the specific problems involved in the present case, for example, it has been held that the juvenile is not entitled to bail, to indictment by grand jury, to a public trial or to trial by jury. It is frequent practice that rules governing the arrest and interrogation of adults by the police are not observed in the case of juveniles.

The history and theory underlying this development are well-known, but a recapitulation is necessary for purposes of this opinion. The juvenile court movement began in this country at the end of the last century. From the juvenile court statute adopted in Illinois in 1899, the system has spread to every state in the Union, the District of Columbia and Puerto Rico. The constitutionality of juvenile court laws has been sustained in over 40 jurisdictions against a variety of attacks.

The early reformers were appalled by adult procedures and penalties, and by the fact that children could be given long prison sentences and mixed in jails with hardened criminals. They were profoundly convinced that society's duty to the child could not be confined by the concept of justice alone. They believed that society's role was not to ascertain whether the child was "guilty" or "innocent," but "What is he, how has he become what he is, and what had best be done in his interest and in the interest of the state to save him from a downward career." The child—essentially good, as they saw it—was to be made "to feel that he is the object of [the state's] care and solicitude," not that he was under arrest or on trial. The rules of criminal procedure were therefore altogether inapplicable.... The idea of crime and punishment was to be abandoned. The child was to be "treated" and "rehabilitated" and the procedures, from apprehension through institutionalization, were to be "clinical" rather than punitive....

Accordingly, the highest motives and most enlightened impulses led to a peculiar system for juveniles, unknown to our law in any comparable context. The constitutional and theoretical basis for this peculiar system is—to say the least—debatable. And in practice, as we remarked in the *Kent* case,... the results have not been entirely satisfactory. Juvenile court history has again demonstrated that unbridled discretion, however benevolently motivated, is frequently a poor substitute for principle and procedure. In 1937, Dean Pound wrote: "The powers of the Star Chamber were a trifle in comparison with those of our juvenile courts...." The absence of substantive standards has not necessarily meant that children receive careful, compassionate, individualized treatment. The absence of procedural rules based upon constitutional principle has not always produced fair, efficient and effective procedures. Departures from established principles of due process have frequently resulted not in enlightened procedure but in arbitrariness. The chairman of the Pennsylvania Council of Juvenile Court Judges has recently observed: "Unfortunately, loose procedures, high-handed methods and crowded court calendars, either singly or in combination, all too often have resulted in depriving some juveniles of fundamental rights that have resulted in a denial of due process."...

It is claimed that juveniles obtain benefits from the special procedures applicable to them which more than offset the disadvantages of denial of the substance of normal due process. As we shall discuss, the observance of due process standards, intelligently and not ruthlessly administered, will not compel the states to abandon or displace any of the substantive benefits of the juvenile process. But it is important, we think, that the claimed benefits of the juvenile process should be candidly appraised. Neither sentiment nor folklore should cause us to shut our eyes, for example, to such startling findings as that reported in an exceptionally reliable study of repeaters or recidivism conducted by the Stanford Research Institute for the President's Commission on Crime in the District of Columbia. This commission's report states: "In fiscal 1966 approximately 66% of the 16- and 17-year-old juveniles referred to the court by the Youth Aid Division had been before the court previously. In 1965, 56% of those in the receiving home were repeaters. The SRI study revealed that 61% of the sample juvenile court referrals in 1965 had been previously referred at least once and that 42% had been referred at least twice before."...

Certainly, these figures and the high crime rates among juveniles... could not lead us to conclude that the absence of constitutional protections reduces crime or that the juvenile system, functioning free of constitutional inhibitions as it has largely done, is effective to reduce crime or rehabilitate offenders. We do not mean by this to denigrate the juvenile court process or to suggest that there are not aspects of the juvenile system relating to offenders which are valuable. But the features of the juvenile system which its proponents have asserted are of unique benefit will not be impaired by constitutional domestication....

Ultimately, however, we confront the reality of that portion of the juvenile court process with which we deal in this case. A boy is charged with misconduct. The boy is committed to an institution where he may be restrained of liberty for years. It is of no constitutional consequence—and of limited practical meaning—that the institution to which he is committed is called an industrial school. The fact of the matter is that, however euphemistic the title, a "receiving home" or an "industrial school" for juveniles is an institution of confinement in which the child is incarcerated for a greater or lesser time. His world becomes "a building with white-washed walls, regimented routine and institutional laws...." Instead of mother and father and sisters and brothers and friends and classmates, his world is peopled by guards, custodians, state employees, and "delinquents" confined with him for anything from waywardness to rape and homicide.

In view of this, it would be extraordinary if our Constitution did not require the procedural regularity and the exercise of care implied in the phrase "due process." Under our Constitution, the condition of being a boy does not justify a kangaroo court. The traditional ideas of juvenile court procedure, indeed, contemplated that time would be available and care would be used to establish precisely what the juvenile did and why he did it—was it a prank of adolescence or a brutal act threatening serious consequences to himself or society unless corrected? Under traditional notions, one would assume that in a case like that of Gerald Gault, where the juvenile appears to have a home, a working mother and father, and an older brother, the juvenile [court] judge would have made a careful inquiry and judgment as to the possibility that the boy could be disciplined and dealt with at home, despite his previous transgressions. Indeed, so far as appears in the record before us, except for some conversation with Gerald about his school work and his "wanting to go to...Grand Canyon with his father," the points to which the judge directed his attention were little different from those that would be involved in determining any charge of violation of a penal statute. The essential difference between

Gerald's case and a normal criminal case is that safeguards available to adults were discarded in Gerald's case. The summary procedure as well as the long commitment were possible because Gerald was 15 years of age instead of over 18.

If Gerald had been over 18, he would not have been subject to juvenile court proceedings. For the particular offense immediately involved, the maximum punishment would have been a fine of $5 to $50, or imprisonment in jail for not more than 2 months. Instead, he was committed to custody for a maximum of 6 years. If he had been over 18 and had committed an offense to which such a sentence might apply, he would have been entitled to substantial rights under the Constitution of the United States as well as under Arizona's laws and constitution. The United States Constitution would guarantee him rights and protections with respect to arrest, search and seizure, and pretrial interrogation. It would assure him of specific notice of the charges and adequate time to decide his course of action and to prepare his defense. He would be entitled to clear advice that he could be represented by counsel, and, at least if a felony were involved, the state would be required to provide counsel if his parents were unable to afford it. If the court acted on the basis of his confession, careful procedures would be required to assure its voluntariness. If the case went to trial, confrontation and opportunity for cross-examination would be guaranteed. So wide a gulf between the state's treatment of the adult and of the child requires a bridge sturdier than mere verbiage, and reasons more persuasive than cliche can provide....

Appellants allege that the Arizona Juvenile Code is unconstitutional or alternatively that the proceedings before the juvenile court were constitutionally defective because of failure to provide adequate notice of the hearings. No notice was given to Gerald's parents when he was taken into custody on Monday, June 8. On that night, when Mrs. Gault went to the detention home, she was orally informed that there would be a hearing the next afternoon and was told the reason why Gerald was in custody. The only written notice Gerald's parents received at any time was a note on plain paper from Officer Flagg delivered on Thursday or Friday, June 11 or 12, to the effect that the judge had set Monday, June 15, "for further hearings on Gerald's delinquency."...

We cannot agree with the [Arizona Supreme] Court's conclusion that adequate notice was given in this case. Notice, to comply with due process requirements, must be given sufficiently in advance of scheduled court proceedings so that reasonable opportunity to prepare will be afforded, and it must "set forth the alleged misconduct with particularity." It is obvious, as we have discussed above, that no purpose of shielding the child from the public stigma of knowledge of his having been taken into custody and scheduled for hearing is served by the procedure approved by the court below.... [Due process] does not allow a hearing to be held in which a youth's freedom and his parents' right to his custody are at stake without giving them timely notice, in advance of the hearing, of the specific issues that they must meet....

Appellants charge that the juvenile court proceedings were fatally defective because the court did not advise Gerald or his parents of their right to counsel, and proceeded with the hearing, the adjudication of delinquency and the order of commitment in the absence of counsel for the child and his parents or an express waiver of the right thereto.... The [Arizona Supreme] Court argued that "The parent and the probation officer may be relied upon to protect the infant's interests." Accordingly, it rejected the proposition that "due process requires that an infant have a right to counsel." It said that juvenile courts have the discretion, but not the duty, to allow such representation.... We do not agree. Probation officers, in the Arizona scheme, are also arresting officers. They initiate proceedings and file petitions which they verify, as here, alleging the delinquency of the child; and they testify, as here, against the child.... A proceeding where the issue is whether the child will be found to be "delinquent" and subjected to the loss of his liberty for years is comparable in seriousness to a felony prosecution. The juvenile needs the assistance of counsel to cope with problems of law, to make skilled inquiry into the facts, to insist upon regularity of the proceedings, and to ascertain whether he has a defense and to prepare and submit it.... [So] we hold now that it is...essential for the determination of delinquency, carrying with it the awesome prospect of incarceration in a state institution until the juvenile reaches the age of 21....

We conclude that the due process clause of the 14th Amendment requires that in respect of proceedings to determine delinquency which may result in commitment to an institution in which the juvenile's freedom is curtailed, the child and his parent must be notified of the child's right to be represented by counsel retained by them, or if they are unable to afford counsel, that counsel will be appointed to represent the child....

Appellants urge that the writ of *habeas corpus* should have been granted because of the denial of the rights of confrontation and cross-examination in the juvenile court hearings, and because the privilege against self-incrimination was not observed. The juvenile court judge testified at the *habeas corpus* hearing that he had proceeded on the basis of Gerald's admissions at the 2 hearings. Appellants attack this on the ground that the admissions were obtained in disregard of the privilege against self-incrimination. If the confession is disregarded, appellants argue that the delinquency conclusion, since it was fundamentally based on a finding that Gerald had made lewd remarks during the phone call to Mrs. Cook, is fatally defective for failure to accord the rights of confrontation and cross-examination which the due process clause of the 14th Amendment of the federal Constitution guarantees in state proceedings generally.

Our first question, then, is whether Gerald's admission was improperly obtained and relied on as the basis of decision, in conflict with the federal Constitution....

Mrs. Cook, the complainant, and the recipient of the alleged telephone call, was not called as a witness. Gerald's mother asked the juvenile court judge why Mrs. Cook was not present, and the judge replied that "she didn't have to be present." So far as appears, Mrs. Cook was spoken to only once, by Officer Flagg, and this was by telephone. The judge did not speak with her on any occasion. Gerald had been questioned by the probation officer after having been taken into custody.... Gerald was also questioned by the juvenile court judge at each of the 2 hearings. The judge testified in the *habeas corpus* proceeding that Gerald admitted making "some of the lewd statements...[but not] any of the more serious lewd statements." There was conflict and uncertainty among the witnesses at the *habeas corpus* proceeding—the juvenile court judge, Mr. and Mrs. Gault and the probation officer—as to what Gerald did or did not admit.

We shall assume that Gerald made admissions of the sort described by the juvenile court judge, as quoted above. Neither Gerald nor his parents was advised that he did not have to testify or make a statement, or that an incriminating statement might result in his commitment as a "delinquent." ...

It would indeed be surprising if the privilege against self-incrimination were available to hardened criminals but not to children. The language of the 5th Amendment, applicable to the states by operation of the 14th Amendment, is unequivocal and without exception. And the scope of the privilege is comprehensive. ...

In fact, evidence is accumulating that confessions by juveniles do not aid in "individualized treatment," as the court below put it, and that compelling the child to answer questions, without warning or advice as to his right to remain silent, does not serve this or any other good purpose. ... [It] seems probable that where children are induced to confess by "paternal" urgings on the part of officials and the confession is then followed by disciplinary action, the child's reaction is likely to be hostile and adverse—the child may well feel that he has been led or tricked into confession and that despite his confession he is being punished.

Further, authoritative opinion has cast formidable doubt upon the reliability and trustworthiness of "confessions" by children. ... The recent decision of the New York Court of Appeals ..., *In the Matters of Gregory W. and Gerald S.,* deals with a dramatic and, it is to be hoped, extreme example. 2 12-year-old Negro boys were taken into custody for the brutal assault and rape of 2 aged domestics, one of whom died as the result of the attack. One of the boys was schizophrenic and had been locked in the security ward of a mental institution at the time of the attacks. By a process that may best be described as bizarre, his confession was obtained by the police. A psychiatrist testified that the boy would admit "whatever he thought was expected so that he could get out of the immediate situation." The other 12-year-old also "confessed." Both confessions were in specific detail, albeit they contained various inconsistencies. The Court of Appeals, in an opinion by Keating, J., concluded that the confessions were products of the will of the police instead of the boys. The confessions were therefore held involuntary and the order of the Appellate Division affirming the order of the family court adjudging the defendants to be juvenile delinquents was reversed. . . .

We conclude that the constitutional privilege against self-incrimination is applicable in the case of juveniles as it is with respect to adults. We appreciate that special problems may arise with respect to waiver of the privilege by or on behalf of children, and that there may well be some differences in technique—but not in principle—depending upon the age of the child and the presence and competence of parents. The participation of counsel will, of course, assist the police, juvenile courts and appellate tribunals in administering the privilege. If counsel is not present for some permissible reason when an admission is obtained, the greatest care must be taken to assure that the admission was voluntary, in the sense not only that it has not been coerced or suggested, but also that it is not the product of ignorance of rights or of adolescent fantasy, fright or despair. . . .

. . . We now hold that, absent a valid confession, a determination of delinquency and an order of commitment to a state institution cannot be sustained in the absence of sworn testimony subjected to the opportunity for cross-examination in accordance with our law and constitutional requirements. . . .

Appellants urge that the Arizona statute is unconstitutional under the due process clause because, as construed by its Supreme Court, "there is no right of appeal from a juvenile court order. . . ." The court held that there is no right to a transcript because there is no right to appeal and because the proceedings are confidential and any record must be destroyed after a prescribed period of time. Whether a transcript or other recording is made, it held, is a matter for the discretion of the juvenile court.

This court has not held that a state is required by the federal Constitution "to provide appellate courts or a right to appellate review at all." In view of the fact that we must reverse the Supreme Court of Arizona's affirmance of the dismissal of the writ of *habeas corpus* for other reasons, we need not rule on this question in the present case or upon the failure to provide a transcript or recording of the hearings—or, indeed,

the failure of the juvenile court judge to state the grounds for
his conclusion. . . .

For the reasons stated, the judgment of the Supreme Court
of Arizona is reversed and the cause remanded for further proceedings not inconsistent with this opinion.

Justices Black and White wrote separate concurring opinions. Justice Harlan concurred in part
and dissented in part.

Justice Stewart dissenting:

The court today uses an obscure Arizona case as a vehicle
to impose upon thousands of juvenile courts throughout the
nation restrictions that the Constitution made applicable to
adversary criminal trials. I believe the court's decision is wholly
unsound as a matter of constitutional law, and sadly unwise as
a matter of judicial policy.

Juvenile proceedings are not criminal trials. They are not
civil trials. They are simply not adversary proceedings.
Whether treating with a delinquent child, a neglected child, a
defective child, or a dependent child, a juvenile proceeding's
whole purpose and mission is the very opposite of the mission
and purpose of a prosecution in a criminal court. The object of
the one is correction of a condition. The object of the other is
conviction and punishment for a criminal act.

In the last 70 years many dedicated men and women have
devoted their professional lives to the enlightened task of
bringing us out of the dark world of Charles Dickens in meeting our responsibilities to the child in our society. The result has
been the creation in this century of a system of juvenile and
family courts in each of the 50 states. There can be no denying
that in many areas the performance of these agencies has fallen
disappointingly short of the hopes and dreams of the
courageous pioneers who first conceived them. For a variety of
reasons, the reality has sometimes not even approached the
ideal, and much remains to be accomplished in the administration of public juvenile and family agencies—in personnel, in
planning, in financing, perhaps in the formulation of wholly
new approaches.

I possess neither the specialized experience nor the expert
knowledge to predict with any certainty where may lie the
brightest hope for progress in dealing with the serious problems

of juvenile delinquency. But I am certain that the answer does not lie in the court's opinion in this case, which serves to convert a juvenile proceeding into a criminal prosecution.

The inflexible restrictions that the Constitution so wisely made applicable to adversary criminal trials have no inevitable place in the proceedings of those public social agencies known as juvenile or family courts. And to impose the court's long catalog of requirements upon juvenile proceedings in every area of the country is to invite a long step backwards into the 19th century. In that era there were no juvenile proceedings, and a child was tried in a conventional criminal court with all the trappings of a conventional criminal trial. So it was that a 12-year-old boy named James Guild was tried in New Jersey for killing Catharine Beakes. A jury found him guilty of murder, and he was sentenced to death by hanging. The sentence was executed. It was all very constitutional.

A state in all its dealings must, of course, accord every person due process of law. And due process may require that some of the same restrictions which the Constitution has placed upon criminal trials must be imposed upon juvenile proceedings. For example, I suppose that all would agree that a brutally coerced confession could not constitutionally be considered in a juvenile court hearing. But it surely does not follow that the testimonial privilege against self-incrimination is applicable in all juvenile proceedings. Similarly, due process clearly requires timely notice of the purpose and scope of any proceedings affecting the relationship of parent and child.... But it certainly does not follow that notice of a juvenile hearing must be framed with all the technical niceties of a criminal indictment....

Adequate Proof of Guilt Required

In the case of *In the Matter of Samuel Winship,* decided May 31, 1970, the Supreme Court ruled, 6 to 3, that juveniles, like adults, are constitutionally entitled to proof beyond a reasonable doubt when found guilty of violating the criminal law. Chief Justice Warren Earl Burger, dissenting, protested the "further strait-jacketing of an already overly-restricted system." The juvenile court systems need "not more but less of the trappings of legal procedure and judicial formalism," he said. "I cannot regard it as a manifestation of progress to transfrom juvenile courts into criminal courts."

Abridgment of the *In the Matter of Samuel Winship* decision (397 U.S. 358, May 31, 1970):

Justice Brennan delivering the opinion of the court:

... This case presents the single, narrow question whether proof beyond a reasonable doubt is among the "essentials of due process and fair treatment" required during the adjudicatory stage when a juvenile is charged with an act which would constitute a crime if committed by an adult.

Section 712 of the New York Family Court Act defines a juvenile delinquent as "a person over 7 and less than 16 years of age who does any act which, if done by an adult, would constitute a crime." During a 1967 adjudicatory hearing, conducted pursuant to § 742 of the act, a judge in New York Family Court found that appellant, then a 12-year-old boy, had entered a locker and stolen $112 from a woman's pocketbook. The petition which charged appellant with delinquency alleged that his act, "if done by an adult, would constitute the crime or crimes of larceny." The judge acknowledged that the proof might not establish guilt beyond a reasonable doubt but rejected appellant's contention that such proof was required by the 14th Amendment. The judge relied instead on § 744(b) of the New York Family Court Act which provides that "[a]ny determination at the conclusion of [an adjudicatory] hearing that a [juvenile] did an act or acts must be based on a preponderance of the evidence." During a subsequent dispositional hearing, appellant was ordered placed in a training school for an initial period of 18 months, subject to annual extensions of his commitment until his 18th birthday—6 years in appellant's case....

We turn to the question whether juveniles, like adults, are constitutionally entitled to proof beyond a reasonable doubt when they are charged with violation of a criminal law. The same considerations which demand extreme caution in fact-finding to protect the innocent adult apply as well to the innocent child. We do not find convincing the contrary arguments of the New York Court of Appeals.... In effect the Court of Appeals distinguished the proceedings in question here from a criminal prosecution by use of what *Gault* called the "'civil' label of convenience which has been attached to juvenile proceedings."... We made clear in that decision that civil labels and good intentions do not themselves obviate the need for criminal due process safeguards in juvenile courts, for "[a] proceeding where the issue is whether the child will be found to be 'delinquent' and subjected to the loss of his liberty for years is comparable in seriousness to a felony prosecution."...

Nor do we perceive any merit in the argument that to afford juveniles the protection of proof beyond a reasonable doubt would risk destruction of beneficial aspects of the juvenile process. Use of the reasonable-doubt standard during the adjudicatory hearing will not disturb New York's policies that a finding that a child has violated a criminal law does not constitute a criminal conviction, that such a finding does not deprive the child of his civil rights, and that juvenile proceedings are confidential. Nor will there be any effect on the informality, flexibility, or speed of the hearing at which the factfinding takes place. And the opportunity during the post-adjudicatory or dispositional hearing for a wide-ranging review of the child's social history and for his individualized treatment will remain unimpaired. Similarly, there will be no effect on the procedures distinctive to juvenile proceedings which are employed prior to the adjudicatory hearing.

In sum, the constitutional safeguard of proof beyond a reasonable doubt is as much required during the adjudicatory stage of a delinquency proceeding as are those constitutional safeguards applied in *Gault*—notice of charges, right to counsel, the rights of confrontation and examination, and the privilege against self-incrimination. We therefore hold, in agreement with Chief Judge [Stanley H.] Fuld in dissent in the Court of Appeals, "that, where a 12-year-old child is charged with an act of stealing which renders him liable to confinement for as long as 6 years, then, as a matter of due process...the case against him must be proved beyond a reasonable doubt."

Chief Justice Burger, whom Justice Stewart joined, dissenting:

The court's opinion today rests entirely on the assumption that all juvenile proceedings are "criminal prosecutions," hence subject to constitutional limitations. This derives from earlier holdings, which like today's holding, were steps eroding the differences between juvenile courts and traditional criminal courts. The original concept of the juvenile court system was to provide a benevolent and less formal means than criminal courts could provide for dealing with the special and often sensitive problems of youthful offenders. Since I see no constitutional requirement of due process sufficient to overcome the legislative judgment of the states in this area, I dissent from further strait-jacketing of an already overly-restricted system. What the juvenile court systems need is not more but less of the trappings of legal procedure and judicial formalism; the juvenile system requires breathing room and flexibility in order to survive, if it can survive the repeated assaults from this court.

Much of the judicial attitude manifested by the court's opinion today and earlier holdings in this field is really a protest against inadequate juvenile court staffs and facilities; we "burn down the stable to get rid of the mice." The lack of support and the distressing growth of juvenile crime have combined to make for a literal breakdown in many if not most juvenile courts. Constitutional problems were not seen while those courts functioned in an atmosphere where juvenile judges were not crushed with an avalanche of cases.

My hope is that today's decision will not spell the end of a generously conceived program of compassionate treatment intended to mitigate the rigors and trauma of exposing youthful offenders to a traditional criminal court; each step we take turns the clock back to the pre-juvenile court era. I cannot regard it as a manifestation of progress to transform juvenile courts into criminal courts, which is what we are well on the way to accomplishing. We can only hope the legislative response will not reflect our own by having these courts abolished.

Justice Black dissented on the ground that the

Bill of Rights does not require proof of guilt beyond a reasonable doubt.

Trial by Jury Not Required

In *McKeiver et al. v. Pennsylvania,* the Supreme Court ruled June 6, 1971 that jury trials are not required in juvenile proceedings. The decision involved these 3 separate cases:

(1) Joseph McKeiver, then 16, charged with robbery, larceny and receiving stolen property after he joined 20 to 30 other youths who took 25¢ from 3 young teenagers. McKeiver was found guilty and placed on probation.

(2) Edward Terry, then 15, charged with assault and battery on a police officer after striking a policeman with his fists and with a stick when the policeman broke up a boys' fight that Terry and other boys were watching. Terry was committed to a youth detention center.

(3) Barbara Burrus and approximately 45 other black children, 11 to 15 years old, ordered to a state institution after being charged with wilfully impeding traffic during a civil rights demonstration. The custody order was suspended, and the youngsters were placed on probation for one or 2 years conditioned on their violating none of the state's laws and attending a school approved by the Welfare Director. The children, who stood trial in North Carolina, faced confinement for up to 10 years, depending on their ages. The maximum penalty that could be imposed on adults for this offense was a $500 fine or 6 months in jail.

Justice Harry A. Blackmun, in his majority opinion, held that a jury was not necessary in juvenile proceedings. A jury is not "a necessary component of accurate factfinding," he said. If the jury trial were to be injected into the juvenile court system as a matter of right, he declared, the result would be "the traditional delay, the formality and the clamor" of an adult criminal proceeding. The requirement of a jury trial would not remedy the defects of the juvenile court system, he said. "Meager as has been the hoped for advance in the juvenile field, the alternative would be regressive, would lose what has been gained and would tend once again to place the juvenile squarely in the routine of the criminal process." If the formalities of the criminal justice system are superimposed on juvenile courts, there would be no reason for their separate existence, Blackmun asserted. "Perhaps that ultimate disillusionment will come one day, but for the moment we are disinclined to give impetus to it."

Justice Douglas, dissenting, said that it was not the responsibility of the court to determine whether a state should use a "clinical" or "punitive" approach to juvenile delinquency. "But where a state uses its juvenile court proceedings to prosecute a juvenile for a criminal act and to order 'confinement' until the child reaches 21 years of age . . . , then he is entitled to the same procedural protection as an adult," Douglas declared.

Abridgment of the *McKeiver et al. v. Pennsylvania* decision (403 U.S. 528, June 6, 1971):

Justice Blackmun, joined by Chief Justice Burger and Justices Stewart and White, delivering the judgment of the court:

Joseph McKeiver, then age 16, in May 1968 was charged with robbery, larceny, and receiving stolen goods (felonies under Pennsylvania law)... as acts of juvenile delinquency. At the time of the adjudication hearing he was represented by counsel.* His request for a jury trial was denied, and his case was heard by Judge Theodore S. Gutowicz of the Court of Common Pleas, Family Division, Juvenile Branch, of Philadelphia County, Pennsylvania. McKeiver was adjudged a delinquent upon findings that he had violated a law of the Commonwealth.... He was placed on probation. On appeal, the Superior Court affirmed without opinion....

Edward Terry, then age 15, in Jan. 1969 was charged with assault and battery on a police officer and conspiracy (misdemeanors under Pennsylvania law...) as acts of juvenile delinquency. His counsel's request for a jury trial was denied, and his case was heard by Judge Joseph C. Bruno of the same Juvenile Branch of the Court of Common Pleas of Philadelphia County. Terry was adjudged a delinquent on the charges. This followed an adjudication and commitment in the preceding week for an assault on a teacher. He was committed, as he had been on the earlier charge, to the Youth Development Center at Cornwalls Heights. On appeal, the Superior Court affirmed without opinion....

The Supreme Court of Pennsylvania granted leave to appeal in both cases and consolidated them. The single question considered... was "whether there is a constitutional right to a jury trial in juvenile court." The answer, one justice dissenting, was in the negative.... We noted probable jurisdiction....

... McKeiver's offense was his participating with 20 or 30 youths who pursued 3 young teenagers and took 25¢ from them;... McKeiver never before had been arrested and had a record of gainful employment;... the testimony of 2 of the victims was described by the court as somewhat inconsistent and as "weak";... Terry's offense consisted of hitting a police

---

* At McKeiver's hearing his counsel advised the court that he had never seen McKeiver before and "was just in the middle of interviewing him." The court allowed him 5 minutes for the interview. Counsel's office, Community Legal Services, however, had been appointed to represent McKeiver 5 months earlier....

officer with his fists and with a stick when the officer broke up a boys' fight Terry and others were watching.

... Barbara Burrus and approximately 45 other black children, ranging in age from 11 to 15 years, were the subjects of juvenile court summonses issued in Hyde County, North Carolina, in Jan. 1969.

The charges arose out of a series of demonstrations in the county in late 1968 by black adults and children protesting school assignments and a school consolidation plan. Petitions were filed by North Carolina state highway patrolmen. Except for one relating to James Lambert Howard, the petitions charged the respective juveniles with wilfully impeding traffic. The charge against Howard was that he wilfully made riotous noise and was disorderly in the O. A. Peay School in Swan Quarter; interrupted and disturbed the school during its regular sessions; and defaced school furniture. The acts so charged are misdemeanors under North Carolina law.

The several cases were consolidated into groups for hearing before District Judge Hallett S. Ward, sitting as a juvenile court. The same lawyer appeared for all the juveniles. Over counsel's objection, made in all except 2 of the cases, the general public was excluded. A request for a jury trial in each case was denied.

The evidence as to the juveniles other than Howard consisted solely of testimony of highway patrolmen. No juvenile took the stand or offered any witness. The testimony was to the effect that on various occasions the juveniles and adults were observed walking along Highway 64 singing, shouting, clapping, and playing basketball. As a result, there was interference with traffic. The marchers were asked to leave the paved portion of the highway, and they were warned that they were committing a statutory offense. They either refused or left the roadway and immediately returned....

The evidence as to Howard was that on the morning of Dec. 5, he was in the office of the principal of the O. A. Peay School with 15 other persons while school was in session and was moving furniture around; that the office was in disarray; that as a result the school closed before noon; and that neither he nor any of the others was a student at the school or authorized to enter the principal's office.

In each case the court found that the juvenile had committed "an act for which an adult may be punished by law." A custody order was entered declaring the juvenile a delinquent "in need of more suitable guardianship" and committing him to the custody of the County Department of Public Welfare for placement in a suitable institution "until such time as the Board of Juvenile Correction or the superintendent of said institution may determine, not inconsistent with the laws of this state." The court, however, suspended these commitments and placed each juvenile on probation for either one or 2 years conditioned upon his violating none of the state's laws, upon his reporting monthly to the County Department of Welfare, upon his being home by 11 p.m. each evening and upon his attending a school approved by the Welfare Director. None of the juveniles has been confined on these charges....

The right to an impartial jury "[i]n all criminal prosecutions" under federal law is guaranteed by the 6th Amendment. Through the 14th Amendment that requirement has now been imposed upon the states "in all criminal cases which—were they to be tried in a federal court—would come within the 6th Amendment's guarantee." This is because the court has said it believes "that trial by jury in criminal cases is fundamental to the American scheme of justice." *Duncan v. Louisiana* ... (1968); *Bloom v. Illinois* ... (1968).

This, of course, does not automatically provide the answer to the present jury trial issue, if for no other reason than that the juvenile court proceeding has not yet been held to be a "criminal prosecution," within the meaning and reach of the 6th Amendment, and also has not yet been regarded as devoid of criminal aspects merely because it usually has been given the civil label....

The Pennsylvania juveniles' basic argument is that they were tried in proceedings "substantially similar to a criminal trial." They say that a delinquency proceeding in their state is initiated by a petition charging a penal code violation in the conclusory language of an indictment; that a juvenile detained prior to trial is held in a building substantially similar to an adult prison; that in Philadelphia juveniles over 16 are, in fact, held in the cells of a prison; that counsel and the prosecution engage in plea bargaining; that motions to suppress are routinely heard and decided; that the usual rules of evidence are applied; that the customary common law defenses are available; that the press is generally admitted in the Philadelphia juvenile courtrooms; that members of the public enter the room; that arrest and prior record may be reported by the press (from police sources, however, rather than from the juvenile court records); that, once adjudged delinquent, a juvenile may be confined until his majority in what amounts to a prison...; and that the stigma attached upon delinquency adjudication approximates that resulting from conviction in an adult criminal proceeding.

The North Carolina juveniles particularly urge that the requirement of a jury trial would not operate to deny the supposed benefits of the juvenile court system; that the system's primary benefits are its discretionary intake procedure permitting disposition short of adjudication, and its flexible sentencing permitting emphasis on rehabilitation; that realization of these benefits does not depend upon dispensing with the jury; that adjudication of factual issues on the one hand and disposition of the case on the other are very different matters with very different purposes; that the purpose of the former is indistinguishable from that of the criminal trial; that the jury trial provides an independent protective factor; that experience has shown that jury trials in juvenile courts are manageable; that no reason exists why protection traditionally accorded in criminal proceedings should be denied young people subject to involuntary incarceration for lengthy periods; and that the juvenile courts deserve healthy public scrutiny....

All the litigants here agree that the applicable due process standard in juvenile proceedings, as developed by *Gault* and *Winship,* is fundamental fairness. As that standard was applied in those 2 cases, we have an emphasis on factfinding procedures. The requirements of notice, counsel, confrontation, cross-examination, and standard of proof naturally flowed from this emphasis. But one cannot say that in our legal system the jury is a necessary component of accurate factfinding. There is much to be said for it, to be sure, but we have been content to pursue other ways for determining facts. Juries are not required, and have not been, for example, in equity cases, in workmen's compensation, in probate, or in deportation cases. Neither have they been generally used in military trials....

We must recognize...that the fond and idealistic hopes of the juvenile court proponents and early reformers of 3 generations ago have not been realized. The devastating commentary upon the system's failures as a whole, contained in the Task Force Report: Juvenile Delinquency & Youth Crime (President's Commission on Law Enforcement and the Administration of Justice [1967]), pp. 7-9, reveals the depth of disappointment in what has been accomplished. Too often the juvenile court judge falls far short of that stalwart, protective and communicating figure the system envisaged.*...

The Task Force Report, however, also said, page 7, "To say that juvenile courts have failed to achieve their goals is to say no more than what is true of criminal courts in the United States...."

Despite all these disappointments, all these failures, and all these shortcomings, we conclude that trial by jury in the juvenile court's adjudicative stage is not a constitutional requirement. We so conclude for a number of reasons:

1. The court has refrained, in the cases heretofore decided, from taking the easy way with a flat holding that all rights constitutionally assured for the adult accused are to be imposed upon the state juvenile proceeding....

2. There is a possibility, at least, that the jury trial, if required as a matter of constitutional precept, will remake the juvenile proceeding into a fully adversary process and will put an effective end to what has been the idealistic prospect of an intimate, informal protective proceeding.

3. The Task Force Report, although concededly pre-*Gault,* is notable for its not making any recommendation that the jury trial be imposed upon the juvenile court system. This is so despite its vivid description of the system's deficiencies and disappointments. Had the commission deemed this vital to the integrity of the juvenile process, or to the handling of juveniles, surely a recommendation or suggestion to this effect would have appeared. The intimations, instead, are quite the other way. Task Force Report, 38. Further, it expressly recommends

---

*"A recent study of juvenile court judges...revealed that half had not received undergraduate degrees; a 5th had received no college education at all; a 5th were not members of the bar." Task Force Report, p. 7.

against abandonment of the system and against the return of the juvenile to the criminal court's.

4. The court specifically has recognized by dictum that a jury is not a necessary part even of every criminal process that is fair and equitable. *Duncan v. Louisiana.* ...

5. The imposition of the jury trial on the juvenile court system would not strengthen greatly, if at all, the factfinding function, and would, contrarily, provide an attrition of the juvenile court's assumed ability to function in a unique manner. It would not remedy the defects of the system. Meager as has been the hoped-for advance in the juvenile field, the alternative would be regressive, would lose what has been gained, and would tend once again to place the juvenile squarely in the routine of the criminal process.

6. The juvenile concept held high promise. We are reluctant to say that, despite disappointments of grave dimensions, it still does not hold promise, and we are particularly reluctant to say, as do the Pennsylvania petitioners here, that the system cannot accomplish its rehabilitative goals. So much depends on the availability of resources, on the interest and commitment of the public, on willingness to learn, and on understanding as to cause and effect and cure. In this field, as in so many others, one perhaps learns best by doing. We are reluctant to disallow the states further to experiment and to seek in new and different ways the elusive answers to the problems of the young, and we feel that we would be impeding that experimentation by imposing the jury trial.... If, in its wisdom, any state feels the jury trial is desirable in all cases, or in certain kinds, there appears to be no impediment to its installing a system embracing that feature. That, however, is the state's privilege and not its obligation.

7. Of course there have been abuses. The Task Force Report has noted them. We refrain from saying at this point that those abuses are of constitutional dimension....

8. There is, of course, nothing to prevent a juvenile court judge, in a particular case where he feels the need, or when the need is demonstrated, from using an advisory jury.

9. "The fact that a practice is followed by a large number of states is not conclusive in a decision as to whether that practice accords with due process, but it is plainly worth considering in determining whether the practice 'offends some

principle of justice so rooted in the traditions and conscience of our people as to be ranked as fundamental.' *Snyder v. Massachusetts* ... (1934)." *Leland v. Oregon* ... (1952). It therefore is of more than passing interest that at least 29 states and the District of Columbia by statute deny the juvenile a right to a jury trial in cases such as these. The same result is achieved in other states by judicial decision. In 10 states statutes provide for a jury trial under certain circumstances.

11. Stopping short of proposing the jury trial for juvenile proceedings are the Uniform Juvenile Court Act, § 24(a), approved in July 1968 by the National Conference of Commissioners on Uniform State Laws..., proposed by the National Council on Crime & Delinquency.

12. If the jury trial were to be injected into the juvenile court system as a matter of right, it would bring with it into that system the traditional delay, the formality and the clamor of the adversary system and, possibly, the public trial. It is of interest that these very factors were stressed by the District Committee of the Senate when ... it recommended, and Congress then approved, as a provision in the District of Columbia Crime Bill, the abolition of the jury trial in the juvenile court....

13. Finally, the arguments advanced by the juveniles here are, of course, the identical arguments that underlie the demand for the jury trial for criminal proceedings. The arguments necessarily equate the juvenile proceeding—or at least the adjudicative phase of it—with the criminal trial. Whether they should be so equated is our issue. Concern about the inapplicability of exclusionary and other rules of evidence, about the juvenile court judge's possible awareness of the juvenile's prior record and of the contents of the social file; about repeated appearances of the same familiar witnesses in the persons of juvenile and probation officers and social workers—all to the effect that this will create the likelihood of pre-judgment—chooses to ignore, it seems to us, every aspect of fairness, of concern, of sympathy, and of paternal attention that the juvenile court system contemplates.

If the formalities of the criminal adjudicative process are to be superimposed upon the juvenile court system, there is little need for its separate existence. Perhaps that ultimate disillu-

sionment will come one day, but for the moment we are
disinclined to give impetus to it.

Justice Brennan concurred in the 2 Pennsylvania cases and dissented in the *North Carolina* case.

*Justice Douglas, whom Black and Marshall
joined, dissenting:*

These cases ... present the issue of the right to a jury trial
for offenders charged in juvenile court and facing a possible
incarceration until they reach their majority. I believe the
guarantees of the Bill of Rights, made applicable to the states
by the 14th Amendment, require a jury trial....

We held in *In re Gault* [1967] ... that "neither the 14th
Amendment nor the Bill of Rights is for adults alone." As we
noted in that case, the juvenile court movement was designed to
avoid procedures to ascertain whether the child was "guilty" or
"innocent" but to bring to bear on these problems a "clinical"
approach.... It is of course not our task to determine as a
matter of policy whether a "clinical" or "punitive" approach to
these problems should be taken by the states. But where a state
uses its juvenile court proceedings to prosecute a juvenile for a
criminal act and to order "confinement" until the child reaches
21 years of age or where the child at the threshold of the proceedings faces that prospect, then he is entitled to the same procedural protection as an adult. As Mr. Justice Black said in *In
re Gault* ..., (concurring): "Where a person, infant or adult, can
be seized by the state, charged, and convicted for violating a
state criminal law, and then ordered by the state to be confined
for 6 years, I think the Constitution requires that he be tried in
accordance with the guarantees of all the provisions of the Bill
of Rights made applicable to the states by the 14th Amendment. Undoubtedly this would be true of an adult defendant,
and it would be a plain denial of equal protection of the laws—
an invidious discrimination—to hold that others subject to
heavier punishments could, because they are children, be denied
these same constitutional safeguards."

Just as courts have sometimes confused delinquency with
crime, so have law enforcement officials treated juveniles not as
delinquents but as criminals. As noted in the President's Crime
Commission Report: "In 1965, over 100,000 juveniles were
confined in adult institutions. Presumably most of them were

there because no separate juvenile detention facilities existed. Nonetheless it is clearly undesirable that juveniles be confined with adults." President's Commission on Law Enforcement, Challenge of Crime 179 (1967). Even when not incarcerated with adults the situation may be no better. One Pennsylvania correctional institution for juveniles is a brick building with barred windows, locked steel doors, a cyclone fence topped with barbed wire and guard towers. A former juvenile judge described it as "a maximum security prison for adjudged delinquents." ...

In the present cases imprisonment or confinement up to 10 years was possible for one child and each faced at least a possible 5-year incarceration. No adult could be denied a jury trial in those circumstances. ... The 14th Amendment which makes trial by jury provided in the 6th Amendment applicable to states speaks of denial of rights to "any person," not denial of rights to "any adult person"; and we have held indeed that where a juvenile is charged with an act that would constitute a crime if committed by an adult, he is entitled to trial by jury with proof beyond a reasonable doubt. *In re Winship* [1970]. ...

PLEA BARGAINING

Court Upholds System

In a series of decisions culminating with *Santobello v. New York,* announced Dec. 20, 1971, the Supreme Court sanctioned the so-called "plea bargaining" system under which a defendant "confesses" by pleading guilty and thus forfeits his right to a jury trial in the hope of receiving a lesser sentence. In *Santobello,* the court held that the prosecutor must honor his agreement with the defendant.

It has been estimated that 90% to 95% of all criminal convictions are by pleas of guilty; about 70% to 85% of all felony convictions are secured from guilty pleas.

The plea bargaining system works as follows: A man charged with burglary, for example, pleads guilty and waives his right to a jury trial in return for which the charge against him is reduced to breaking and entering or illegal entry.

One difficulty with that arrangement, according to the *Harvard Law Review,* is that "the primary purpose of plea bargaining is to assure that the jury trial system established by the Constitution is seldom utilized."

Plea bargaining can pressure a defendant into pleading guilty to a crime that he did not commit. It can also encourage the prosecutor to inflate or to multiply the original charges in an effort to force a guilty plea. On the whole, however, plea bargaining, according to Abraham S. Blumberg in his book *Criminal Justice,* "probably tends to serve better the interests and requirements of the guilty." Chief Justice Warren Burger has said that a reduction in guilty pleas from 90% to 80% would require doubling the current number of judges, lawyers and courtrooms.

In *North Carolina v. Alford,* the Supreme Court ruled May 4, 1970 that a judge could allow a guilty plea from a man, who, in pleading guilty, told the trial judge that he was innocent. The Court of Appeals had found the guilty plea involuntary because it was motivated principally by fear of the death penalty. (North Carolina law then provided for [a] the penalty of life imprisonment when a plea of guilty was accepted to a first-degree murder charge but [b] the death penalty following a jury verdict of guilty, unless the jury recommended life imprisonment.) In the Supreme Court's 6-3 decision, Justice Byron R. White wrote for the majority that courts can accept guilty pleas from defendants who simultaneously maintain their innocence if the plea is not coerced and there is "strong evidence of actual guilt," as in *Alford.* The consequence of *Alford,* as it relates to the plea bargaining system in general, was considered minimal, however, for it was assumed that had the court ruled that a defendant who wanted to plead guilty must say he had committed the crime, the defendant would probably make the confession having concluded that it was in his interest to plead guilty. Critics held that the most significant aspect of the decision lay in its failure to establish procedures or standards for judging the voluntariness of guilty pleas.

Abridgment of the *North Carolina v. Alford* decision (400 U.S. 25, Nov. 23, 1970):

Justice White delivering the opinion of the court:

On Dec. 2, 1963, [Henry C.] Alford was indicted for first-degree murder, a capital offense under North Carolina law. The court appointed an attorney to represent him, and this attorney questioned all but one of the various witnesses who appellee said would substantiate his claim of innocence. The witnesses, however, did not support Alford's story but gave statements that strongly indicated his guilt. Faced with strong evidence of guilt and no substantial evidentiary support for the claim of innocence, Alford's attorney recommended that he plead guilty, but left the ultimate decision to Alford himself. The prosecutor agreed to accept a plea of guilty to a charge of 2d-degree murder, and on Dec. 10, 1963, Alford pleaded guilty to the reduced charge.

Before the plea was finally accepted by the trial court, the court heard the sworn testimony of a police officer who summarized the state's case. 2 other witnesses besides Alford were also heard. Although there was no eyewitness to the crime, the testimony indicated that shortly before the killing Alford took his gun from his house, stated his intention to kill the victim and returned home with the declaration that he had carried out the killing. After the summary presentation of the state's case, Alford took the stand and testified that he had not committed the murder but that he was pleading guilty because he faced the threat of the death penalty if he did not do so.* In response to the questions of his counsel, he acknowledged that his counsel had informed him of the difference between 2d- and first-

---

*After giving his version of the events of the night of the murder, Alford stated: "...I pleaded guilty on 2d-degree murder because they said there is too much evidence, but I ain't shot no man, but I take the fault for the other man. We never had an argument in our life, and I just pleaded guilty because they said if I didn't they would gas me for it, and that is all."

degree murder and of his rights in case he chose to go to trial. The trial court then asked appellee if, in light of his denial of guilt, he still desired to plead guilty to 2d-degree murder and appellee answered, "Yes, sir. I plead guilty on—from the circumstances that he [Alford's attorney] told me." After eliciting information about Alford's prior criminal record, which was a long one, the trial court sentenced him to 30 years' imprisonment, the maximum penalty for 2d-degree murder....

. . . That he would not have pleaded [guilty] except for the opportunity to limit the possible penalty does not necessarily demonstrate that the plea of guilty was not the product of a free and rational choice, especially where the defendant was represented by competent counsel whose advice was that the plea would be to the defendant's advantage....

In addition to Alford's statement, however, the court had heard an account of the events on the night of the murder, including information from Alford's acquaintances that he had departed from his home with his gun stating his intention to kill and that he had later declared that he had carried out his intention. Nor had Alford wavered in his desire to have the trial court determine his guilt without a jury trial. Although denying the charge against him, he nevertheless preferred the dispute between him and the state to be settled by the judge in the context of a guilty plea proceeding rather than by a formal trial. Thereupon, with the state's telling evidence and Alford's denial before it, the trial court proceeded to convict and sentence Alford for 2d-degree murder....

. . . [W]hile most pleas of guilty consist of both a waiver of trial and an express admission of guilt, the latter element is not a constitutional requisite to the imposition of criminal penalty. An individual accused of crime may voluntarily, knowingly, and understandingly consent to the imposition of a prison sentence even if he is unwilling or unable to admit his participation in the acts constituting the crime.

Nor can we perceive any material difference between a plea which refuses to admit commission of the criminal act and a plea containing a protestation of innocence when, as in the instant case, a defendant intelligently concludes that his interests require entry of a guilty plea and the record before the judge contains strong evidence of actual guilt. Here the state

had a strong case of first-degree murder against Alford.
Whether he realized or disbelieved his guilt, he insisted on his
plea because in his view he had absolutely nothing to gain by a
trial and much to gain by pleading. Because of the overwhelming evidence against him, a trial was precisely what
neither Alford nor his attorney desired. Confronted with the
choice between a trial for first-degree murder, on the one hand,
and a plea of guilty to 2d-degree murder, on the other, Alford
quite reasonably chose the latter and thereby limited the
maximum penalty to a 30-year term. When his plea is viewed in
light of the evidence against him, which substantially negated
his claim of innocence and which further provided a means by
which the judge could test whether the plea was being
intelligently entered..., its validity cannot be seriously questioned in view of the strong factual basis for the plea demonstrated by the state and Alford's dearly expressed desire to
enter it despite his professed belief in his innocence, we hold
that the trial judge did not commit constitutional error in
accepting it.

Relying on *United States v. Jackson* [1968],... Alford now
argues in effect that the state should not have allowed him this
choice but should have insisted on proving him guilty of murder
in the first degree. The states in their wisdom may take this
course by statute or otherwise and may prohibit the practice of
accepting pleas to lesser included offenses under any circumstances. But this is not the mandate of the 14th Amendment and
the Bill of Rights. The prohibitions against involuntary or
unintelligent pleas should not be relaxed, but neither should an
exercise in arid logic render those constitutional guarantees
counterproductive and put in jeopardy the very human values
they were meant to preserve.

The Court of Appeals for the 4th Circuit was in error to
find Alford's plea of guilty invalid because it was made to avoid
the possibility of the death penalty. That court's judgment
directing the issuance of the writ of *habeas corpus* is vacated,
and the case is remanded to the Court of Appeals for further
proceedings consistent with this opinion.

Justice Brennan, whom Douglas and Marshall joined, dissenting:

Last term, this court held over my dissent that a plea of

guilty may validly be induced by an unconstitutional threat to subject the defendant to the risk of death, so long as the plea is entered in open court and the defendant is represented by competent counsel who is aware of the threat, albeit not of its unconstitutionality. *Brady v. United States...; Parker v. North Carolina....* Today the court makes clear that its previous holding was intended to apply even when the record demonstrates that the actual effect of the unconstitutional threat was to induce a guilty plea from a defendant who was unwilling to admit his guilt.

I adhere to the view that, in any given case, the influence of such an unconstitutional threat "must necessarily be given weight in determining the voluntariness of a plea." *Parker v. North Carolina...* (dissent). And, without reaching the question whether due process permits the entry of judgment upon a plea of guilty accompanied by a contemporaneous denial of acts constituting the crime, I believe that at the very least such a denial of guilt is also a relevant factor in determining whether the plea was voluntarily and intelligently made. With these factors in mind, it is sufficient in my view to state that the facts set out in the majority opinion demonstrate that Alford was "so gripped by fear of the death penalty" that his decision to plead guilty was not voluntary but was "the product of duress as much so as choice reflecting physical constraint." *Haley v. Ohio...* (1948) (Frankfurter, J., concurring). Accordingly, I would affirm the judgment of the Court of Appeals.

In *McMann v. Richardson,* decided May 4, 1970, the court refused, 6-3, to invalidate a guilty plea on the ground that the plea was motivated by a previously obtained illegal confession. Justices Brennan, Douglas and Marshall, in dissent, charged the majority with moving closer "toward the goal of insulating all guilty pleas from subsequent attack no matter what unconstitutional action of government may have induced a particular plea."

Abridgment of the *McMann v. Richardson* decision (397 U.S. 759, May 4, 1970):

Justice White delivering the opinion of the court:

...The principal issue before us is whether and to what extent an otherwise valid guilty plea may be impeached in collateral proceedings by assertions or proof that the plea was motivated by a prior coerced confession. We find ourselves in substantial disagreement with the Court of Appeals....

Since we are dealing with a defendant who deems his confession crucial to the state's case against him and who would go to trial if he thought his chances of acquittal were good, his decision to plead guilty or not turns on whether he thinks the law will allow his confession to be used against him. For the defendant who considers his confession involuntary and hence unusable against him at a trial, tendering a plea of guilty would seem a most improbable alternative. The sensible course would be to contest his guilt, prevail on his confession claim at trial, on appeal or, if necessary, in a collateral proceeding and win acquittal, however guilty he might be. The books are full of cases in New York and elsewhere, where the defendant has made this choice and has prevailed. If he nevertheless pleads guilty the plea can hardly be blamed on the confession which in his view was inadmissible evidence and no proper part of the state's case. Since by hypothesis the evidence aside from the confession is weak and the defendant has no reasons of his own to plead, a guilty plea in such circumstances is nothing less than a refusal to present his federal claims to the state court in the first instance—a choice by the defendant to take the benefits, if any, of a plea of guilty and then to pursue his coerced confession claim in collateral proceedings. Surely later allegations that the confession rendered his plea involuntary would appear incredible, and whether his plain bypass of state remedies was an intelligent act depends on whether he was so incompetently advised by counsel concerning the forum in which he should first present his federal claim that the Constitution will afford him another chance to plead....

What is at stake in this phase of these cases is not the integrity of the state convictions obtained on guilty pleas, but whether, years later, defendants must be permitted to withdraw their pleas, which were perfectly valid when made, and be given another choice between admitting their guilt and putting the state to its proof. It might be suggested that if *Jackson* had been the law when the pleas in these cases were made—if the judge had been required to rule on the voluntariness of challenged confessions at a trial—there would have been a better chance of keeping the confessions from the jury and there would have been no guilty pleas. But because of inherent uncertainty in guilty plea advice, this is a highly speculative matter in any particular case and not an issue promising a meaningful and productive evidentiary hearing long after entry of the guilty plea....

Justice Brennan, whom Douglas and Marshall joined, dissenting:

In this case the court moves yet another step toward the goal of insulating all guilty pleas from subsequent attack no matter what unconstitutional action of government may have induced a particular plea. Respondents alleged in some detail that they were subjected to physical and mental coercion in order to force them to confess; that they succumbed to these pressures; and that because New York provided no constitutionally acceptable procedures for challenging the validity of their confessions in the trial court, they had no reasonable alternative to pleading guilty. Respondents' contention, in short, is that their pleas were the product of the state's illegal action. Notwithstanding the possible truth of the claims, the court holds that respondents are not even entitled to a hearing which would afford them an opportunity to substantiate their allegations....

The court's formalism is symptomatic of the desire to ignore entirely the motivational aspect of a decision to plead guilty. As long as counsel is present when the defendant pleads, the court is apparently willing to assume that the government may inject virtually any influence into the process of deciding on a plea. However, as I demonstrated in *Parker* and *Brady,* this insistence upon ignoring the factors with which the prosecution confronts the defendant before he pleads departs broadly from the manner in which the voluntariness of guilty pleas has traditionally been approached. In short, the critical question is not, as the court insists, whether respondents knowingly decided to plead guilty, but *why* they made that decision....

In *Santobello v. New York,* the Supreme Court Dec. 20, 1971 described plea bargaining as "an essential component of the administration of justice," which, if "properly administered," should "be encouraged." The court said, however, that plea bargaining "must be attended by safeguards to insure the defendant what is reasonably due in the circumstances." Those circumstances vary, the court said, "but a constant factor is that when a plea rests in any significant degree on a promise or agreement of the prosecutor, so that it can be said to be part of the inducement or consideration, such promise must be fulfilled."

The case concerned Rudolph Santobello, who had pleaded guilty to a lesser gambling offense after an assistant New York district attorney agreed to make no recommendation as to the sentence. When Santobello appeared for sentencing, a 2d Assistant Attorney General, who did not know about the agreement, recommended that Santobello receive the maximum one-year sentence, and the judge imposed it.

The Supreme Court ordered the case back to the state courts to determine whether Santobello should be permitted to withdraw his guilty plea or whether he should be resentenced before a different judge. Justices Marshall, Brennan and Stewart argued that Santobello should be permitted to withdraw his guilty plea as he requested.

CASES ABRIDGED OR CITED

445

INDEX

451